Making It Big in Software

Get the Job. Work the Org. Become Great.

Sam Lightstone

PRENTICE
HALL

Upper Saddle River, NJ • Boston • Indianapolis • San Francisco
New York • Toronto • Montreal • London • Munich • Paris • Madrid
Cape Town • Sydney • Tokyo • Singapore • Mexico City

Library of Congress Cataloging-in-Publication Data

Lightstone, Sam.
  Making it big in software : get the job—work the org.—become great / Sam Lightstone.
    p. cm.
  Includes index.
  ISBN 978-0-13-705967-6
  1. Computer programming—Vocational guidance. 2. Computer software industry—Vocational guidance. 3. Computer software developers—Interviews. I. Title.
  QA76.25.L54 2010
  005.1023—dc22
                            2010000235

ISBN-13: 978-0-137-05967-6
ISBN-10: 0-137-05967-1

Text printed in the United States on recycled paper at R.R. Donnelley & Sons, Crawfordsville, Indiana

First printing March 2010

Associate Publisher
Greg Wiegand

Senior Acquisitions Editor
Katherine Bull

Development Editor
Kendell Lumsden

Marketing Manager
Judi Morrison

Publicist
Heather Fox

Technical Reviewers
Joseph Hellerstein
Rasekh Rifaat
Danny Sadinoff

Managing Editor
Kristy Hart

Senior Project Editor
Lori Lyons

Copy Editor
Hansing Editorial Services

Indexer
Publishing Words

Proofreader
Language Logistics, LLC

Publishing Coordinator
Cindy Teeters

Cover Designer
Alan Clements

Compositor
Nonie Ratcliff

Manufacturing Buyer
Dan Uhrig

To my wife and children, Elisheva, Hodaya, and Avishai.
Thanks for making our home a place of perpetual fun and love.

To my high school English teacher, Mr. David Aldwinckle.

Contents

Preface xi

Acknowledgments xiv

About the Author xvi

Part I   **Fundamentals**

Chapter 1   **Making It Big** 2

  What Do "Big Shots" in Software Do? 3

  Follow Your Bliss 5

  Why Bother? 7

  It's Not as Hard as You Think 9

Chapter 2   **What Good Software Is Really About** 10

  Software Projects Gone Bad and Other War Stories . . . 11

  The Marketplace Is the Driving Force Behind
  Everything We Do 13

  Two Kinds of Customers: Ones You Have
  and Ones You Want 15

  Winning Strategies and Tactics 16

  When (Not) to Listen to Your Customers 21

Interview   *Marissa Mayer: Google VP and
First Lady of Software* *23*

Chapter 3   **School Versus Job** 31

  Limited Field of Vision 32

  School Is a Fishbowl 32

  Industry Is a Fishbowl 33

  Leveraging the Differences 34

Interview   *Jon Bentley: Author, Programming Pearls* *37*

Chapter 4   **Mission Impossible? Getting a Job in Software
Development** 43

  Choosing Wisely 43

Resumé Realities for New Graduates 46

Killer Resumés for Software Development 47

Beyond the Resumé–Way Beyond 49

The Value (or Not) of Grades 52

The Value of Extracurricular Activities 54

Why Student Positions Dramatically Improve
Your Odds 55

Fifteen Points to a Great Interview 56

Interview   Bjarne Stroustrup: Inventor of the
C++ Programming Language 62

Chapter 5   Making the Most of the Early Years As
a Software Developer 68

Tradecraft 69

The Business of Software 70

Build Domain Expertise 70

What's Old Is New 71

Watch the Leaders 72

Start Building Your Network 72

Who Do You Want to Be? 74

Everyone Needs a Mentor 74

Fun Breeds Success 75

Interview   Richard Stallman: Founder of the Free Software
Movement 79

Chapter 6   Essential Skills. Some Are Even Technical 84

Hard and Soft Skills 84

Technical Skills for Career Growth 85

Programming Languages: What's Hot
and What's Not 86

Debugging 88

Surviving Spec, Design, and Code Reviews 91

The Growth Skill 92

Soft Skills at the Top of Most Organizations 95

The Ultimate Soft Skill: Emotional Intelligence 95

Interview   Ray Tomlinson: Inventor of Email 100

Chapter 7   The Sweet Science of Software R&D
            Organizations 110
                Who Does What in Software? 110
                The Good and the Great 115
                Three Laws of Career Effectiveness 116
                Four Modes of Business Conversation 118
                Never Surprise Your Boss 120
                Impressions and System Tolerance 121

Interview   Peter Norvig: Google's Director of Research 122

Chapter 8   Career Killers 127
                People Problems 127
                Team Problems 131
                Productivity Problems 133
                Growth Problems 135
                Fundamentals Versus Incidentals 137

Part II   Leadership

Chapter 9   Working the Org 139
                Getting Buy-In and the Myth of Electronic
                    Communication 140
                Give to Get: Building Emotional Caches 140
                Leveraging Your Social Network 143
                Negotiating 101 144
                Communication That Gets Results 149
                Dress for Success: Wear Running Shoes 150
                Getting Agreement Isn't Enough 151

Interview   John Schwarz: CEO, Business Objects 154

Chapter 10 Successful Software Project Proposals 161
                Core Competencies 162
                How Successful Proposals Are Really Made 163
                The Art of the Pitch 166

Personal Tenacity 168

Getting to the Next Steps 169

Interview   Linus Torvalds: Mr. Linux 170

Chapter 11   Career Advancement 176

Why Evaluations and Advancements
Are So Unscientific 177

Track Record Is Credibility—Credibility
Is Everything 178

Communicate Your Accomplishments 179

Goal-Oriented Careers 180

Your Manager's Influence on Your Career 185

The Secret Impact of Management Peers 187

Promoting Others Sincerely 189

The Secret of Promotibility Inversion 189

Interview   Mark Russinovich: Windows Guru,
Microsoft Technical Fellow 192

Chapter 12   Time Management 201

Goal-Centric Time Management 202

Task-Centric Time Management 203

Circles of Influence and Concern 205

Indecision May or May Not Be Your Problem 207

Act with a Sense of Urgency 208

How Much Time Wasting Is Reasonable? 209

The Scourge of Email 210

Interview   David Vaskevitch: Microsoft CTO 214

Chapter 13   Avoiding Software Development Overruns 219

Don't Be Moe 219

How Common Are Software Project Overruns? 222

Why Software Project Overrun Occurs 224

We're Late—Now What? 232

Final Thoughts on Software Development
Overruns 235

Interview   *Grady Booch: The Sage of Software Architecture* *236*

Chapter 14   **Zen and the Critical Art of Balance** **244**
Work-Life Balance 245
Organizational Culture Affects Balance 246
Life Impacts Work 247
Patterns, Possibilities, and Defining Yourself 248

Interview   *Tom Malloy: Adobe Chief Software Architect* *251*

Chapter 15   **Secret Insights on Software Project Management** . . **260**
Goal-Oriented Project Management:
Lessons from Space 261
Managing Human Nature 264
Making Use of Students 266
The Value of Measuring Value 267
Of Mice, Men, and Project Plans 269
Assessing Your Development Maturity 270
Software Defects and Costs and Efficiencies 276
You Can't Test In Quality 279

Interview   *James Gosling: Inventor of the Java*
Programming Language *281*

Chapter 16   **The Big Leagues: From Medium-Shot**
to Big-Shot **288**
Leading Versus Managing 288
Leadership Styles 290
Be an Authority 293
Shoot First, Take Questions Later 294
Building Teams and Recruiting the Best 295
Follow the Money 300
You Get What You Reward 301
Creating Shared Values 302
Effective Delegation 303
Directing Others 304

Part III   Greatness

Chapter 17   **Leadership in Software Innovation** 306

Why Innovate? 306

Software Innovations That Succeed 308

The Opportunity to Innovate 311

Brainstorming 312

The Value Perception Cycle 313

The Innovator's Twelve: Fostering Successful
Innovation 315

99% Perspiration 322

Interview   *Robert Kahn: Co-inventor of the Internet* 323

Chapter 18   **The Big Leagues: From Big-Shot to Visionary** 333

Be the Authority 333

Personal Breadth 334

Believe in Your Ability to Master New Ideas
and Technology 336

Business Fluency 337

Patenting 338

Publishing 341

Public Speaking 345

Success Is a Lousy Teacher 348

Advanced Social Networking (Social Steroids
for Nerds) 349

Passion and Process for Your Art 350

Interview   *Steve Wozniak: Inventor of the Apple Computer,
Co-founder of Apple Inc., Pop Icon* 352

Chapter 19   **If I Knew Then What I Know Now** 360

The First Few Months on Any Software Job 361

Who You Work For 362

Who You Work With 364

Managing Your Manager 364

Creating Opportunities 366

Waiting Until You're Ready Is Waiting Too Long 367

Interview   *Marc Benioff: CEO, Salesforce.com* 369

Chapter 20   Going Out on Your Own: The "Software Startup" ... **379**

              Good Ideas Versus Good Business 380

              The Plan and the Pitch 381

              Bootstrapping Your R&D 382

              Financing 383

              Getting to Revenue 385

              Crossing the Chasm 386

              Be Nimble, Be Quick 389

              Growth Versus Acquisition 390

              How to Get Acquired 392

Interview   *Diane Greene: Co-founder and
Past CEO of VMware* *396*

Chapter 21   Compensation: Kuh-ching! **404**

              Compensation Differences Between
                  Company Types 405

              Impact of Graduate Degrees on Compensation
                  and Career Potential 405

              Stock Options 406

              Stock Grants 407

              Bonus Plans 408

              Retirement Plans 408

              Typical Salary Ranges (2010–2013) 409

              Indirect Compensation 409

              Fatherly Thinking 411

Chapter 22   Making It Big? **413**

              Who Makes It Big? 413

              What Does Making It Big Look Like? 414

              Why Some People Don't or Can't 415

              Final Thoughts 416

Index **418**

Preface

"Thus the sage Chaninah would say:
Much have I learned from my teachers and even more from my
friends but from my students I have learned the most of all"
—Ethics of the Fathers, circa 200 CE

You went to university to study a profession, but they were hell-bent on giving you an education instead. Unfortunately, there's a gap between the formal education we receive in school and the skills we need to build truly successful careers. Not only are many of the basic skills for professional growth not taught in school, but to a large degree they aren't taught anywhere. The dynamic and somewhat bohemian quality of the software industry introduces unique career challenges. Our industry includes many of the trappings of corporate American culture, but many odd divergences. It's a domain where teenage hackers compete head-to-head with MIT Ph.D. graduates and where crinkled T-shirts and unlaced running shoes coexist with stock options and executive titles. *Making it Big in Software* is my attempt to share strategies for traversing these unique dynamics and maximizing your professional potential. This book also includes interviews with some of the most influential software innovators and leaders of the past 30 years—people who literally changed the world.

In 1991, I was a fourth-year electrical engineering student at Queen's University, trying to finish up my degree and get a job. Every Friday afternoon the electrical engineering school invited a guest speaker to inspire and enlighten our young, impressionable minds. These talks covered a wide range of technological topics; we discussed everything from high voltage transmission lines to CMOS VLSI circuit design. I confess that most of these sessions were less than inspirational for me. One day, a guest speaker arrived with a radically different message. He spoke to us about "life in the real world" and what we could expect after we graduated. I was riveted. This is the only fourth-year seminar from which I still have the notes. Most of my classmates, like me, were in the dark about what our lives might be like after graduation. Even those students who had managed to find summer positions in engineering were limited in their experiences by the normal constraints of student positions.

I decided then that if I ever could, I would return the professional courtesy and volunteer to speak to university students. In the late 1990s and early 2000s, I began a series of career talks at leading universities. The lecture notes from my talks, often delivered to capacity-filled auditoriums, became the basis for this book. Some of the ideas are my own, but many are culled from the leading business thinkers and software development evangelists of the past three decades. Hopefully, this book succeeds in providing you what school and daily work life generally cannot: the tools with which to make it BIG.

Audience

This is a book for software professionals of all ages and levels, whether they're just trying to break into the field or have decades of experience. Writing a book with that range isn't easy; every age group and community has a different set of concerns that affect what's interesting to them. After nearly two decades of recruiting, managing, and mentoring software professionals, there are some common themes I've found that cross most boundaries of age and experience. I've tried to make those themes central to the book. I hope this book will also be of interest to students and teachers of computer science, providing a colorful look into the less mathematical aspects of the profession.

Organization of This Book

The book is divided into three major sections: fundamentals, leadership, and greatness. "Part I, Fundamentals," discusses the major building blocks of a great career in software, including the fundamentals of good software products, major skills and leading programming languages, how to land a job, and how to operate effectively within a software team (including some pitfalls to avoid). "Part II, Leadership," takes the reader into a series of topics around driving and leading change and operating in a much more harried professional environment. Leaders, almost by definition, need to multitask and drive parallel agendas forward while deflecting myriad forces of negativity. This section covers important topics related to "working an organization," how to build and pitch successful project proposals, career advancement, time management, avoiding software project overruns, work-life balance, and higher-level management and leadership insights. "Part III, Greatness," discusses topics around innovation—how to reach the pinnacle of the profession (becoming a software visionary or guru), how to start your own business, a review of compensation rates, and a retrospective on things I wish I had known earlier in my career.

Between the chapters you'll find a number of interviews I did with leading personalities. These interviews deliberately include a mix of business executives, researchers, and industry leaders. I feel it's important for readers to get perspectives broader than my own. To enhance the structure of the book, the interviews are all marked with a gray bar along the leaf edge of their pages, including the interviewee's name. I've made a moderate effort to place the interviews near related chapters (for example, two startup sensations, Marc Benioff CEO and founder of Salesforce.com and Diane Greene past CEO and co-founder of VMware, frame the chapter on software startups). Some interviews didn't have a clear correlation to a specific topic, so there's an admittedly arbitrary aspect in the placement of a few. It's absolutely not the case that interviews placed in the Fundamentals section are any less profound than those in the Greatness section. I think it's fair to say that everyone I interviewed has reached the heights of the profession. After all, that's what made them such interesting people to speak with.

Feedback

If you have feedback on the book or find any errors, please contact me. You can send feedback to feedback@makingitbigcareers.com. Although I can't guarantee a reply to every email, I'll make sure that every email is read.

Sam Lightstone

To learn more about *Making it Big in Software*,
including upcoming events and additional publications,
please go to:
www.MakingItBigCareers.com

Acknowledgments

A special thanks to my acquisition editor at Prentice Hall, Katherine Bull. Katherine had faith in this project and put up with a tremendous number of questions from me. Thank you to the production staff at Pearson Education that helped so much with layout, flow, and copyediting, including Kendell Lumsden, Lori Lyons, and Krista Hansing. Thank you to Susan Visser at IBM Press, whose encouragement was nothing short of relentless. For the past three years, there hasn't been a single time I passed Susan in the hallway at IBM when she didn't ask me about this book! Thank you to Carole Jelen McClendon at Waterside Productions, who provided valuable insight into the publishing process and whose ideas helped improve the initial book proposal. Thanks to Randall Craig from PineTree Consulting, who provided valuable suggestions on the initial proposal. My thanks as well to Scott Woodrow, Director at Lions Peak Capital Corporation, Anthony Ciccone of the IBM Business Development Group, and Allan Friedman, Business Development Executive with the IBM Global Technology Unit, who each provided valuable insight into the business of software startups and acquisitions. Thank you to Robert Begg of IBM and Scott Ambler of Dr. Dobb's fame, both experts in agile development, who added critical insights around software development processes. A thank you to the reviewers of the proposal and the manuscript, Dr. Joe Hellerstein from Google Inc., Dr. Pat Martin of Queen's University, Danny Sadinoff, CTO of Conveycentric Limited, and Rasekh Rifaat of Google Inc. Your critical feedback helped significantly improve the quality of this book.

This book includes the thoughts and ideas of some of the industry's greatest luminaries. We are very fortunate (myself as the author and you as reader) that these brilliant and charismatic personalities agreed to share their histories and personal thoughts with us. A hearty thank you to Marc Benioff, Jon Bentley, Grady Booch, James Gosling, Diane Greene, James Hamilton, Robert Kahn, Alan Kay, Tom Malloy, Marissa Mayer, Peter Norvig, Mark Russinovitch, John Schwarz, Richard Stallman, Bjarne Stroustrup, Ray Tomlinson, Linus Torvalds, David Vaskevitch, and Steve Wozniak.

I'd like to thank some of my mentors, whose insights and personal coaching have helped me over the years and whose ideas permeate the pages of this book. Thank you to Berni Schiefer, Matt Huras, Sal Vella, John McPherson and Pat Selinger of IBM.

Most important, thank you to my wife and children. None of us could have imagined how time-consuming this project would be. Borrowing a quote from my interview with Jon Bentley, "Writing code is a joy; writing English is just plain hard work." When I look back at this project and what you put into this as a family, it's fair to say your names deserve to be on the front cover. I truly appreciate your love, support, and patience. Thank you for allowing me the time to write this book when I should have been spending more of it with you.

About the Author

Sam Lightstone is the creator of MakingItBigCareers.com as well as Program Director and Senior Technical Staff Member with IBM's Software Group, where he works on product strategy and R&D for one of the world's largest software engineering teams. Sam is a sought-after public speaker, author, and prolific inventor who still spends a good part of his professional time recruiting and mentoring software engineers. Sam has presented to dozens of Fortune 500 companies, industrial and scientific conferences, and major universities on topics related to careers, technology trends, and emerging research needs. Sam has been quoted in *eWeek*, *InformationWeek*, *InfoWorld*, and the *MIT Technology Review*. His management career has spanned from small high-performance applied research teams up to large-scale projects with more than 200 staff across multiple geographies.

Sam is the founder of the IEEE Data Engineering Workgroup on Self Managing Database Systems and a member of the International Advisory Committee of the IEEE Computer Society Technical Committee on Autonomous and Autonomic Computing Systems. Sam is inventor and co-inventor of more than 30 patents and patents pending and author of several books and scientific papers. He has a Bachelor of Applied Science in Electrical Engineering from Queen's University and a Master of Computer Science & Software Engineering from the University of Waterloo. Sam is a former national class competitive foil fencer and enjoys spending time with his family, cycling, and playing guitar.

PART I

Fundamentals

CHAPTER 1

Making It Big

"Success didn't spoil me, I've always been insufferable."
—Fran Lebowitz (1950–)

Software is an amazing place to build a professional career. In few other domains can you have so much fun with so much positive potential to change the world, while pulling down a decent living to boot. Software has made complex technology accessible, and allowed us to control systems and processes in a way that manual operators could once only dream about. We've shrunken the world, brought people and societies to greater common understanding, and allowed families and friends to connect when they are apart. Business and researchers have faster and more accurate access to strategic business information, historical records, data analysis, and mathematical optimization. The world is creating nearly 15 petabytes of digital information daily, and by 2011 an estimated 2 billion people will be connected to the Internet.[1] Almost everything that has an electrical power source, from handheld phones to refrigerators, is running software. That's what I call demand. All that demand means a world of opportunity for software professionals. With all that potential, it's worth knowing what it takes to evolve your career to its highest possible potential for impact, leadership, innovation, freedom, financial compensation, and fun.

Making It Big in Software is a book about maximizing your career success and your professional impact. From getting a job and honing key skills to becoming a leader and innovator, this book walks you through the skills,

---

[1] Steve Mills, Senior Vice President IBM Software Group, Keynote address, IBM Analyst Connect Symposium, Stamford CT, Nov 2009.

behaviors, and personal qualities you need to reach your professional potential. In addition to my own thoughts, stories, and metrics, I've included a number of interviews with industry-leading luminaries between the chapters. These interviews with major executives, innovators, and researchers provide fresh insights into the art and business of the software professional. Their ideas are often profound and sometimes controversial. Having gone through the extraordinary process of interviewing all of them, I found it profoundly interesting to see the points of convergence and variation among them on topics from time management to the value of graduate degrees. One of the major points of convergence is that all these leaders and innovators clearly love what they do. It's both a cause and an effect: Loving what you do is the most necessary of all ingredients for success, but it's also true that being successful allows people to spend more of their time on things they love.

What Do "Big Shots" in Software Do?

Success means different things to different people. For many people, the first and most important meaning of success is financial compensation. The more money you earn for what you do, the more "successful" you are. "He's a very successful lawyer, a partner in the firm." "She's a successful entrepreneur. Her business grew into an international conglomerate." "He's a successful surgeon. He earns enough in six months to spend the rest of the year traveling." We're all accustomed to that way of thinking about success. Make no mistake about it, financial rewards are indeed a very significant part of what most people consider career success, and for some this is the most important component. However, it's a shallow mind indeed that considers it the only component. Beyond financial rewards lie several other measures of success, and the relative value of each varies from one person to the next. Here are some other hallmarks of success gleaned from the interviews in this book, as well as from decades of discussion with industry leaders at major software companies around the world:

- Fun and interesting work
- Corporate and industrial influence
- The betterment of society
- Freedom to work on what you want, when you want
- Fame
- Travel

Successful people in software are defined by some or all of the attributes in this list, and financial rewards follow as a result. For example, most of the software giants interviewed in this book define their own success by their contributions to the industry and their impact on society rather than by their bank balances. Even so, several of them are very wealthy. Although relatively few people in the software industry become fabulously rich, it's a surprising and hopeful fact that the short list of the world's wealthiest people contains several notable software gurus: Microsoft founder Bill Gates, Google founders Sergey Brin and Larry Page, Oracle founder Larry Ellison, and Facebook founder Mark Zuckerberg, just to name a few. Microsoft's success created many millionaires in the 1980s and 1990s through employee stock option programs, as did several other high-flying software firms of the period. Indeed, if becoming rich is your goal, there's precedent for doing it through a career in software. Many a software millionaire has been made by software developers just doing their thing, writing great code and marking just the right time to "cash out."

Corporate and industrial influence comes after you have made a reputation for yourself as an industry expert in a technical field or as an executive with a track record of leading great success. When that happens, your opinion is sought to direct the strategic investments in new technologies, to approve standards, and to help foster industrial research efforts. This gives you significant influence over how technology evolves, not only in your own company, but also across the world.

Technology aids in the betterment of society, though many people feel that it continues to be our downfall and that in some pockets of life technology will always do more harm than good. Even so, the general purpose of technology is the betterment of society: reducing humankind's labor and suffering, engendering freedom, and advancing our exploration and understanding of the universe. Software big shots, our business strategists and technical architects, are the people who have the greatest influence on technology. Okay, it takes a village to raise a child, and it takes a wide range of professionals to successfully bring good software to market, including wise investors, savvy managers, salespeople and sales channels, and a lot of luck. But nobody influences the shape of technology more than those who create it. Having read this, the venture capitalists are now red-faced and fuming, the salespeople are pounding their tightened fists, and the project managers are rolling their eyes, but I stand by it. Certainly, without these people, most projects never achieve lift-off. But although they enable, they do not shape, define, or mold the creative expression of the engineering team the way the technical and executive visionaries do.

Follow Your Bliss

Software is one of the few professions that allows its practitioners to come to work and dream, solve puzzles, surf the Internet, and then collect a handsome paycheck at the end of the day. Whether you're writing your very first "Hello world" program in a new computer language or putting the finishing touches on a new cloud computing infrastructure for your corporate data center, every programmer has enjoyed the remarkable sensation of seeing technology spring to life when their software runs for the first time. Not only is software fun, but having fun in software is a catalyst for a successful career. It was striking to me how often this theme came up in the interviews for this book. Almost everyone I interviewed commented on the importance of finding enjoyable work. If all the gurus seemed to agree on one piece of advice, this was it. Check out the consistency across these statements:

> "If you are entering the field, find something that you really love doing and get excited about doing, so that you almost feel as if you should be paying them to come to work. I think you need to be happy to be successful, not successful to be happy."
> —David Vaskevitch, Microsoft CTO

> "Be sure that you like what you do at work and that you like the people you work with—you'll have to live with them for a long time."
> —Bjarne Stroustrup, inventor of C++

> "The more you can merge what you want to do with your job, the better."
> —Steve Wozniak, inventor of the Apple computer

> "One piece of advice I would give people is to always make sure you're in an environment that leaves you feeling empowered to fully use your talents, and that you feel appreciated for the work you do."
> —Diane Greene, co-founder and past CEO of VMware

> "I believe that I just work better if I enjoy what I'm doing. I suspect that if anybody wants to be 'the best' at whatever they do, they have to realize that it takes decades of hard work. And the main way to actually keep doing decades of hard work is to simply enjoy it so much that you don't want to stop."
> —Linus Torvalds, original author of GNU/Linux

"...if you can find a job that you really like, the better you're gonna be. You're gonna be more productive. You're going to be happier. You're going to be more satisfied in general with what's going on."
—Ray Tomlinson, inventor of email

"Follow your bliss."
—Jon Bentley, author of *Programming Pearls*

"For me, work is really enjoyable, making it hard to define where work ends and fun begins."
—Marissa Mayer, Google VP

"That's what's great—my career is a lot of fun. I don't view it as work. Computers have always been my hobby. The fact that I get to go to work and work on my hobby and get paid for it is just fantastic."
—Mark Russinovich, Microsoft Technical Fellow

"What is really important is to make sure that they are growing, contributing, and enjoying what they do."
—John Schwarz, CEO Business Objects

"My number one piece of advice is to have fun."
—James Gosling, inventor of Java, Sun VP and Fellow

"...follow your passion. Most of all, be sure you have fun in the process."
—Grady Booch, IBM Fellow

"Any career is a marathon race, not a sprint. For it to be rewarding over years and decades, it has to be something you like to do. As you consider career decisions, listen to your heart as well as your head. Your head will tell you how to succeed in a traditional sense. Your heart will tell you what fulfills you, what you find fun. Here is a simple metric: Ask yourself how fast the time passes at work. If you "lose yourself" in your work—that is, if time passes quickly—that is a powerful, positive message."
—Tom Malloy, Chief Software Architect for Adobe Systems

Having fun is critical to career success in any profession; those of us in software are fortunate to be in a place where having fun is easy. When you're having fun, you'll work with more enthusiasm and more energy, and you'll get more done. The natural frustrations of professional life will slide past you, paled by the enthusiasm and excitement of your work. As Grady Booch told me in my interview with him, "I can't think of any other industry that has impacted every other business in the way that we as humans and civilizations connect. What a cool business to be in."

Why Bother?

But with long hours, considerable stress, and no guarantees, the obvious question is whether it's even worth trying to make it big. I believe the answer is unequivocally yes. The most compelling reason is that, in most cases, you have to show up to the office and work like a lunatic anyway—it's really not optional (if you want to eat). So if the difference between being a midlevel career programmer and making it big is an incremental strategic investment of time and energy, then it's more than worth it for you and for your family. In the long run, the benefits are significant: a more satisfying career, greater influence and impact within your company and the industry, more fun, and more money. And while there may not be less "crap" to do, at least it's strategic work rather than "grunt" work. How much more money is there really, after all that effort? According to data at PayScale.com and the United States Bureau of Labor Statistics, in 2007, the lowest-paid software engineers earned approximately $38,000, while senior architects earned more than $211,000, a difference of 5.55 times. If you add to this the benefits from bonuses, preferred stock, and stock options that are always dolled out more generously to the senior staff, the variance in compensation between the ends of the job performance spectrum can be pretty astounding.

Plus, making it big gives you the freedom to work on what you want to. That broad statement is true in degrees, depending on just how big you make it. The higher up the totem pole of technology you climb, the more freedom you can have in what you work on. The late computer scientist Jim Gray, who was one of the founders of modern database systems and a leader in scalable computing before his mysterious disappearance in a boating accident on a clear, calm day in 2007, was a great example. Before recruiting Gray, Microsoft had always resisted the pressure to establish R&D sites outside of their core location in Redmond, Washington. Gray just wasn't interested in living there. No problem. In 1995, they built their new laboratory, called the Microsoft Bay Area Research Center (BARC), around him. Some may believe that Microsoft had decided to finally tap into the incredible pool of software talent and dynamism in the Bay area, but in truth, the move to open BARC was motivated heavily by a desire to attract Gray to Microsoft. According to Senior Vice President of Microsoft Research Rick Rashid, "If Jim had wanted a lab in Monte Carlo, we would have built a lab in Monte Carlo." That's the freedom to work not only on what you want, but where you want! Why does this happen? This kind of freedom comes with the value you provide through your creativity, insight, and industrial influence.

Big shots in technology have more "eureka moments" per unit time than the little shots. They are leaders and connectors. They are the charismatic inspirations for new ideas who build consensus to forge ahead on new technology initiatives. They have the ideas that create and shape the technology of the future. This makes them sensationally valuable assets to any enterprise. The more valuable you are, the more control you have over your destiny. Your employer, colleagues, and industrial associates will do more for you and give you that freedom, to keep you happy and focused on what you have excelled at. Notice that I said "freedom to work on what you want," but I did not say the freedom to work the amount you want. In software, successful people generally work hard. The climb to fame and fortune in software generally exacerbates this fate until you decide you have climbed enough, done enough, and earned enough, that you're willing to let your contributions plateau.

Fame awaits those who make it big. When *eWeek, TechWorld,* and other magazines want to get the inside scoop on emerging technology, they turn to the technical gurus. Big shots in software write the books, publish the papers, present the lectures, and are interviewed for columns that present technology to the world. Fame isn't all it's cracked up to be, but whatever it is, the big shots get a larger share.

Finally, I contend that those who make it big have more meaningful and fulfilling jobs. More satisfying work means you'll have more enthusiasm for what you do. Enthusiasm means you'll work harder and be more profoundly inspired. As a result, you'll not only be more successful, but you'll have a good time doing it. Why is that?

▶ The most successful people have larger degrees of control on what they work on, so they can bias their work toward the things they enjoy. Perhaps just as important, when you work on the things you enjoy, your enthusiasm will rub off on others, and that's a kind of leadership, too.

▶ Big shots don't do grunt work. The least pleasant and lower-skilled tasks are delegated to the junior employees, while senior folks focus on the strategic items. This is a gross oversimplification. After all, senior staff also gets involved in decisions to cancel technology projects, meetings to lay off staff (possibly including co-workers they have known for years), and painful arguments over technical strategy.

It's definitely not all fun and games. Some of these responsibilities include miserable experiences you wouldn't wish on your worst enemy, even after he'd stabbed you in the back, kicked your dog, stolen your life savings, and burned down your home. As miserable as some of the tasks of senior staff can be, they tend to be strategic in nature. Their influence is large and profound. The process of executing these tasks can be gut-wrenching, but there's a concomitant sense of accomplishment of having made a radical and profound difference. Okay, it's hell, but it's hell that matters. In contrast, some of the miserable tasks relegated to junior staff are more likely described as just plain miserable.

One constant runs throughout: Nobody makes it big without a large and sustained outlay of effort. Success in achieving your long-term goals always means hard work for several years.

It's Not as Hard as You Think

Throughout the chapters ahead, you'll see that making it big isn't the impossible elusive dream that some people think it is. Making it big requires a moderately consistent effort and the careful and strategic use of time to focus your energy and talents in meaningful ways. Yes, it's true that most successful people in software tend to work longer hours than career journeymen, but you don't need to be a workaholic to get to the top. Working smart is always more important than working hard. In fact, although the most successful people work hard, long hours, their career success is gated more by what they do than by how much of it. The chapters ahead tell the tale.

CHAPTER 2

What Good Software Is Really About

"Mustard's no good without roast beef."
—Chico Marx (1891–1961)

Everyone thinks they know good software when they see it. What businesses consider good software can be very different from what end users value. It's not as simple as "great function, no bugs" (though that's certainly a good starting point). Microsoft has been a leading software company in the world since 1983, despite a reputation that not all of their products were built to the highest-quality standards. Conversely, some of the seemingly most boring software products in the world have been great business successes for providing precious little more than extreme reliability.

For example, IBM's mainframe IMS product is a highly available hierarchical database. IMS was first developed in 1966 to help manage the Saturn V moon rocket and Apollo space programs. While few of us experience euphorial elation when discussing IMS technology, the IMS product is still going strong after 40 years. It might not be sexy, but IMS provides tried-and-true reliability and is still delivering new versions to market.[1] Depending on the target audience, the need for function, innovation, ease of use, and reliability vary dramatically. Despite our natural intuition to the contrary, good software—software that the market embraces—depends heavily on context. Sigh ... if building software were easy, talented programmers, software architects, and product strategists wouldn't be so desperately needed.

---

[1] IMS shipped version 11 of its product in October 2009 and remains a popular and reliable software product used by financial institutions around the world.

To advance in your career, it's powerfully important to develop a strong intuition about what good software really is. Understanding good software allows you to pick the winners by sensing which projects are on to something valuable, avoid work on doomed projects, and help refine good projects into great ones. Dr. Robert Kahn, co-inventor of the Internet, noted during his interview with me the career importance of sensing where things are going:

> You have to be at the right place at the right time.... The hockey player Wayne Gretzky is reputed to have said that the essence of hockey is knowing where to be! I think that's the best you can offer. You need to have a sense of where things are going. If you know where the puck is going to be, it prepares you to be in the right place to take the right shot.

Software Projects Gone Bad and Other War Stories

Everyone has a war story about a software project gone awry. Your career success hinges very strongly on your ability to pick and create the winners. By that, I mean your career depends on your ability to work on successful software projects and, through your talents, help them become even more successful. Your career is at least loosely defined by the sum of your successes. The war stories we all hear about—infamous software projects gone bad—are always someone else's fault and never the fault of the guy telling the story. The stories come in three canonical forms:

1. "We built a great product, but the market wasn't ready for it yet. It was ahead of its time."

   Reality check: It didn't meet the customers' needs.

2. "We built a great product, but the sales and marketing teams dropped the ball."

   Reality check: Nobody wanted it.

3. "We had a great product, but the executives canned it before we could get traction."

   Reality check: It was taking too long to generate value.

These kinds of stories are thinly veiled excuses for a product development team that failed. An engineering team is never at liberty to blame the marketing team or the sales team for the fact that the product wasn't compelling to the marketplace. Internalize this, believe it, and live it, and you will rise far above the unwashed masses of software's middle-management hordes who are all too quick to deflect blame for their product development failings. Truly great software is about providing value to the marketplace at the right time. Valuable software always makes it possible to do something more easily and more quickly than possible without it.

James Hamilton is Distinguished Engineer and Vice President of Amazon.com's cloud computing technology. He's also been a senior architect at Microsoft and IBM. I asked James for some of his ideas about bringing quality software to market, and he was quick to point out that good software is pretty much by definition software that the market embraces. When the market accepts a product with enthusiasm, it will quickly overshadow a host of engineering overruns and other sins.

> Bad software, software that doesn't sell, and software that doesn't solve the problem that the development set out to solve is wildly expensive. Bad software shipped on time is still wildly expensive. Great software, software that sells in millions of copies, can be a wonderful development cost bargain, even if it's late. I've seen slips of better than times two still work out to be wild successes. Great software is profitable even with huge cost and schedule over runs. Bad software can never be profitable.

How common is project failure? The Standish Group has been collecting data on this topic for more than 12 years, published in their *CHAOS Report*. The analysis covers more than 50,000 IT projects worldwide. The results show a huge rate of project failure or semi-success (what Standish calls "challenged," meaning that the project was completed but was late or failed to provide critical function). The good news in the historical data, evidenced by Figure 2.1, is that the trends have improved significantly since the mid 1990s.

The good news is that between 1994 and 2006 project success rates nearly doubled. Even so, only ~35% of 2006 projects were completely successful.

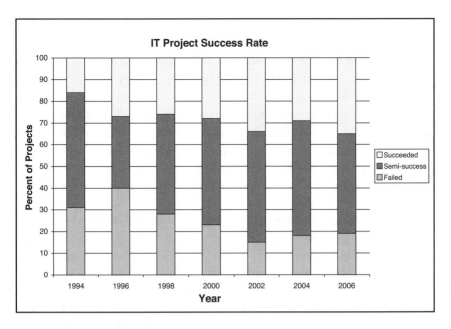

FIGURE 2.1   IT project success rates

The Marketplace Is the Driving Force Behind Everything We Do

1990 was IBM's most profitable year ever, to date, with corporate revenues of $69 billion. Only three years later, in 1993, things had changed dramatically and IBM was staggering under its own weight on a path to lose $16 billion. The end was near, and IBM was on its way to suffer the same fate as Steller's Sea Cow, the Irish Deer, and the Caspian Tiger when John Akers was removed as CEO and Lou Gerstner was brought in, as part of a clear salvage attempt. Gerstner left his position as CEO of RJR Nabisco, with the grand challenge to resuscitate one of the world's greatest technology companies, a company that, despite serious financial difficulties, was still pulling in about $60 billion. The first thing Gerstner did was assess the root causes of IBM's fall from grace— and there were several. Among his chief observations: IBM had become an insular corporation accustomed to telling other companies what they should buy and investing heavily in advanced technology without clear market goals. To shake things up at IBM Gerstner instituted a set of mantras, guiding principles for everyone in the company to follow.

Gerstner's #1 principle was perhaps the most poignant:

The marketplace is the driving force behind everything we do.

Gerstner didn't mean that IBM would no longer invest in speculative technology unless existing customers were demanding it. He meant that, from hardware to software to services, everything that IBM was to do from that point onward needed to be grounded in their best understanding of the market direction and requirements. The market would drive IBM, not the other way around.

Great innovations, brilliant new technology, and breakthrough ideas are truly great only if people use them and find them valuable. Marketing and hype help to spin that perception, but they provide only a bias in the process, not the substance. Ultimately, consumers are the real decision makers on whether products have merit. It's a profound and subtle point: A great idea ahead of its time is not a great idea—it's a useless one. Similarly, a great idea without great execution, usability, and reliability will flop. Everyone who works in software, from the product strategy planners to the function testers, needs to understand this. Understanding that good ideas alone aren't enough is the single greatest epiphany an organization can have toward collectively channeling energies into a deliberate successful software R&D development cycle.

As a leader, your job is both to operate with that knowledge and help others internalize it. If you find yourself in an organization that "just doesn't get it," continuing time and again to invest in bad ideas that are out of synch with market needs, you can help establish your leadership by explaining how the right course corrections can act as a catalyst for product success. Failing that, you might be in a losing organization, and your career would be better served somewhere else. No organization makes the right decisions all the time, and a few missteps are healthy. But constantly being out of touch with both where the market is and where it's heading are hallmarks of an organization sailing off the end of a precipice to its peril.

If you look at any large-scale software development effort, you'll inevitably find people working hard on features that have tiny and almost insignificant benefit to the end user while deferring other features of far greater urgency and consequence. This happens because engineering teams get hyped to work on exciting features but not necessarily those that are most important to the market. Cool engineering projects don't make good business based on the cool factor alone. One of the hardest and most critical ideas for us to come to terms with as software developers is to internalize that we are not our own customers. To help your own career, avoid working on projects or features with microscopic benefit, no matter how interesting they may be in terms of scientific computing or cutting-edge technology. As you advance to a level of organizational and strategic influence, you should strongly discourage your teams from spending time and money on anything that provides benefit measured in fractions of a percentile or moderate benefit to only a tiny segment of your market.

Two Kinds of Customers: Ones You Have and Ones You Want

You need to keep your existing customers happy because the stream revenue they provide pays the bills. Love 'em to death. On the flip side, stream revenue is not a growth mechanism, so attracting new customers, so-called transactional revenue, *is* critical when you want to put your product on a path to higher long-term revenue. Many times, keeping the old and attracting the new are conflicting goals because existing customers will have extensive requirements for completeness and reliability, whereas potential customers might be looking for disruptive technology features, or dramatic cost savings.

For example, customer ABC needs a specific extension to your high-availability solution or will move to a competitor. New customers are overwhelmingly asking for a new encryption feature. If the features are about the same size and you can't afford to build both, the choices become very hard. These problems have no silver bullets. Ultimately, you need to make a Solomonic decision about the cost-benefit of the potential growth versus the loss of the existing revenue stream (and possibly the loss of a valued reference account or negative optics in the marketplace). One thing is certain: The best software development organizations carefully track stream and transactional revenues distinctly and plan their product development strategy around goals for each.

A classic problem in North American executive leadership is focusing engineering and sales efforts on existing customers. Executives do this for two reasons:

▶ The relentless corporate focus on revenue generation. Short-term revenue growth is usually dominated by the existing customer base.

▶ The squeaky wheel gets the oil. Existing customers have connections in corporations that potential customers do not. They have the ear of the executive, so their requirements get disproportionate attention.

Focusing on existing customers is a myopic business behavior that drives short-term revenue growth but leads inexorably to long-term limitations in growth, creating a ceiling to your product's revenue potential. It takes a nearly superhuman strength of character to set aside the revenue pressures of the coming fiscal half to direct the majority efforts of an engineering team or a sales team toward net-new accounts, but the best and brightest leaders do it.

Commercial products always need to keep a focus on both new and existing customers. The challenge is to get the balance of investment right. As a leader in an organization, you can help set the tone and advance your career by helping your organization understand that during the emerging growth years of your product, the focus needs to be slightly heavier on net-new accounts and should migrate to an existing-account focus as your market share matures.[2]

Winning Strategies and Tactics

Good software is about bringing value to the market, but value is relative. A prototype is "good" if it is compelling and easy to show off. In contrast, how "good" a mission-critical software product such as a web server or a relational database is might be measured more by its performance (speed) and availability (up-time). The strategies you use depend on what kinds of products and services you are offering and the customers you are going after. The definition of *value* changes significantly depending on your audience and where your product sits in the maturity lifecycle.

Loosely, in the software world, the audience can be divided into a small range of categories:

1. Customers with IT infrastructure

2. Independent software vendors who sell or resell software and services

---

[2] It's worth pointing out that many software projects are not developed for sale. Many relate to custom applications developed exclusively for a single organization (such as an in-house application developed by a bank for its own use), research projects developed by universities, or federal research projects. Software development isn't only about creating software that can be sold to others.

3. Customers via hosted services (cloud computing)

4. Consumer software for personal computing

Each of these target audiences has a range of personalities and risk tolerances, from very adventurous companies that like to try out the latest and greatest product to be on the cutting edge of operational efficiencies, to the most conservative companies that adopt only proven and mature technologies. In his classic book on technology adoption, *Crossing the Chasm,* Geoffrey Moore categorizes risk toleration as a normal distribution he calls "the technology adoption lifecycle." The most aggressive technology adaptors, called "innovators," will always be the first to try new products, although they represent the smallest community and a community that doesn't expect to pay much (or anything) for their dabbling with emerging technology. The next group, which is larger, is the early adopters, followed by the early majority, then the late majority, and, finally the most conservative group: the adoption laggards. The majority of your revenue stream for any software product will come from the last three communities. The early and late majority represent the bulk of paying customers. The laggards, although somewhat smaller in number of paying customers, often include some of the most conservative and risk-averse consumers. This group might include banks and insurance companies, who are also famous for having deep pockets. The innovators and early adopters represent the most critical communities for brand-new products, especially those that will introduce disruptive technology.

To simplify this discussion, let's compress Moore's categorization of the technology adoption lifecycle to three categories instead of five, as shown in Figure 2.2: early adopters, majority adopters, and late adopters.

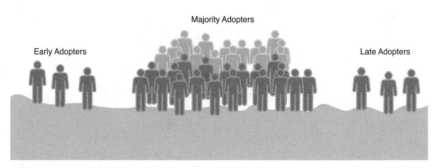

FIGURE 2.2   Adoption cycle by risk tolerance

The software technologies you can offer these groups can also be categorized as follows:

▶ **Disruptive technology.** These are sea-changing technologies that create new markets and often replace old ones. For example, the NPN transistor created a completely new market and caused the vacuum tube market to virtually disappear overnight. It offered dramatically superior size, power consumption, and speed for switching and amplification.

▶ **Incremental improvements.** These are improvements to your existing products and services that help solidify your existing customers and, hopefully, attract new ones. They do not create new markets, but they expand and cement the existing ones. An example here might be adding a high availability feature to an existing relational database product or adding grammar checking to an existing word-processing application.

▶ **Competitive offerings.** Many software companies have made their fortunes not by constantly introducing disruptive technology, but simply by following the leaders. Watching the leader and being quick to provide competitive and, hopefully, leapfrog technology is a great way to make money while reducing risk. The challenge is timing: If you wait for a disruptive technology to take hold—perhaps an 18-month cycle, at which point you begin your own 18-month cycle to develop a competitive offering—by the time you reach market, you'll be three years behind with very little hope of catching up without a large, disproportional investment in R&D.

So we've now defined four separate customer criteria, shown in Table 2.1.

TABLE 2.1   Customer Criteria

CRITERIA	DESCRIPTION
Target platform	Customers with IT infrastructure, ISVs, SaaS users, and personal computing
Software or service impact	Disruptive, incremental, competitive
Customer's risk tolerance	Early adopters, majority adopters, late adopters
Type of sale	New customers, existing customers

For each combination of these axes, the market will be looking for eight quality characteristics most significantly (see Table 2.2).

TABLE 2.2   Quality Characteristics

CHARACTERISTIC	DESCRIPTION
1) Unique technical and business value form	This is provided by function, performance, or factor.
2) High reliability	This is measured potentially by both the rate of apparent failures or Mean Time to Failure (MTTF) and availability, which measures the system's ability to keep running (even in the face of errors).
3) Referenceable customer base	This helps define how believable and trusted you are.
4) Market share	The larger your share, the lower the perceived risk in buying your product.
5) Ease of use	Everybody hates software that's complicated to use. Some companies tolerate it more than others, depending on their needs.
6) Ease of administration	How much effort is there for your customers' IT staff to administer your product? IT staff are expensive, but these costs gets amortized over many users and servers.
7) Cost	Everyone is concerned about cost, but there's a huge range. Large banks will pay a lot more for the exact same software than home users if they see a business need.
8) Solution completeness	Early adopters will tolerate incompleteness more than others. You don't need to be fully functional to be a success.

For example, depending on the kind of software we're providing, the earliest adopters may put up with more bugs, expect few or no references, and tolerate a less complete solution. (That's not always true, especially if our software is mission critical or has important security or safety considerations). In return, they expect pretty low cost and substantial business value from the new technology. Conversely, the late adopters will expect a very complete solution with high reliability and lots of reference accounts before moving to the new technology. Software as a service (SaaS) users and ISVs will place a premium on ease of use, which is the nature of their business space. Mission-critical systems with life-threatening consequences will place a huge premium on reliability, and so on.

Here's an example to illustrate the process. Let's assume you and I have founded a company together, GroovyData Co., which develops a new database product to provide SaaS-like access to data while keeping all data persistent in main memory for ultra-fast access. We plan to scale this with a huge data center of ultra-cheap machines. Because we're running our business on cheap machines, we provide availability by keeping four copies of every record over three geographies. If a server fails, two or three others always remain to keep servicing requests. Our business idea is to save customers the fuss and bother of having their own internal database systems while providing five nines of availability and ultimate ease of use. What we lose in network latency we hope to gain in the efficiency of main-memory access. We hope this will disrupt the USD 23 billion database market. Even a small slice of that will make us happy, but we're new on the scene. Table 2.3 describes the profile of our initial customers.

TABLE 2.3   SaaS User Example

CUSTOMER CRITERIA	OUR TARGET
Target platform	SaaS
Software or service impact	Disruptive
Customer's risk tolerance	Early adopters
Type of sale	New customers

With these in mind, we can easily think through the quality characteristics that will initially matter to GroovyData Co., as shown in Table 2.4.

TABLE 2.4   Quality Characteristics That Matter

QUALITY	IMPORTANCE	DESCRIPTION
Technical and business value	High	We're offering hosted main-memory database processing with super-high availability. It's important that we make this noticeably unique from other database experiences.
High reliability	High	This is a huge part of our value proposition. Because we're not storing anything on disk, eyebrows will be raised about data persistence. We need this to be compelling.
References	Low	Not necessary to attract the early adopters. We hope to create a reference base from them. We'll need these over time, but not now.
Market share	Low	We're new on the block.
Ease of use	High	We're offering a hosted service. Our value proposition is that we're going to handle all the difficult administration pieces. What the user experiences needs to be super easy.
Ease of administration	Low	Because this is hosted, in the short term we can hide a lot of the administrative complexity in the data center and manage it with our own staff.
Cost	High	Right now we need to get some momentum going and generate excitement and references. It's critical that we make this inexpensive.
Solution completeness	Low	Just the bare-minimum database function will do. We'll stick with ODBC and JDBC interfaces for now.

It was a pretty simple analysis, but it helped clarify for us who we're selling to, what we're selling, and the quality attributes we need to focus on in the short term. It wasn't all obvious—for example, we realized through this that we needed to place a super-high focus on reliability, something that most new entries into the market would have felt they could compromise on. We also realized that completeness was not a critical point for us and finally that we could bury some administrative complexity behind our firewall as long as the user experience remains simple.

If product development has one truism, it is this: You won't be able to be all things to all market segments in a single product release. Whether you are a software developer, a product architect, or a project manager, your goal should be to understand the quality characteristics of your market or desired market. It is critical to your success that you do your part to help your organization internalize these. Clever companies and savvy teams understand this and make deliberate choices about what they are trying to deliver to the market. These are the companies, the teams, and the individuals who are on the path to success.

When (Not) to Listen to Your Customers

The problem with the marketplace is that it can't tell you if there is demand for a product that doesn't yet exist. The marketplace responds strongly and decisively to products and services that exist, but it's an opinion-free zone about hypothetical product ideas. To quote Apple Computer CEO and co-founder Steve Jobs, "A lot of times, people don't know what they want until you show it to them." When you depend on your customers to tell you what they want or need, then you are, by definition, setting yourself up to be a follower. As Henry Ford said, "If I'd listened to customers, I'd have given them a faster horse." What the marketplace can tell you is whether they like what you've done.

Starting a new project requires a leap of faith—there is always risk associated with creating an initial service or product offering, even a simple prototype. Once you have an actual implementation, however rudimentary, then the market can tell you everything. When I interviewed Marc Benioff, CEO of Saleforce.com, he was emphatic that the success of his now-billion-dollar-a-year company was directly linked to its strategic focus on listening to users. They didn't ask the market if it wanted or needed CRM in the cloud, but once they built their hosted CRM software as a service offering, you bet they listened very carefully to what their users had to say about it—and they still do.

From the very beginning, we enlisted the insight of the people who would use our service, and we listened to their advice. As a result, we built something customers loved, and they were eager to talk about their experience using the service. I had never seen this in the enterprise software world. Customers actually stood up at our events and talked about their experiences with our service. There was an evangelistic feel to it that was very positive and very contagious. In that way, our customers taught us that the best way to sell the service was not by selling features, as most companies did, but by selling the customers' success with our unconventional model. We never stopped listening to the customer, and we used their feedback to evolve our service as well. Once customers were successful, they asked for more: more customization, more integrations, more applications. They pushed us. We created only what they wanted, not what we thought they wanted.
—Marc Benioff, CEO and founder, Saleforce.com

Things are pretty similar at Google. Marissa Mayer notes that innovation at Google has been driven from conception through successful productization by heavy use of user feedback. Google uses its software as a service platform to quickly float new product concepts on Google Labs, garnering immediate feedback from its huge worldwide user base. Their development model is all about iteration, revising the initial kernel of an idea based on user feedback. The kernel, the initial seed of a new idea, comes from innovation: creative ideas that smart people dream up without the market telling them what's needed. These seedlings require intuition, creativity, and vision to conjure up enough passion to convince others they are worth pursuing. The refinements, often major, come largely from listening to users.

Good software has a very different meaning, depending on where your software is in the maturity cycle, your audience, and how you want it to evolve and grow. When you start thinking about what your customers really need from your software and where both you and they are sitting on the maturity cycle and risk tolerance, you can make much better strategy decisions and deliver truly great software to market. Helping your product stay focused on the right qualities is a leadership activity that, when well-timed, will help identify you as a strategic business thinker. Perhaps more important, you can personally have a very large and positive impact by helping refine these attributes, leading to better project/product results for everyone involved, including shareholders and employees alike. On the flip side, understanding when your leadership team is far off the path to success because they're consistently reading the markets wrong should signal you that you're riding a flailing stallion and that it might be time to find a better race horse.

An Interview with Marissa Mayer

Google VP and First Lady of Software

CURRENT POSITION

Vice President, Search Products & User Experience, Google, Inc.

CLAIM TO FAME

Google Vice President, Google's 20th employee, and arguably the most powerful woman in software today

DATE OF BIRTH

May 30, 1975

EDUCATION

M.S. in Computer Science, Stanford University, 1997–1999
B.S. in Symbolic Systems, Stanford University, 1992–1997

FAVORITE PASTIMES & HOBBIES

Traveling, skiing, running, flying kites

BIOGRAPHY

Marissa leads the company's product management efforts on search products—web search, images, news, books, products, maps, Google Earth, the Google Toolbar, Google Desktop, Google Health, Google Labs, and more. She joined Google in 1999 as the company's first female engineer and led the user interface and web server teams at that time. Her efforts have included designing and developing Google's search interface; internationalizing the site to more than 100 languages; defining Google News, Gmail, and Orkut; and launching more than 100 features and products on Google.com. Several patents have been filed on her work in artificial intelligence and interface design. In her spare time, Marissa organizes Google Movies—outings a few times a year to see the latest blockbusters—for more than 6,000 people (employees plus family and friends).

Concurrently with her full-time work at Google, Marissa has taught introductory computer programming classes at Stanford to more than 3,000 students. Stanford has recognized her with the Centennial Teaching Award and the Forsythe Award for her outstanding contribution to undergraduate education.

Before joining Google, Marissa worked at the UBS research lab (Ubilab) in Zurich, Switzerland, and at SRI International in Menlo Park, California.

Marissa has been featured in various publications, including *Newsweek* ("10 Tech Leaders of the Future"), *Red Herring* ("15 Women to Watch"), *Business 2.0* ("Silicon Valley Dream Team"), *BusinessWeek, Fortune*, and *Fast Company.*

Graduating with honors, Marissa earned her B.S. in Symbolic Systems and her M.S. in Computer Science from Stanford University. For both degrees, she specialized in artificial intelligence.

"...My first computer was a Macintosh Centris 610"

How did you get started in software?

Growing up in Wisconsin, I saved all my babysitting money—I was a prolific babysitter from age 13 to 18—to buy my first computer, which was a Macintosh Centris 610. I remember having to be taught how to turn my Centris on! Before going to Stanford, the most sophisticated computers I had worked on were the Commodore 64 and very simple early PC computers that ran things like Bank Street Writer. At Stanford, I had my first experience with a mouse—I didn't know what it was or how it worked. At the end of my freshman year, I took CS105A, a computer science course for nonmajors. I entered all the course's programming competitions, did all the extra credit, and really loved the experience of programming. When I came back my sophomore year, I changed my major to symbolic systems so I could study computer science, philosophy, psychology, and linguistics. I started taking the computer science core courses, where I learned how to program in C and later LISP, concurrency, and object-oriented programming.

Was there an event in your life that had a pivotal effect on your career?

Two teachers at Stanford put me on this path. One was Tom Wasow, and the other was Eric Roberts. After I had my really good experiences with my computer science course, I came back that fall and was considering either computer science or symbolic systems as a major. I met with Tom Wasow, who was the director of the symbolic systems department and also a professor of linguistics. I asked him a lot of questions about how symbolic systems worked, what was interesting about the major, and whether it was applicable as a career after graduation. At the end of the meeting, he said, "I love running this major because all the most interesting students at Stanford are in it. And you should want to be in the symbolic systems major because you should want to be around all those interesting people. And you yourself should want to be an interesting person." I liked the idea that being a symbolic systems major just magically makes you interesting! So I remember that quite fondly. And that really did inspire me and helped me understand that a lot of what I could take from my classes was from my peers.

The other influential teacher was Eric Roberts. After I took my computer science course, I won a programming contest for the introductory graphics part of the course. I wrote a screen saver because I loved the graphics package. I was the first person to enter the graphics contest with a screen saver, which has now become a standard assignment for computer science graphics introductory classes. One part of the prize was a 100% on the final, in advance. The other prize was an invitation to Eric's house for dinner, and it was then that I really connected with him. He's been a big proponent of women in technology throughout his career, so he sort of scooped me up and really encouraged me. He told me, "I think you're really good at this. I think you could be really good at teaching this. I think it's really good to have more women involved." And he encouraged me to be a section leader. After I proved to be a good section leader, he made me a head teaching assistant for the course, which is how I started writing a lot of the tests and exams, grading, and managing people. Eric eventually gave me my first teaching experience. So I think that meeting with Tom Wasow, winning the contest, and getting to go to Eric's house for dinner were pivotal moments.

Do you have a pet peeve in any aspect of the software world?

For me, there are probably two. I don't understand the religious wars surrounding rendering engines in browsers. When you talk to people who are using KHTML, Konqeror, or another engine, and when you talk to people from Firefox or Safari who are doing the browsers, the conversation quickly devolves into which rendering engine is superior and why they won't contribute to the other rendering engine. As a designer, I am simply frustrated that presentation elements are not consistently rendered by the different renderers. I'm hoping that the software world will settle on a single renderer and have everyone contribute to that, but it has been slow to congeal. That's been one frustration of mine. The other frustration is the lack of women in

Marissa Mayer

Marissa Mayer

computer science. I'd like to see the industry encourage women to contribute software in more significant numbers.

Why do you think there are few women in computing? Where does the problem originate? The industrial level? The educational level?

A lot of people define their career pursuits in the teenage years and college years. Women may choose to avoid computing partly due to stereotyping and partly because this is what girls are coached to do. Video games, for example, were geared to males, which may have made software tangible for a lot of men: They could see in games how programming could generate things. For women, the ways computer science could touch their lives hasn't always been as cogent. But I believe the Web is making technology more tangible for women. With the growth of the Web, we've seen an increase in the number of women entering computer science. Every day, they use sites like Flickr, Google, and Facebook, and now they can see how computer science can have a meaningful impact on their lives.

"Some of the code I wrote still exists today"

What do you consider your greatest accomplishments or contributions to software?

I think this kind of question is always hard for people who are midstream in their careers because it's difficult to foresee which contributions will prove meaningful. And since you're still in the middle of it, you hope there are bigger accomplishments to come. Technically, I wrote a good chunk of the Google web server, the scalable web server that answers the user's query and writes the results pages for things like the main web search and image search. It's how we interface to the back ends and do the presentation to the page. I understand that some of the code I wrote still exists today—I feel that's a hearty contribution. I also believe that an important part of software is the interface design—how people interact with software—and my contribution there has been to try to elevate interface design to more of a science than an art. For example, Google was an early proponent of split A/B testing and one of the largest companies to run it. Early on, I helped with programming the web server to take a percentage of the traffic and give users a new interface experience, and then to measure how that interface experience changed their overall behavior and happiness. But we also use split A/B testing in a data-driven framework to inform the design for the home page or the main search engine, or iGoogle and Google Toolbar, Google Maps, Google News ... those are all interfaces that I helped design.

What makes you feel successful in your work in software?

For me it's ultimately about the opportunity to touch people's everyday lives. Being at Google has been really meaningful. People really need information—about health problems, about career decisions—because it helps inform them. That fundamental element of information retrieval coupled with the fact that it affects people's everyday lives is very compelling to me.

"Work for people who invest in you and challenge you"

What suggestions do you have for others on being successful in software (either R&D or business)?

I would offer four pieces of advice that are not necessarily restricted to software.

1. Find somewhere you feel extremely comfortable because that will help you participate. You want to be at a place where you can think out loud and share your opinions and your thoughts, be it on software architecture decisions or company strategy.

2. Work for people who invest in you and challenge you. You want people who are strong mentors. Tom Wasow and Eric Roberts changed my life. Jonathan Rosenberg, Eric Schmidt, Larry Page, Sergey Brin, and other people here at Google have given me a ton of responsibility because they believed in me and wanted to invest in me.

3. Try to work with the smartest people you can find, since they challenge you to think and work better. I came to Google because I wanted to work alongside Craig Silverstein, who, to this day, is one of the five smartest people and one of the best coders I have ever met. For my first three years here, I was Craig's coding partner. Craig did all my code review and made me a much stronger programmer. When you work with really top-notch, smart engineers, it will fundamentally change the way you think and the way you program.

4. Always do something that you're not ready to do. Doing something that scares you a little bit means you're taking a step forward, you're going to learn something new, and you're going to grow.

Marissa Mayer

You have a B.S. in Symbolic Systems and an M.S. in Computer Science from Stanford University. Larry and Sergey also have graduate degrees. Do you feel graduate degrees in computer science (or an MBA, for that matter) are beneficial to career success in software?

I think the unique thing about my educational background is that I did things in the reverse order. Most people would do an undergraduate computer science major that would teach them a lot of the fundamentals of computing—how you write a compiler, how you write an operating system—and then go on to earn a master's degree and specialize. Interestingly, my concentration in symbolic systems allowed me to take upper-level computer science courses in artificial intelligence as part of my undergraduate degree. Then when I was graduating, I thought, "I'd really like to market myself as a computer scientist and software engineer, but what kind of software engineer has never written a compiler or never written an operating system?" So I went back as part of my master's degree to do those programming-intensive elements that weren't part of my undergraduate degree, to build out more of that specialization. Ultimately, I think having worked on large-scale systems that have been under load, that have many lines of code, and that are complex really helps computer scientists be successful. When you've been in school for a long time, you typically get exposed to projects like that. But I think the same is true of people in the industry, where the challenge is pushing yourself to work on complicated systems and being able to contribute to that code base. Whether it comes from academia or commercial experience doesn't matter so much as the sheer breadth of experience you have.

How do you stay on top of technology trends and innovation?

My current role is in product design and product management, and I try to extend the product strategy for the company. But I still like to write some programs every year. I do some programming on the weekends. Lately it's been more web-centric, using PHP and MySQL. The next thing I'll try to tackle is the Google App Engine. I'm looking to do a little more programming with Python and Ruby on Rails. But I think it's just an element of keeping my skills fresh by exploring some of these new trends and keeping my hand in coding, even if it's on the side of core Google work.

"...Play off the opportunities presented through work"

Time management ... technical leaders and executives are famous for being time-strapped. What strategies do you use to stay sane and use your time effectively?

One of my friends in college, Eleanor, would rank a list of things she needed to do by priority. She put them in order and started working on them from the top down. Naturally, the more important things push down less important things. But instead of being frustrated that you never get to the bottom of the priority queue, you can revel in the fact that you never have to work on things that weren't that important! So the fact that you never get to the bottom of your to-do list is actually a good thing because it means you are thinking about how to use your time. You're using your time in the most important, high-leverage way, and you're not letting yourself get distracted by things that won't have that big of an impact. Some people find it depressing when they are in that state and can never get to the bottom of a long to-do list. But my friend Eleanor's approach is a refreshing perspective. Either you can get overwhelmed with all the work there is to get done, or you can recognize that this is an opportunity to do the big and important things.

How do you achieve a work-life balance? How do you keep your professional life from dominating everything?

For me, work is really enjoyable, making it hard to define where work ends and fun begins. Not that I like to work too hard! I travel a lot—I'll travel for work for two or three days and decide to stay an extra day to experience a place I'd never visited. I look for ways to play off the opportunities presented through work, to get the most out of life.

What do you see as the coming changes in the software field over the next 10–15 years that will impact career opportunities or the way we develop software?

The Internet will fundamentally change the way software is developed, and, in many ways, it already has. Release cycles have accelerated, and new features are being developed all the time, which is a very different case than with shrink-wrapped software. When we look at our best products, including

Marissa Mayer

Marissa Mayer

YouTube and some of the acquisitions we've made, they are on weekly—if not daily—release cycles. We are constantly working to improve, and it's a much more iterative process. I also think that the data housing structures and basic server warehouses that are being built up will fundamentally change the way people access data. If a piece of information really matters to you, be it a picture or a document, it's foolhardy even in today's day and age for you to be storing it only on your computer and not also on the Web. These server warehouses enable you to store your data in a way that is replicated, maintained, and guaranteed to ensure that your data continues to live on. Everyone should be leveraging the cloud, as it's a much better place to store data. User names, passwords, and securities keep it completely within your control. It's actually a lot safer than your laptop, which could be subject to hardware failures, loss, theft, and accidents.

What final words of wisdom or caution do you have for people entering the field?

I have felt very lucky during my nine years at Google to be a part of something that is so much a part of people's daily lives and that, in some respects, has changed the world. I think that's what software offers to people, the opportunity to make a broad impact on the world. I encourage all those entering the field to embrace opportunities to work on really big and hard problems that will affect people's everyday lives, and then be thoughtful and respectful of the fact that you've been able to participate in such an amazing and revolutionary time.

CHAPTER 3

School Versus Job

"Every person takes the limits of their own field of vision for the limits of the world."
—*Arthur Schopenhauer (1788-1860)*

School is very different from professional work. Some people stumble in their early professional careers by failing to transition from the school environment they've been immersed in for nearly twenty years into the brave new world of software professionalism. Students operate in a world of highly constrained, well-defined workloads (though it certainly doesn't feel that way when you're a student). As a student your scope is limited to a set of courses that are intended to address your professional needs upon graduation. In short, school is about learning. Professional life is more about getting things done, being both productive and innovative in a way that jells with the people you work with. It's not uncommon for junior staff to treat the workplace as though it were simply the next phase of school. Few things could be more disastrous.

I also believe that a great weakness of many middle managers is failing to understand the differences between the academic and corporate skills requirements, leading them to hire the best and brightest students rather than the best and brightest professionals. A good student is usually smart, hardworking, and conscientious. But success in scholastics doesn't guarantee an ability to innovate, learn independently, work in a team, or show leadership—which are all critical skills for professionals. Hiring the wrong skill set means hiring less effective people, and when that phenomenon is multiplied over many people in an organization, the net result is a marked reduction in the effectiveness and talent of the entire organization. Put another way, hiring the wrong people for the job is a bad way to run a company. On the flip side, when new graduates position themselves for the workplace, assimilating the culture and needs of a professional life, and managers learn to recruit the best employees for their needs rather than the best students, the mixture forms a potent brew for the rapid success of individuals and organizations alike.

Limited Field of Vision

Whether you're in school studying the art and science of computer programming or working as a software professional, you exist and function in a largely constrained and somewhat artificial environment. Life is a kind of fishbowl. Fish in a bowl can swim and explore, up to a point, but their view of the world is remarkably limited. The fish sees almost nothing beyond the glass of the fishbowl, in part because its eyes can't focus that far and in part because of the diffraction of light as it crosses the boundary from water to glass to air. If the fish could see beyond the fishbowl, at most, its view of the world would be limited to the room the bowl resides in: a few chairs, a sofa, a bookshelf. The real world outside of the fishbowl is far larger and more profound than the tiny colored glass stones and rocks that have been artificially placed in the fish's manufactured domain. But, for better or worse, the fish is blissfully unaware. Software professionals are fish, too.

School Is a Fishbowl

School is a highly artificial environment where the workload is relatively well controlled, where all participants have similar work challenges, and where people are encouraged to do individual work. If you are a student, you probably think I've completely forgotten what school is all about because what I've described is nothing like the world you're living in. Very true, but it's a relative comment. Even though some professors demand a far heavier workload than others, the reality is that these variations are small compared to the variation that would occur without a fixed curriculum, such as in the environment outside of school. You'll protest: "But if there were no set curriculum, that wouldn't be fair!" and you'll be 100% correct. That's one reason schools must have a set curriculum—because school needs to be fair. The process of making school fair leads to a wide array of artificial constraints and behaviors that, although fair, necessarily create a framework of a highly constrained fishbowl.

Second, although schools encourage students to do their own work, on penalty of expulsion or severe reprimand, professional work is saturated with the ubiquitous mantra of "teamwork." In school, your success depends on individual effort, whereas professional life depends frequently on your ability to work in teams.

Finally, very little that students experience in school is directly influenced by market pressures. There is some indirect influence, as the market drives new technologies to the fore, which, over time, influences curricula. Professors get involved in new technologies and introduce these themes into the courses they teach. Over time, the system of professors, industrial grants, the drive for publications, and review committees will ensure that the educational process stays reasonably connected to current industrial trends. All the while, the student body is happily oblivious.

Welcome to the fishbowl. While you're in it, you won't be able to see too far past the glass. That's fine, as long as you realize that there is a world outside the fishbowl that's a rather different place, then you're well positioned to try to learn more about it.

Industry Is a Fishbowl

How in the world could industry be considered a fishbowl? Isn't industrial work the definition of the real world? It's time for a reality check! The software industry is sensationally complex, and it requires a broad range of skills and disciplines to construct a successful business (the larger the enterprise, the more this is true). People become specialized and focus on a narrow scope of the industrial machine. Every employee has a domain. High up in the organizational hierarchy, people working on the big picture can't possibly know all the little details. At the other end, the detail workers, down in the trenches, have a very hard time understanding the broader scope of every project that is related to them.

Second, if you're like most software developers, your compensation is only loosely tied to the market success of the projects you work on, unless you are an owner in the company (such as owning stock or stock options) or have a compensation plan that is directly tied to quotas or business performance. Similarly, your compensation is only loosely connected to years of service or the technical depth of your job.

Your compensation at work will never directly increase with your productivity or the success of your product. Employees who work five times more will not get paid five times more than others. If your company revenue soars and revenues increase by tenfold, don't expect employee salaries to increase by a factor of ten. If this sounds discouraging, it shouldn't be—remember, the sword cuts both ways. Just as you are unlikely to see your salary grow 300 times in size when your product begins to sell and earn 300 times more revenue, your salary will not be cut to 1/300th if the inverse befalls you. And although the most productive and valuable people might not get compensated proportional to their contributions in a literal measurement, they do get paid substantially more. Over time, they will accrue much more accomplishment, fame, money, and freedom of movement for their efforts.

Professional software positions almost always limit the software developer from the sales and marketing world, and in larger companies, software developers can be heavily isolated from customers, business strategy, and product planning. In short, it's a controlled and not truly reflective environment. So it's a fishbowl—what you see is not a reflection of reality.

By understanding and being sensitive to the artificial limitations of your environment, you can begin an active effort to extend your skills and expand your professional potential.

Leveraging the Differences

These fishbowls are very different both in style and in kind. The most dramatic difference is the approach to collaboration and teamwork. School teaches you technical skills in software development and software engineering and some teamwork and social skills along the way. The 18 or more years you spent in school deeply entrench within you expectations and values that are sometimes at odds with the expectations of the workplace. For example, at school we are taught that our work must be our own and that reusing the work of others is a serious crime that can lead to suspension or expulsion from the institution. Conversely, in a professional software development company, few things propel a software development project more effectively and reduce time to market than code reuse. Code reuse is an objective in the workforce but a serious liability at school. Similarly, at school, people are required to do their own work, except in the cases of a few group projects. Within corporate software projects, people are expected to work together and help others with some fraction of their time even when they are not directly assigned to a project. The scope of teamwork ranges from small groups to team efforts measured in dozens or even hundreds of people working toward a collective goal to deliver a project or a product.

Many new software developers cripple their careers by clinging to the entrenched ideology they were immersed in for years that "your work must be your own." For good reason: From early childhood until our mid-20s, this is the message we are all consistently given and ordered to follow. Post-graduation, this edict dissolves and is replaced by the belief that work should *de rigueur* be shared and collaborative. It's critical to your success that you rapidly adopt a collective model for success, code and documentation reuse, and skills sharing. You should collaborate, share, and team with others as much as possible and give as many people credit for that effort as is reasonable.

Table 3.1 lists some other key differences in the school versus work paradigm.

TABLE 3.1   Differences Between School and Industry

CHARACTERISTIC	DIFFERENCE
Drivers and shapers	School requirements are defined by a committee of academics who define the course curriculum. Successful businesses are always driven by market demands: customers and business climate.
Freedom of motion	Within a computer science (or related) major, the range of courses is fairly limited. You can usually take a few electives each term, but they represent a small diversion from your major. In contrast, the range of what you can work on in industry is profound, crossing deeply technical development work, research, business development, management, marketing, and sales. Even within the technical space, there is a huge range of roles, from quality assurance to development, from architecture to innovation and new product generation.
Innovation	The level playing field that school provides limits the opportunities for technical innovation. Exceptions exist, particularly in graduate school thesis programs, which allow students an opportunity to do independent research. By contrast, industry thrives on innovation; it is the distinguishing feature that separates one high-tech company from another.
Interpersonal networking	Networking is useful at school, especially if you need help from classmates to stay on top of assignments. The best and brightest students don't rely heavily on networking with others. In industry, social networking is essential because it connects you to people and ideas that are necessary to help channel the organizational energy of the business.
Leadership	School is largely a level playing field, and the institution works hard to create a common circumstance for all the students within a specific major. Although some opportunities for leadership exist within school (captain of a sports team or student council), schools generally are hierarchy free within the student body. Students do not lead other students. Within industry, leadership skills and leadership roles are prized and encouraged.
Learning and doing	School is about learning, and work is about producing. It's true that school requires students to produce and industry requires employees to learn, but the focus is heavily inverted.
Payment	You pay to go to school, but you get paid to work. That means your college or university works for you, but after graduation, you work for your employer.

TABLE 3.1   Differences between School and Industry (continued)

CHARACTERISTIC	DIFFERENCE
Productivity	Educational institutions reward students with grades. The reward for doing well is a higher grade on a project or an exam. Your GPA is the measure of your success. In industry, the measurement is "contribution," which loosely translates to "productivity" in the broad sense of producing code, designs, technical innovation, new business, improved organizational efficiency or capacity, and so on. Businesses value productivity, whereas educational institutions do not.
Recognition	In school, your evaluation is designed to be fairly quantitative and measurable. Your grades on assignments, tests, and exams define your GPA. Within a professional software development organization, people have widely varying roles, and the evaluations become much more qualitative and subjective.
Risk and impact to others	The risks of messing up your education are serious, but they predominantly affect you and your family. In industry, large projects depend on the skill of the engineering team, and if you screw up, the consequences can affect the entire corporation, many of its employees, and a broad range of customers and business partners.
Personal portfolio	Neither school nor industry requires you to have a personal portfolio of any kind. By "portfolio," I mean a collection of externally visible accomplishments. Having an impressive portfolio won't help you be a better student (though, in some cases, it can help buttress your candidacy for scholarships or graduate school admittance). In a professional setting, however, having a portfolio of major innovations, successful programming projects you've delivered on time and with high quality, trade publications, scientific papers, public speaking engagements, and positions on industrial committees can help propel your career and open new opportunities for collaboration and engagement.

The greatest challenge of your first few years in industry is to unlearn what the educational environment of the past 18 years or more has drilled into you. Understand that you have entered a brave new world with radically different rules of engagement.

Unquestionably, school and industry both require a lot of hard work and are very competitive environments. Many career paths in fields other than software have a slower pace of learning and change following graduation. The rules of the game change less frequently in most professions. The software industry is distinguished by its dynamism and rapid evolution. Everything can change in a few years. The rapid changes that characterize high tech mean that software professionals are necessarily life-long learners. One thing is certain: If you were hoping for a gently loping career that largely takes care of itself, something akin to a warm, comfortable bath, then software is the wrong place for you. Expect a wild ride.

An Interview with Jon Bentley

Author, Programming Pearls

CURRENT POSITION

Distinguished Member of Technical Staff, Software Technology Research Department, Avaya Labs Research

CLAIM TO FAME

Author of *Programming Pearls* and *Writing Efficient Programs*; developer of several widely used data structures and algorithms; recipient of the Dr. Dobb's Excellence in Programming Award in 2000 for "advancing the craft of computer programming."

DATE OF BIRTH

February 20, 1953

EDUCATION

Ph.D. in Computer Science, University of North Carolina, 1974–1976
M.S. in Computer Science, University of North Carolina, 1974–1976
B.S. in Mathematical Sciences, Stanford University, 1972–1974
A.S. candidate, Long Beach City College, 1970–1972

FAVORITE PASTIMES & HOBBIES

Hiking, climbing, and mountaineering; volunteering as an emergency medical technician

BIOGRAPHY

Jon started programming computers in 1969 and was first paid to write programs in 1970 as a student employee at Long Beach City College. After two years, he transferred to Stanford, where he completed his undergraduate degree in 1974. Jon had many exceptional opportunities as an undergraduate: He worked as a programmer at Xerox Palo Alto Research Center when they were developing the personal computer as we know it, and his under-graduate paper on "k-d trees" (under the supervision of Don Knuth) proposed a geometric data structure that has since found wide use. Jon attended grad school at the University of North Carolina and then taught at Carnegie Mellon University from 1976 to 1982, where he had many excellent colleagues and students. At Carnegie, Jon concentrated his main research on algorithms (with a focus on geometry) but also branched out into many other areas and wrote *Writing Efficient Programs* (Prentice Hall, 1982), a book on code tuning.

Jon started working at Bell Labs in 1982 and found a wonderful home in the Computing Science Research Center, the group that gave the world UNIX, C, and C++. He worked in many different areas there, including theoretical algorithms, applied algorithms, software tools, and products such as tele-phones and switches. For several years, he wrote the "Programming Pearls" column in *Communications of the ACM* and compiled selected columns in the books *Programming Pearls* (ACM Press, 1986; second edition Addison-Wesley Professional, 1999) and *More Programming Pearls* (Addison-Wesley Professional, 1988).

After retiring from Bell Labs in 2001, Jon took two-and-a-half months off to "play in the mountains" and then joined Avaya Labs Research. There he has worked in many areas, including algorithms, software engineering (with Dave Weiss), human authentication, and enterprise communication systems. In 2007, he filed about a dozen patent applications.

"…The favorable termination of an attempt"

How did you get started in software?

When I was a junior in high school, I found myself doing repeated calcula-tions involving the shape of an aircraft wing as I worked on a Boy Scout merit badge. Rather than doing boring computations for 20 minutes, I spent several hours learning FORTRAN and writing a program to do the job. I was able to sweet-talk my way into an account at Long Beach City College (just a few houses down the street from my home), wrote the program on punched cards, and had the answers just a few short hours later. I've been hooked ever since.

What do you consider your greatest accomplishments or contributions to software?

Books: *Programming Pearls* and *Writing Efficient Programs*

Theoretical algorithms: k-d tree, scan lines for geometric intersections, mul-tidimensional divide-and-conquer, multikey quick sort and ternary search trees, and locally adaptive data compression

Applied and experimental algorithms: analysis of bin packing; books, papers, and columns that bridge theory and practice

Software tools: UNIX grap, anim, l2fit, and qsort

Software techniques: Systematic code tuning, little languages, back-of-the-envelope calculations, and minimalism

Products: PRL 5.0 (a domain-specific language used in the 5ESS) and AT&T Computer Telephone 8130

Do you have a pet peeve in any aspect of the software world?

The struggle in software between simplicity and completeness will not—and should not—end. I would, however, like to see elegance and simplicity triumph a bit more often.

You've had distinguished contributions to software algorithms and some important products, but you've also invested time and energy into writing. Why?

Writing code is a joy; writing English is just plain hard work. When I took Don Knuth's data structures course at Stanford, we were required to write a term paper. Ray Finkel and I wrote ours together on quad trees, although we originally called them "2-4" trees. At a meeting in his office, Knuth pointed out that the name clashed with "2-3" trees, so we quickly thought of their four-way branching and the central area of the Stanford campus, and renamed them "quad trees." That paper later appeared in Acta Informatica as my first publication; when I held the journal in my hand, I had no doubt that the hard work of writing was worth it. When I was a teacher, I followed in Knuth's footsteps and required a term paper in my undergraduate classes on algorithms and combinatorial analysis.

What makes you feel successful?

My dictionary defines *success* as the "favorable termination of an attempt." Since I'm not yet finished with my attempt at software, I have no idea whether I'll be successful, and I therefore can't answer the question. I can identify, however, three different activities that have given me great personal fulfillment.

1. Solving a hard problem. It might involve code, mathematics, or English prose. It is most rewarding after you have butted your head against it for a long time before it finally succumbs.

2. Seeing your work widely used. The PRL 5.0 language that I helped design was used to generate code for AT&T's 5ESS switch, which was

connected to about half the telephone lines then in use in the United States.

3. Having an impact on the technical community. It is incredible when your work is published, read, understood, and acted upon.

Some work wins big and scores in all three areas. Other times I have been quite satisfied popularizing the ideas of others or doing work that I knew was important yet very few others would ever see.

"...The harder I work, the luckier I get"

How do you stay on top of technology trends and innovation?

The Web is a great start, but it is rarely the end. I'm a big fan of conferences and workshops, where you can see the latest and greatest and hear the buzz in the corridors about what is coming soon. But the only way to keep up-to-date in any field is by hard work—lots of it—and by pounding on your keyboard until everything comes together gracefully.

Technical leaders and executives are famous for being time-strapped. What strategies can one use to stay sane and use one's time effectively?

A good worker always keeps all tools in fine working order. The most valuable resource you have is you; take care of yourself. It's fine to sprint every now and then, but remember that a technical life is a marathon; pace yourself. And then pamper yourself—give yourself the time to do what you love. I now find that I get at least half of my good technical ideas while hiking in remote mountains or driving back from the hospital after an EMS call. Sometimes I'll go into the backcountry or off to an EMT class for a week without ever once thinking about computing and then return to work to find that a really hard problem has an unexpectedly simple solution that I had just been unable to see.

How can one achieve a work-life balance? How can one keep professional life from dominating everything?

Set inviolable rules (the easy part) and then don't violate them (always much harder). In the mid-1990s, I was simultaneously involved in rushing a product to market and being the full-time single dad of a middle-school son. I made a point to take my son to school every morning, to pick him up most afternoons, and to have dinner with him and lots of other "quality time" every evening. At the slight expense of my pulling all-nighters on a weekly-or-more basis, everything worked out okay: We shipped the product without delay, it won national recognition, and my kid turned out okay (except, of course, for becoming a software engineer). A few months after the product was shipped, my company cancelled it, and a few years later, I had a heart attack at age 46. Since then, I've been willing to draw much more reasonable rules and abide by them, well, like my life depended on them. Think very, very hard about the word *life* in the phrase "work-life balance!"

What do you see as the coming changes in the software field over the next 10–15 years that will impact career opportunities either positively or negatively?

I won't try to predict the future. In the past, though, there have always been wonderful opportunities for people with the attitude of "The harder I work, the luckier I get."

"Do what you love!"

What suggestions do you have for others on being successful in software (either R&D or business)?

Here are some suggestions that have worked for me so far:

- Follow your bliss.

- Learn everything you can; it is all relevant to software, somewhere, someday, somehow.

- Try new things; stick with (and return to) old things.

- Work with the very best people.

- Get a mentor; learn from someone you admire.

- Give something back to your team, company, technical community, or neighborhood.

- Practice writing and coding; review the work of your peers and have them review yours.

- Be cool to your school—or your company, team, or whatever. Loyalty goes both ways.

Jon Bentley

Jon Bentley

- Read great books. Some of my favorites include Strunk and White's *Elements of Style* on writing English; Polya's *How to Solve It*, on mathematical problem solving; and R. E. D. Woolsey's *The Woolsey Papers*, on solving real problems.

I've not always been able to follow such laudable advice, but it has worked pretty well every time I've tried.

What final words of wisdom or caution do you have for people entering the field?

A wise word of caution: Do what you love! My passion for programming has been quite rewarding on many levels; if you follow your dream, I wish you as much luck and joy as I've had.

CHAPTER 4

Mission Impossible? Getting a Job in Software Development

"I don't want to achieve immortality through my work ...
I want to achieve it through not dying."
—Woody Allen (1935–)

Whether you are looking for your first major permanent job upon graduation or going through a job search later in your career, I can guarantee that finding a job is hard work. Fortunately, in our profession for the past few decades, demand has been high for software developers, and getting a job has been easier for us than many of our friends and neighbors in other fields. Whether it's hard or just plain impossible, you can use some tricks to improve the effectiveness of your hunt. In this chapter, I share some tips for new grads and seasoned professionals alike.

Choosing Wisely

Perhaps more important that getting a job is the question, what job do you want? During my interview with Marissa Mayer, she described her reasons for choosing her major at university and, ultimately, her choice to work for Google. Her reasons for both decisions were similar:

> I met with Tom Wasow, who was the director of the symbolic systems department and also a professor of linguistics. I asked him a lot of questions about how symbolic systems worked, what was interesting about the major, and whether it was applicable as a career after graduation. At the end of the meeting, he said, "I love running this

major because all the most interesting students at Stanford are in it. And you should want to be in the symbolic systems major because you should want to be around all those interesting people. And you yourself should want to be an interesting person." I liked the idea that being a symbolic systems major just magically makes you interesting! So I remember that quite fondly. And that really did inspire me....

Try to work with the smartest people you can find, since they challenge you to think and work better. I came to Google because I wanted to work alongside Craig Silverstein, who, to this day, is one of the five smartest people and one of the best coders I have ever met. For my first three years here, I was Craig's coding partner. Craig did all my code review and made me a much stronger programmer. When you work with really top-notch, smart engineers, it will fundamentally change the way you think and the way you program.

Ultimately, if you join a company with experts, their styles of thinking and their approaches to problem solving will rub off on you. The fear people have is that they won't be able to compete. How can I get ahead in a place like that, where everyone is so impressive? First, it's very important to come to terms with the fact that it's a problem you want to have. In the long run, the skills you develop, the tactics for innovation, and the strategies for success will propel your career. Even if you don't thrive in that environment, you'll emerge a far better and more capable employee for the next position you get. You'll also probably have a lot more fun working with people who are more interesting. Finally, don't sell yourself short. All those people who are so brilliant, creative, and interesting have often had the benefit of life experiences and personal mentors who helped shape their outlook and strategies to life. If some of that rubs off on you, you might be surprised to see what heights you can reach.

On the flip side, if you love software but also want to get rich through it, or be in a position of great influence, it's arguably the case that the fastest path to those goals may be to join (or start) a growing technology company with explosive disruptive technology. Mayer got lucky by being one of Google's first 20 employees—she joined a company with both attributes. If you take a look at the people I interviewed in this book, you'll notice a mix of people; some who climbed the corporate ladder and others who were early participants (or founders) of a new venture. It's a small sample and, of course, far from being a random selection. (I deliberately picked the people to interview.) Even so, there's clearly a skew toward founders of organizations or companies:

1. Marc Benioff: Founder and CEO of Saleforce.com

2. Grady Booch: Co-founder of Rational Software

3. Diane Greene: Co-founder and former CEO of VMware

4. Merissa Mayer: One of Google's first 20 employees

5. Peter Norvig: Joined startup Google as Director of Research

6. Mark Russinovitch: Founder of Winternals, which led to his being recruited as a Microsoft Fellow

7. Richard Stallman: Founder of the Free Software movement

8. Linus Torvald: The original author of GNU/Linux

9. David Vaskevitch: Microsoft CTO who joined Microsoft around the time of its IPO in 1986

10. Steve Wozniak: Co-founder of Apple

Of the 17 people I interviewed, fully 59% of them founded or were early members of an organization that propelled their success.

Climbing to the top of the corporate ladder in a large company such as Microsoft, Sun, HP, or IBM is a much slower and more incremental process. John Schwarz did it, and so did James Gosling. Climbing the corporate ladder is doable and, in many ways less risky, but it's a process that's hard to shortcut.

Look for ten attributes in a software company:

1. Is this a company that has experience in building professional, high-quality systems?

2. Are there really talented people here I can learn from?

3. Is the position I'm being offered one that is interesting, with long-term growth potential on something I can believe in?

4. Do they have savvy business executives who really understand the business requirements for success and have a track record for delivering it?

5. Does the company have clarity of vision for the product it produces?

6. Is there an independent research arm?

7. How does the company innovate, and how profound has their innovation been?

8. Is the work environment pleasant and flexible, and does it suit my lifestyle?

9. Does the company seem stable? Do I believe it will still be around in ten years?

10. Is the pay in line with industry standards?

Taking the job that offers the most money is almost always a poor choice. Let compensation be a tie breaker for you, if all other qualities seem to balance. On the flip side, don't let yourself get paid significantly below market norms. The best companies won't pay their employees poorly because talented software developers are crucial to their business success. If you get a lowball offer, it's a warning flag that the hiring organization is neither a very professional software development group nor a savvy business team.

Resumé Realities for New Graduates

The sad reality is that although school performance is a very loose indicator of job performance, for all the reasons outlined in Chapter 3, "School Versus Job," unfortunately, when recruiting new grads, there is often little else by which to measure candidates, aside from their academic performance. Even worse, most computer science schools offer fairly similar curriculums, so as a graduate from any reputable school, you can be pretty confident that the skills you've picked up through your formal education are virtually identical to the skills of most other graduates across the country. To be sure, there are variations, and some schools are better than others. But the differences in the quality of your education tend to be small when compared to the differences in talent that you personally bring to the table.

The resumés of most applicants vying for positions in software development will be pretty similar. You've all taken courses in operating systems, structures, and algorithms. You all know the major programming languages, including Java, C, and C++. You've had an introduction to machine language programming, TCP/IP, and on and on. I say this tongue-in-cheek, of course, because these are all good skills worth including on your resume. These skills communicate that you have a solid foundation in computer science, the kind that can be expected from a student graduating from a good school. Don't expect these things alone to land you a job with a major firm such as Microsoft, IBM, or Google, nor make you attractive to the next hot startup looking to push the envelope of technological innovation by recruiting the best and brightest new hires. These are a basic starting point for your resumé, but list them concisely so you can dedicate more of the precious real estate on the page to what really distinguishes you from others. Call out job experiences, leadership experiences, academic and nonacademic awards and distinctions, professional activities (ACM, IEEE, and so on) sports involvement, and hobbies.

Killer Resumés for Software Development

Whether you're a new grad or have worked professionally for some years, creating a great resumé as a software professional involves some basic rules. If your resumé doesn't list your degrees, your GPA (for new graduates), your employment history, and the programming languages you know, the absence will imply a negative reason for the omission. The obvious mechanical stuff needs to be there in the normal format. (You can find many examples of resumé formats on the Web, so I don't bother creating examples here.) A killer resume concentrates on highlighting the distinctive accomplishments of the job seeker:

- ▶ **Leadership roles.** Include every managerial, technical, or organizational leadership you've had, including extracurricular positions, such as serving on a board of directors for an organization or organizing a community sports league.

- ▶ **Deep technical domain skills.** Everyone applying for a software position has programming experiences, but some people have had the chance to go very deep on certain areas. If you've had some experiences like that, make sure it comes through on your resumé. You don't want your deep experiences and know-how to read the same as someone who has dabbled superficially in the same area. For example, many programmers include TCP/IP on their resumé, but although some have done socket programming, a small minority have actually developed their own implementation of the protocol. There is a world of difference.

- ▶ **Awards.** Awards are one of the most compelling aspects of any software development resume because they indicate that a third-party organization has selected you from a broader community for distinction. Remember that awards distinguish you even if they aren't academic awards. New grads are, quite justifiably, so wrapped up in the academic experiences and indicators that have dominated their lives for nearly two decades that they often forget to mention (or fail to realize the importance of) awards that are not academic in nature. Many computer science and math contests are not formally part of the academic process, but these can be strong indicators of your potential. Awards for community service can distinguish you as a team player, and awards in musical performance can make a very strong impression about your ability to use both left and right sides of your brain and apply discipline. Every award you've been granted since the age of 15 is probably worth mentioning.

▶ **Innovation.** Especially include patents or scientific papers you have authored. List every one of these, with a full bibliographic-styled citation.

▶ **Professional activities.** Examples might include membership in the ACM or IEEE or participation in computer science clubs.

▶ **Extracurricular activities.** Make a point to list the ones that demonstrate leadership, creativity, or intellectual prowess. For example, if you are a musician, a soccer star, or a champion debater, make sure it's well near impossible to read your resumé and miss it.

I've seen tens of thousands of resumés in which candidates have worked hard to make their resumés stand out using impressive paper, stylish fonts, and other eye-catching strategies. What you need to know is that these techniques work only on the most inexperienced and inept recruiting managers. Nobody who has sifted through hundreds of resumés is impressed or captivated by the eye candy. In many cases, it makes a resumé look less professional—even desperate. By contrast, deep technical accomplishments, distinctions, awards, leadership roles, publications, patents, and public speaking roles make a massively positive and arguably disproportionate impression.

One other point is important: You might have heard that resumés should be kept short, to one or two pages. Frankly, that's old-school poppycock. Let the first page of your resumé be the summary, but if you've been in the business for five years or more, it's perfectly reasonable for your resume to be longer. Include a few sentences about each major project you've worked on, plus a listing of your distinction (awards, papers, publication, patents, speaking engagements) and a point form list of professional activities outside of your day job (such as work with standards bodies, international organizations, conferences, and journals)—you'll definitely need more than two pages. Keep the major messages to the first page so that someone sifting through hundreds of resumes will get the basic idea quickly and then treat the rest of the content as appendixes for people who want to know more. Remember that if they read the first page and aren't captivated, they may never get to page 2.

Beyond the Resumé—Way Beyond

What are key strategies that really help people land a good job in software development? Not surprisingly, most of the "classic" strategies that have involved spraying your resumé around are among the least effective. Make no mistake, your resumé is critically important; no matter who you are or what job you apply for, somebody somewhere is going to need to see and review it. Let's assume you have a solid resumé that positions you in the best light while still being honest and authentic. What next?

For people looking for a job in software development, there are generally ten different ways they get through the process and successfully land an offer.

- ▶ **Career planning and placement.** Universities and colleges generally have a career planning or placement office that helps new grads find work. Companies with positions for new grads coordinate with these schools to advertise their positions and coordinate reviews of candidates and interviews. The biggest and most successful software companies—Microsoft, IBM, Google, Adobe, Sybase, and many others—recruit heavily through this method. A large percentage of new grads will find their first jobs this way. The downside to this process is that landing an interview will be heavily skewed by your GPA, and it is useful only for new grads.

- ▶ **Friends and contacts.** It might not sound scientific, but using your network of friends and family to find a suitable available position remains the single most effective way to get a job in almost any industry. First, and most important, when you reach out to your network of contacts, you are dealing largely with people who know you, have a degree of comfort with you, and can vouch for you. You become a known quantity, and employers always prefer a known quantity over mysterious strangers, no matter how well they do on an interview.

- ▶ **Employment agencies.** Private job-placement firms, the so-called "head hunters," match companies looking to recruit with job seekers. They make their money by taking a commission when a candidate is successfully placed (one or two months' pay is typical). The hiring firm pays the commissions. The good news is that because head hunters are incentivized by commission, they will try their best to negotiate a top-level salary for you. In practice, companies approach head hunters for recruitment help only when they need either very specialized skills (such as experience with a programming language that has been unused for more than ten years) or when the market is hot and there is a serious skills shortage in their geography. (The mid to late 1990s were a boom for these agencies.)

▸ **Government agencies.** Most states, provinces, and large cities have government employment agencies that help job seekers find work. These agencies are biased toward blue-collar positions, and the best of the high-tech companies don't recruit from these venues. Even so, these governmental agencies can be a great source for job seekers for software development positions in governmental projects—and there are many. A huge percentage of people in North America are employed by some level of government.

▸ **Professors.** Professors in computer science generally do some degree of collaborative work with partners in industry. It helps them get funding for research, as well as keeps their research work grounded in practical problems. A reference on your behalf from a professor to a well-placed decision maker in the industry can go a long way to helping you get a job. The downside: Most professors have a very small list of industrial connections, and they each make recommendations for, at most, a couple students each year. On the receiving end, companies take careful notice of candidates who are recommended by professors. Unlike the normal recruitment process, in which student applications are filtered through an HR process, professors usually send the student's resumé and a recommendation directly to the senior technical staff they've done joint research with. It's a fast path to the decision makers. If you can be one of the few, it's a great way to get yourself noticed.

▸ **Cold calls.** Calling a company and asking about jobs is a shot in the dark. You can expect to make dozens of calls before finding a company that's hiring. Most of the time, you'll be speaking to a receptionist. Large companies don't recruit this way, and small companies generally recruit through word-of-mouth or campus hiring. If you try to target medium-sized companies that are experiencing growth, you'll have the most success with this strategy.

▸ **Internet searches.** Several online sites provide help for job seekers and recruiting companies alike. Does it work? You bet. Every year there are stories about people who posted their resumés online and got a job interview within hours. But while there are constant success stories, it's definitely a long shot. Thousands of people post to these sites, and it's pretty hard for employers to make a match.

▶ **Job postings in newspapers.** The thing you need to know about job posting in the newspaper is that many of these postings are compulsory: A public posting may be an obligatory step in the recruitment process of the hiring company. In many cases, the employer has specific candidates in mind for the position before the ad is placed. Second, if the posting looks good, you can expect dozens or hundreds of applicants to apply, so competition will be stiff. But people do find jobs through this path.

▶ **Visits to companies.** Visiting companies in person and dropping off a resumé and using the face time to try to arrange a subsequent interview or meeting with recruiters is a strategy some have used successfully. It's time-consuming because of the travel involved, even if you limit this to companies in your community. Again, if you limit this to companies that you know are experiencing growth, it has a higher chance of success.

▶ **Resumé mailings.** Mailing your resumé to companies you'd like to work for gets your resumé into their hands, and someone at the company will certainly take a look at it. The bad news is that, in most cases, it will be glanced at and thrown into a pile with several hundred others, never to be looked at again. People do get follow-up calls and positions using this tactic, but it's a long shot.

Table 4.1 summarizes the effectiveness of these job-hunting strategies.

TABLE 4.1   Ways to Get a Job

	METHOD	DESCRIPTION	EFFECTIVENESS (THE HIGHER THE NUMBER, THE MORE EFFECTIVE)
1	Career planning and placement	For new or recent graduates your school will likely have a placement office that helps students connect with employers who are hiring.	9
2	Friends and contacts	Asking people you know about job opportunities.	8
3	Employment agencies	Using private "head hunters" who take a commission on the salary of professionals they place. They're very motivated to get you a job.	5

TABLE 4.1   Ways to Get a Job (continued)

	METHOD	DESCRIPTION	EFFECTIVENESS (THE HIGHER THE NUMBER, THE MORE EFFECTIVE)
4	Government agencies	Using government job-placement agencies	4
5	Company visits	Making cold visits to companies you want to work with.	3
6	Professors	Professors often have links to industry through joint research projects.	3
7	Cold calls	Calling companies you want to work for.	2
8	Internet searches	Searching and using job sites like monster.com, careerbuilder.com, and simplyhired.com.	2
9	Job postings in newspapers	Looking for jobs in the newspaper.	2
10	Resume mailings	Sending your resumé and a cover letter to companies you want to work for.	1

Which of these should you pursue? Ideally, all of them; the more of these you pursue, the better your odds of finding a great position. There's absolutely no harm in doing several of these concurrently. The first two on the list should be a minimum for new grads.

The Value (or Not) of Grades

Your grades will be important for landing your first job. Over time, they have increasingly little bearing on job opportunities, but if you happened to have been an A+ student, it never hurts to include that on your resume, even when you are several years into your career. Your grades in school represent your ability to absorb information, stick to the tasks assigned to you, think on your feet, and be responsible and complete. Grades are loosely correlated with aptitude because people with higher aptitude get high grades more easily; the material you've learned will help you professionally, and the dedication and work ethic are very transferable. However, the correlation is weak because people with low aptitude can get high grades by working exceptionally hard, and people with very high aptitude can get mediocre grades because they are slacking. Regardless of how much grades reflect your future potential with a prospective employer, the sad fact is that, for the majority of new graduates, GPA is the only real distinguishing attribute you'll have prior to an interview.

Your resumé will have a long list of impressive skills in programming, operating systems, databases, and so on—and, of course, you know Java, C, and TCP/IP. So do all your classmates. So does every single graduate from every respectable computer science or related degree program across the free world. Getting a job depends a lot on getting an interview and the kind of impression you make there. A good impression during the interview supersedes almost everything you had to produce through your academic career. For new graduates, grades will be a factor in getting that first interview, especially when applying for a position at one of the large software firms, such as Microsoft, Google, IBM, HP, and Sun.

The more you have on your resumé to distinguish you from the pack, the less important your grades will be. Not all employers ask about grades before the interview process, so if your grades are not in the top third of your class, there's still a lot of opportunity.

A final point, especially for those of us where weren't A+ students: Grades are a very poor indicator of your potential and future success because they don't measure how hard you work or your ability to work in a team, to lead others, or to be creative and innovative. School is about none of these things. If you survey the great software innovators and CEOs of our times, you'll find that most of these people weren't top students, and some were notably bad students—even dropouts. Bill Gates was a dropout. Oracle founder, CEO, and multibillionaire Larry Ellison dropped out of University of Illinois and then again out of the University of Chicago. Apple co-founder and CEO Steve Jobs was a dropout from Reed College in Portland. These impressive people succeeded because they had ability, drive, and business sense. Their lack of academic prowess was almost certainly caused by their being distracted by business interests or a lack of maturity and focus at that stage of their lives, not by their lack of ability.

Bill Gates reportedly scored 1590 out of 1600 on the SAT, which at that time was equivalent to an IQ of about 170, or roughly one in a million. Larry Ellison was working as a junior programmer developing software for a CIA database when he read a research paper from IBM about relational databases and decided to form his own company to develop the first UNIX-based relational database product. How many junior programmers spend their time reading IBM research papers? These are exceptional people with exceptional stories who were also fortunate to be launching their careers at the very outset of the computer revolution. What truly matters in the long run are the things that academic grades don't necessarily reflect: your willingness to learn, your attention to detail, your work ethic, your creativity and innovativeness, your smooth relations with co-workers, your emotional intelligence, and your ability to lead others. Even if you're not an A+ student, the sky is still the limit to what you can do and who you can become.

The Value of Extracurricular Activities

Software is teamwork and innovation. This is a creative field, and employers are always looking to attract the best minds to their teams. Reading through the interviews in this book, you'll see that the greatest leaders and innovators are characterized by a scope of interest that extends far beyond software. Grady Booch studies physics and chemistry and plays the Celtic harp. Marissa Mayer flies kites. John Schwarz goes sailing. James Gosling is a 3D graphics hobbyist who regularly designs the T-shirts for the JavaOne conference. David Vaskevitch is a competitive equestrian rider and digital photographer. Diane Greene is a sports and fitness enthusiast who was the women's National Doublehanded Dinghy Champion in 1976 and three-time women's division winner of the San Francisco Classic, a long-distance windsurfing race. It's not coincidental that people with such interesting successful careers are also people who have interesting and successful side interests. Employers understand that the best employees are dynamic people with broad interests. Hobbies and interests outside of work have large positive value because they extend your life and skills in the following ways:

▶ Stimulate other parts of the brain and allow you to approach problems from different and new perspectives

▶ Give you a work-life balance that allows you to unwind, rejuvenate, and energize

▶ Provide a level of emotional and intellectual distraction and release

▶ Generally make you a more interesting person

The correlation is very strong, and most employers understand that a well-balanced person with really good technical and leadership potential can be a greater boon to their team in the long run than someone who presents a narrower technical skill set. You don't need to have a funky hobby to get a good job or to advance in your career, and, truthfully, at the end of the day, these are simply bonus points on your resumé. Generally, your hobbies and interests will have a small but occasionally balance-tipping effect on getting noticed and landing a job. The real benefit of having these outside interests in the long run is the profound value they can add to your life and your long-term breadth of thinking.

Why Student Positions Dramatically Improve Your Odds

Software companies are all about people and very little else. The office space and the hardware and software that the company uses are all minor costs and considerations in the overall success of a company compared to the human talent and skill that comprises the team. No matter how detailed your resumé is or how grueling of an interview process a company throws at you, employers will still know relatively little about you when they make a decision to extend a job offer. After all, they've spent only a few hours with you, and you've never done any work for them. Recruiters know that even the most impressive candidates are a gamble. Gambling on who they recruit is costly to companies. Getting rid of poor performers is an emotionally and financially painful process. Perhaps worse than the poor performers are the clock-punching journeymen who come to work every day and do little more than a passable job, providing no energy or leadership in what they do. They fail to provide the energy that teams need to compete on an aggressive market, but they do just enough work that it's very hard, if not impossible, to remove them with cause.

Student positions change the recruiting dynamic completely. As a student working for a firm as a co-op placement (4–8 months) or an internship residency (8–16 months), your employer is giving you an opportunity to know you and see your work directly. By the end of the work term, you will no longer be a candidate they know only through your resumé and a few hours of interviews; you'll be a known quantity. They'll know what you can produce, how hard you work, how innovative you can be, and how you work and get along with others in the team. Even the best and most impressive candidates with years of experience, top grades, and graduate degrees will be higher risk than you. Student positions tend to be a little easier to get than full-time positions because the majority of students aren't interested in taking the time off school to pursue these jobs—a co-op program or an internship will add a year to your degree program. When you have a student position, you'll have increased your odds of landing a full-time offer by about

100 times. People sometimes call these positions "a foot in the door," but student positions are really two legs and an elbow into a full-time career.

Fifteen Points to a Great Interview

Cynthia Shapiro is a leading career coach who is regularly featured on CNN, in the *Wall Street Journal* and DowJones Market Watch, and author of *What Does Somebody Have to Do to Get a Job Around Here?* With her permission, I've included her 10-point list for a top-notch interview (items 6–15), along with another 5 of my own (1–5) that are current trends for interviews in the software business. This is the 15-point master list to a foolproof interview for any software position.

1. **Research the domain and the interviewing company's position in it.**

   You should be able to find out about the technology the company is working on from their public information, and in many cases, prior to the interview, you can find out specifically what technology you're about to be interviewed for. Use the days leading up to the interview to expand your understanding of the technology the company develops, the marketplace for it, and the strengths and weaknesses of competitors. You don't need to become an expert overnight, but demonstrating a little bit of understanding and curiosity during the interview will make a big impression.

2. **Be prepared for skill-testing questions, brain teasers, and programming on the spot.**

   Almost all software companies now use some combination of an aptitude test and skill-testing questions to help assess the thinking style and potential of new employees. These are often conceptual questions that have no bearing on computer science (such as "Why are manhole covers round?") or algorithmically intense problems that you should be able to solve in a few minutes (such as "Design a routine to randomize an array of integers, assuming you have a rand() function," or "Given pointers to each of two nodes in a binary tree, efficiently find their nearest common ancestor"). IBM made these kinds of testing strategies de rigueur with its Programming Aptitude Test in the late 1980s, and Microsoft made this a common part of its face-to-face interviewing process in the early 1990s. Today it has become ubiquitous among all the major software firms. There are common patterns in these questions, and by practicing samples available on the

Internet, you'll better prepare yourself for the questions they'll throw at you during the interview. Almost as important as how you answer the problems is how you deal with the experience. Your interviewer is looking to see that you enjoy thinking through hard problems. Some interviewers will give you at least one super-hard problem you can't possibly answer in an interview just to gauge your reaction to it. They're looking for people who enjoy the thrill of the hunt.

3. **Exude simultaneous confidence and humility.**

People often come into interviews without a clear vision of how they should behave. After watching a few Hollywood movies, you may get the impression that your best strategy is to come in showing super-high energy, enthusiasm, and enough bravado to conquer the world (or at least take over the company). Nothing could be further from the goal. Software is teamwork, and your employer will be looking for someone who energetic and hardworking, but humble and pleasant enough to work well with the rest of the team.

4. **Demonstrate that you can communicate clearly.**

If you visit computer science classes across North America, you'll see a very high rate of enrollment of students who don't communicate well in the local language, and it doesn't seem to be hampering them too much in their schoolwork. Even for the native speakers, you'll find that the typical computer science majors lag behind their counterparts in liberal arts degrees in communication clarity. That might be bearable during your school years, but after graduation, the ability to communicate clearly in the local language becomes critically important because a large amount of software development is teamwork. When recruiting software specialists, employers are always watching for clear communication during the interview. This isn't about your accent; it's about your ability to understand and communicate clearly. As long as you can do that, nobody will worry too much about your accent, your spelling, or even your grammar. If you have trouble with spelling, don't worry—chances are, the people interviewing you can't spell, either. It's not a coincidence that computer scientists invented spell checkers!

5. **Show your breadth of interest in software.**

For most positions, you'll be interviewing for a very specific role, such as software developer, software tester, or project manager. You certainly want to focus your energy during the interview on the core skills needed in that role, but don't let the discussion limit itself only to that scope. For example, if you are interviewing for a position as a programmer, it would be valuable to show some interest in and awareness of software engineering, quality assurance, and project management.

6. Know your opponent.

Most candidates go into an interview thinking the person behind the big desk is looking to include them as a candidate, but the opposite is actually the case. Most interviewers are, first and foremost, looking to exclude you. They are looking for red flags that will tell them you are someone to discard. They are looking to avoid the potential liabilities and inconveniences that a poor corporate fit could cause. If no red flags pop up, you get to move on to the next step. So don't volunteer additional information. Every interviewer has experienced having a candidate come in and spew his life story, sharing inappropriate information and hanging himself before the interview even gets going. The rule of thumb is, let the interviewer lead the process and don't share your personal information.

7. Stick to the positive.

Think of this like a first date. You wouldn't tell someone on a first date all the terrible things you've done in your life, that you can't cook, and that you're a real slob, would you? So definitely don't do it in an interview. Make sure everything you share puts you in the best light possible. All an interviewer has to go on in this delicate hiring process is the piece of paper you've handed them (your resumé) and what you say in this one meeting. So if you want a second date, you'd better put your best foot forward. And don't ever say anything bad about your previous employers or bosses. This is a major red flag that makes you look like a negative, possibly bitter, and unsuccessful candidate. Beware of trick questions such as "Tell me about the most difficult work experience or boss you've ever had"—they are trying to see if you will go into negative territory. At the most, if you find yourself cornered over a delicate past issue, you can say something like, "That experience was challenging, to say the least, but I learned a lot from it, and I believe it has made me a better employee."

8. Be enthusiastic.

Most employees go into an interview unsure of whether they really want to work for this mystery company. Unfortunately, that tends to come through and can make you seem like a lackluster candidate. So save all decisions about whether you really want to work there for after the interview, during the offer negotiations, when you have some real data. In the meantime, it's critical that you show enthusiasm for the company and the position during the interview. Treat every job interview like it's for your dream position. You can always turn it down when you have an offer in hand if you decide it wasn't the one for you. Interviewers are looking for people who show enthusiasm for the opportunity, are certain they want to work for the company, and are really excited to occupy the position.

9. **Don't ask negative questions about the company.**

    Don't ask about their dicey reputation for overworking their employees or bad press they may have had recently. This will make them very nervous. Stick to the positive here, too.

10. **Don't give any personal or medical information.**

    The small talk before the interview "gets started" is where most people get trapped. Beware small talk and make sure you redirect it to your work experience and/or the company. Once you set foot in the door and begin speaking with people (even the receptionist), the interview is on—and everything you say could be held against you. If you talk about how hard it is to be a single mom, how devastated you are by your recent divorce, or how difficult it's been coming back from a recent surgery, you will be sidelined. Yes, it is illegal for an HR person or interviewer to discriminate based on these things, but the truth is, they'll make a mental note and never tell you why you weren't called back for another interview. You will get the standard line: "We felt your skills did not match the position, and we wish you well." This kind of secret criteria is never written down and not openly spoken about, but it's there.

11. **Be prepared to sell yourself.**

    Get your ego going before you start interviewing. Make a list of all your best qualities and why a company would be lucky to have you. Be prepared to work those into the conversations with your interviewer. Write down your success stories at the various companies you've worked for, the things you are most proud of, so they are fresh in your mind and you can work them into answers.

12. **Don't falsify.**

    In this day and age, it is too easy to check every last detail. Even the smallest mistake could put you out of the running. Most companies today hire private investigators to run complete background checks on potential candidates.

13. **Know the follow-up etiquette.**

    When the interview is over, don't bug them with follow-up phone calls and emails. If they want you, they will hunt you down. If they disappear, you have to assume they lost interest for whatever reason. No company will let their top candidates get away, believe me. The only follow-up should be a thank you note or email full of enthusiasm for the job and thanking the interviewer(s) for their time. That's it—that's all you get.

14. **Interview coaching.**

    Just as a resumé is your calling card representing all you've accomplished in your career, the interview process is a delicate dance that can stand between you and your dream job. You may want to invest in some interview training so you are always your calm, collected best in these situations. A skilled interview coach can help you learn to avoid and recognize the trick questions and turn every answer into a showcase for your wonderful experience. One can also help you learn how to negotiate for the highest salary and best benefits.

15. **Some additional tricks can make the process easier:**

    ▶ Always drive to the location a day or two before the interview. Then you'll know where it is and you won't be stressed on the day of the big event. Watch the people coming in and out to get a feel for the company culture. Are they casual or formal? Getting a feel for the place and the people will allow you to look like a good corporate fit when you show up for your interview.

    ▶ You'll look more confident if you take up space. Don't be afraid to drape your arm over the chair next to you or lean forward.

    ▶ Say something nice about the company right off the bat, even if it's just "Great location" or "The people look happy" or "I love your product and use it often."

▶ Always bring a copy of your resumé—it will help with filling out the application and will make you look prepared if someone needs it.

▶ Always take notes and get the business cards of each person you spoke with. This will help tremendously when you write your thank you notes.

You have a lot of things to consider when searching for a software job: the company, the people, the technology, the location, the organizational culture, and, yes, the compensation. Study each of these carefully while preparing yourself for the interview process, and you'll be considerably further ahead in your search.

An Interview with Bjarne Stroustrup

Inventor of the C++ Programming Language

CURRENT POSITION

College of Engineering professor in Computer Science, Texas A&M University

CLAIM TO FAME

Inventor and original implementer of the C++ programming language

DATE OF BIRTH

December 30, 1950

EDUCATION

Ph.D. in Computer Science , Cambridge University, 1975–1979

Cand. Scient. (Master's degree), Mathematics and Computer Science, University of Århus, Denmark, 1969–1975

FAVORITE PASTIMES & HOBBIES

Reading (light literature, popular science, history), running, traveling and hiking, listening to music (classical, rock, and more), dining with friends

BIOGRAPHY

Bjarne is the designer and original implementer of C++ and the author of *The C++ Programming Language* (Addison-Wesley Professional, 2000), *The Design and Evolution of C++* (Addison-Wesley Professional, 1994), *Programming: Principles and Practice Using C++* (Addison-Wesley Professional, 2008), and many other research and popular publications. His research interests include distributed systems, design, programming techniques, software development tools, and programming languages. He is actively involved in the ANSI/ISO standardization of C++.

From 1979 to 2002, Bjarne worked at Bell Labs and AT&T Labs Computer Science Research as a researcher and, later, department head. Since 2002, he has been a professor in the Texas A&M University Department of Computer Science. He retains a link to AT&T Labs–Research as an AT&T Fellow.

Bjarne's honors include the Dr. Dobb's Excellence in Programming Award, the William Procter Prize for Scientific Achievement from Sigma Xi, the IEEE Computer Society's Computer Entrepreneur Award, and the ACM Grace Murray Hopper Award. He is an elected member of The National Academy of Engineering, an IEEE fellow, an ACM fellow, an AT&T Fellow, and a Bell Labs Fellow.

"I signed up for 'mathematics with computer science' … I mistakenly thought it was some kind of applied math"

How did you get started in software?

After high school, I signed up for the "mathematics with computer science" degree at the university in my hometown, Århus. I mistakenly thought it was some kind of applied math. There I discovered programming and was hooked. After my second year, I was able to finance my studies by programming small commercial applications. That taught me a lot about the complete scope of software development and its importance in society.

What do you consider your greatest accomplishments or contributions to software?

My greatest accomplishment was getting C++ into real-world use, thereby making object-oriented programming mainstream. Before C++, few people in the computing industry had heard of object-oriented programming (OOP), and most of those who had heard of it considered it to be unbelievably slow, manageable only in the hands of Ph.D.s from top universities, and impossible to fit into real-world execution environments. A popular "definition" of OOP was "slow graphics." C++ was by no means the first language to support OOP (Simula has that honor); many other languages supported variants of the idea, including Ada, Eiffel, Objective C, Smalltalk, and various Lisp dialects. However, C++ was the language that broke through the barrier of ignorance, resistance to change, and scale of projects. The strengths that allowed C++ to succeed were performance in time and space, capability to fit into a variety of systems, C compatibility, the generality of the language mechanisms (not just OOP), and limited goals (C++ is a language, not a complete system). The

Bjarne Stroustrup

Bjarne Stroustrup

reasons were not "marketing might" (what marketing? what development budget?), "being first," or "just luck" (over 25 years?). The C++ community grew by word-of-mouth, technical papers and talks, and my book.

Designing a language is easy, compared to getting it into use. I could have designed a cleaner/prettier language than C++, but abstract beauty wasn't the primary aim—usefulness was. Now, I'm working to do the same for generic programming (GP). GP is an essential part of the current C++ standard library, but it will receive better support in the next C++ standard.

What makes you feel successful?

I feel successful when I see my work used for something exciting or important. For example, I'm thrilled that C++ is used for the scene analysis and autonomous driving subsystems of the NASA Mars Rovers. I can hardly do anything without stumbling into yet another use of C++ (see www.research.att.com/~bs/applications.html). C++ had a major role in the Human Genome Project. I'm also writing this in a C++ application and will mail it using a mailer written in C++—and, undoubtedly, the book you are reading was produced using some C++ programs.

"Take five papers and a manual, add water, and stir"

You published your classic book The C++ Programming Language *and made the commercial version of C++ available at the same time. I'll bet there's a story in there.*

One day in 1984, I was standing in the doorway of my next-door office neighbor, Al Aho, complaining that the C++ users kept asking the same questions and that answering them was beginning to be a real burden. "Bjarne," Al interrupted, "you have to write a book!" That was a new idea to me. Al explained that by collecting the answers in a book, I would no longer have to spend time answering them and could move on to new projects. Great idea! The next day, I presented the book project to my department head, Sandy Fraser, along the lines, "Take five papers and a manual, add water, and stir." Two days later, that project was approved. Bell Labs had excellent technical management. Writing turned out to be not that easy, though, and I also had to complete the C++ compiler, modify the C++ language along the way to benefit from experience, help users, write documentation, and more. But in October 1985, that book, *The C++ Programming Language*, appeared on the same day as the first commercial release of C++. Al was wrong, though:

Writing the book didn't give me more time—it simply encouraged users to ask more and harder questions.

How do you stay on top of technology trends and innovation?

With difficulty. I talk to people, I travel to do so, seeing a variety of software-development organizations. I email a lot and read a fair bit. The problem with reading is that there is far too much information out there for an individual to comprehend, so the problem becomes what to believe and what to consider important.

What's a pet peeve of yours in any aspect of the software world?

Too many managers and executives try to reduce programming to a low-level assembly-line activity. That's inefficient, wasteful, costly in the long run, and inhumane to programmers. One size does not fit all in software development. You need to give people room to use their talents and encourage them to grow.

Do you think graduate degrees are professionally valuable? Why?

Yes. Without a solid technical/scientific foundation, you are lost in fads and fashions. Graduate education is also one of the few places left where you can think, experiment, and learn things that are not immediately useful. I think that it is important to spend time being not very focused and looking at things just because they appear to be interesting. A good degree program allows for that, in addition to giving rigorous technical/scientific foundation.

"Multitasking is not for serious work"

Technical leaders and executives are famous for being time-strapped. What strategies do you use to stay sane and use your time effectively?

I'm not sure I'm good at that. I work best at one thing at a time; multitasking is not for serious work.

How do you achieve a work-life balance? How do you keep your professional life from dominating everything?

I read a lot of nontechnical stuff. I run. I like good food in good company. I try to add nonwork days to my travel schedules. This all helps keep a balance. However, research is not a 9-to-5 job. I'd love to do three-quarters of my work in three-quarters of the time, but it takes almost 95% of my work time just to keep up; after that, there is so little time to push the envelope.

Bjarne Stroustrup

What suggestions do you have for others on being successful in software (either R&D or business)?

Be lucky. Do what you are good at. Work hard but not always obsessively. Be human.

You cannot be lucky if you are too focused, too obsessed, or too sure of yourself to notice and explore new opportunities. You cannot be lucky if you don't have the time and skills to take advantage of an opportunity when you see it. You won't be good at something you don't like because becoming good at something (at a level where "good" means something in a competitive world) takes years—if you don't like it, you'll become miserable. Also, you are far more likely to have a talent for something you like doing. Talents are there to be built upon.

Work is a major part of life. If you want a 9-to-5 job and live for the weekend, I'm not writing for you. Think of the absurdity of people describing Mozart without considering his music central to his life! Be sure that you like what you do at work and that you like the people you work with—you'll have to live with them for a long time. Don't choose a field full of people you couldn't respect or wouldn't like to spend spare time with (people in advertising really are different from engineers). Trust your colleagues.

"Predictions are notoriously hard to make, but ..."

What do you see as the coming changes in the software field over the next 10–15 years that will impact career opportunities or the way we develop software, either positively or negatively?

I wonder. So much of what we see and what we see discussed in the media has a very short horizon—maybe three years—and trends and fads tumble over each other. I'll try to step back and ponder.

Predictions are notoriously hard to make, but anything deployed on a worldwide scale within the next 10–15 years exists in a lab somewhere today. Actually, much of what we'll see in 10 years' time has already been deployed now. Software has an enormous inertia, so we'll see lot of Fortran, Cobol, and C code. Some will be stale, minimally maintained true legacy code, but a fair bit will be actively maintained and interacting with more modern software parts.

I think we might see a clearer separation between infrastructure and application work. This would show up in the use of languages and tools, in education, and in the growth of two increasingly different development communities. I'm extrapolating from the differences we see between infrastructure builders (today mostly using close-to-the-hardware languages, typically C or C++) and application builders (today mostly using dynamic languages, such as JavaScript and Ruby). Java is in many ways in between; time will tell whether it is in a sweet spot or is falling between two stools. It is increasingly difficult to bridge those cultures. I suspect that 10 to 15 years from now, each community will be supported by massive toolsets: the infrastructure world aiming for performance, correctness, and security; the application world aiming for flexibility and time to market (relying heavily on the infrastructure world for security and performance).

Into this picture we throw heavily concurrent hardware and a need for geographical distribution. My guess is that there will be a huge demand for highly skilled developers with traditional computer science skills (for the infrastructure work) and for a huge number of developers with skills geared more toward their application areas. I hope to see greater professionalism, especially in the infrastructure areas—our civilization depends on that. In particular, I hope to see a greater emphasis on correctness, verifiability, and fundamental soundness of system components. I think this will require more rigor (including mathematical reasoning) and fewer ad hoc approaches than we see today.

If I'm wrong in my guesses about technology—and most such guesses turn out to be widely off the mark—I suspect we will still be in a variant of the current confused mess and need significantly more developers of all sorts. In either case, there will be layers of technical management needed, opening opportunities to those who prefer promotion to technical work. In either case, the software development industry will be larger than today and more central to society.

Any final words of wisdom or caution for people entering the field?

When you find something worth doing, work hard at it, persist, and ignore fashion.

CHAPTER 5

Making the Most of the Early Years As a Software Developer

*"If living conditions don't stop improving in this country,
we're going to run out of humble beginnings for our great men."*
—Russell P. Askue

Software development is a wonderful field in part because it's always so fresh and dynamic. The dynamism of the industry and the rapid pace of change keep everyone focused on personal growth and learning—there's absolutely no escaping it. Some people thrive on the elements of change and constant learning, whereas others struggle. But throughout the churn and the constant refactoring of best practices, one constant holds true across the industry: The first five years of professional work are always the most educational. During these years, you get exposed to corporate culture, organizational dynamics, and their politics. You'll need to work as a member of a team rather than as an individual, and in so doing, you'll thrive on the sharing of information, skills, and assets (documents, code, presentation materials) with your colleagues. You'll see the mundane aspects of the field up close (and will probably have many of them assigned to you—somebody's gotta do it, so it might as well be the newbie). On the technical front, you'll be exposed to how industrial-strength software is built and witness firsthand the dynamics of working in larger teams. These are years to value and capitalize on. Time spent in professional growth during these years is time well spent.

Tradecraft

"Programmers are not to be measured by their ingenuity and their logic but by the completeness of their case analysis."
—A. J. Perlis, Epigrams on Programming

Most new graduates have fairly strong skills in programming, although they have not yet worked on large-scale projects. When you join a new company, you might expect to learn about its impressive technology and incredible sophistication, and you might be underwhelmed to find that although the code developed in industry is larger and more complex than what you developed in school, it is not fundamentally otherworldly. The things that bedazzle new employees are the tradecraft skills. By "tradecraft," I mean skills that are very technical in nature but probably weren't taught in much depth at school. These are skills you need on large-scale projects with many developers touching the code over time. Real-world projects often have much higher requirements for reliability, availability, concurrency, or performance efficiency than what most of us dealt with at school. Some of these topics are taught in graduate-level courses, but even the lucky few who hold Master's degrees and Ph.D.s in computer science will have only grazed the surface.

Some of the skills are related to how we plan and develop code; others are related to how an organization of many people (5, 50, or 500) collaboratively develops code. Yet other issues are related to the scale of the systems that the software must run on, with perhaps hundreds of CPUs and tens of thousands of concurrent users operating on terabytes or petabytes of data. The tradecraft of software is much less technical and abstract than the raw academic skills, but as with learning to play the piano, they require years of experience to fully master and appreciate.

I recommend that every software expert pick up these experiences and skills in their first five years of professional work. If you haven't had the chance to pick up these skills already, it's never too late:

- Learn at least four different programming languages and at least four different data formats (such as JPEG, XML, delimited text, and MPEG).

- Develop software that is suitable for at least a thousand people to use concurrently.

- Develop software that can scale to more than 1TB of data.

- Work on a project with more than ten programmers.

▶ Work on extending code that someone who is no longer available to ask questions of wrote more than five years ago.

▶ Fix at least 40 defects in code you did not author.

▶ Write code that supports international languages, including UNICODE input, and more than one language of generated user output (error messages, GUI text, and so on).

▶ Study the performance characteristics of the following:

— Data fetched from memory with and without a CPU cache miss

— Reads of consecutive blocks from disk versus random I/O seeks

— Large block I/O versus small-sized I/O

— Three popular languages (such as Java, C/C++, and PHP)

The Business of Software

If you've graduated from a degree or diploma program in computer science, computer engineering, or a related field, you've acquired an impressive list of technical skills that you now will use in the exciting and dynamic field of software development. Chances are your school hasn't taught you much about the business of software—the way software is sold, the nature of the market, and how the sales and marketing processes work. The most successful people in software work hard to develop a working knowledge of the process even if it's not where they spend the bulk of their time. The reason, of course, is that everything you do in software is enhanced by having a clearer understand of how the process works and who your audience is and what they are looking for.

Build Domain Expertise

In the long run, your career success will be most heavily influenced by your ability to be an expert in something: an expert programmer, manager, tester, or technology evangelist, or an expert in a specific technology area (such as databases, virtual reality, real-time communications, CRM systems, mobile devices, or more). It takes a career of focus and effort to develop world-class expertise, and in most cases, the technology areas you start off in will not be the ones that define your career. However, everything you learn in the early years of your career will serve you well in the future. Programming languages change (who uses FORTRAN or Pascal anymore?), and so do the operating systems, the technology platforms, and the kinds of devices that can be programmed. But despite the changing paradigms, the fundamentals of specific domains such as telecommunications, gaming, image processing, databases and how we operate as an industry change slowly.

What's Old Is New

Remember that what is low-level today will become obsolete in the future as programming abstractions and the power of our programming interfaces evolve. Few people today make a career from assembly language programming because the power of the modern CPU and the efficiency of our language compilers have removed the need for programming at such an intimate level of control between the programmer and the CPU. But those who once learned and mastered the skill remain powerful programmers today because they understand systems with a level of intimacy that few of us will ever attain. The assembler guru reads core dumps with ease and debugs memory corruption problems through a maze of hexidecimal code and register entries the way most us read the *Sunday Times*. If he lets his skills stop there, they remain an oddity, good for occasional circumstances, but not a particularly mainstream skill for achieving primary business objectives. For the subset of assembly programmers who made the transition to C/C++, Java, and beyond, their deep understanding of the CPU and its interaction with the operating system and memory remains a powerful extension of their skills. It allows them to combine the best of old and new, designing, programming, and debugging systems with greater elegance and ease than others. Just as assembly language was once a core programming skill in the 1980s, the low-level programming skills of today will one day be abstracted away. The understanding you gain from mastering these skills now will magnify and expand your power as a software professional in the future.

Ray Tomlinson was the original inventor of email. He's not only a pioneer in software, but he's one of the few technical gurus who has kept his career focused on the technical track. He's still working on software projects today. When I interviewed Ray for this book he commented that the more things change in software development, the more they stay the same. New technologies intending to simplify aspects of a process often introduce new complexities, more memory is consumed by software bloat and larger data volumes, and, in the end, although the tools, platforms, and languages change, the fundamentals of the discipline remain the same.

Often with software there's some new wonderful thing that's going to make what programmers currently do doable by some lesser individuals, and programmers can then get on to some other thing. But this never happens. Whatever you invent of that sort just turns into the same problem all over again—it's just got a different name. It's just as hard, and you're working with different kinds of tools, different kinds of objects, different kinds of programming entities, and a different language, but it's still the same kind of thing. You are still trying to assemble things that have all these edges that make them not want to fit together, and finding ways to make them fit.
—Ray Tomlinson, inventor of email, BBN Technologies

Watch the Leaders

You might be surprised to find that many of the career gurus surrounding you in an organization are more than a little behind the times. They're still talking about technology from five years ago. They don't seem to know much about some of the current programming paradigms you studied in school or the hot new platforms your programming buddies tinker with in their spare time. It's easy to dismiss them. However, these people reached their positions for good reasons, and although they might not know what you do, they usually know a lot of things that are qualitatively more important to a career in software. They know how to build large-scale systems. They know good code from bad. They know where corners can be safely cut and where you do so at your peril. They understand the process of software development and software team dynamics. Perhaps most important, if they've been with your particular company for a while, they know the organization and the corporate culture in which the team operates. You can learn immensely from these people by learning from their experience and wisdom. You can learn how to survive, how to work the system to achieve success, and how to avoid pitfalls (technical or political) that most junior programmers fall prey to.

Start Building Your Network

Use these early years to start to develop a network of contacts throughout the business who you'll be able to reach out to in the future. Remember, it's not what you know, but who you know. The friends and relationships you form in your career will be useful later. Many of the people you'll work with will be relatively junior during these early years—we always work most closely with our peer group. You can be lulled into a false sense of being in a network-free zone. After all, how will any of these junior people be useful as a professional network in the years ahead? But the beauty of life is that we all grow old together. Ten years down the line, you'll have advanced in your career and so will many of your peers. Some of them might be working for you; others might be your executives. Some will have left and moved to other companies or started companies of their own. One thing is for sure: Your peers will move on with their careers, and some of those people will end up in positions where someday, some time, they'll be able to help you. That's why this can't just be a receiving relationship—you have to give to get. Find ways to do small favors for others and build a cache of trust and emotional debt. In the long run, these relationships will propel you in your career. You'll be able to get more things done because, in the fullness of time, you'll be building a large cadre of people who support you. Perhaps more important, you'll be building that same cadre of people who you are able to help. This is a classic model for building win-win scenarios.

In his classic book *The Tipping Point: How Little Things Can Make a Big Difference,* Malcolm Gladwell describes how social interactions lead to profound change. One of the core agents of change he suggests is the "Law of the Few," which suggests that major change depends on three specific kinds of people: connectors, mavens, and salesmen. Connectors have wide-reaching social networks and connect people with one another. These people span many communities and draw across normal boundaries to connect people who otherwise would not meet. Mavens understand a vast array of information about domains and share it widely. Prolific bloggers can be thought of as mavens. Salesmen are the persuasive charismatic people who can motivate others to see a shared viewpoint. Collectively, the connectors, mavens, and salesmen of the world effect change. Building your social network helps make you a connector. Over time, if you can become a maven and a salesman, too, then your combined attributes position you as a kingmaker and a rainmaker. If you fail to become a charismatic salesman or an information maven, you can build your success with the help of some friends who are. If you know enough people in enough interesting places, your network will help you get things done. That's especially true if you can infuse your network with a healthy dose of quid pro quo—engage in acts of kindness to others, and when the time comes that you need something from them, they'll (hopefully) be glad to return the favor. What goes around comes around. If your network is broad and far reaching, you can generate a lot of good coming your way.

Who Do You Want to Be?

Your first few years in industry will expose you to the process of software development and the business of software. Through these years, you'll learn the different roles that exist in the industry and the stresses, challenges, opportunities, and delights that come with each. The single most important thing you can do to help define the success of your career is to determine where you want to end up. Many people try to think about their future objectively in terms of what technology they would work on, but that's a difficult path to analyze because technology keeps changing. Another reasonable way to plot your course is to look around the organizations in which you find yourself, observe the daily rigors of the senior people around you, and consider two questions:

1. Which of these people would I most like to emulate in my career because I believe I would enjoy doing what they do?

2. Which of these roles suits me to the point I can imagine doing that job as well as or better than the senior person who is doing it now?

Thinking about these questions will help you begin to define a vision of your future professional self. Once formed, this image can direct your professional development. Nothing is carved in stone, and most of us change our goals over time. Having an initial vision of where you want to get to is the first and most critical step in the process of career development.

Everyone Needs a Mentor

A mentor is a professional guide who can share pearls of wisdom with you (not that you'll need any after reading this book) and can offer some personal feedback to you on your own behavior. Your manager is always a mentor, but it's useful to have a mentor outside the manager–employee relationship. There are a few reasons for that, but perhaps the most important is that, in most organizations (both large companies and small), a manager has numerous employees and can't always see the intimate technical contributions of each in the same way peers might. Second, many benefits of a mentor are day-to-day insights on coding tricks, or debugging strategies, or where to find tools and people that your manager might not be readily available to provide. My first mentor at IBM taught me tons about the art of programming and gave me deep insights into the C language and programming tools, which greatly improved my productivity. My second mentor taught me everything I know about relational database systems and their internal architecture. Later mentors gave me career direction, political insight, and sometimes hard-hitting constructive feedback. I never would have risen to much in IBM without these mentors. A good mentor shows you the ropes along several dimensions: technical, organizational, and political. Whether you're in a small startup or a large corporate entity, it's good to have someone to help direct your efforts. All this may be obvious, but I'll close with a few points that aren't:

▶ You have to make a mentor. Don't expect to be assigned an all-knowing guru who will spend large swaths of time looking after your career. Seek out for yourself a person you feel is suitable and likely has a reasonable amount of time for you.

▶ If the mentoring process works well, you'll be consuming time and energy from your mentor, particularly if you're new to the team. Make sure you show constant appreciation for it and look for things you can do in return.

▶ Make sure you have an arrangement with your mentor that allows you to get input regularly and sporadically (perhaps twice a day or more if you are new to the team) either through face-to-face discussion or electronic communication (IM or email). Setting expectations up front is important. If you start asking lots of questions every day and your mentor was expecting a formal meeting once every three months, the mismatch in expectations will lead to frustration and resentment by the mentor.

▶ At different points in your career, you'll need mentors for different things. Early on, you might need a mentor to coach you in technical matters or to teach you about the processes in a new group you've joined. As your career progresses, you might need career guidance or business strategy insight.

Fun Breeds Success

In 2005, Google Vice President Marissa Mayer gave a keynote lecture at her alma mater, Stanford University, where she'd studied computer science and artificial intelligence. During the question-and-answer session following her talk, she was asked what she attributed her own career success to. She had an answer on the spot: "I like to work. That helps a lot."

Time flies when you're having fun, and it's easy to be focused and work harder and longer hours when it's pure enjoyment. Significant work in the field of cognitive and industrial psychology has studied the relationship between job satisfaction and productivity. Intuitively, we all seem to sense that we do things better when we love doing them; we have more energy and more interest in what we do. However, a scientific relationship was elusive until a large study in 2001 by Judge et. al.[1] found that job satisfaction and productivity are tightly correlated for specific job classes—namely, jobs involving intellectual complexity. It seems that, most of all, what we need to ignite, inspire, and enthuse ourselves to get peak performance is our brain. That's why software positions, notorious for their job complexity, are among the most affected by job satisfaction.

Not only will job satisfaction make you more productive, more innovative, and more enthusiastic, but it will give you the legs to endure for decades. Many people think of their work as a job, but yours is a career that will span decades. With a timeline that broad, keeping enthusiasm high over such an extended period is a challenge in itself—and an important one. Career success is bidirectionally coupled with job satisfaction. Being successful will give you the opportunities to do more enjoyable things, and doing enjoyable things will help make you more successful.

An ancient Zen aphorism reads "Pain is inevitable. Suffering is not." Unfortunately, every job has unhappy responsibilities, painful obligations, and occasional failures. These are the unpleasant necessities of software. Fortunately software organizations usually provide an environment where employees also have a range of more pleasurable (or entertaining) activities that are not officially part of their formal responsibilities. Although it would be wrong and even unethical to spend the majority of your time on items outside your official responsibilities, you can usually manage to spend 10%–20% of your time on these and perhaps even more if you supplement the efforts

---

[1] T. A. Judge, C. J. Thoresen, J. E. Bono, and G. K. Patton, "The job satisfaction-job performance relationship: a qualitative and quantitative review." *Psychol Bull*, vol. 127, no. 3, pp. 376-407, May 2001.

with after-hours work. Fun, of course, depends greatly on the individual, so scan this list and consider which of these you would enjoy:

▸ Spinning off a whole new technology or project as a skunkworks[2] effort.

▸ Inventing something patentable.

▸ Publishing a trade paper, whitepaper, or technical article.

▸ Publishing a scientific paper at a prestigious academic conference or in a scientific journal.

▸ Writing a book.

▸ Speaking at a conference (or perhaps helping to run a conference) in an exotic location. There's always a way to sneak in time at the beach or an archeological tour.

▸ Helping your company close a multimillion-dollar deal.

▸ Chairing an industrial committee that is helping to set an industry-wide direction or standard.

▸ Mentoring more junior employees and nurturing the next generation of leaders.

▸ Organizing social events for co-workers both at and outside of work.

▸ Organizing a distinguished speaker series for your company or a local consortium of software companies and universities.

▸ Helping to produce a new YouTube video showcasing technology you worked on. You've always wanted to be a movie producer!

I know many people who've tackled almost everything in this list, and doing so has made their careers much more enjoyable. These are just examples; you could probably add others to it. Sidebars like these are a kind of spice you add to your work. They're optional, but they can bring a lot of zest to your work life. Consider a few interesting observations about these kinds of tasks:

---

[2] Skunkworks: Unofficial projects that employees work on (often bootstrapped using after-hours time) with or without formal management approval. As the project matures and builds momentum, the people involved might receive leeway to spend an increasing amount of their official hours on it. Some companies have semi-institutionalized this informal dynamic by encouraging employees to spend a set percentage of their week on skunkworks initiatives.

1. Successful people are usually able to accomplish these kinds of tasks using just a fraction of their time at work and with a small amount of overtime hours for the rest. Most employers smile on these kinds of activities, and why not?

2. These are all tasks that look good on your resumé and indirectly advance your career. Although nothing is a substitute for a strong track record of high achievement and good old-fashioned project success, they can be the icing on the cake that makes a solid career look and feel like a career of far greater industry-spanning leadership. Compare the resumés of Bob Smith and John Doe in Figure 5.1. Bob and John have had very similar educational and work experiences. They are both very solid performers, but John made time over the years to do some fun professional stuff on the side. Over the course of a decade, these have started to accumulate. If you were a hiring manager reviewing resumés, which candidate would you more likely bring in for an interview for a top position? (Note the "Distinctions" section on John's resumé.) If you were evaluating employees to promote, how significant would John's advantage be to you?

Bob Smith	John Doe
E-mail: BobS@rogerst.com	E-mail: JohnD@rogerst.com
Education:	**Education:**
B.Sc. Computer Science, MIT, 1995	B.Sc. Computer Science, MIT, 1995
Employment History	Employment History
2005-2008 Senior Architect, Microsoft	2005-2008 Senior Architect, Microsoft
2002-2005 Senior Programmer, Microsoft	2002-2005 Senior Programmer, Microsoft
1996-2002 Programmer, AT&T	1996-2002 Programmer, AT&T
Skills: C, C++, Java, Eclipse, Cloud	Distinctions:
Computing, AI algorithms.	Coinventor of 12 software patents
	Coauthor of 15 scientific papers
Awards:	Founder, IEEE committee on Green Computing
ACM programming award 1995	
	Skills: C, C++, Java, Eclipse, Cloud
	Computing, AI algorithms.
	Awards:
	ACM programming award 1995

FIGURE 5.1   Fun can benefit your career success.

An Interview with Richard Stallman

Founder of the Free Software Movement

CURRENT POSITION

President, Free Software Foundation

CLAIMS TO FAME

Founder of the Free Software Movement and the GNU operating system; founder of the GNU Project in 1984; and principal or initial author of GNU Emacs, the GNU C Compiler, the GNU Debugger GDB, and parts of other packages

DATE OF BIRTH

March 16, 1953

EDUCATION

B.A. in Physics, Harvard University, Cambridge, 1970–1974

Honorary doctorates from University of Glasgow (2001), Vrije Universiteit Brussels (2003), Universidad Nacional de Salta (2004), Universidad de Los Angeles de Chimbote (2007), and University of Pavia (2007)

FAVORITE PASTIMES & HOBBIES

Listening to music, reading, protesting, eating, travel, cooking, sharing affection

BIOGRAPHY

Richard is a software developer and software freedom activist. In 1983, he announced the project to develop the GNU operating system, a UNIX-like operating system meant to be entirely free software, and he has been the project's leader ever since. With that announcement, Richard also launched the

Free Software Movement. In October 1985, he started the Free Software Foundation.

The GNU/Linux system, a variant of GNU that also uses the kernel Linux developed by Linus Torvalds, is used in tens or hundreds of millions of computers and is now preinstalled in computers available in retail stores. However, the distributors of these systems often disregard the ideas of freedom that make free software important. That is why, since the mid-1990s, Richard has spent most of his time in political advocacy for free software and the ethical ideas of the movement; he also campaigns against both software patents and dangerous extension of copyright laws. Before that, Richard developed a number of widely used software components of the GNU system, including the original Emacs, the GNU Compiler Collection, the GNU symbolic debugger (gdb), GNU Emacs, and various other programs for the GNU operating system. Richard also pioneered the concept of copyleft and is the main author of the GNU General Public License, the most widely used free software license.

Richard gives speeches frequently about free software and related topics. In 1999, he called for the development of a free online encyclopedia by inviting the public to contribute articles.

In Venezuela, he has promoted the adoption of free software in the state's oil company (PDVSA), in municipal government, and in the nation's military. Richard is on the Advisory Council of TeleSUR, the television station launched by Venezuela and other countries to counter the biased news of the corporate stations.

During his college years, he also worked as a staff hacker at the MIT Artificial Intelligence Lab, learning operating system development by doing it. He wrote the first extensible Emacs text editor there in 1975. He also developed the AI technique of dependency-directed backtracking, also known as truth maintenance. In January 1984, he resigned from MIT to start the GNU project.

"Freedom!"

How did you get started in software?

When I was around 9 years old, I went to summer camp. A counselor had a manual for 7094 assembler language. I read it and began writing programs on paper because I was fascinated.

What do you consider your greatest accomplishments or contributions to software?

My principal accomplishment has been to make it a common practice to develop and release freedom-respecting (free) software. Free software existed in the 1960s (and in the 1950s, I think), but by 1980, nearly all software was proprietary—and it was impossible to use a computer without proprietary software.

Free software is a matter of freedom, not price. It means the user has these four essential freedoms:

- Freedom 1: The freedom to run the program as you wish

- Freedom 2: The freedom to study the source code of the program and change it so that the program does what you wish

- Freedom 3: The freedom to help your neighbor—that is, the freedom to make and distribute exact copies when you wish

- Freedom 4: The freedom to contribute to your community—that is, the freedom to make and distribute copies of your modified versions when you wish

If a program doesn't come with these four freedoms, you can use it only at the cost of your freedom, and you shouldn't do that.

Do you have a pet peeve in any aspect of the software world?

I have two:

1. Proprietary (nonfree) software, which tramples the user's freedom.

2. Foolish users who don't appreciate freedom and trade it for some sort of short-term convenience that they get from proprietary software

What makes you feel successful?

What makes me feel successful is to see freedom triumph as a result of my work. I am disappointed when people express appreciation for purely technical achievements such as GNU Emacs and GCC because it means they don't appreciate freedom.

Richard Stallman

What set you down the path of becoming a champion for free software?

Around 1978, the AI lab got a new printer, the Dover. It was much faster than the old XeroGraphic Printer, but it often got paper jams and stayed jammed for a long time. It was very frustrating to use.

With the XGP, I had added some convenient features. For instance, the system displayed a message on your screen each time a file of yours finished printing. And if you were waiting for printing, it displayed a message on your screen if the printer got in any trouble so you could immediately go fix it. I was able to do this because the control software for the XGP was free software—in particular, we had the source code. I wanted to add the same features for the Dover, but that was impossible because the software for the Dover was not free.

Then I heard that someone at Carnegie Mellon University had a copy of that source code. Eventually, I visited there, so I asked him for a copy of the source code. But he refused; he said he had promised not to give me a copy. By my standards, this was a betrayal. But he did not do this to just me—worse, he had betrayed the whole world.

This made me think of the evil Chinese emperor Cao Cao (pronounced Tsow Tsow), who said, "I would rather betray the whole world than have the whole world betray me." But Cao Cao only talked about betraying the whole world. That man at CMU had actually done it.

This was not the sole incident that taught me to recognize the injustice in the licensing of nonfree software, but it was an important part. Eventually, I realized that it was my duty to respect the freedom of others by developing only free software. And so I could actually live in freedom, I decided to develop free software systematically, enough so that a person could use software in freedom.

"I always have my computer with me"

How do you stay on top of technology trends and innovation?

People forward me articles from various web sites that they think I would be interested in.

*Time management ... technical leaders are famous for being
time-strapped. What strategies do you use to stay sane and
use your time effectively?*

I always have my computer with me, and I squeeze in some work whenever
I have a few minutes to sit and not do anything else. I work in cars, buses,
trains, airplanes, and airports. When you are waiting for your luggage to be
delivered, do you stand anxiously watching for it? I always work or at least
read.

*How do you achieve a work-life balance? How do you keep your
software life from dominating everything?*

Why would I want to do that? My work is not programming; it is campaign-
ing for freedom for software users. This is not just a pastime and not just a
job. It's the most important thing I know any way to do. I'm proud of it, and
when I achieve something, I am very satisfied. It should be the main focus of
my life, and it is.

"What sort of achievements should a person be proud of?"

*What do you see as the coming changes in the software field over
the next 10–15 years that will most heavily impact what software
does or how it is developed either positively or negatively?*

I can't see the future, but sometimes I am aware of present trends. One such
trend is that of doing your computing on a web server belonging to someone
else instead of running your copy of a program on your own computer. Many
people have noted this trend, but few have noted how, in some cases, it completely denies users the control of their computing. I intend to do more to
warn people about this problem.

*What suggestions do you have for others on being successful
in software?*

The crucial question is, what sort of achievements should a person be proud
of? If you develop a nonfree program that is so attractive that a million people cede their freedom in order to use it, should you be proud? I would be
ashamed if I did that. It's better to do a small amount of a good thing, such
as free software, than a large amount of a bad thing, such as proprietary
software.

Richard Stallman

CHAPTER 6

Essential Skills.
Some Are Even Technical

"Masochism is a valuable job skill."
—Chuck Palahniuk (1962–)

Two kinds of skills define employees: hard skills and soft skills. The hard skills are the technical skills you learn at school, such as requirements planning, software design, programming, debugging, software engineering, operating systems, and so on. Soft skills refer to everything else you need to know about working in an organization, such as teamwork, communication (written and oral), public speaking, organizational etiquette, negotiating, mentoring, recruiting, managing, and leading. Both sets of skills are always important, but early in your career, the hands-on technical skills are a little more dominant. As your career advances, the soft skills become more important. Senior people are always expected to be leaders and to play a strategic role in the team; those expectations set a higher emphasis on soft skills. Both hard and soft skills are needed at every level of your career, but the balance changes over time.

Hard and Soft Skills

During the first five years of a career, the challenge is typically on developing soft skills because the nature of our work during that time forces technical skills upon us. After ten years in the business, the converse is true. Soft skills are thrust upon us by virtue of the situations we are put in and the roles we play, and most people find that staying current in their technical skills is the harder challenge. Wherever you find yourself in the path of your career, you'll get a head start by sensitizing yourself to your need to develop your-self along both dimensions and finding time to make that happen. Most people develop skills "on the job," which means they wait for the job circum-stances to present a need for them to grow in some aspect of their skill set (soft or hard) and develop the skills at that time. That's the default strategy most people use, and it's a fairly poor one. First, when you need a skill, it's already too late to start learning it. Second, one of the great secrets of career success is to develop skills and perform beyond your expected job level because it helps distinguish you from the crowd. The best technical and busi-ness leaders make time for skills growth on a regular basis, including skills outside their immediate business need.

Technical Skills for Career Growth

Your technical skills depend in part on what job you have, where you want to get to in your career, and where the industry is moving. In the software business, the market changes so fast that you should always be developing new skills to stay current and valuable. In general, technical skills growth can be categorized as in Table 6.1.

TABLE **6.1**   Technical Skills for Career Growth

SKILL	DESCRIPTION
Fundamentals	These are the core development skills you should have learned at school. They need constant upgrading because the industry is in a state of perpetual change. These include core languages (Java, C/C++, PHP), operating systems, CPUs, object-oriented design, GUI programming, storage systems (RAID), solid state storage devices (SSDs), storage area networks and networked attached storage (SAN/NAS), memory management, structures and algorithms, databases, XML, and web programming. Add at least one user-friendly programming language, from LISP, Perl, Python, or Ruby.
Development skills	Development skills, beyond the basics, fall into three categories: coding skills, quality assurance (QA) skills, and strategic planning skills.
	Coding: Requirements planning, feature specifications, unit testing, software architecture design, encapsulation, reuse, debugging, diagnostics, extensibility, review methodologies, usability design

SKILL	DESCRIPTION
Development Skills (cont.)	**QA:** Function verification testing (FVT), system verification testing (SVT), stress testing, performance quality assurance (PQA), statistical testing, software reliability engineering process (SRE), formal methods, code and branch coverage theory, quality measurement, control and management, risk analysis
	Strategic planning: Requirements gathering, market segmentation, resource planning, sizing, and estimation
Domain expertise	Whatever field you are working in, you should strive to become an expert in that domain, not simply the domain of software design and construction. For example, if you work on a product for social networking, such as Plaxo or Facebook, you should try to become an expert in the domain of social networking technology. If you work on a relational database engine such as Oracle, DB2, SQL Server, or Sybase, try to become an expert on relational databases. Expertise sets you apart and, in many ways, makes you a leader.
Tradecraft	Agile development, iterative design, rapid prototyping, waterfall development process. (More on these in Chapter 15, "Secret Insights on Software Project Management.")

Programming Languages: What's Hot and What's Not

"A language that doesn't affect the way you think about programming is not worth knowing."
—*Alan Perlis*

Alan Perlis (1922–1990) was a pioneer of programming languages. In 1966, he became the first recipient of the now-coveted ACM Turing Award. He once said, "You can measure a programmer's perspective by noting his attitude on the continuing viability of FORTRAN."[1] Although the heyday of FORTRAN has passed, aspiring programmers should be constantly asking themselves what programming languages and paradigms are at the fore. Let's face it, if your technical skills are based on FORTRAN or COBOL, your job prospects in the twenty-first century are pretty limited. Software development is, first and

---

[1] Perlis, Alan J. "Epigrams on Programming," *SIGPLAN Notices* 17, no. 9 (September 1982): 7–13.

foremost, about programming; if you can't speak in the currency of the business, your career along any technical path will be limited. Programming skills become much less important as you reach the level of software architect or executive, and many people in those positions have a fairly limited repertoire of programming skills. Even so, most of these folks (and, I would argue, all of them who are architects) were deeply proficient in the key languages of the day during their early professional years. So which languages are really hot these days?

One strategy is to study the frequency of references to programming languages on the Internet. I'm not the first to suggest this approach, but I've used that strategy to do a quantitative analysis summarized in Figure 6.1. I also included XML in the analysis; even though it's a data format instead of a language, it represents a very popular coding model that was worth exploring in the mix. Programming platforms, such as .NET and Eclipse, were included because they are just as fundamental to programming as the base programming languages they support. What's interesting about this strategy is that although it doesn't tell you which languages and platforms have been used most extensively over the past 30 years, which have been used for the largest projects, or which are better than others in any engineering sense, it does tell you the relative popularity of these languages being referenced on the Internet. There's a currency to that strategy that I find appealing because it sifts through the politics and engineering issues and speaks purely to metrics. That kind of bias-free analysis is exactly what you want to really get insight into when you examine what's hot and what's not. Some interesting results surface when you look at the top 24 languages and platforms in 2009, as shown in Figure 6.1.

First, Java is the world's most popular programming language, but if C and C++ are taken together, they cumulatively surpass Java. The second interesting point is that the top six languages (Java, C, C++, .NET, PHP, and VB) completely dominate the marketplace, representing 62% of the popularity index. Of these, recent reports from *eWeek* indicate that PHP is by far the fastest growing. XML comes in at a startling sixth place, right after PHP, and SQL and HTML rank just after Python and Perl, with similar statistics. It's good advice to make sure you're fluent in at least two of the top six languages. Every few years, it's worthwhile to do a reality check and make sure you've still got fluency in two of the major languages.

In addition to the powerful and intimate languages such as Java and C/C++, I think every programmer should know at least one higher-level language suitable for building tools, such as LISP, Perl, Python, or Ruby. Perl has shown significant traction in recent years. When I joined IBM in 1989, people were using REXX for a similar purpose (it's hard to find REXX programmers outside the mainframe today, although they do exist). These higher-level user-friendly languages come and go more frequently over time than the mainstay languages. Even so, you always need to have one of these in your back pocket for building tools, scripts, and small applications.

Also very significant in the data is the relative use of object-oriented (OO) languages. Java and C++ are two of the top three languages. PHP includes OO support as well. If you want to stay current on programming languages, you really ought to stay abreast of the top five languages shown, know your way around XML, and keep your OOD/OOP skills up-to-snuff.

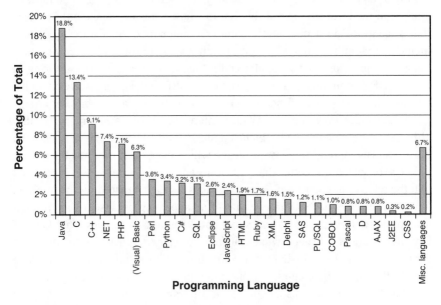

FIGURE 6.1   Internet frequency of the top 24 programming languages and platforms

Debugging

Programming is an absolutely humbling experience because there is just no bluffing your way around busted code. Every typo and snippet of broken syntax will cause a program to fail. If you're lucky, your errors will be of the simplest type, those that the language parser or compiler finds. Most of us, even the best of us, will introduce a dozen syntactical errors in our code for every few hundred that we write. I've often wondered whether this rate of error happens in other fields but is masked by the bravado and rationalization of the practitioners in a way that the brutal mechanical honesty of computers doesn't allow. Finding and fixing defects can be as simple as fixing a syntax error from an ever-watching C compiler, to correcting a subtle timing problem in a multithread high-concurrency program that can take weeks or even months to derive the root cause for. Most software developers have had these experiences, so there's no need to elaborate. Debugging problems is a key skill—and, unfortunately, not one that is taught explicitly. Most programmers are familiar with using debuggers or trace facilities or mocking up their own diagnostics logs to help identify problems. But are these experiential tactics that we've embraced by force of need really the best practices in defect discovery? Are there better strategies and methodologies for finding problems than what we typically do as a community?

The first trade secret is to avoid the urge to fire up a debugger as the first step in the debugging process. The debugger is a powerful but inefficient tool that should be used as a last resort. Two tactics have emerged as best practices to mitigate the need to fire up the debugger: self-asserting code (and Design by Contract™) and code walkthroughs. By using both of these fairly religiously, you can produce much higher-quality code and become a far more productive programmer. Fewer defects means more time for design and coding, along with a shorter test cycle; this is time well spent that pays back tenfold in programmer efficiency. As a manager, encouraging your teams to use these processes with discipline helps you transform an average development team into a high-performance one.

Self-Asserting Code and Design by Contract™

Assertions allow code to test itself by checking (asserting) that conditions in the code, including state data, ranges of input and output variables, and intermediate results and return codes, are within sensible ranges. Assertions allow programs to validate themselves at runtime. Typically, assertions are implemented using a macro that is disabled in production code, so the runtime overhead of the assertion is incurred only during in-house execution, never by customers. Assertions can find problems that could be extremely hard to identify through external observation during test or customer use. Most programmers use assertion checking in a fairly arbitrary way, scattering assertions throughout their code. Adding some rigor to their use goes a long way.

A formalization I'm fond of is a methodology called Design by Contract, introduced by Bertrand Meyer, who is also the progenitor of the Eiffel programming language. Design by Contract is based on the notion that all functions and methods have a signature (or specification) that defines their inputs and expected output. Assertions should be rigorously used to enforce that the inputs to a method or function match the supported contract (that is, speci-fication) of the function, as do the outputs. When using Design by Contract, functions and methods are heavily asserted at the entry to the routine and at their exit, to enforce the terms of the specification. It's a powerful idea that lends itself to a consistent programming style: lots of asserts at the start and at the end.

Code Walkthroughs and Code Reviews

Code inspections, or the process of having human reviewers walk through source code listings, remain the single most efficient way to identify defects. Design reviews are often cited as the most effective process for removing sys-tem problems, but although design reviews can find the more egregious prob-lems, they find a minority of the coding problems (you can't find code defects before you have written code). A bad design will give you more grief than bad code, but pound for pound, the number of defects you can detect is much higher with code reviews. In 1976, a landmark paper by Michael Fagan[2] found that code inspections can remove the overwhelming majority of code defects (up to 90%); no other quality assurance technical comes close.

Code inspections are largely divided into three categories:

1. Formal code reviews, by a group of reviewers. In the case of the pair programming development model, this is done in pairs.

2. Informal code walkthroughs, usually by the author and one other pro-grammer, as a sanity check on the author's work.

3. Personal walkthroughs, in which a programmer walks through his or her own code, tracing the logic flow. If you know the code segment that is failing, you can usually better identify the defect causing the fault by examining the code visually than you could through firing up the debugger and producing a repeatable scenario.

Writing code is much easier than debugging it. A top programmer might be able to write a thousand lines of source code in a day, but a single defect buried within it could take weeks to find and fix. Assertions, Design by Contract, and code inspections can collectively reduce the number of times

---

[2] Fagan, Michael, "Design and Code Inspections to Reduce Errors in Program Development," *IBM Systems Journal* 15, no. 3: 182–211.

per year a programmers needs to fire up the debugger by an order of magnitude. I also believe that they noticeably reduce the number of defects that get shipped to customers and dramatically improve programmer efficiency. Do yourself and your career a favor, and avoid firing up the debugger when possible.

Surviving Spec, Design, and Code Reviews

One of the more brutal experiences that separates industry from school is the technical review of your work. Product specifications, design specifications, test plans, product code, test code—everything is subject to review. Depending on the organization you've joined, some or all of these will be reviewed 100% of the time. These reviews typically involve a small team of people who are assigned to review these pieces of work in excruciating detail and pick apart your work with finely pointed cast-iron pliers. This is approximately as much fun as having your...okay, I'll spare you the biological analogies, but it's not pleasant.

Although at first the process is humbling and downright humiliating, it has a therapeutic and emboldening quality: You'll never want to go through it again. After the first experience, your attention to detail in subsequent projects is always dramatically improved. Reviews make you a better, more reliable, more cautious, and more accurate professional. They also make you a more compelling professional because, knowing that your work will be scrutinized by a group of your peers and superiors, you'll want to prepare for the inevitable questions about the choices you made that appear in the material under review. Why did you choose to design it like that and not like this? Why don't you have test cases to cover scenarios a, b, and c? Why did you use a recursive implementation instead of a simple looping structure? In your first few reviews, these questions will hit you like a ton of bricks, but in subsequent reviews, you'll be ready.

Even after a few years in the business, every review brings with it questions, challenges to your ideas, criticisms, and valid observations. The only valid path through the review is to modestly accept the valid criticism and calmly but determinedly defend the choices you believe in. Never defend your initial choices purely to save face—remember, most of the people in the review know how to program as well as or better than you. At the same time, don't let yourself be unduly swayed by the opinions of senior people only by virtue of their charisma or political schlep. There is a time and place to defer to authority, but technical reviews need to be about open discussion. Many times the senior people raising questions have been studying the material for only a few hours, whereas you've been developing it for weeks or months. They may be more senior, more forceful, more charismatic, and perhaps even more intelligent, but none of these necessarily makes them right. If you truly believe you are right, then in a calm and polite manner, hold your position. You'll be amazed at how often you can convince others that what you believe is right by showing a little bit of polite and courteous backbone. You'll be more respected in the team for behaving that way. If your expression turns to anger or frustration, not only are you on a path to thoroughly unimpress the reviewers, but by forcing the discussion into a conflict of ideas rather than a discussion of merits, you'll have moved everyone into a combative mode, leading to entrenched positions and a far less receptive audience.

The Growth Skill

Moe was out for a walk in the woods and came upon a woodcutter working furiously to cut down a large tree. He was so impressed by the woodcutter's effort and determination that he decided to watch from a distance to see how the sawing event would unfold. Several minutes passed, and the woodcutter was still sawing furiously with every ounce of strength and skill that he had. Moe noticed that the woodcutter had been working so hard to cut down trees over the past several days that the saw blade he was using had become dull. Thinking it might be helpful to point this out, he approached the woodcutter, who was drenched in sweat and still working furiously.

"Excuse me, sir. I noticed that the saw you're using has become dull. If you stop for a moment to sharpen it, you'll probably be able to finish the job much sooner."

The woodcutter replied, "Stop to sharpen the saw? Can't you see how busy I am? I don't have time to stop!"

This story, and variations of it, has become a classic in the business world and is generally referred to simply as "Sharpen the Saw." It illustrates the importance of skill building and business process optimization. "Sharpen the Saw" is about the skills people have and the tools they use to do their work. Taking the time to improve ourselves as individuals and organizations pays off in the long run. In computer science, this can be tooling optimization, such as finding and adopting a superior debugger, or skills development, such as learning a new programming language. One of the characteristics most successful people in software share is that they all spend time regularly sharpening the saw. Some do it deliberately, and others have come to do it habitually without realizing it. It's also a process that is easier for senior staff to do than for junior staff because the nature of their jobs forces senior staff to regularly review and to be consulted on new technologies and business paradigms.

In order to reach the ranks of the senior staff where this becomes an easier process, the trick is to structure your professional life to deliberately make time to regularly develop yourself and the organizational processes you operate within. The challenge is that these skill-building and process-optimization efforts take time—and they're never as urgent to get to as the project tasks you've been assigned. If you wait for a lull in your day job when you can get to these things, then like Vladimir and Estragon in Samuel Becket's "Waiting for Godot," you'll be waiting forever. How do you make time for something that is never more urgent than what you are working on but is crucial for your professional success? Make no mistake about it—in the software business, where tools, languages, best practices, and underlying technology change almost completely every few years, your long-term success absolutely depends on your ability to stay on top of technology and sharpen the saw.

The secret to building time to sharpen the saw is to sensitize yourself to how you spend your time. You can divide all the time you spend at work into four quadrants. Along one axis, you have the categories of Urgent Work and Nonurgent Work; along the other axis, you have the categories of Important Work and Unimportant Work. Your core job, the tasks at hand and the deliverables you commit to the business, generally fall into the Urgent and Important quadrant. These tasks include critical meetings, work you are doing to help meet an upcoming deadline, and so on. These tasks are urgent because they can't wait, and they are important.

Not everything is urgent and important. Some things are just urgent, such as answering a ringing phone. We've been conditioned to drop everything we're doing to answer a ringing phone, a social habit dating back to a time when there were no asynchronous communication modes such as voice mail and email. Many of the meetings we attend in a large organization are similarly urgent (the meeting is now—you can't attend it tomorrow or next week) but perhaps not very important. Of course, someone felt the meeting was important enough to schedule—that's how you got invited—but their sense of urgency may be different from yours. Then there are things we do at work that are complete time wasters, neither urgent nor important, such as taking a two-hour lunch, spending time playing a video game, or surfing the Web for a new camera. Spending too much time in that quadrant will definitely get you fired!

The fourth and final quadrant is the magic quadrant of Important but Not Urgent. Time spent in this quadrant separates the winners from the losers, the people with big-shot potential from the career middlemen. As a software pofessional, this is where you expand your career and develop your potential. Growth activities, the activities that sharpen the saw, generally fall in this quadrant. They are rarely urgent–they can wait a week, a month, or longer, in most cases. But although these tasks aren't urgent, they define the scope and potential of your career. Spend time in this quadrant as follows:

▶ Recognize its relative importance to you personally and professionally and develop strategies for spending time here on a regular basis.

▶ Purge or bypass activities in your schedule that are really in the unimportant categories. The less time you spend in quadrants 2 and 3, the more easily you can justify to yourself and others time that you'll spend in quadrant 4.

Take a look at Figure 6.2.

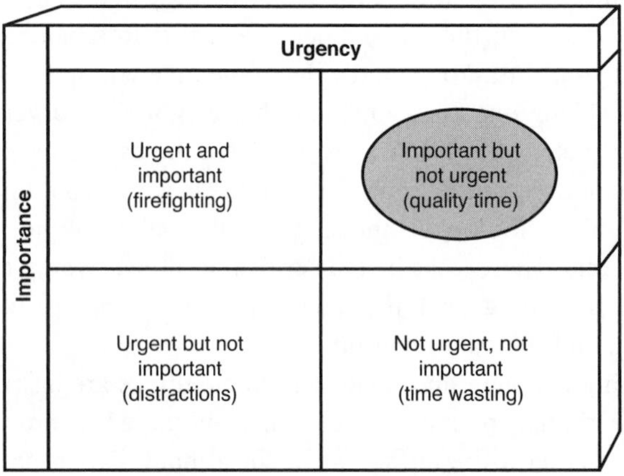

FIGURE 6.2   Quadrants of time (From *The 7 Habits of Highly Effective People*, by Stephen R. Covey New York: FreePress, 2004, reprinted with permission from Franklin Covey Co.)

Individuals and corporations have varying strategies for getting quality time in quadrant 4, the magical zone of Important but Not Urgent. For some people, it's a daily event; for others, it's a weekly or monthly routine. If you're not finding time in the Important but Not Urgent zone on a regular basis, it will definitely lower your career potential. *Carpe diem*–seize the day.

Soft Skills at the Top of Most Organizations

Look around any organization, and you'll notice that the people at the top are characterized by certain common qualities:

- ► They are socially aware, generally avoiding verbal gaffs and political missteps. They are good at making professionally appropriate conversation.
- ► They communicate well (or, at least, clearly) in small groups, in large groups, and in writing.
- ► They use their time efficiently.
- ► They are well connected within the organization (if they're new to a group, they form connections rapidly)
- ► They act with a sense of urgency, attacking important matters with vigor.
- ► They are relatively calm under fire, facing problems as a matter of due course.

These aren't skills you'll learn in a school curriculum, but they are indeed powerful skills for any professional. In fact, soft skills are so dominant that you can often identify the future leaders and managers of an organization within the first two years of their career simply by looking for these personality traits. The sad thing is that for most people, these truly are personality traits more than learned skills. However, I have come to believe that a conscientious professional can learn all of these attributes over time. Soft skills are always important, but they rise in value in senior positions. Why? Simply because senior positions are usually filled with responsibilities related to managing people (or in the case of senior architects, interacting with people) and resolving problems. Focus on your soft skills, and you'll be building a foundation for future career growth. Exceptions exist to every rule, and it's true that people can rise to the higher echelons of an organization even if they lack one or more of these qualities—but it's harder.

The Ultimate Soft Skill: Emotional Intelligence

Emotional intelligence (EI) is a measure of several noncognitive mental and emotional skills that strongly affect people's ability to cope with and succeed in a wide array of practical situations. EI isn't about how smart you are in the normal sense of remembering information accurately or solving challenging technical problems. You'll find a wide range of definitions for EI, but I believe it is an attempt to measure maturity and common sense. Maturity and common sense take you far in life, giving you the ability to deal with emotionally challenging business and organization situations. In fact, if you look around any organization in corporate America, you'll find that the senior management teams of most organizations include people with a wide range of technical and organizational skills, but successful senior managers are people with clear operational maturity and common-sense business acumen. IQ is important (it's hard to get ahead if you don't have a modicum of analytical, logical, and rational thinking), but it's simply not sufficient on its own. Research over the past decade has shown that IQ alone is a weak predictor of career success, influencing outcomes on average by only 6%. Studies on EI have a dramatically stronger influence on employee success, showing anywhere between 27% and 45% correlation with job success. Put this into the context of software development, and you'll pretty quickly observe that a hot programmer who can code 35,000 lines of high-quality code every year with an uncanny knack for upsetting every single co-worker he or she encounters will never get promoted to senior levels as quickly as a consistently solid (but not genius) programmer who demonstrates common sense, maturity, and business acumen—in short, high EI.

Consider the case of the following two employees, Moe and Curly working at SuperDuperTech Inc. A new management position has opened up within their organization, and a strong leader is needed to fill the position and lead a team of software developers. Moe and Curly have both been brought forward as candidates. Based on the comparison shown in Table 6.2, who would you pick?

TABLE 6.2   Moe and Curly: A Side-by-Side Comparison

	MOE	CURLY
Productivity	Super high	Medium high
	Moe produces huge amounts of high-quality, innovative code consistently.	Curly is a solid performer; she knows her stuff and gets good work done but is not in Moe's league.
Years in the business	8	7

(continues)

TABLE **6.2** Moe and Curly: A Side-by-Side Comparison *(continued)*

	MOE	CURLY
Business acumen	Medium	High
	Moe is passionate about the software business and seemed to understand the nature of the industry ever since joining. However, he doesn't like to learn from others. Whatever he doesn't pick up on his own, he'll probably never learn.	Curly didn't start as a business guru, in terms of either corporate culture or the nature of the software industry, but she takes feedback to heart. She has been on a steady path of growth since graduation.
Technical skills	Super high	High
	Technical depth will be a great asset in leading the new engineering team.	She displays solid skills, although she's not a rainmaker.
Interpersonal	Very low	Very high
	Everyone has a hard time working with Moe, because he considers everyone a moron; despite consistent mentoring, he can't seem to stop sharing those views. He's a consistently negative influence on the team.	Curly is a pleasant person to be around, and everyone likes working with her. She always has a smile on her face.
Leadership	Low	High
	Moe has a vision of what an engineering team needs to do but has never been successful in motivating others. He doesn't understand the dynamics of people and teams.	Curly is a people person and understands what makes people tick. She's good at rallying the troops.

Why would most companies choose Curly, and what are the ramifications of choosing Moe from a business/success perspective? Although it's tempting to select Moe because of his technical prowess, Moe is a one-man show, and he won't be effective in leading a team. Curly's technical skills are good, and what she lacks in depth she can compensate for by recruiting top-notch talent to her team. Moe can't compensate for his failings in the same way because leadership isn't something you can delegate: Leaders need to lead. As a manager and leader, Curly will need to bring together the best people, motivating them and managing their operations to achieve a goal. Everything about Curly's profile suggests she'll be able to do that. Because Curly can leverage the strength of her team, her chances of establishing a solid technical direction for the project are about as good as Moe's. Conversely, selecting Moe would be a disaster for the project and the individuals working for him. He's unlikely to focus the team energy, coordinate the work, and navigate the organizational and political issues. Not only will the project be hampered by his style, but he'll be a poor role model for his staff on all the nontechnical issues.

EI has a lot to do with emotional maturity and common sense and, therefore, is tightly linked to personality. Harnessing and nurturing your own personal maturity and common sense is hard, but it's also fairly mechanical. Most of us don't have the ability to make our brains larger, dramatically improve our memory, increase our ability to think through analytic problems, or raise our IQ by a factor. But with effort, we can reduce how often we get angry, whether we examine problems from an objective perspective or a selfish one, and whether we ask what's in it for us versus what's best for the team. The wonderful thing about EI is that it's not just a catalyst for professional success; it's a strategy for whole-life improvement. Higher EI makes you a better and more well rounded, balanced, and emotionally resilient person, not only in a professional sense, but in your personal life as well. People with high EI are also more willing to learn, more willing to focus on self-improvement, and more receptive to constructive feedback. They create a spiral of self-improvement that leads to increasing successes in life.

Another interesting finding in the cognitive research literature, described in a 2006 paper by Brackett et. al.,[3] is that people are particularly poor at assessing their own EI. That means that you can have a very low EI and think you are an emotional genius, or you can have a very high EI and still think you are low in the pack. Several possible reasons for this exist, not the least of which is probably that EI is needed to assess deficiencies in EI. People with low EI are hopeless at self-assessment, and people with high EI understand how much they really need to grow and mature.

There's a huge body of literature on this field, and it's still developing rapidly. Here are some tips for developing your own EI over time.

1. Understand yourself. Throughout the day, try to be aware of the emotions you are feeling in different situations. Keep a mental note of situations that cause you negative feelings. Over time, try to understand why you feel the things you do.

---

[3] Brackett, M.A., Rivers, S.E., Shiffman, S., Lerner, N., & Salovey, P., "Relating Emotional Abilities to Social Functioning: A Comparison of Self-Report and Performance Measures of Emotional Intelligence," *Journal of Personality and Social Psychology* 91 (2006): 780–795.

2. Sensitize yourself to others. In discussions or meetings with others, ask yourself what each person in the room might be feeling. How do you know? Are they giving off indicators through facial expressions, body language, inattentiveness, or enthusiasm?

3. Exude positive emotions. Make a deliberate point of smiling throughout the day. Try to encourage yourself to exude a modest amount of enthusiasm most of the time.

4. Commit to never expressing anger. Translate the situations that used to evoke anger into completely objective moments.

5. Identify the professional aspirations of others. Understand what others around you want and try to encourage their engagement and enthusiasm by creating situations in which they have opportunities that fulfill their goals and desires.

6. Frequently thank your co-workers for their contributions.

7. Help others. Engage in acts of selfless generosity without expecting reciprocation.

8. Show sincere interest and caring in the lives of others. Make other people more interesting to you by imagining that they are close (or closer) friends or relatives.

9. Make a point of studying the high-EI people around you. Every organization has some people who are naturally more emotionally mature, sensitive, and in control. Try to observe how they do what they do and imagine yourself reacting as they do in difficult situations.

10. Be sociable. Talk with others and form relationships outside of the mechanics of getting tasks done (this does not require your work relationships to extend outside the office). Develop yourself as a person who is pleasant to be with.

Your skills as a software professional are a combination of many technical skills, domain expertise, and soft skills. Software professionals need a broad array of talents, but the two big secrets to maximizing all of these are to build time for the important but not urgent tasks that lead to professional growth (skill building) and to develop your EI, which, over time, will dramatically improve your professional suitability for senior positions.

An Interview with Ray Tomlinson

Inventor of Email

CURRENT POSITION
Principal Engineer, BBN Technologies

CLAIM TO FAME
Inventor of email

DATE OF BIRTH
April 23, 1941

EDUCATION
M.S. in Electrical Engineering, Massachusetts Institute of Technology, 1965
B.S. in Electrical Engineering, Rensselaer Polytechnic Institute, 1963

FAVORITE PASTIMES & HOBBIES
Reading, music, writing programs (Kaleidoscope program, puzzle simulations) for fun

BIOGRAPHY
Ray is associated with many of BBN Technologies' most significant networking innovations. He has contributed to the design of several network protocols, including the ARPANET host-host protocol, NVT protocol, TCP and IP protocols, packet radio protocols, and multimedia email protocols. He designed and implemented the first network email system, participated in the design of a secure network communication system, and implemented the first electronic key distribution. Although his accomplishments are numerous, Ray is perhaps best known as the creator of the @ protocol for addressing email. Ray has also played a key role in the development of time-shared computing. He developed the software for the real-time input-output system of a time-shared SDS-940 computer system and was one of the principal designers of the TENEX time-sharing monitor for the DEC PDP-10 computer.

During his 32 years at BBN Technologies, Ray made significant contributions to many additional projects. He was the principal designer of Jericho, a single-user computer for use by BBN scientists, and he implemented a large portion of its operating system. As a member of the Monarch team, Ray developed the instruction sequencer for a large, shared-memory parallel processor computer using custom-designed VLSI circuits. He was the principal software architect for the Pathfinder project, which developed systems for health and status monitoring of and communication between members of special teams operating in situations with inadequate information infrastructure. Ray has also worked on a video information server and multimedia conferencing systems. For the past 17 years, he has held the title of Principal Engineer, a position of distinction at BBN Technologies.

More recently, Ray developed a Logistics Anchor Desk (LogAD) to provide a situation awareness display and other tools that integrate database information on the location of critical resources to aid logisticians in discovering problems and creating solutions. Ray also spent a year revising the CyberTrust software architecture to make it more effective. Currently, he is working on the Advanced Logistics Project (ALP), an agent-based logistics planning system architecture aimed at incorporating adequate persistence to survive an outage without data loss.

Ray has published and presented extensively on processor hardware design, distributed architecture, networking protocols, time sharing, and speech synthesis.

"That's kinda neat"

How did you get started in software?

That stands out quite prominently in my mind. I was working as a coop student for IBM. I was in Poughkeepsie, New York, in the memory technology group. We were designing technology for new memories for computers, obviously. But I had never actually used a computer, and I wasn't really too interested in them, but I discovered that we had access to a computer for doing things like solving transmission line problems. I said, "Well, that's neat, and that's just down the hall"—it wasn't one of these batch-operated systems where you had to submit your job; you just walked up to the machine and did whatever you wanted. So I said, "That's kinda neat." I got the hardware documentation for it that described what the bits and bytes did in the machine, and I punched the codes onto cards, basically writing the equivalent of binary, except that it was a BCD machine. I didn't know about assemblers, I didn't know about compilers. I was just writing as close to the hardware as you can get. I wrote a program to compute Pi, and that was my first program. I said, "Hey, that was neat!" Then I learned about compilers, and I said, "Hey, that makes it easy!" because I had been doing all the memory allocation and stuff all by myself.

You are most famous for your work on networked email. Do you consider that your greatest accomplishment and contribution to software?

Yes, I think it's quite significant, but there have been some others that were quite significant at the time as well. They tend to be just not very exciting in that sense, things like some aspects of the TCP protocol that everybody uses now; I looked at that in the early proposals and said, "There's something missing here," and figured out what was missing.

The specific thing missing had to do with the three-way handshake. It was sufficient for the two ends to agree on what the other end wanted to do during the communication, but because of the possibility of duplicates arising in the network, there needed to be a third part of the handshake. In essence, the responding party had to say, "Here's where I'm going to start my communication of the sequence numbers, and, furthermore, here's where I understand you are starting." If the other party doesn't understand that, because of the possibility of a duplicate being thrown into the mix, then the other end can say so: "Whoa! You're agreeing to do something that I didn't ask you to do." So there was a third handshake, and there were some details to be worked out, and that's what I did. That's a single fairly small thing, and I don't think that anyone even realizes it's there. I did a lot of interesting things over my career. I didn't spend my whole time working on email. I had a major role in writing TENEX, the OS we wrote for the PDP-10 computer in 1969 or so, that preceded the email thing. Two of us worked on the operating system, and three or four more worked on other subsystems. It was a significant effort, and we got it done in a fairly short amount of time, and it filled a niche. At the time, it was the idea of using virtual memory, and using an age form instead of another form of virtual memory; using hardware support for that was all new at the time.

I'm guessing that you didn't realize at the time that email would become so ubiquitous in society.

Yeah, what was hard to imagine was the ubiquity of computers themselves because at the time they were very expensive to buy. At the time, the smallest computer you could buy was over $100,000. So you just couldn't imagine that being in every living room in a good portion of the world. Certainly, at the time I said, "This is a neat thing you can do, and if you have one, why not send messages to other users?" I figured it would be ubiquitous, but in a very small community.

What makes you feel successful about your own work in software?

That answer is going to be different for everybody. For me, I like to write code. I like to design systems and write code. I'm not terribly interested in management or customer interactions and other things like that. I feel best when I'm getting a lot of code written that works well and then being able to build on that to do the next thing. Also, I really like solving hard problems—typically a bug, something that's not working in a piece of software. I like hearing a problem described and then, after listening for many an hour, being able to ask questions, to illicit more information or offer suggestions on what might be going on. I like being able to grasp the situation and understand it in short order and then contribute to a solution to whatever the problem is.

"Oh, the @ sign!"

I'd love to hear the story of how you invented networked email. Can you tell me about it?

The email story was fairly interesting because, at the time, I was reading the Requests for Comment (RFCs). There was one particular RFC that Richard Watson wrote (he was at SRI at the time). He was proposing what amounted to an email protocol, except that his focus was on printing paper on a line printer and stuffing the paper into numbered mailboxes. So he had provisions for using up to 255 mailboxes (because he had 1 byte for a mailbox number). Most of it had to do with formatting the pages for the printer, line feed, form feeds, indentation and tabbing, and all that sort of stuff. It wasn't addressed to an individual, but rather a mailbox. The overall complexity of it struck me, and I thought, "We can do better than that." We already had mailboxes on almost all the systems of the time; they just weren't networked. So we had to come up with an addressing scheme that would uniquely identify the mailbox. Then we had to address the actual transfer of the data from one machine to the other, which was before FTP was specified, so I made up a file transfer protocol that I had already implemented, so that part was easy; I just had to glue things together. Probably the entire code wasn't more than one or two pages beyond what was already there in the file-transfer and the mail-sending programs. Then it caught on. When I was first asked this question in 1994 or maybe 1995, it was about a year before the 25th anniversary of the ARPANET. Someone called me and said, "Didn't you write an email program back in the early days?" And I said "Yeah, I did," and they said, "Well, when did you do that?" I said to myself, "Hmm, I really don't know. Maybe around 1972?" And for a while, 1972 was the year being bandied about as the date that email was invented, but after thinking about it for while and asking some questions of some other people, I realized lots of things had happened. For example, we had to have a piece of hardware to have our computer connected to the IMP, which was in a different building, and that hardware hadn't even been designed. So I asked when that had happened, and I figured it was within 6 months of our having gotten our connection. I also knew it hadn't been too long after Richard Watson's paper was published in June 1971, so I finally settled on the end of 1971. Shortly after I had that version running, we were delivering 10x to our customers on a fairly regular basis, so that went out with the next release probably in 1972. About three or four months later, in April, the working group for FTP was putting mail commands into the FTP protocol.

These were both eureka moments. You read something and you say, "I can do better—I know I can do better." Then you need to have the freedom and the time to pursue it. Then there's a lot of false starts. You debug, you do it again, you do it again, and then finally it works. With any program, you work on a bug for a day or three, and then finally it works and you go, "Aha!" and then you go on to the next thing. I don't think that one is more of a eureka moment than another. You need to have a problem to solve. If you don't have a problem to solve, you're not going to get to the second eureka moment.

You had this seminal contribution to email, and I'm sure you've watched with interest as it has evolved from a text-based system to a multimedia communication medium. Do you think it will become more powerful and evolve into something new, or will it be supplanted?

I don't really know. It's certainly possible for it to be supplanted. The generations coming up are using other forms of communication more and more. Whether that will ever dominate, I don't know. Email fills that nice asynchronous communication that is relatively quick but doesn't require an instant reply. I think that will stay, but some of these other modes might morph into having that kind of behavior as well.

What has your involvement in the beginnings of email meant to you personally?

You have to remember that nothing really happened until the mid-90s. Suddenly email was famous. That was very gratifying, although it was somewhat belated! I think overall it has been very gratifying, especially when I see some of the uses that are made of email outside the work atmosphere. I had an exchange with a woman who was reference librarian for the National

Institute of Standards and Technology, someplace in the D.C. area. As part of her job, she was producing this monthly newsletter and looking for stories. She contacted me, did an interview for her newsletter, and sent me a copy. I said, "That's a nice article," and I didn't hear anything from her for a while. About four or five months later, I got this email from her, and the subject was "Thank you! Thank you! Thank you!" I thought that was a bit extreme, and it was a bit late if she was thanking me for the interview. But then I read the email, and she was actually saying through an email list that she had found a group of people who were dealing with the same medical health problem her sister-in-law was dealing with. She was trying to get involved in this, to find out what other people were doing about this situation. And she said, "It was wonderful because I could talk to these people. They were dealing with the same problem I was dealing with." It was a kind of support group. "Thank you! Thank you! Thank you!" And I thought to myself, "That's wonderful." That's the kind of thing you like to hear when you work on something that is actually benefiting someone. It was a very interesting and very gratifying moment.

I don't think it affected my career all that much. I do get visits from our new employees, when the HR person brings them around and says, "Here's the person who invented email." It's interesting—it hasn't really advanced my career much. That was one event, and I guess to some extent BBN gets a little recognition from that point. It's another one of those one-liners they can put in about what the company has done—but it's what you're doing today that's really important.

I can't not ask you...Tell me about the @ sign.

[chuckles] Oh, the @ sign! Well, the @ sign was just there on the computer. If you look at the keyboard, it's the only preposition on the keyboard. The rest are all conjunctions, or disjunctions, or things of that sort. I was trying to think of a person being at or on or somehow associated with a computer, and that's the job of a preposition. So since it was the only one, in some sense it was inevitable that I should choose it. However, I really chose it because it wasn't used in any login names on any computer I was aware of. If it's not used in a login name, then you don't need to distinguish between a character that's in a login name and a character that is distinguishing between a user and a server.

You had all these logical and sensible reasons for choosing it. Now it has become this world-spanning pop icon: Everything in society is @ something! I guess it was impossible to predict at that time.

For a brief period, I was advocating using a word, like <space> at <space>, because it looked more like English, more like prose. But enough people said they really liked it this way, we're not going to change it. So I said OK, and

I gave up. That was only a brief period, but it was a little ironic since it turned out to be one of the most distinguishing features of the whole thing!

"Prove that you can do what you need to do"

What suggestions do you have for others on being successful in software (either R&D or business)?

Personally, I'm more interested in doing things I'm really interested in doing. I've seen some people who just seem to be able to get the job done, but they don't really enjoy the work. I understand that not everybody can enjoy their jobs, but if you can find a job that you really like, the better you're gonna be. You're gonna be more productive. You're going to be happier. You're going to be more satisfied in general with what's going on. I don't know how to find that job. I just happened into it here. There are lots of opportunities to do things if I don't like the particular task I'm working on. But you have to work yourself into that position; you're not going to get those opportunities up front. You have to prove that you can do what you need to do, and then you can start spotting opportunities and saying, "Well, I did a great job on this— I should be able to do a great job on that. Why don't you give me a chance on it?" It's not so much advice as much as recognizing your abilities and recognizing what you like and looking for places where they overlap and pursuing that as your goal.

You have a graduate degree in electrical engineering. Do you think graduate degrees are professionally valuable? Do you see them as a substantial benefit to a candidate when recruiting?

I think that as you progress to the various degree levels, the kinds of problems you are ready to tackle change. If you have a bachelor's degree, you can be a very good programmer. If you have the capability, you can rise above whatever degree you have. To some extent the degree you have is a measure of how far you are willing to go. For example, if you have a Ph.D., most Ph.D.s have had to solve all kinds of problems that may not have had anything to do with what they've really wanted to do—but they've tackled them and found ways of dealing with these issues. They can generally do similar things when they get to their job. With a bachelor's degree, you can be quite competent, and you may have the skill to go on to do some advanced stuff, but you probably will not progress as far. I won't say you *can't,* but the probability is that you *won't.* I won't say you need to pursue a degree to do something, but if you want to get that degree, you'll probably want to do the things that are compatible with that degree. So it's more a measure of the same aptitude and abilities as doing the job and getting a degree. I don't think one causes the other to happen. You get a leg up in some ways if you have an advanced degree, but if you have the ability to get that degree and you don't get that degree, you still have the ability to do whatever that degree would allow you to. You just come in at a lower level and have to work your way up. It's just a matter of getting a leg up.

"Sometimes you just have to put in the extra time"

How do you stay on top of technology trends and innovation?

I don't do a lot. Typically, if I'm working on a project, somebody will come along and will seem to understand something that I don't know anything about. To me, that is a kind of red flag—that's something I should know something about, even if I'm not working on the same part of the project. It's noticing things you don't know and then taking the time to find out about them, even if you don't have a working knowledge of it—at least you'll have a cursory knowledge so you can understand what someone else is talking about. And then when the time comes and you need to really understand it, you'll at least have a starting point and can do the research you need to discover some of the details of that technology.

I almost always start with a Google search. Then, of course, you've got to find the right document, the one that is really definitive about the topic, and that sometimes is hard. A lot of dead ends are out there. You find that this person does really seem to know it—he's found a solution, but he doesn't really seem to understand why the solution works.

Time management ... technical leaders and executives are famous for being time-strapped. What strategies do you use to stay sane and use your time effectively?

I'm not sure I'm really good at that. One thing that leads to an inefficient use of time is working on too many things. It's much better to do them sequentially than in parallel. Most people can deal with two fairly readily. When they get to three, they start spending all their time keeping up with what's going on in the project and not doing anything themselves. So when I find myself with three programs, I find that one of them suffers. I'll do enough to keep up-to-date, but I won't be really able to contribute unless somebody says, "We need this solved," and then I'll switch priorities. Limiting what you

Ray Tomlinson

take on is important. Working extra time ... sometimes you just have to put in the extra time to get caught up.

Do you feel that programming as a discipline is not by its nature a 9 to 5 job? Because a lot of the problems we work on require a certain uninterrupted attention, you just can't stop because of the clock time.

I agree with that. When I leave at night, I like to have checked all my software into the version control system and have no compilation errors even if it doesn't quite work yet. Sometimes that happens by 5:00, and sometimes it doesn't. So, yeah, I think a rigid schedule is not really compatible with programming. Nothing about it means it needs to be 9-to-5. You can work when you want to work. I think having a certain amount of discipline certainly helps. When you have to work with others, being on a compatible schedule is quite important—but I don't think it's a 9-to-5 job.

How do you achieve a work-life balance? How do you keep your professional life from dominating everything? Do you have a life outside of work?

Sure. Because I like to program, part of my life outside of work involves programming, but I consider that distinct from whatever I'm doing for my work. Right now I have as a goal to visit all 44 autobahn sanctuaries in Massachusetts. I'm not thinking about programming when I'm out there in the woods walking the trails.

"Learn how computers work"

What do you see as the coming changes in the software field over the next 10–15 years that will impact either the technology we work on or career opportunities, either positively or negatively?

I'm sure it will change to some degree. Often with software there's some new wonderful thing that's going to make what programmers currently do doable by some lesser individuals, and programmers can then get on to some other thing. But this never happens. Whatever you invent of that sort just turns into the same problem all over again—it's just got a different name. It's just as hard, and you're working with different kinds of tools, different kinds of objects, different kinds of programming entities, and a different language, but it's still the same kind of thing. You are still trying to assemble things that have all these edges that make them not want to fit together and finding ways to make them fit.

Do you have a pet peeve in any aspect of the software world?

Everyone's style of doing software tends to have aspects that grate—little things like coding conventions and lack of adherence to coding conventions and writing ugly code. I've written my share of ugly code, but that doesn't mean I can't object to it! The dearth of women in the field is another pet peeve.

What final words of wisdom do you have for people entering the field?

I think they should learn how computers work. You asked me about pet peeves before. One of my pet peeves is that programmers sometimes don't even know how computers work! I once had a high school student come in for some parent's day at work. I was talking about email in front of about three or four dozen young people. I said, "Does anyone have any questions?" One of the young kids said, "What happens when I press the Enter key?" I thought about it for a couple seconds. Well, that's a really a deep question when you get right down to it because all sorts of things happen inside that computer. But I figured that wasn't the answer that was being looked for. That's the sort of thing programmers don't know themselves when they initiate an action of some sort. They don't know what parts of the computer are doing what—they don't even realize whether the network is being used. Sometimes that manifests itself as really weird questions, and it's clear that somebody has not figured out how a computer works!

This is an observation: I think it's true about technology in general, not just software. All technology and software has a stated purpose of making somebody's job easier. It's supposed to be a benefit from it, and somehow there should be benefit from what you do. The software you write should help somebody get something done more easily, more efficiently, faster, or whatever. Somehow that never seems to happen because once you can get to do things faster, then somehow you have more things to do! There's an old maxim that the size of your program will grow to exceed the amount of memory you've got. It's the same kind of thing. If you add more memory to a computer, suddenly all the applications get bigger. If you make it easier for people to do things, suddenly they all just do more of them instead of using the time to do something else.

How should we react to that as a society or as a profession?

I don't think we can. It seems to be somehow wired into humans that if they can drive a car, they have to go farther. We invented an automobile, and then suddenly we had a bigger world instead of focusing on covering our own world more quickly. It must be wired in, and I don't think we can do anything about it.

CHAPTER 7

The Sweet Science of Software R&D Organizations

> *"Insanity in individuals is something rare—but in groups, parties, nations and epochs, it is the rule."*
> *—Friedrich Nietzsche (1844–1900)*

Software organizations are a fantastic and bizarre fusion of people who are notoriously poor communicators, far more interested in fun than finance, bad dressers, great puzzle solvers, and famously indignant. Understanding the complex and bohemian world of the software development organization is central to navigating your career through it.

Who Does What in Software?

It takes a village to raise a child, and it takes many professional roles to make a successful software company or to bring a single software product successfully to market. In smaller companies, you'll find that people might wear many hats. In a company of two, the product architect, lead programmer, CEO, and marketing team might all be the same sorry chap. Here's a quick rundown on the main roles you'll see in a typical software organization. Most software companies have people who effectively perform more than one of these roles. Only the very largest companies have distinct job positions for each of the roles outlined in Table 7.1.

TABLE 7.1 Roles in a Software Organization

ROLE	DESCRIPTION
CEO	**Role:** Executive role responsible for the business success of the company. **Seniority:** Head of the organization. **Scope:** Overall business strategy and success. Answers to the board of directors.
CTO	**Role:** Executive role with overall technical leadership for the company. **Seniority:** Highest technical member on staff but answerable to other C-level executives and vice presidents (VPs). **Scope:** Technical strategy, often called on to support business opportunities.
Fellow	**Role:** A strategic technical thinker and innovator. This is usually the highest technical level in a software company. Generally fewer than 1/10th of a percent of employees can reach this level. This is often an executive position. **Seniority:** The top of the technical chain. Depending on the company, this position might not be higher than the CTO. However, unlike a CTO, Fellows may not directly control technical teams. **Scope:** Domain-specific, based on expertise. For example, Fellows usually are associated with a specific field, such as compilers, operating systems, mobile computing, etc.
Vice President (of development, marketing, sales, and so on)	**Role:** An executive responsible for the success of an entire function within a brand or a large portion of the company, such as R&D, marketing, or sales. **Seniority:** Reports to either a C-level executive or a more senior VP. **Scope:** Product or brand level.
Director of engineering	**Role:** An executive responsible for the R&D team, in part to ensure that strategy is well defined but more specifically to ensure that the product development is well managed. **Seniority:** Reports to a VP. Most of the development team will be under the director's control. **Scope:** The entire R&D organization.
Director of marketing	**Role:** Responsible for the marketing team, in part to ensure that the marketing strategy is well defined but more specifically to ensure that the execution of the strategy is well managed. **Seniority:** Reports to a VP. Most of the development team will be under the director's control. **Scope:** An entire marketing organization.

ROLE	DESCRIPTION
Chief architect	**Role**: Architectural responsibility for a product or brand. **Seniority**: A senior role, similar in stature to Director. Sometimes termed Distinguished Engineer if the role is an executive position. **Scope**: The chief architect is the architect for the architects. All technical design decisions are under his/her purview.
Release manager	**Role**: A project manager who has the overall responsibility to ensure a product ships. **Seniority**: Usually depends on the scope of what is being managed. For a small product this can be similar in standing to a senior programmer or department manager. For a very large product this can be equivalent in standing to a second-line manager. **Scope**: Product level.
Second-line manager	**Role**: A manager of managers. Second-line managers usually manage an organization of 50–200 people. **Seniority**: A senior management role, usually reporting to a director or VP. **Scope**: Responsible for the success of the team(s) managed as well as the personnel needs of the direct reports.
Architect	**Role**: Architectural responsibility for a large part of a product or an entire product. Sometimes referred to as Senior Technical Staff Member (nonexecutive) or Distinguished Engineer (executive). **Seniority**: Similar to a second-line manager or 1st line manager, depending on scope. **Scope**: All technical design decisions for a specific domain are under his/her purview. A component or product architect is answerable to the Chief Architect for design integrity and efficiency.
Technical manager	**Role**: Manages staff doing actual productive work but also acts as the senior technical leader on the team. **Seniority**: Mid-level manager, reporting to either a second-line manager or another senior staff member. **Scope**: Responsible for the deliverables of the employees, technical leadership for the department, and the department's personnel needs. Technical managers tend to manage somewhat smaller departments than ordinary department managers, as their role includes technical leadership.

(continues)

TABLE 7.1   Roles in a Software Organization *(continued)*

ROLE	DESCRIPTION
Program manager	**Role:** Combines the roles of Product Manager and Project Managers. Ensures that that resources are being applied to the right things and, to a lesser extent, that things are being built right. **Seniority:** Usually a mid-level position, similar in standing to a department manager, although there is a range depending on scope. This can be a very senior position, comparable to a Director. **Scope:** Product or brand level.
Department manager	**Role:** Manages staff doing actual productive work. **Seniority:** Mid-level manager, reporting to either a second-line manager or another senior staff member. **Scope:** Responsible for the deliverables of the employees in the department as well as their personnel needs. Handles recruiting and coaching.
Research staff member	**Role:** Full-time researcher. This position generally requires a Ph.D., although there are exceptions. **Seniority:** Highly regarded, but with moderate to little control over teams of people. This is the corporate equivalent of a university researcher. **Scope:** Usually focused on an area of research expertise, such as operating systems, mathematical optimization, database, etc. Success is measured both by impact on real product innovation and by traditional metrics for research, such as patents and tier 1 publications.
Product manager (or product planner)	**Role:** Defines the strategy and content of a product with input from multiple sources (R&D, marketing and sales). Also helps define pricing and packaging (license terms and bundling). **Seniority:** Usually a mid-level position, similar in standing to a department manager. **Scope:** Product level.
Usability engineer	**Role:** A cross-disciplinary role that helps design and/or validate the ease of use of a product or a feature. **Seniority:** A range of levels, including associate, intermediate, and senior. The degree of design responsibilities and team leadership increases at each level. **Scope:** Product- or feature-level responsibilities.
Programmer	**Role:** Designs and programs new software. **Seniority:** A range of levels, including programmer, intermediate, and senior. The degree of design responsibilities and team leadership increases at each level. **Scope:** Specifications, design, code development, and associated tasks.

ROLE	DESCRIPTION
Function verification tester	**Role**: Functional verification. **Seniority**: A range of levels, including tester, intermediate, and senior. The degree of design responsibilities and team leadership increases at each level. **Scope**: Test plans, test design, test development and execution, and associated tasks specifically focused on functional verification.
System verification tester	**Role**: System verification. Unlike functional verification, which examines the function of a product, system verification examines the interactions of the components when they are integrated and operated under stress. System testing includes user profile testing, stress testing (concurrency, volume, scale), and integration testing. **Seniority**: A range of levels, including tester, intermediate, and senior. The degree of design responsibilities and team leadership increases at each level. **Scope**: Test plans, test design, test development and execution, and associated tasks specifically focused on functional verification.
Technical salesperson	**Role**: Sales to either business partners, resellers, Independent Software Vendors (ISVs), or customers **Seniority**: A range of levels, including associate sales specialist, intermediate, and senior. **Scope**: Technical sales staff represent a subset of the sales team. They are typically more deeply skilled in specific product lines and assist the broader sales team in handling detailed accounts. May work with a broader community to lead proof of concept implementations.
Direct salesperson	**Role**: Sales to customers. **Seniority**: A range of levels, including associate sales specialist, intermediate, and senior. **Scope**: Introduces products and brands to prospective customers. Travel is common, and it can be regional or international.
Channel salesperson	**Role**: Sales to business partners, resellers, and ISVs **Seniority**: A range of levels, including associate sales specialist, intermediate, and senior. **Scope**: Introduces products and brands to companies that will resell the product either directly (reseller) or in conjunction with their own (such as bundling a database with an accounting package). Travel, either regional or international, is common.

(continues)

TABLE 7.1   Roles in a Software Organization *(continued)*

ROLE	DESCRIPTION
Technical evangelist	**Role:** Evangelist who builds community enthusiasm for a product or brand. Supports the marketing and sales teams.
	Seniority: A range of levels, including associate, intermediate, and senior.
	Scope: Product or brand level. Scope is both inward-facing toward the R&D, marketing, and sales teams, as well as outward facing toward communities of users. Often responsible for creating demos, whitepapers, and other publicity collateral.

The Good and the Great

Software teams are like soccer teams. The collective effort of the group affects the success of the group. You will not succeed as a lone superstar in a team of incompetents. However, whereas the group survives, thrives, or dies as a collective, the organization's success also depends heavily on keeping its best and brightest people happy and motivated. As a result, the best people are cared for disproportionately. Although programming is just one aspect of what goes on in a software organization, in no other discipline is the gap between high and low performance starker. Microsoft founder Bill Gates once said, "A great programmer is worth a hundred good ones." Differences between high and low performers can typically be an order of magnitude in most professions, but only in software programming has the gap been found to be so dramatically higher. The gap is not just a gap in productivity, but a difference in quality and sophistication. The best programmers not only do things more quickly, but they also do them more elegantly. They produce superior designs and write code with better attention to extensibility, scalability, performance, and maintainability. Companies are right to focus their attention on the best programmers because, let's face it, at a hundred times the value, they typically pay one only two to five times as much over the course of the programmer's professional career. For the employer, it's as good as a fire sale: more quality code for a lot less expense. This leads software professionals to a healthy sense of combined cooperation and competition between colleagues, or simply "co-opetition." The co-opetition model of teamwork requires members of the group to work together effectively to achieve success for the product, but they also compete for the optics of being viewed as a top performer. Some call it a healthy tension, others a sickness.

Either way, it's the dominant way organizations operate today, so we all need to come to terms with it.

To achieve freedom, control, work on fun projects, or be promoted to leadership positions, your primary goal is to stand out as a top performer while maintaining all the social connections among your peers as cordially as possible. That's easier said than done, but the ideas in this book will help. Unfortunately, doing a great job isn't enough because a great job that nobody notices won't help drive your career. Executives value some roles much more than others, and it's important to be sensitive to that dynamic. Typically, the roles that get the most visibility are the ones that either solve major problems for an organization or drive major innovation. Look for major problems you can fix or ask for a project that offers room for innovation. It takes time and a successful track record to pull this off, but success leads to more success. If you can build a track record of success, you'll be trusted with ever-bigger projects and challenges.

Three Laws of Career Effectiveness

In real estate, they say the only three things that matter are location, location, and location. In software organizations, the three laws are similar:

Communicate.
Communicate.
Communicate.

Keep people informed about what you are doing. From a technical perspective, they might need to know, to avoid overlap and duplication of effort. For your career advancement, you can't expect to get credit for work that nobody knows about.

Ask others for their opinions if you aren't getting them voluntarily. Most people don't like to volunteer their opinions and thoughts.

Look around any organization, and you'll find that almost nobody makes it to a senior position without excellent communication skills. What do people mean by communication skills? Simply, it's clear, effective communication in speech, text, email, phone, and technical writing. It's easy to give up on being an effective communicator, especially if your organization operates in a language that isn't your mother tongue. Communicating in a second language is always hard. You will never master the accent, have a vocabulary as broad, or master all the nuances and minor insinuations that various words have. Even so, being a clear communicator doesn't mean you need to be an eloquent communicator. The need for clarity in communication isn't a tantamount obligation to speak like Winston Churchill or Barack Obama, and it's not about your accent. Clear communication is about simplicity and frequency of your message. Most people don't communicate enough—not because they can't, but simply because they don't.

Tips for Better Communication

Communicate frequently and in different ways. For whatever reasons, the simple and undeniable fact is that different people consume information best in different ways. Some people are more visual, and others are more verbal. Some people prefer the back-and-forth dynamism of a conversation, while others like having the ability to read and reflect on an email before replying. The most important thing you can do to become an effective communicator is to sensitize yourself to the fact that, in any group of people, there will be subsets of people who receive and communicate information best in different ways. Try to communicate your messages using a variety of media:

▶ Phone conversations

▶ Meetings

▶ Presentations (visual)

▶ Documents

▶ Email

Avoid using email for significant discussions. Unfortunately, email, which was established in the business world as a mechanism for sending memos, has evolved into an abusive medium for discussion. When you find yourself using email for discussion, stop yourself immediately and schedule a phone call or meeting to get the right people together. Email is a terrible discussion medium because it is processed asynchronously. It's even worse as a software design forum because it doesn't lend itself easily to graphic representation of ideas so common in engineering problem solving. Some people take hours or days to reply. That's one inefficient way to have a discussion. In fact, with the modern onslaught of email, many emails don't get read at all. Most tragically, the sender often has no way to know. At its core, software design remains a teaming activity best suited to face-to-face brainstorming around a whiteboard.

Keep emails short. Long emails often don't get read at all. I've seen too many keen, energetic, and well-intentioned software professionals seriously damage their careers by conscientiously sending detailed emails. Worst of all, when they discover their message isn't reaching the desired audience, they react by sending an even more detailed email! As a rule of thumb, try to ensure that you can see the first word at the start of your email and your signature at the bottom on the same screen.

Make personal requests in person. If you need to ask someone for a favor, such as asking your boss for a day off to attend an important family event, make the request face to face, if possible, or at least by phone. After all, the request is personal, so have the courtesy to ask in the most personal medium possible.

Four Modes of Business Conversation

Only four modes of in-person communication are used commonly in industry. Not surprisingly, each of us tends to be better at some modes than others. Master all four, and you'll have developed a powerful set of career skills.

1. The Face-to-Face Private Meeting

This is a private meeting between you and someone else. It's intimate, and although it has the illusion of being confidential, things you say in this mode can leak. This can be a meeting between you and your manager, a meeting between you and an employee, or just a discussion between peers. Emotional intelligence is important here—try to be sensitive to what the other person wants and feels.

Key skills: Charm, straight talk, EI

2. Small Group Discussion

This is a meeting with a group of people, usually between 3 and 15. It can be hard to get your ideas on the table, especially if there are charismatic and outspoken people in the room who dominate.

Key skills: Loud speech (or you might not get a word in edgewise), straight talk. Airtime is divided among everyone, so limit your comments to only the most important things.

3. Small Group Presentation

This is a presentation you make to a group of people, usually between 3 and 15. In this case, you have the floor, but the small group setting makes it possible for you to get some brutal questions and challenges. You will never be able (nor should you try) to hold questions until the end. Your material should cover about 40% of the allotted time, with the remaining 60% being used for discussion. Make sure the goals of your presentation are clear to everyone in the meeting from the start. Be explicit about what you are presenting and why and what you are hoping to get from them. Is this a status update or a proposal? Are you looking for their approval or just informing them? Don't keep them guessing or waiting too long for the punch line. A common error in this venue is for the presenter to build up to conclusions: Here's the problem, followed by all the issues, followed by all the things we considered and tried—and, finally, on chart 4,153, here's the conclusion. By the time you get to the conclusion, everyone will be either confused or asleep. Include a summary of the topic and the conclusions up front, to set the stage. Use graphics to illustrate complex ideas. A picture is worth a thousand words. Use metrics to support your positions. Data is always compelling and interesting. Watch the body language in the room to gauge whether you are getting buy-in, moving too slowly, or confusing people. Avoid theatrics but keep it lively and personal.

Key skills: Clarity of purpose, pace, body language interpretation (yours and theirs)

4. Large Group Presentation or Lecture

This is a presentation you are giving to a large group, usually 20 to 250 people. The large format generally means that you can hold questions to the end, and this is advisable. If you're giving a lecture or a presentation, the charts should be mostly graphical. People don't need you up there just to read a bunch of text. Your value as a presenter comes in being able to present the material, act as an expert, and keep people excited and engaged. Don't assume that people know what you know (if they did, they wouldn't need to attend your talk), so be careful to explain terms and ideas briefly, even if they are not brand new. Keeping people engaged in a lecture is an art, but some basic tactics include these:

▶ Start by summarizing what you are about to present. Present it. Then summarize the conclusions. This is often coined in the business lingo as follows: "Tell them what you're going to tell. Tell them. Then tell them again." This helps the audience follow your talk and consume the core messages.

▶ Tell a joke or two. It does wonders to keep the mood up and the audience engaged.

▶ Be enthusiastic. Keep the message as exciting as possible and make sure you seem excited to give it. After all, if you don't seem excited, why should anyone else?

▶ Have some kind of graphic on almost every page. Charts are *supposed* to be visual. The facts are supposed to come from the speaker, with graphical support from the charts.

▶ Carefully control your own body and hand motion. Too much, and you'll look like a nervous wreck; too little, and you'll appear rigid and nerdy.

One strategy I strongly recommend for people who need to do public speaking is to spend some time watching experts doing it. If you attend an organized religious congregation, your pastor, priest, rabbi, or imam might be a local example. Watch your company's executives give business talk whenever possible. Study television footage of presidents and prime ministers, especially if they are renowned for their public speaking prowess. Bill Clinton and Barack Obama are both excellent examples. Watch what these people do with their hands, their body motion, their use of eye contact, their pace and use of language, and their vocal inflection. Watch the body language in the room to gauge whether you are getting buy-in, moving too slowly, or confusing people. Practice in front of a mirror until you are polished.

Key skills: Humor, modest amount of theatrics. Keep the audience engaged. Body language interpretation (yours and theirs). Demonstrate domain expertise. Hold major questions and comments until the end.

In a room of blind men, the one-eyed man is king. The stereotype of the classic software developer is of a tediously poor communicator, and although that label might be somewhat overstated, it does have a few molecules of truth in it. If you can develop effective strategies for communication, especially in the personal modes of communication just described, you'll immediately have a big advantage over the majority of people in the software industry.

Never Surprise Your Boss

Managers, by their nature, do not like to be surprised. They hate finding out important news about their own staff through the grapevine or in the middle of a cross-departmental meeting. That's true for both good news and bad news. Aside from avoiding "the wrath of boss," in most cases, you'll find that your manager has a history in the business that you can use to your advantage. A good manager can help shape and position good news into something great, help clear obstacles to progress, and find creative strategies for resolving problems. When you surprise your boss by exposing news (good or bad) to others, you've removed the possibility for the manager to help position the good or address the bad. You've also done your manager some professional harm if he or she is made to appear uninformed on important activities in his or her department.

The last thing you want at evaluation time is a manager who's grumpy with you because you, however unwittingly, made him or her look bad. Let your manager be the first to know about the good news and the bad, and take advantage of his or her talents and position in the organization to nurture the situations to its best possible outcome. Your career success is always most immediately determined by your manager. If your goals aren't aligned with your manager's, you're definitely going to run into problems in terms of performance evaluations and advancement. Remember, your manager is the most significant determiner of your near term career advancement.

Impressions and System Tolerance

Corporations succeed on meritocracy and production. Just a few sentences ago, I wrote that your track record is credibility. A solid track record is gold to your career; even so, if you have a perfect track record and you've never failed at anything, you probably aren't trying hard enough and taking on big enough challenges! Stretching yourself and pushing your limits is part of professional growth, and it comes with occasional failure. None of us can succeed all the time while still pushing our limits and working outside our comfort zone. The interesting issue is how the "system" responds to failures and successes.

The reality is that organizations of people have short memories for facts and long memories for impressions. The sword cuts both ways—your mistakes will be easily forgotten if they are few, but so will your successes. Build up a good name and positive image within the group, and you'll create an immunity for yourself against the mistakes. This is the so-called halo effect. Conversely, if the organization has a negative image of you, it can be extraordinarily difficult to recast yourself in a positive light. After you've created a strong image within an organization, it will generally have a stickiness factor of about two years. That means every two years it's good to revitalize your image with another successful hit.

An Interview with Peter Norvig

Google's Director of Research
(responsible for answering more
queries than anyone in the history of the world)

CURRENT POSITION

Director of Research, Google

DATE OF BIRTH

December 14, 1956

EDUCATION

Ph.D. in Computer Science, University of California, Berkeley, 1980–1986
B.S. in Applied Math, Brown University, 1974–1978

FAVORITE PASTIMES & HOBBIES

Photography, travel, Frisbee

CLAIM TO FAME

Head of search at Google from 2002 to 2005, responsible for answering more
queries than anyone in the history of the world; also the author of the leading textbook on artificial intelligence.

BIOGRAPHY

Peter is a Fellow of the American Association for Artificial Intelligence and
the Association for Computing Machinery. At Google, Inc., he was Director of
Search Quality, responsible for the core web search algorithms from 2002 to
2005; he has been the Director of Research since 2005.

Previously, Peter was the head of the Computational Sciences Division at
NASA's Ames Research Center, making him NASA's senior computer scientist.

He received the NASA Exceptional Achievement Award in 2001. Peter has served as an assistant professor at the University of Southern California and as a research faculty member at the University of California, Berkeley, Computer Science Department, from which he received a Ph.D. in 1986 and earned the distinguished alumni award in 2006. He has more than 50 publications in computer science, concentrating on artificial intelligence, natural language processing, and software engineering, including the books *Artificial Intelligence: A Modern Approach* (Prentice Hall, 2009; the leading textbook in the field), *Paradigms of Artificial Intelligence Programming: Case Studies in Common Lisp* (Morgan Kaufmann, 1991), *Verbmobil: A Translation System for Face-to-Face Dialog* (CSLI Publications, 1992), and *Intelligent Help Systems for UNIX* (Springer, 2001). He is also the author of the Gettysburg PowerPoint Presentation and the world's longest palindromic sentence.

"...Her algorithm was O(n^2) and mine was O(n)"

How did you get started in software?

My high school offered a computer course in 1973. I thought it was great fun. I remember a moment that, in retrospect, meant that I might be a computer scientist: The teacher was explaining an algorithm for shuffling a deck of cards. She said to pick two cards and swap them, and keep going until every card had been swapped. I had an immediate reaction that this was terribly wrong, that it could potentially take forever to do that—and besides, there's a straightforward approach that is much faster. I didn't know then that her algorithm was $O(n^2)$ and mine was $O(n)$, but I did know right from wrong, and I couldn't stand for the wrong.

What do you consider your greatest accomplishments or contributions to software?

My biggest accomplishment was directing the development of the Google search engine in its early to mid years, 2002–2005, because of the number of people it serves, its impact on the world, and the sheer difficulty of doing what it does.

I'm also proud that I had a small part to play in the development of autonomous planning software for use on Mars rovers and spacecraft, including Remote Agent, the first AI program ever to control a spacecraft. I didn't specify or write any of the software myself, but I served as an advocate for its

Peter Norvig

Peter Norvig

development and deployment; when NASA threatened to cancel the project, I helped successfully argue to the understandably conservative project managers that the software was, in fact, safe and effective.

Do you have a pet peeve in any aspect of the software world?

Programmers and product managers who can't think about their product from the user's point of view. As Alan Cooper puts it, "The inmates are running the asylum." If everyone would design from the point of view of a user who has a busy life and not from their own point of view of being immersed in the product for years, the world would be a better place.

"Go out and solve some problems!"

Can you tell me about an event in your professional history that readers might find interesting?

I remember in one of my first job interviews, the interviewer was describing the work he did. I wasn't sure if I really understood it and commented, "Oh, that sounds similar to the work of so-and-so on such-and-such." The interviewer was very interested and started to take notes on what I was saying. That was a moment when I thought, "Hey, maybe I really can play at this game; maybe the reading and thinking I've done over the years does have some value to others."

What makes you feel successful about your work?

I'm very pragmatic and try to measure the impact I've had by multiplying the number of people I've done something for by the average impact on them. That's one of the things that makes it rewarding to work at Google: I can say that over a certain period of time, I've helped improve the response for a trillion queries. Even if each query saves the user just 5 seconds of time, that's 2,000 lifetimes we've saved over that period. And of course, we've had a much bigger impact on many users—we've helped them reunite with missing loved ones, find diagnoses for debilitating diseases, and so on. But ultimately, a purely numerical score is unsatisfactory. So I also forget about those hundreds of millions of anonymous users and focus more carefully on the impact I've had on those closer to me—whether I have made life better for the few hundred people in the company I interact with, the few dozen I work the most closely with, and the few others in my immediate family.

What do you see as the coming changes in the software field over the next 10–15 years that will impact career opportunities either positively or negatively?

I think it is a great time with a lot of opportunities. The necessity for capital is less than it has been in any time in history. With a stipend of $5,000, a couple of college kids with a good idea can buy some laptops, create a solution, rent web servers from Amazon or some other service on a pay-as-you-go basis, and create the next big product. Or company. Or industry. More and more types of businesses are relying on software as a key ingredient to what they do, whether it be a movie rental business, a robotic vacuum cleaner, the discovery of new medicines or fuels, or a thousand other opportunities. Go out and solve some problems!

How do you stay on top of technology trends and innovation?

Talk to people you respect and ask them what they're doing and what is interesting. Then read about those topics. When it makes a sense, you learn a lot more by actually doing a project in an area than by reading about it.

"Do the things that matter"

How do you achieve a work-life balance? How do you keep your professional life from dominating everything?

People get out of balance when they see their value as being able to respond quickly. If I see myself as a machine for answering email, then my work life would never stop because my email never stops. If instead I see my value as separating the important from the unimportant and making good decisions on the important, then I can go home at a reasonable hour, spend time with my family, ignore my email and phone messages all weekend long, and make sure that when I return to work, I am in the right mood to make the good decisions.

Time management ... technical leaders and executives are famous for being time-strapped. What strategies do you use to stay sane and use your time effectively?

Do the things that matter, stop doing the things that don't, and continuously examine your use of time so that you can tell the difference. Don't waste time on something just because that's the way it has been done.

Peter Norvig

Peter Norvig

"Make sure you play in the big leagues"

What suggestions do you have for others on being successful in software (either R&D or business)?

One thing I think is very important in life: Make sure you play in the big leagues. There's only so much you can learn or accomplish by yourself. For many attributes, you will be about the average of your peers, so make sure you have great peers. When I was in grad school, I played on a club Frisbee team that was competitive at the national level. Just for fun, I also played in a much less competitive intramural league. I tried to recruit the best athletes from that league to join my club team, but I ended up recruiting a player who was not the tallest, fastest, or strongest athlete. But he watched, learned, strived hard to improve, and, by virtue of playing with great teammates and great opponents, became a world-class player, leaving his old peers behind. I've always remembered that, and at every opportunity I tried to work with people who were better than me, from whom I would be able to learn and raise my game.

On the other hand, at some point it is useful for you to be the best person on a team, the one others look to to get things done. You improve basic skills by watching others who are more experienced, but you improve decision making by being the go-to person, by feeling the burden of responsibility and living up to it.

What words of wisdom or caution do you have for people entering the field?

To paraphrase my friends at Y-Combinator, "Make something people want, and have some guts." Life is too short to waste it on doing something that is not important. If you're in this field, you have the privilege of getting paid well to do interesting work with a variety of choices; you have the responsibility to choose wisely.

CHAPTER 8

Career Killers

"You are what you do. If you do boring, stupid, monotonous work, chances are you'll end up boring, stupid, and monotonous."
—Bob Black

We all make mistakes, but some mistakes have greater impact than others. To avoid serious career-limiting maneuvers, it helps to understand what one looks like. In this chapter, I point out common mistakes many of us stumble over throughout our careers. Some career killers are spectacular and volcanic, erupting and destroying a career overnight. The harder ones are the problems that creep up on you over the course of years. Some unlucky souls wake up after years of ponderous work and loyalty to their employer and wonder quizzically, "Why am I here, and what did I do wrong?" Career-development problems fall into some basic categories, including social interactions, teamwork, productivity, and professional growth.

People Problems

Software teams are all about people. Even the code that software teams produce is largely a representation of team thinking: You work with people, you work for people. People might work for you. Your customers are even people. That's why in software, when you have a problem in how you deal with others, you have problems with virtually everything.

Burning Bridges

Overall, your ability to get things done and receive good evaluations and timely promotions depends on real people working collaboratively with you to produce a strong set of accomplishments every year, or every software product cycle. When you're focused on a project and operating in a goal-oriented manner of getting to task and reaching milestones, there are always times when it's tempting to bypass people who are obstacles to progress. It's tempting to escalate issues to their management chain and apply uncomfortable pressure to help motivate and modify their behavior, or find ways to work around them. This is a fallacy of thinking. Memories are long, especially when people feel they've been slighted. If you've upset people in the past, it'll be hard to get their help on future projects or garner their buy-in when you're making a proposal or deserve a positive evaluation, a raise, a bonus, a promotion, or just a helping hand. The problem compounds over time because if you upset a couple of coworkers every year, then after a decade you could end up with 20 people who are deeply unmotivated to work with you. Here's the catch: someone who today is your peer or junior may tomorrow be your manager, your employee, or someone you have a dependency on. Your career is a long-term event, and over time, people jockey for positions. The players, including you, are always in motion, but each with a different trajectory and velocity. The more you can do to keep your relations with others on a positive tone, the better you'll be able to protect your career.

Gossiping

Don't assume that what you say about others behind closed doors will remain a secret. If you make negative comments about coworkers or management in a hundred private conversations over a year (that's just a couple innocent conversations per week) and as many as 90 of those stay secret, you'll have ten conversations floating around the team that can seriously damage you. Be nice both privately and publicly—even to the jerks and slackers. End of story. Consider our programmers at SuperDuperTech Inc. Curly, frustrated with Moe's contributions, starts venting her frustrations with other colleagues. "Moe's such a dweeb—he can't code his way out of a box. We're going to be late on this project thanks to him. While we're all working late hours that lazy fool leaves at 4:30 every day." There's also a reasonable chance that whatever Curly says about Moe, either to her manager or to coworkers, will eventually get back to Moe. Even if the news reaches Moe anonymously, Moe won't have much trouble figuring out who the source was. When it comes to gossip, you just can't trust anyone to keep a secret—and corporate gossip has no special semantics. Now Curly will need to undo the damage she's done to her own professional image, and she also has burned the bridge with Moe. Good luck getting Moe to do any extra favors or help in the future. More likely, Moe will start thinking of places and ways to sling some mud back in Curly's direction.

Getting along with your coworkers is important on so many ethical and moral levels that the temporary benefits of going gossiping and badmouthing others are never worth it. If you do feel the irresistible need to vent your frustration, vent upward not outward—vent your frustrations to your superiors not your peers. Your superiors are more likely to keep sensitive information private.

Becoming the Complaints Department

Everyone hates a "yes man," a sycophant. The only thing *worse* than a sycophant is a chronic complainer. People commonly feel that by making constructive, well-intended observations, they are helping the process along, but complaining frequently will just make you an annoyance to your peers and managers. With so many problems to solve in any organization, surely there's some reasonable way to bring your ideas to the fore. Indeed there is. First, when you raise a concern, make sure you also have at least one suggested solution. Having a recommendation changes you from a complainer to a potential fixer. Second, be prepared to volunteer to help with any action items related to the solution. If you are perceived as a complainer who doesn't have ideas and is never willing to get involved, you'll definitely be reviled across the board.

One of the most insidious and ugly behaviors is the tendency to snitch on coworkers. This behavior usually comes from two misplaced feelings. First, the snitch might think that he'll elevate himself by deriding his peers. Nothing could be further from the truth. In fact, managers hate this kind of backstabbing so much that it always reflects negatively on the snitch. Second, the snitch might falsely think that his manager has no idea what's really going on, so he needs to play the informant lest all the unprofessionalism of incompetent coworkers continue unabated. Any manager worth his or her salt is usually completely aware of the strengths and weaknesses of his or her employees. Remember that just because your manager isn't discussing your coworkers' professional weaknesses with you doesn't mean your manager is clueless. You wouldn't want your manager to discuss your professional failings with your peers. Don't confuse your manager's politeness with cluelessness. Imagine our hypothetical employee Curly, who meets with her boss and tells him, "Moe can't code for beans. We spend half our time just teaching him what to do and correcting his mistakes. Now our project is late, and it's his fault!" The manager will hopefully do some investigating to determine the veracity of the statement. More than likely if it's true, it probably wasn't news to the manager. But as much as this may hurt Moe, consider how it affects Curly: She's whining and complaining and clearly frustrated. She's not leaving her manager with a professional image of an employee under control. She's not in control of the situation or herself, and instead she has stooped to making damaging remarks about her colleague. For whatever damage Curly has done to Moe, she's also done a fair bit against herself.

Telling your boss that someone isn't pulling his or her weight or has done a bad job on a project will always reflect badly on you. If you really see an urgent need to notify management about a problem, try to cast your observations in the *context of the project* instead of the *context of the person*. For example, instead of saying that "Moe is doing a bad job at testing," say "I'm concerned about our test coverage."

Helping Too Much with Suggested Improvements

No person or organization can afford to spend too much energy on self-improvement, refactoring, and new initiatives. An appropriate amount of energy should be spent on these things, but the amount that's appropriate depends on many factors, ranging from the organizational culture to the business pressures the team is under. Being an overbearing fountain of new ideas and process improvements is neither helpful nor appreciated. Instead, pick just a few to champion each year. By doing so, you'll be less annoying to folks around you, and you'll probably still be making a larger contribution in these respects than most.

Watch your manager's reaction to the first one or two suggestions you have. If your manager springs on them and works to implement them, it's a good sign that the suggestions were highly appreciated. If your otherwise spot-on, absolutely undeniably good ideas were ignored, your manager might simply not be a person who's interested in change. If so, further "constructive feedback" from you will not only likely lead to similar results (that is, none), but your manager will pretty quickly start thinking of you as a first-class bother. It's time to cease and desist with the new ideas for a while.

Displaying an Inability to Work the Org

As a junior employee a lot depends on your ability to produce as an individual. You produce designs, specifications, code, test units, or product plans. As you advance, your role becomes more about leveraging the strength of the team to get things done, regardless of whether anyone explicitly tells you this. This is partially about increasingly leading others, but it's more about your ability to remove roadblocks and push through agendas so your team can operate as efficiently as possible. If you remain an individual contributor who lacks the wherewithal to work the organization, your career will probably stall. More on this topic comes in Chapter 9, "Working the Org," but, in short, don't expect people to work on your agenda. Everyone is busy working plenty hard on their own problems. Successful careers require artisanship in coordinating and motivating people with other agendas toward a common goal (of course, yours). Rarely is it enough to drive people and resources toward your needs by convincingly showing that it's the right choice for the business; keep in mind that the other stuff they're working on is, too. You need to align your needs with others' goals, give them something back as compensation (quid pro quo), agree on timelines for delivery, follow up with them regularly to make sure it's happening, and, perhaps most important, be effusive in sharing the glory by publicly thanking them for their efforts. If they get large doses of positive feedback from having helped you, they'll be more inclined to help you again in the future.

Exhibiting Inappropriate Decision Making

Business life is filled with tough questions surrounding ethics, people management, and strategy. If every question you face requires an escalation to senior management, you'll clearly display that you don't have the business acumen required to make these decisions on your own. Conversely, if you make all the tough decisions on your own, chances are, some will have serious consequences you won't be able to walk away from. How can you strike the right balance? Take some time to understand your organizational culture and decision-making process so you can see which kinds of questions really need to be raised to senior management. Then develop the skill to make the others on your own that mesh with your company's corporate values. When something does need to go to a higher decision-making body, come prepared with a recommendation to help frame the discussion. If you consistently make bad decisions about technical or nontechnical issues, it speaks heavily against your being chosen for positions of responsibility. That's a tough image to shake.

Team Problems

It takes a team to get anything substantial done. Only the most trivial projects can be handled by a single person working alone. You can be a nice person, a hard worker, and a brilliant computer scientist, but without teamwork you're just an army of one. As a lone soldier there's a pretty narrow limit on the territory you can cover and the amount of responsibility you'll be asked to bear.

Showing Lack of Teamwork

Software is a team sport. In Chapter 3, "School Versus Job," I discussed how this quality fundamentally separates professional software development from school. Not everyone makes the change smoothly, and failing to do so will definitely hurt your career in several ways. Senior positions are usually reserved for people who work well in a team. Make sure you are getting along nicely with and helping your peers. Carry your share of the work—more, if you can. Look for ways to help everyone by being a source of information, productivity, or new tooling for others. Be willing to sacrifice your own projects within reason for the benefit of the team.

Failing to Give Credit

If you take appropriate credit for your own work while failing to give credit to others who worked on the same project, you can be certain that your commentary will somehow get back to your teammates and leave a negative impression. You might not have intentionally excluded someone, but by commenting on what you've done without mentioning the contributions of others, the rest of the team will perceive that you're attempting to take credit for their work. Once broken, this is a hard fence to mend.

This happened to me early in my career as a junior employee at IBM. We were developing a number of demonstration programs. One of my colleagues, another junior programmer, had an obvious use for a feature I had developed. The feature allowed images to be re-blit to the screen at the coordinates of a mouse click. I was happy to share, and he quickly integrated my code into his demonstration and began showing his very impressive demo program around IBM, screen blits and all. The screen blits were a small feature, but one that was quite visual and showed well in the demo. Unfortunately, my colleague told everyone that he had developed this demonstration application himself. After a few days, frustrated, and lacking the maturity to deal with the problem in a more sophisticated way, I met with my manager and told him I'd developed that particular feature. In the end, it just reflected badly on my colleague—and probably on me as well (see "Becoming the Complaints Department," earlier).

Looking back on the scenario, I would have been better off just discussing the matter quietly with my coworker. I also could have found a way to get the word out with more subtlety, perhaps in the form of a friendly up-beat casual comment, rather than raising it behind closed doors as an issue. A casual comment at lunch would have gotten the message across without creating as much fuss or airing feelings of negativity. Clearly, both of us handled the situation poorly. If my coworker had more readily given credit where it was due, not only would I have felt better, but he would have scored brownie points as a team player and somebody who reuses code assets instead of reinventing the wheel. We both would have gained. The funny and wonderful thing is that being effusive with your praise of others is not only neighborly and good team behavior, but it almost never hurts how your contributions are perceived. Knowing the kind things you've said of them, your teammates will be more open and communicative about the excellent contributions you've made. Everybody wins.

Productivity Problems

Software really is about people and the teams they form. Within those teams everyone has to carry their weight. The benefits of the team are real: When we slip, the team catches us. When we fall, they pick us up. But if we're a constant drag, we can do more damage than good. Weak players spend more time on the bench, are placed in less valuable roles, and ultimately might get cut from the team. Being likeable, smart, and a team player isn't enough. You've got to be a doer.

Writing Buggy Code

Bugs come in many shapes and sizes, whether from bad logic, missing requirements, poor runtime performance, or misunderstood project goals. If you're a programmer and you get a reputation for writing buggy code, you won't likely get promoted to a position of leadership responsible for the design, planning, and execution of a team of programmers. Senior technical positions will elude you. A developer on my team once had an excellent reputation for innovative research and team collaboration, but his code was consistently buggy and late. He told me he really wanted to manage a software R&D team. I explained to him that as long as his own code was buggy and late, he wouldn't likely be put in charge of overseeing the code quality of an entire team. On the flip side, these kinds of problems are fairly mechanical. A sloppy programmer can learn to be a little more diligent, develop a more complete design, follow coding standards, review logic flow, and do more complete unit testing. You can't teach someone to be dramatically more intelligent or innovative, but you can teach the art of quality software R&D. If you have this problem, you should be able to fix it.

Displaying a Lack of Productivity

Employees get paid to produce work for their employers. Productivity is measured in different ways, and because everyone has a slightly different working style, this varies considerably among people. Some people are prolific programmers; others make their mark through innovation or team leadership. One truth is certain, though: If you fail to produce on a significant axis—creativity, code development, leadership, or something else—your career will decline. Most people have considerable ups and downs in their productivity over the course of time. Life situations shift, and major events such as a death in the family, change in marital status, serious illness, or new home can temporarily impede productivity and mental focus. Fortunately, the system seems to be quite tolerant of periodic productivity swings, and a few low points over your career won't hurt you much. However, sustained low productivity over a couple years can be damaging. The remedies are straightforward. First, make sure you are working on things you enjoy because it's hard to be productive if you're working on things you hate. Second, know yourself and understand the axes along which you naturally are most productive. Try to align your natural gifts (programming, creativity, team leadership, organizational management, or strategic planning) with your role definition, and you'll be better oriented to showing results. Above all, work hard.

Missing Your Dates Consistently

Few things destroy a career in software more quickly than consistently missing dates. This maxim is true for programmers, testers, planners, marketers, and managers alike (remember that managers carry the blame for all the missteps of their employees). On the R&D side, the problem is particularly painful (and notoriously endemic) because of the huge uncertainty related to software development cycles. Software development is complex and difficult to project; I've dedicated Chapter 13, "Avoiding Software Development Overruns," to this topic. In a nutshell, consistently overrunning your target dates year after year will have a deleterious impact on your career and will almost certainly preclude you from project-management positions. Always being late is a guaranteed way to make sure you never get a senior position.

Getting Stuck in the Wrong Time Quadrants

In Chapter 6, "Essential Skills: Some Are Even Technical," I talk about divisions of time—urgent versus nonurgent and important versus unimportant tasks. The most effective people divide their time between "important and urgent" tasks and "important but not urgent" tasks.

Spending too much time on urgent but unimportant tasks is a fairly common problem. Don't let yourself spend a lot of time reading email you needn't, attending meetings you shouldn't, and answering phone calls you oughtn't. A lot of these things are urgent but not very important, and they take you away from the important things you could be doing. The net result is a stalled career. Review your use of time periodically to make sure your time is dominated by important tasks. Life is more interesting when it's spent doing important things, and people who spend their time that way are usually valued highly in the eyes of others.

Focusing on Sidebars and Skunkworks

Side projects, sometimes called *skunkworks projects*, have been the genesis of many great software innovations. These projects can form the foundation of a new product line or a new company. It's healthy to spend some of your time on these over the course of your career, especially if you develop a knack for maturing them to fruition. Some companies explicitly encourage this. However, as with anything off the beaten path, the time you spend on these projects is perceived as time you haven't spent on something that more officially needs doing. If you spend most of your time on a skunkworks project that bombs, you can expect a blow to your career progression. Make sure skunkworks projects never consume more than 10%–20% of your official time (depending on your organizational culture).

Growth Problems

Letting Technical Skills Slide

It probably goes without saying, but in software, you need to keep your skills current. That's easier said than done in an industry where everything you know can be obsolete in a few years. Fortunately, many of the fundamentals about operating systems, algorithms, structures, programming languages, and development processes have significant longevity, even though the details change rapidly. If your technical skills lapse, you can find yourself a dinosaur in an exponentially evolving high-tech world. If that happens, your career will begin a serious decline unless you've climbed to a point at which technical skills are of minimal value. I would argue there are very few places in the software world where technical currency isn't needed to some degree. Whether you are in technical support, sales, or marketing, you will always need to speak the lingua franca of IT. The key to staying current is to always work on something cutting edge and to spend regularly in the "important but not urgent" time quadrant, building new skills.

Engaging in Excessive Self-Promotion

Self-promotion is necessary. If you fail to let your peers and management know about your accomplishments, they'll have no reason to be impressed by them. Although it's critical to communicate your own accomplishments in a modest and appropriate way, there's a fine line between modestly communicating your accomplishments and outright tooting your own horn. People hate self-centered personalities. If you blow your own horn too much, you'll create an image of yourself as a self-serving, self-interested, egocentric narcissist that will do far more damage than the few brownie points you score. Always keep your self-promotion modest and professionally appropriate.

Self-Marketing Off-Message

Unfortunately, most of us are poor judges of our own accomplishments. Sometimes we attach more value to achievements that others consider less significant, and less value to those that others consider more profound. Consider a scenario with our favorite programmer, Moe, tasked to develop a new feature for the company's flagship product. Moe is excited about the opportunity, and he develops an elegant implementation using a straightforward design. The coding effort was large, resulting in 20KLOC of new code. Moe is so proud of his design that he waxes on about it to his manager and others. They smile and nod politely, but frankly they really aren't impressed; the design is nice but unspectacular. Moe's real accomplishment is the 20KLOC he developed in short order with high quality. If he was a little more sensitive, he'd realized that his productivity and quality accomplishments were the real achievements. Because he's highlighting the design work instead, Moe is pushing the wrong message and risks not getting the recognition he deserves.

Getting Stuck in an Unimportant Role

Everyone needs to be challenged, to grow, and to find opportunities for professional advancement. In most sensible companies, a manager's job is to help ensure that, over the course of time, employees have those opportunities. Sometimes it doesn't pan out. If you get stuck in a role your company doesn't view as having strategic importance, it will impact your career growth. Don't expect anyone to come to your rescue—if you're not voicing concern, why should anyone else complain on your behalf? You owe it to yourself to make sure you're generally in a role with a future. Be polite, but work to ensure that you're on a growth path.

Fundamentals Versus Incidentals

We all make mistakes, and we all fail. In fact, I've come to believe that if you don't have a few things fail every year, you probably aren't pushing your limits. Fortunately, the system is very tolerant of mistakes because it's filled with so many of them. Ultimately, what counts is your track record. If you have a track record for being productive and innovative, working as a good team player, and delivering on the important things, all the periodic errors will be forgiven and forgotten.

PART II

Leadership

CHAPTER 9

Working the Org

*"Never doubt that a small group of thoughtful,
committed citizens can change the world.
Indeed, it is the only thing that ever has."*
—*Margaret Mead (1901–1978)*

Getting things done in an organization depends heavily on your ability to "work the org," or collaborate across boundaries and negotiate with others to make projects and events happen. The smaller the organization, the easier this is, and that's why large organizations seem so bureaucratic. The problem of getting things done in an organization isn't just one of logistics; it's more one of competing objectives. Everyone in the organization is driving toward a goal, hoping to make a good impression at what they've been assigned to deal with. Often when you need something from someone else, it's at the expense of what he or she is focused on. You might be asking for someone's time, staff, or physical resources. Assuming that your colleagues are decent people and that they even like you, why should they risk their own success to help yours? The challenges of working the organization grow dramatically with the size of the organization, but I believe organizations of every size, even the smallest startups, struggle with these dynamics. Having the skills to work the org is critical to your career success.

Getting Buy-In and the Myth of Electronic Communication

Getting people's help and getting people to see your point of view about project or organizational needs is always about convincing people. Convincing people is only partially about facts and figures. A lot of what we call "getting people on-side" involves passion, comfort, and personal trust. Think about the people in your life whose advice you accept and ask yourself why you value their opinion over others. A big part of why we all value the opinions of certain people is related to how much we trust them. Trust counts for as much or more than the facts and figures people spout. Trust is something you build through repeated success and by following through with your commitments to others. It's also something you convey in a very personal way, face to face. It's hard to engender trust with an email. When you need others to believe in your viewpoint—for example, a new design idea for a product feature or a marketing proposal—you won't likely get them on-side with a text message. Email has no heart and lacks soul. It doesn't convince anyone of anything. Meet face to face, and you not only stand a better chance of explaining the ideas to someone, but you can have a dialogue with that person about questions, concerns, and ideas of potentially improving on what you're proposing. When it comes to getting buy-in, a five-minute face-to-face meeting is always more effective than a multiday email thread. Of course, you can't build deep trust in a five-minute discussion, or even an hour. But you begin a path of trust-building with face-to-face discussions that text-based communication never can.

Give to Get: Building Emotional Caches

How do you get what you want from people and organizations? It's not about good looks and charisma (fortunately for me). Nor is it about having the best and most compelling business ideas. The emotional motivators that compel people to help one another are actually quite simple. By understanding them and using them honestly, you can dramatically motivate the people and teams around you to work with you and help you on a wide range of needs. Emotional strategies might sound unprofessional and unnecessary. After all, in a professional business environment, you shouldn't have to play to people's emotions. Everyone should be motivated to do what's right for the business. This isn't kindergarten; these are grownups in a professional workplace earning professional income, right? Regardless of how people *should* operate professionally, you can always count on people to be human, and humans are emotional beings with ego and self-conceptions.

Five simple ideas lie at the root of motivating collaboration and assistance:

▶ **Give something for nothing**—When you help others repeatedly, you build trust and an emotional cache of debt. People get that feeling of "I owe him one." Over time, you'll make friends and be able to call in favors. This is the most fundamental way to build up your emotional cache with someone else because it's clear you have helped someone without an expectation of return.

You can't always count on busy professionals to remember everything you've done for them, but emotions have a long memory because *impressions* last much longer in most peoples' memories than *facts*.

▶ **Quid pro quo**—This literally means "something for something"—you scratch my back, and I'll scratch yours. Sometimes you'll need help from people you don't have a long history with and have no emotional cache to draw from. Depending purely on their professionalism, there's no guarantee they'll make time for your needs; they might not share your view of what's critically important. In addition to leaning on compelling arguments about how important their help is to the business, you should look for win–win scenarios for how you can help them in return. When you help others in return for their help, it creates a synergistic codependence. Almost all cooperation in organizations is explicitly or implicitly arranged this way. The trades might not always be fair, and they might be separated in time by months, but *quid pro quo* makes the world go 'round. Think win–win and, to really make it pay off, try to give others the better end of the deal.

▶ **Inspire self-worth in others**—Everyone has an ego, and people like to be around others who inspire their sense of personal value. It's not complicated: People like people who make them feel good. Be kind to others and give compliments generously—not just about work, but compliments about your coworkers' work, jokes, home, children, and intellect. Of course, you need to do this with complete sincerity—everyone hates a phony. Most people smell adulated cajolery and sugar-coated jive from a mile away. Believe what you're saying, or you're probably better off not saying it. Most of us can find characteristics in our coworkers that we admire, but we often don't say them because it's just too corny or out of context. If you invest a small amount of energy in bringing up these compliments during conversation, you'll be doing something good for your coworker and adding installments to the emotional cache. Just like doing something for nothing, building up others isn't just practical at work—it's also just plain nice.

▶ **Share the glory**—When you need someone's help to make an important project successful, you can help motivate him by telling him explicitly how important the project is to the leadership team, how his contribution will make a notable impact, and how you will certainly make sure his contribution is visible and appreciated. The more people care about their careers, the more motivated they'll be to volunteer to help on projects, especially if you can position their help as visible and valued to the leadership team. Naturally, when you tell people you'll ensure that their contributions are visible and appreciated, you absolutely need to follow through and do it. This can be as simple as sending out an email of thanks, clearly identifying the contributions of others, and putting in a few good words about their contribution to your manager and theirs. Not only will you have gotten their help, but by throwing in some well-deserved words of praise and thanks, you'll be adding to the emotional cache for the next time.

Remember that it's not about you. Saying "this is really important to me" or "You'll be helping me out a lot" provides weak motivators. These are useful to a point because they illustrate a sense of urgency, and they can tug at the heart strings to some degree, but they provide little reason for people to turn their worlds upside down, drop what they are working on, and chip in. If you fail to build up the emotional cache you have with others, your interactions will become mechanical and sterile. Getting people to work with you will be like pulling teeth— not because they don't like you, but simply because you've given them no motivation to trust you and invest in you. Offer something to others at both the emotional and practical levels, and you'll have much greater success in leveraging the power of the group and multiplying your impact on the organization. Your colleagues will let all your little errors slide and will barely notice them.

▶ **Make face time**—Software teams are increasingly allowing employees to work remotely either from home or from a remote offsite location. In fact, it's not uncommon for staff on the same project to work from different continents. The wonders of electronic communication make this possible to a large degree, but not without penalties. As human beings, we do connect emotionally with people we interact with in a tactile way. The ability to see someone's face, experience their moods, and chit-chat about mundane things works poorly without physical collocation. It's hard to build emotional caches with people and form personal connections over email or even the telephone. Out of site, out of mind; if you work remotely, your career will face a penalty. You can compensate to a degree by making deliberate trips to the office periodically and using the precious on-site time to store up face time with your colleagues. If you're particularly far away, such as in a different state or country, consider making a few trips per year to meet locally. In my opinion, it's important enough that you should consider doing it on your own dime if your employer won't cover the expense.

In 2005, while working for IBM, my family and I had an opportunity to live overseas for several months. My wife and I both felt it would be a wonderful life experience, and our kids were at just the right age for it. I knew that working in another country with another time zone wasn't going to help my career. While abroad, I deliberately adjusted my work hours so they aligned with Eastern Daylight Time (which meant I started work in the afternoon and worked late into the evening). I made periodic trips back to the IBM Lab in North America to stay personally connected with my team. I still suffered from being a remote employee, but my efforts to stay connected definitely mitigated the effect. I considered it the cost of the opportunity, and looking back, it was well worth it. If you're the manager of a remote team, one of the healthiest things you can do to build esprit de corps and keep your team running on all cylinders is to find ways to bring them together. Even if only a few times a year, face time is bonding time.

Leveraging Your Social Network

Everyone has a social network of colleagues, former bosses, and school friends who have a cross-section of talents, interests, and resources. In Chapter 5, "Making the Most of the Early Years As a Software Developer," we talked about the idea of building and expanding your professional social network. When you need things done at work, your social network should be the first place to look to resources and talent because these are people with whom you have a personal connection—and that means there's some emotional currency in the cache.

Like the *Law of the Few* in Gladwell's *The Tipping Point,* getting things done effectively in an organization of people requires you to be an effective connector and a reasonably good salesperson. Your professional social network connects you with a wide pool of people you can look to for help, and the emotional cache you have with each of them means you've got a better chance for having a successful conversation with them about getting their help.

Social networks take time and energy to maintain. Online social networking sites such as LinkedIn and Facebook can effectively enable you to stay in touch with a much broader circle of contacts than your normal daily activities allow. These social sites allow you to reach more than just a circle of friends, to also include friends of friends. In addition, you can use email distribution lists to build larger outreach lists for people at work, so you can keep in touch without the risk of forgetting someone.

Negotiating 101

The business world is filled with scenarios that require negotiation. Negotiating who gets the new laptop or the new server. Negotiating who gets to work on the best software project or who gets the window office. Negotiating your salary or negotiating days off. The list is never-ending. Negotiations unfortunately are more art than science, but there are some general guidelines than can help even the novice negotiator. Here's a crash course you can think of as "negotiating for dummies."

Seek First to Understand

The worst negotiations are deadlocked from the beginning because parties are focused on entrenched positions. They are optimizing for winning solutions, without considering the other party's needs. To make progress in a negotiation, you always need to address some of the other person's needs. That's why the first thing you should begin any negotiation with is a discussion to try to understand what the other person is looking for. What does success mean for him or her? Of course, it's not easy; a shrewd negotiator won't tell you the real truth about the bottom line, and if you're equally crafty, you won't want to tip your hand too soon, either. But in a civilized world of colleagues and coworkers, negotiations are usually less brutal because you're in the same company, even if your departments or organizations are far apart.

Seeking first to understand is unnatural—it's human nature to want to be understood. While forcing yourself to do this can be difficult, it can serve you well in a negotiation. Because it's a natural human tendency to want first to be understood, you usually won't have much trouble getting the people you're negotiating with to start talking. Once you've culled some facts, you'll have at your disposal a short list of the things that really matter to them and some sense of the lines they can't cross. You're armed to start positioning your own arguments and maximize the results.

Estimate Your Outcome

Depending on how flexible the people you're dealing with are and the strength of their negotiating position versus yours, your ability to achieve a positive negotiated solution could be limited. If you're negotiating from a strong position, you won't have any reason to compromise much; conversely, if you're in a weaker position, you might be able to hope for little. As the old saying goes, beggars can't be choosers. In the early parts of any negotiation, it's worthwhile to quickly assess the best possible outcome you can reasonably hope for (emphasis on the word *reasonably*). You need to know that so that if the negotiations get close to that point, you can make the wise decision to accept the offer and close. Persisting far beyond the point of a reasonable deal will not only *not* result in what you want, but you'll rapidly exhaust the emotional cache you have with others and leave them with a very bad impression. Be happy with what's reasonable, if you can get it. If you do better than you expected, consider that a bonus, but don't force the discussion to the point of frustration, hatred, and ruin in an attempt to get there.

Plan to Meet in the Middle

Almost all negotiations meet in the middle. When it's a question of money, the parties usually meet at the midpoint. If it's a question of things that can't be scaled up and down (such as who gets the new laptop), the result is almost always based on a *quid pro quo* solution: Moe gets the new computer, but Curly gets the new 28-inch flatscreen display. Knowing in advance that negotiations almost always work this way, you can generally achieve your goals if you know the opening position of the other before you state yours. For example, let's say you have a laptop you want to sell for $800, and a coworker named Moe happens to be in the market for one and hears you've got one to sell.

> Moe: How much for the laptop?
>
> You: I dunno. How much will you give me for it?
>
> Moe: How about $500?

Now you know that Moe's opening position is $500, and you've read this book, so you know the negotiation will probably close in the middle. Since you work in software, your analytic mind quickly computes that in order to "meet in the middle" and still get $800 in your pocket, you'll have to ask for $1,100.

> **You:** You can have it for $1,100. Come on, it's got a really great sound card and quad-core CPU. The hard drive is three times the normal size.
>
> **Moe:** No, $1,100 is way too much. I could get a new one for that much. I'll give you $750, tops.
>
> **You:** Okay, okay, I see your point about a new one. But really, $800 is fair.
>
> **Moe:** It's a deal.

Best of all, poor Moe thinks he negotiated you down from $1,100. I don't recommend you use those tactics to sell Moe a $500 computer for $800. The ethical thing to do is to sell Moe the computer for what it's worth. But knowing how the process of negotiations typically works can help you get there a little more quickly and painlessly.

Separate people from the problem. It's critical in any negotiation to keep the discussion civilized. Even if the party on the other side of the table is the personification of the words *malevolent, pernicious,* and *vile,* you won't be doing yourself any good by making the discussion emotional or personal. Compliments and flattery will be received as disingenuous once negotiations begin, so don't waste your time on them. Be civilized and polite; be friendly, but neither suck up nor get fired up.

Find the common ground. When parties are really having a hard time getting to closure, it's usually because they haven't found common ground to build a solution around. Finding some piece of common ground, something fundamental you can agree on, is critical to the negotiating process. Finding common ground is so fundamental, you'll find it's a central theme in every book and course on negotiation. As you find the points of commonality, you can build on them. Let's replay your negotiation with Moe about the computer and see if common ground can help if Moe wants to play a little tougher.

> **Moe:** How much for the computer?
>
> **You:** I dunno. How much will you give me for it?
>
> **Moe:** How about $500?

> **You:** You can have it for $1,100. Come on, it's got a really great sound card and quad-core CPU. The hard drive is three times the normal size.
>
> **Moe:** You're nuts. Paying $500 is plenty for a secondhand laptop.
>
> **You:** I agree, $500 is reasonable for a normal, run-of-the-mill secondhand laptop. But, Moe, you have to agree, this machine isn't typical—it's got some very special features.
>
> **Moe:** I agree, the quad-core CPU is sweet, and that's worth something. The extra hard drive was good in its day, but on today's systems, that much is just normal. I don't know much about sound cards, so I'm not willing to pay extra for it.

Moe wasn't willing to budge from $500, but now you've found some common ground, and things can progress. You both agree that you've got a computer that Moe wants. You both agree that a typical laptop would be worth about $500 and that yours is something better than that.

> **You:** The quad core alone is worth an extra $250 over the usual dual core. Listen to the sound system [you start playing Moe's favorite band]. You can see on this web page that the sound card is worth at least $60.
>
> **Moe:** Okay, I'll throw in $200 for the quad core. That's sweet, and an extra $40 for the sound card. That's my limit.
>
> **You:** Deal.

It didn't turn out quite as well this time, but you did fine, considering that Moe wasn't initially inclined to pay a penny over $500. Finding the common ground helped close the deal, and at $740, you achieved most of your objective.

Invent Options for Mutual Gain

Sometimes parties are just too far apart and don't have enough common ground to build a complete solution around. When that happens, it's time to start thinking of *quid pro quo*. What can you throw in to sweeten the deal? You're asking for more from them than they're willing to give, but in return, you can help them with something that wasn't originally on the table. Let's go back to Moe and the computer.

Moe: How much for the computer?

You: I dunno. How much will you give me for it?

Moe: How about $500?

You: You can have it for $1,100. Come on, it's got a really great sound card and quad-core CPU. The hard drive is three times the normal size.

Moe: You're nuts. Paying $500 is plenty for a secondhand laptop.

You: I agree, $500 is reasonable for a normal, run-of-the-mill secondhand laptop. But, Moe, you have to agree that this machine isn't typical. It's got some very special features.

Moe: The quad core thing is sweet, but no deal. I can go as high as $600, but I just don't have more than that, and it doesn't sound like you're willing to sell it for that little. I guess you'll have to sell it to someone else.

Moe might be bluffing, but he's drawn a very hard line in the sand. He claims he doesn't have a penny more than $600 for this purchase. It's not about features and value anymore. It's time to start inventing options for mutual gain.

You: U2 is coming to town in three weeks. I was going to use the money I got from selling my computer to get some tickets and take Sue to the concert. Isn't your dad connected with the concert hall?

Moe: Yeah, my dad runs the box office. He gets free tickets for him and mom for all the shows, but he's not gonna want to see U2!

You: How about you throw in a couple of tickets to the concert and the $600, and we'll call it a deal?

Moe: Yeah, that works. The tickets are worth about $200. As long as my dad agrees, you can have the tickets and $600 in exchange for the laptop.

You: Deal. Let me know once you've checked with your dad.

The negotiations were just about dead, but you salvaged the deal by pulling in an inventive idea that had nothing to do with the laptop. In the end, you got $800 in value and Moe got the computer for $600, so everyone was happy.

Quit While You're Ahead

In any negotiation, you need to know when you've reached the end of the line and further negotiations will lead to minimal advances. At that point, you have to make a decision to either close a deal or walk away. If the other party has a strong bargaining position, you might not be able to get what you think is fair. Life isn't always fair. Welcome to one of the most consistent hard realities and brutal truisms of the real world. Keep the negotiations civilized, no matter what, and if you see they aren't progressing beyond a certain point, be prepared to accept what's on the table or walk away. Sometimes you'll find that by walking away, the other party will in due time come scurrying back, with a more congenial attitude and a better offer. Either way, don't get sucked into perpetual deadlock.

Communication That Gets Results

People communicate in business in many modes, and different people prefer to communicate through different media. Even so, some modes of communication are more effective than others in getting results. People rarely read all their email and certainly do not respond to every message, but senders love to believe that their email is different. The sender believes his or her email will be received instantaneously and acted on immediately. We are a generation of delusional communicators! The asynchronous nature of email means it is easily ignored, and there's no possible way to know if it will be read or responded to. When you really need an answer fast, email is a rotten method. In general, the more personal and the more synchronous you can make your request, the more likely you'll get a professional response quickly. In rank order, here's how you should communicate with others when you really need a response:

- ▶ Stop by someone's office and discuss the topic face to face.
- ▶ Telephone discussion.
- ▶ Communicate through instant message (real time).
- ▶ Set up a meeting (this delays the process, but the discussion will be effective).
- ▶ Send your question or request by email (most appropriate when the topic is not time-critical). If you don't hear back within two days, you probably never will, and then it's time to escalate to one of the previous strategies.

Dress for Success: Wear Running Shoes

If you want to be a sartorial sensation as a techie in the software business, you need to dress like you're in college. The software business is absolutely one of the strangest businesses on earth when it comes to dress code. The Bohemian nature of the Silicon Value startups of the 1980s and '90s set a standard corporate attire that was driven in part by the fact that the kids who started all these brilliant startups out of their garages simply couldn't afford to buy ties, and in part by a kind of youthful disdain for corporate establishment. The theory goes that high tech is about revolution, and revolutionaries don't wear suits. It's about disruptive technology that will change the world, and we want to value our people the same way we value our products: based purely on merit. Style has nothing to do with it. Well, that's the theory, but in practice, style has a lot to do with it. If you do show up in a suit, expect a pretty negative reaction. The fact of the matter is that somewhere in the early 1990s, software went mainstream, and what you should wear depends a lot on who you are and what your role is in the organization. If you are a corporate executive, you probably need to dress a little better—at least business casual (wear a shirt with a collar, and leave the jeans at home).

On the flip side, if you're a senior architect or a technical guru, T-shirt and jeans remain de rigueur. If you take a look at the head-and-shoulders photos of the gurus interviewed for this book, you'll see that most are wearing T-shirts with or without a collar—and several are in desperate need of ironing. I still remember James Hamilton giving a keynote address to the DB2 Technical Conference in 1996 wearing jeans and a snugly fitting Harley-Davidson T-shirt. James Gosling, Sun VP and Fellow, consistently gives keynotes wearing a T-shirt. John Wilkes, HP Fellow, gave a keynote at the SMDB workshop of ICDE wearing a T-shirt and jeans. Apple CEO Steve Jobs and Facebook founder Mark Zuckerberg do this, too. When Google founders Sergey Brin and Larry Page were featured on the front cover of *Time* on February 20, 2006,[1] they made a point of being featured in T-shirts. I'll stop there, but the list is infinite. Dressing down is cool for technical gurus in the software business. It says, "My quality stands on its own merits. I don't care about corporate pomp and circumstance, and neither should you."

Conversely, business executives in software usually dress a bit more upscale, almost always wearing a collar and a jacket for business presentation. You'll notice that on the cover of *Time*, although Larry and Sergey are

---

[1] You can see an official image of this *Time* cover at www.time.com/time/covers/ 0,16641,20060220,00.html.

boasting black T-shirts, their CEO, Eric Schmidt, is wearing business attire. Friends of mine who work at Google tell me Eric is fond of saying, "At Google, we have a dress code: You have to wear something." I'm not passing judgment on software corporate culture or endorsing bad dress as good business. This is just an observation of the way things are. Adjust your dress code based on where you are in the company and the role you play.

This chapter has looked at some of the factors in motivating people to collaborate, support your needs, and respond to your requests. We communicate not only by what we say or write, but also by who we say it to (a junior staffer or a senior manager), by our clothing, and by our ability to align our needs with the goals of others to create networks of mutual gain. To make it big, you need to do more than just get your work done—you need to become a catalyst for change by aligning and motivating others through frequent and appropriate communication.

Getting Agreement Isn't Enough

Even if you get another person or team's agreement that they should do something for you, your request will be competing against a full plate of work they are already committed to doing. The subtle part of the equation is that, in most cases, getting agreement just isn't enough. When push comes to shove, the work they have an official commitment to usually trumps whatever work they agreed to do for you. The biggest mistake people make in effectively leveraging the power of an organization is thinking that getting someone's agreement is sufficient to effect change. "But won't he get a bad evaluation if he fails to deliver what he promised?" Not always, particularly if the other person produces the rest of their commitments in impressive shiny spades. Your requests might not matter much to another team or the people who evaluate them. Someone might accept the responsibility to help you, with positive intentions, but if that person comes under time pressure, the things they agreed to do for you can easily move lower on the priority list.

Let's take a look at our heroes, Larry, Moe, and Curly, at SuperDuperTech, Inc., who are working hard on a new project. The Chief Technical Officer (CTO), Larry, is expecting the engineering team to finish the new compression algorithm and have it ready for launch in four months. Moe is assigned to lead the project. He's excited and has some brilliant ideas for new compression algorithms. But Moe knows he's not a performance analysis guru. He's going to need help from the performance analysis experts in another group to make sure the compression algorithm he designs not only saves space, but does it with minimal CPU consumption. Moe meets with the team's performance specialist, Curly, and explains his predicament. Curly agrees that if Moe can get working compression code to her within two months, she'll be able to analyze it and work with Moe on refinements before the product ships to market. Two months later, Moe sends Curly the code and awaits news. After a month goes by he's hopeful Curly has made some impressive progress, so he sends her an email requesting an update. Curly replies that she'd completely forgotten about Moe's request and apologizes profusely. It's now unlikely she'll have time to do the work before product delivery because she's swamped with other projects. She offers to give Moe a crash course on the performance-analysis tools and help Moe install the required utilities so he can do the analysis himself. Moe feels really let down. The analysis will take him ten times longer than it would Curly. Even if he manages to complete it, there's no way he'll have time to optimize the compression algorithm by redesigning the weakest code segments before delivery.

Moe failed to do three things:

1. Think win-win by aligning his needs with Curly's goals. Curly was already bogged down with lots of work to do. While Curly sincerely intended to help Moe, it wasn't a high-priority goal for her. At the end of the year Curly wants to be able to show her leadership the significant contributions she's made on the projects she's been assigned. Moe offered her very little in return for her efforts; he didn't think about how to make this a win for her. When push came to shove her commitment to him got short shrift. Knowing that Curly wants to show her value to the organization as a performance expert, Moe could have leveraged his in multiple ways by explaining how the compression project was important to the business and emphasizing that Larry has been actively following it. He could also have explained how significantly the compression algorithm would impact performance both negatively and positively, so there was a large opportunity for Curly to make a serious impact through her performance analysis. It might also have helped to engage Curly's management in the discussion because resource planning and project scheduling would be impacted. Making this a formal part of Curly's job would have changed it from a perceived favor to a job requirement. Finally, Moe could have offered some of his own time or resources (such as servers he has access to) to Curly to help with other projects she had on the go, achieving a degree of *quid pro quo*.

2. Follow up regularly to make sure the performance work was moving forward. After Curly agreed to the work, Moe shouldn't have let the first meeting end without coming to an agreement on follow-up and checkpoints. With only two months between the time Moe would have the code available and the delivery date, a weekly meeting (or possible daily scrum) was certainly in order to keep things moving forward and resolve issues quickly.

3. Share the glory. Periodic emails to both Curly and Moe's managers thanking Curly for her contribution would certainly have showcased her contributions in a positive way and made her feel appreciated. It would also have gently but indirectly reminded Curly that the project had managerial attention.

Working an organization is as much art as science. It usually requires you to keep other peoples' interests in mind and relate to both their practical and emotional needs. With some artistry you can leverage the strength and breadth of your organization to achieve great things far beyond your individual scope, while building emotional caches and personal relationships for the future.

An Interview with John Schwarz

CEO Business Objects

CURRENT POSITION

Member of the Executive Board of SAP AG, SAP BusinessObjects, Ecosystem & Corporate Development; CEO of Business Objects

CLAIMS TO FAME

CEO of Business Objects; former executive at Symantec and IBM; business thought leader in relational databases, information security, and business analytics

DATE OF BIRTH

September 24, 1950

EDUCATION

Honorary Doctorate of Law, Dalhousie University, 2004

MBA, University of Toronto, 1979

B.Sc. in Computer Science, University of Manitoba, 1972

FAVORITE PASTIMES & HOBBIES

Sailing, environment, evolution of social systems

BIOGRAPHY

In 1968, John fled Czechoslovakia to Germany as a result of the Soviet invasion. Within weeks, he and his family met up in England and together relocated to Winnipeg, Canada. John graduated from the University of Manitoba's computer science program in 1972 and moved to Toronto. Two years later, in 1974, he was hired by IBM. In 1991, he became the Director of IBM's Toronto software lab, one of IBM's premier software laboratories, with 1,500 employees. This was just one of several executive roles John held with

IBM before his departure in 1999. In 2001, he became the President and Chief Operating Officer of IT security leader Symantec Corp., and in 2005, he became the CEO for Business Objects. John led Business Objects through major revenue growth and several key acquisitions before SAP bought the company in 2008.

John is a member of the Executive Board of SAP AG, reporting to Leo Apotheker and Henning Kagermann, co-CEOs of SAP AG. John is also the CEO of Business Objects SA. He is responsible for all aspects of the SAP Business Objects division, including product development, go-to-market activities, and customer service and support, as well as for all external SAP relationships leading the Global Ecosystem and Partner Group and the Corporate Development Group.

John joined Business Objects in September 2005 as its CEO. During his tenure, he oversaw seven strategic acquisitions, including Cartesis and Firstlogic. He drove revenue growth to more than U.S. $1.5 billion. Before Business Objects, he was the President and Chief Operating Officer of Symantec Corporation. While at Symantec, he played a key role in tripling the business to more than U.S. $2.7 billion in revenue and was instrumental in the successful combination of Symantec and VERITAS.

Before joining Symantec, John spent 25 years at IBM Corporation, working in various development, manufacturing, sales, and marketing roles. His last position was general manager of IBM's Industry Solutions unit, a worldwide organization focused on building business applications and related services for IBM's large industry customers.

John currently serves on the board of directors of Synopsys Corporation.

"I had no idea what I was doing or supposed to do"

How did you get started in software?

I was taking geology as my major at Manitoba, and we were asked to use a computer program to do some analysis. I became enamored while working with this particular program, and I wanted to know more about what was behind it and how it was built. I ended up switching majors from geology to computer science, much to my father's dismay!

First of all, getting a job in the industry wasn't easy. I graduated in 1972; I think I applied to something like 60 or 70 companies. I wanted a computer science job, and I did not get a single offer. It was only after I moved to Toronto and spent six months working as a sales clerk at Hudson's Bay that

John Schwarz

I finally found my way into the industry. I loved my first job and realized this is not only a good way to make money, but it's also a great way to have fun.

I was hired by IBM in 1974, just two years after I graduated. IBM put me in charge of a massive manufacturing re-engineering project. I was a kid out of school and had no idea what I was doing or supposed to do. Jumping into this role became an opportunity to learn, in essence, the entire manufacturing process. That led me, some years down the road, to actually go into manufacturing proper. I managed a plant, which was perhaps one of the most fun jobs I've ever had.

However, running a plant is great for a time, but it's pretty repetitive after a while, so I went back to my alma mater (IBM) and got involved in some pretty heavy-duty software development, such as DB2, compilers, and OS/2—stuff that made a real difference in the marketplace. I became interested in the commercial aspect of software, not just in the engineering content.

What do you consider your greatest accomplishments or contributions to software?

I would put a couple points on the map. I brought the DB2 (for OS/2, Linux UNIX, and Windows) project to being at IBM. I was one of the drivers, with Janet Perna, of making relational databases on a PC possible. There was not a lot of belief that it would work, and we made it work. Second, I was one of the people who took OS/2 from DOS to a graphical user interface. I was not the engineer who coded it, but I was the catalyst and the executive who had that responsibility.

At Symantec, I contributed to the idea of data management and security to be seen as related disciplines. And at Business Objects, my greatest product contributions have been to expand from pure business intelligence reporting and analytics, to forward-looking business-management tools—in other words, using business insight from past experience as a method for planning, forecasting, modeling, and predicting future trends, processes or instances of a given execution point. I also initiated the foray into financial performance management, which was a critical competitive move to put Business Objects on par with, and eventually ahead of, Cognos.

Some people get to be CEO the easy way, by starting their own company. You climbed the ranks and got there on pure merit. I believe that's a much harder path. Was there an event in your life that helped you reach the level of CEO?

When I was at IBM, I think a year into the job, IBM had a program they called "Skip Level Interviews." I was an associate engineer and was interviewed by the vice president responsible for the division in which I worked. He was about my current age today: He was in his 50s and had spent his whole life at IBM. He asked me, "What do you want to be when you grow up, or at the end of your career?" I didn't really have a very good answer, but he'd upset me with the things he had said before, and so as a kind of a flippant thing to say, I said, "I want to be the president of IBM." He first fell off his chair, and then he looked at me and he said, "You know, if you're serious, there are about 15 steps between where you are today and that job, and each step will take you between two and three years. It's the difference between two and three years that will decide whether you make it to CEO or not. If you make it in 30 years, you are probably okay; if you take 45 years to get there, forget it." That gave me the roadmap for how to build a career plan. I actually built that roadmap, and I stuck with it, and I made it in 20-some years. If he hadn't done that, it would have taken me so long to figure it out that I might have never made it.

"Reconcile yourself to not being an expert on most topics"

How do you stay on top of technology trends and innovation?

First of all, I don't worry about it unduly. In my view, the amount of new information coming out today relative to the amount of information that already exists is no different than it was 10, 50, or 100 years ago. I'm sure it seemed just as overwhelming to people then to deal with the influx of new data as it feels to us today. And by the way, technology allows us to consume information far more efficiently and effectively than it ever did. So I would say we are no worse off than our predecessors in this regard.

My personal strategy is to track the four or five areas that I am particularly interested in (not all of which are directly related to my job or my area of expertise). I have a Google page set up on my computer that constantly tracks these four or five areas. If anything seems interesting and worth investigating further, I'll drill down. I don't read many industry or technical journals because I find some of them to be too biased and pushing certain views which I don't appreciate. Instead, I read generic business publications such as *The Economist, Newsweek,* or *Time.*

Mostly I go to the Internet today. The Internet is the source of most of my news—I like the ability to drill down and find out what I want to read. I like to be able to find and explore the news that interests me—I don't like being pushed; I like to pull. When it comes to my job and my business, my staff also helps me to digest, prioritize, and point out what's worth reading and

John Schwarz

important for me to know. I also use the SAP Business Objects portfolio to sort through or find information. But in my personal life, I pride myself in being very broad—I'm interested in history, global affairs, health, the environment, and education. For those topics, I do my own research.

What do you see as the coming changes in the software field over the next 10–15 years that will impact career opportunities either positively or negatively?

I would say that mobility is perhaps the single biggest change because it will free us from being tied to a wire or being tied to a PC. I think that wireless mobility will enable us to consume software and computing services anywhere, anytime, with any device. I think that is probably the single biggest change because you will no longer have to sit down in a specific place to use a computer. You'll be able to use it from your cell phone, from your car, from your boat, from your refrigerator. From a usability perspective, that is perhaps the single biggest change.

The second-biggest change is that I think we will stop buying software as a license to use something, but rather as a service that happens to use software to deliver certain value. In that context, the software industry will be remade into a services industry. The payment is for the service, and the payment may come in the shape of an explicit service charge attached to a given session or transaction, or it may be paid through an advertising model.

The third change is collaboration. Today software is primarily a single-person, individual experience. I think increasingly and dramatically, software is becoming a social tool—it becomes a collaboration tool; Facebook and YouTube being good examples of that. Software will be used in business to create a persona and an environment, a problem-solving area where you invite other people to help.

Technical leaders and executives are famous for being time-strapped. What strategies do you use to stay sane and use your time effectively?

Work very long hours. Reconcile yourself to not being able to be an expert on most topics. Live with that knowledge and rely on other people to be the experts to support you when needed. Become very good at synthesizing information; learn to be able to connect the dots with relatively limited information. Surround yourself with people who are able to understand what is important to you and what your priorities are. Rely on them as an extension of yourself, to help surf through the mass of information and bring forward those things that are truly important to understand.

Finally, I find that, in any situation, after about six months of being in that role, I know enough about the organization, the people, the processes, the products, and the market and business environment to then zero in on those things I should be spending the most time on. I delegate the things I should not be spending as much time on to people I trust. But the first six months in a new role can be tough. You're still learning enough so you can make good calls and getting to know the people and the business so you can set priorities.

How do you achieve a work-life balance? How do you keep your professional life from dominating everything?

I wouldn't say I do a particularl good job of that. I'm not sure I'm going to be able to give great advice. However, I have a couple of passions that are sufficiently different from my job and that require me to unplug completely. One of those is sailing. I have always managed, with some exceptions, to find the odd weekend or week to go to my boat and get out on the water. When I'm out there, I cannot afford to do anything but focus on sailing because the consequences of not being focused are potentially disastrous. So I have found that a forcing function is a very helpful tool.

I've also been extremely lucky with my wife, who has offloaded virtually all the family-related matters off my shoulders, yet doesn't make me feel like I'm not a part of the family. So being lucky in the choice of your partner is, in my view, a life-and-death situation for CEOs, for sure. You cannot be a CEO without having that arrangement, unless you want to be single. When my children were young, it was hard to find enough time to spend with them, and I regret that very much.

"Jump in with both feet"

What suggestions do you have for others on being successful in software (either R&D or business)?

It doesn't matter what profession or what discipline you choose. What matters is your commitment to excel in that discipline. A lot of kids I talk to today look at their work as a means to make money so they can survive. What I tell them is that the income will come. What is really important is to make sure that they are growing, contributing, and enjoying what they do. Otherwise, spending 12 hours a day at it is a waste of time. So pick something that you have aptitude for and that you have reasonable confidence will be sustainable in the long run—it doesn't have to be exactly any one specific thing; and then drive like a person possessed to be the best there is.

John Schwarz

Do you think graduate degrees are professionally valuable? Do you see them as a substantial benefit to a candidate when recruiting?

They're incredibly valuable. First of all, the person demonstrates the ability to stick to the discipline long enough to get a graduate degree. Second, the degree proves to me that that person has the degree of gravity, perseverance, and organizational smarts to be successful. Of course, there are always exceptions, like Bill Gates or other people who dropped out and made it nevertheless, but I think those are very unique instances.

Do you have a pet peeve in any aspect of the software world?

Lack of standards! And the insistence on solving every problem from scratch because it can be done more elegantly instead of using the best of what exists and building on top of that.

What makes you feel successful about your work in software?

The ability to communicate ideas and direction. The ability to motivate people to join me in pursing that direction.

What final words of wisdom or caution do you have for people entering the field?

Jump in with both feet. Be as assertive and as aggressive as you know how, without upsetting relationships with your colleagues. If you do this, the dynamism of the software industry will look after your future.

CHAPTER 10

Successful Software Project Proposals

"Don't worry about people stealing an idea.
If it's original, you will have to ram it down their throats."
—Howard Aiken (1900–1973)

One of the hallmarks of leadership in software is the ability to identify and successfully bring forward new technology ideas. It's one of the few characteristics that unifies all leaders in the software business, whether their jobs find them on the technical track or the business executive track. All successful leaders have a share of winning project proposals under their belts. Nobody hits a homerun every time, but the best leaders have the best track records.

The illusion presented to the world is that clever people with good ideas bring ideas forward to a decision-making body for evaluation and consideration, whether this be in the format of a board meeting, a house of representatives or parliament, or a meeting of senior managers and corporate executives. After hearing the pitch and asking critical questions, the decision makers determine whether to proceed and what kind of support they will offer. The little-discussed truth is that few proposals get approval through this kind of naïve approach. Before proposals come to decision makers for a group review, there's work going on that sets the scene and, in most cases, predetermines the outcomes. Why does life have to be so complex and clandestine all the time? Well, the real process for successful proposals isn't clandestine at all. It's an iterative process that leads to deeper buy-in, more excitement, superior proposals, and a far more certain outcome.

Our friends Larry, Moe, and Curly at SuperDuperTech, Inc. will help illustrate a number of points throughout this chapter. SuperDuperTech develops and sells embedded relational database products as its core competency. Our protagonist, Moe, is one of the company's top architects hoping to convince the company to invest in a new project. Larry is the company's CTO, and Curly is a peer architect who leads one of the engineering teams. Moe knows that if Larry and Curly both believe in his proposal, it will likely get support and funding. Moe needs more than a good idea to convince Larry and Curly—he needs just the right amount of spin and positioning.

Core Competencies

Companies always have core competencies, or what those companies do best. Seagrams makes whiskey. Microsoft makes software. Sony makes digital equipment. Boeing makes airplanes. If Boeing wanted to make software, Sony wanted to make whiskey, Seagrams wanted to make digital equipment, and Microsoft wanted to make airplanes, could they succeed? Not likely. Each of these companies has built a set of competencies required for them to succeed in their domains. Those core competencies have critical components to them. For example, consider the case of building an airplane:

Technical know-how: Do we have people who know how to do this?

Infrastructure: Do we have a manufacturing facility that can produce it?

Sales channels: Do we have people to sell planes to and people who know how to sell them?

Credibility: Do we have a track record for selling planes?

Companies can't easily branch into new domains outside their core competencies. Most software teams struggle with the dichotomy of encouraging their engineering teams to think outside the box and be innovative, while being unable to leverage the new, creative ideas if they aren't closely related to the company's fundamental self-conception and capabilities. Consider our hypothetical company, SuperDuperTech. One fine day, Moe has a new business idea for a virtual reality social networking product that runs on a wrist-worn form factor, much like a conventional wristwatch. Moe develops a crackerjack highly compelling proposal and even finds a manufacturer in China that will mass-produce the devices cheaply. Although none of the engineers at SuperDuperTech knows much about the required technology, Moe is a hobbyist in this field and is willing to bootstrap the engineering effort personally. He'll help build a skilled team over time.

His proposal sounds good, but SuperDuperTech will still likely fail because they have no experience in selling software of this kind—or in selling physical devices. In most companies, proposals outside the company's core competencies are shut down, much to the disappointment of the passionate people who develop them. The ideas may be brilliant and, under the right circumstances, could sell like hotcakes, but the right circumstances also require a clear channel to market and a skilled sales force. If Larry has his head screwed on, Moe's proposal in its current form will, correctly, go nowhere. One of the secrets to successful proposals is to make sure they don't require skills, talents, or infrastructure outside the company's core competencies. Sensitizing yourself to this reality can save you considerable grief.

Company culture is also hugely important, affecting how core competencies are perceived. A company might be good at multiple things, but its culture may include a strong (often historical) bias. For example, a company that prides itself on the prowess of its search algorithms might be more receptive to a new proposal related to extending the technological boundaries of search, even preferring it over a database proposal that would leverage existing competencies and sales channel. Put simply, not all core competencies are equal. Company decisions are tightly related (rightly or wrongly) to their self-image and passions.

Exceptions do exist. When an idea is compelling enough, some companies look for ways to test it in the market, even if it means going against their core competencies. A common strategy is to seed a startup around the emerging division to see whether it can fly on its own. The startup model disencumbers the new division from the momentum and biases that exist around the core competencies, but the fledgling startup faces the brutal challenges of building a go-to-market plan and sales channels with potentially little support.

How Successful Proposals Are Really Made

The corporate world is filled with xenophobic nihilistic naysayers. Get used to it. Plenty of people with power, conviction, and influence will tell you why you won't succeed and why you or your ideas aren't any good. Their naysaying comes from a dark place. Either they are afraid you will succeed and siphon off resources from their part of the business, or they're simply pessimistic—they've seen too many radical ideas fail, and they simply don't believe that bold ideas ever take flight except in unforeseen ways that are so equally rare and random they never warrant planning and investment.

Your ability to get your proposals accepted and get necessary buy-in requires you to convert a good chunk of the naysayers to believers. I discussed the first set of tools early in this book, such as giving to get so that you fill the emotional cache and also build your track record. Remember that your track record is your credibility, and credibility is everything. No matter how extreme or crazy your latest idea is, people's willingness to let you try (using their money) depends more than anything else on whether they trust you. This trust is born of the emotional cache you have with them and your track record of continued success.

But there's more to it. The bigger the proposal, the more detail and supporting data it needs. However, you must be able to explain every good idea to others in a few seconds. This is often called the elevator pitch because you need to be able to articulate the idea in less than a minute, as if you had a rare opportunity to present to the CEO in an elevator while going from ground floor to the eighth floor. A compelling elevator pitch with some cold, hard facts is not enough, but it's a necessary start. The hidden secret of a successful proposal is iterative discussion before any decision making is done. By the time a meeting of decision makers is scheduled to review your proposal, you should already know how most of the leading personalities in the room view the idea. If you're going in cold, you might have blown it before the meeting begins.

Connecting privately with decision makers in advance is the key. Figure 10.1 illustrates the process. Each person you meet with can help you understand the strengths and weaknesses of the proposal so that the next person you present to gets a more complete, sophisticated, and higher-value version of the idea. Your elevator pitch evolves rapidly. Decision makers usually reached their positions of influence because they have considerable talent and insight. After speaking with a few of them privately, it's virtually impossible to not end up with a better proposal. In addition, because each decision maker you review with adds their wisdom and improvements, subsequent decision makers will hear the proposal with the combined insight of the previous decision makers. They're guaranteed to be amazed by how someone like you has thought through the ideas so thoroughly with such maturity and sensitivity to the business factors!

By including others' ideas in the proposal as much as possible, you increase the emotional cache you have with them because you're sharing the glory. People hesitate to do this because they worry that it diminishes them as the progenitor and visionary of the proposal. In fact, it has the opposite effect. It engenders the most senior people in the organization to feel a part of what you are proposing. Because all of them know it was originally your idea (you discussed it with them personally), no significant threat arises that one of them will claim to be its originator. It's not usually a serious concern. The benefits you'll accrue from including senior people's ideas and refinements into your proposal far outweigh any risks. Make sure you give them credit, too.

Getting the proposal right might take a couple iterations with these folks. For example, some of the early discussions you have might raise serious issues that you address later. You'll want to go back to those people with the improved version, to make sure they're on board.

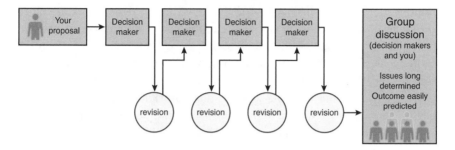

FIGURE 10.1   Effective proposal process

When your proposal finally does come down to a decision-making moment (usually in the form of a meeting between decision makers, with you present), you shouldn't face any surprises. Not only is the idea familiar to the key people, but in many cases, when they see their own ideas included, they'll feel a significant emotional attachment to the work. The proposal is, in a real way, their proposal, too. What a wonderful situation to be in when you're hoping to get someone's vote of confidence. Let's see how this could help Moe with his idea of virtual reality social networking on a watch.

Moe starts his proposal by meeting with his co-worker Curly. Curly sees the promise but points out that hardware isn't what they do—and, fundamentally, the watch bit isn't necessary to the project success because the software could run on a laptop as well as on a wrist-worn device. She suggests that Moe consider staging this as a software-only solution for personal computers as phase 1 and advancing to wrist-worn form factor if it takes off. She also points out the value in leveraging SuperDuperTech's existing software and suggests that SuperDuperTech's database be used as a back end to the new social networking software, perhaps with a logo such as "Powered by SuperDuperTech." Moe takes the revised idea to Larry, who likes the "Powered by SuperDuperTech" tag (Moe aptly gives Curly the credit). Larry wants to invest, but there's no market analysis to suggest that this will be a winner—it's just gut feeling. Moe agrees and spends a few days studying the market opportunity. After some research with the help of analyst reports on social networking and virtual reality software, Moe determines that there's a large untapped market, especially in northern Europe, that will easily justify the project. By the time Moe takes his proposal to a group meeting, he has a proposal that both Larry and Curly feel attached to and have already given their tacit approval to—but, more important, the proposal is much more compelling because it's aligned with SuperDuperTech branding, it sticks initially with a software-only solution, and it has supporting market analysis.

This is the way the real world works. It's a bit like votes at the United Nations. Do you truly believe that UN votes on national decisions are left in the hands of ambassadors in attendance or that major resolutions are brought to the UN without first vetting the ideas with key voting parties? When the United States or another major power brings a resolution to the floor, you can rest assured that the political machinery has vetted the proposal with allies well in advance and that the key positions are known before the voting begins. Iterative review and refinement before the decision making always leads to better proposals and improved acceptance rates.

The Art of the Pitch

Woodrow Wilson, 28th president of the United States, once said: "If I am to speak ten minutes, I need a week for preparation; if an hour, I am ready now."

Truer words were never more plainly said. Speaking for a short time is much harder because you need to organize and prepare your thoughts much more judiciously to get the central points across quickly. Your proposal has two primary media before you can get approval:

1. An elevator pitch—just a couple of minutes (or less) and optionally a couple of supporting charts.

2. A review meeting, with most of the time dominated by discussion. Your actual speaking and pitching time could be as little as 15 minutes.

Like Woodrow Wilson, you'll need a lot of practice to get the message compact enough without losing clarity of purpose or dropping key points. How fast can you get the idea across with clarity? In the movie business, they say the proposal for the movie *Speed,* with Keanu Reeves and Sandra Bullock, was pitched simply as "Think *Die Hard* on a bus."

At the most senior levels of your organization, the people making the decision to proceed with your proposal may or may not be business leaders, but you can be certain they're thinking like them. Every manager and architect is keenly aware that new projects bring cost and risk. You can think of your decision makers as a small venture capital firm wondering why to invest.

If you're proposing a new product and you have only five minutes or less, what people really want to know is who you built your product for and how you plan to make money with it. Proposals aren't just about making money; they can also be about cost savings and operational efficiency. For example, maybe you're proposing a better test strategy or a better customer support idea. Cost savings proposals are always a harder sell because they won't generate new revenue, and revenue generation is top-of-mind for business growth. Proposals can also be about risk reduction, which is an indirect kind of cost savings. Second, if you have the time to help your audience visualize your proposal in the form of a mocked-up graphical storyboard or a mock demo, it's worth its weight in gold.

A picture is worth a thousand words, but a demo is worth a thousand pictures.

Getting the visual storyboard of a mock demo into your pitch usually requires only another 3–4 minutes on the agenda, so it's well worth adding when you've got 15 to 30 minutes for the pitch. Software is a complex business, and helping people visualize what you're proposing by literally showing a visual representation goes a long way toward getting their buy-in.

Finally, the critical point in pitch success is to pitch it differently depending on who the audience is. Architects will always want to know what's under the hood; unless you explain the underlying technology in enough detail that they could start building their own, they won't truly believe what you're telling them. Architects want to know what the components are, how they are hooked together, and whether the solution will be scalable, reliable, and robust. They'll be looking for indicators in your ideas that demonstrate you've thought through what's needed to make the idea real, not just a toy. Of course, they'll be expecting all that in just a few minutes.

Technical architects will typically be much less skeptical about your revenue projections and field studies.

When presenting to business and executive leaders you'll be under less scrutiny to explain how technology works; you can merely allude to the major components (for example, it uses a Web 2.0 infrastructure to interface with a MySQL relational database and a data mining engine—throw in a picture, for good measure, and that level of definition will be adequate for business folk). If you can assure them that the viability of your proposal has been vetted by a few senior technical leaders they know and respect, that will usually be sufficient. They'll be much more critical of revenue projections, market analysis, and case studies to determine their veracity. If you're making a technical proposal, you'll compromise your credibility by dressing up, so for heaven's sake, don't wear a jacket and tie. If it's a sales proposal, the rule is inverted: Wear jeans and a T-shirt at your peril. Never be better dressed than the people you are presenting to; it just makes you look desperate.

A successful pitch is information dense and compact and answers these key questions:

- ▶ What is it?

- ▶ Why should I care?

- ▶ How much will it cost?

- ▶ How much will it save or garner?

- ▶ What are the indicators of success, and how credible are they?

If you can fit in all that, plus a storyboard or demo, and save half the time for discussion, then you've got a crackerjack proposal in hand.

Personal Tenacity

Finally, the single most important ingredient in getting new ideas off the ground is simply your own personal tenacity in forcing the topic without expressing frustration or anger. It's a tenacity that usually requires weeks or months of sustainment, unless you are working in a company of ten people or less, because good ideas almost never get real traction in a day or a week. The xenophobic nihilistic naysayers take time to win over. In many cases, the only way to get them on board is through the charismatic support of others they admire. In other words, the process needs to be iterative and can snowball; the more people you get excited and supportive, the more people you can potentially get excited and supportive. If you let the naysayers depress you or persuade you against your better judgment, then your proposals will always be stillborn. Successful proposals require tenacity to go back and make the case for a good idea several times over, and the willingness to articulate convincingly and unemotionally even against people far more senior and more charismatic. In my interview with James Gosling, Sun Vice President and Fellow and inventor of Java, he offered the following powerful advice, well worth heeding:

> Be really stubborn. A lot of these things are really easy to give up on. Whether it's organizations that you give up, or APIs, or software, a lot of times, it's too easy to give up too early.

Getting to the Next Steps

Having your executives or senior architects buy into your proposal is a first-order objective. However, if you let them leave the room with smiles on their faces but without committing to invest in your proposal (or at least set a date when they will), your good idea is about to die. Your first job is to make their decision easy by showing them how they can either deliver your proposal for free (enough people are willing to develop a beta version as a skunkworks project using only a few hours of their time per week) or with low-risk/high-return potential (for example, you need two people, but this could lead to as much as $10 million in revenues next year). Getting commitments to proceed and to provide the required staff and components is absolutely necessary. Business executives and product architects have a lot on their minds, and they rely on your passion to keep the wind in the sails of your proposal. Don't expect them to leave the room and start making things happen without you. You need to get their commitment on staffing and any capital requirements for servers and software and then keep pushing the agenda forward with reminders and updates.

Let's go back to Moe's proposal at SuperDuperTech. In Moe's case, as a hobbyist with passion, he can do a lot of the heavy lifting on his own, but he knows he needs help around the edges for some of the AI and graphics, as well as beta launch activities. Larry and Curly are part owners in the idea now, so they're easily convinced to lend a few hours from the staff they manage to get this beta going and see where it can go. They readily agree to it in the group decision meeting, and Moe leaves the meeting with approval and agreement to get four hours a week in help from each of four additional engineers.

After you've made a few proposals in your organization (or watched others try), you'll get a sense for the company's political attitude toward them. What attributes are they looking for? Is there tolerance for new proposals at all? If you're lucky, have a good eye for some creative and useful ideas, make the effort to iterate with key people in advance, align your projects with core competencies, and are fiercely tenacious, you'll certainly get some proposal accepted over the course of your career. Remember, most proposals go nowhere, so if you get traction with 20% or better, you'll be doing extremely well. With a few of these tucked under your belt, projects you actually got going and drove to success, you'll have built a significant track record for leadership and success that is certain to propel your career forward.

An Interview with Linus Torvalds

Mr. Linux

CURRENT POSITION

Fellow, Linux Foundation

CLAIM TO FAME

Originator of Linux, the popular open source UNIX-like operating system kernel

DATE OF BIRTH

December 28, 1969

EDUCATION

M.Sc. in Computer Science, Helsinki University, 1989–1997
Honorary degrees include Ph.D. H.C., Stockholm University, 1999; and Ph.D. H.C., Helsinki University, 2000.

FAVORITE PASTIMES & HOBBIES

Reading and computers. Things I wish I had the time/energy for: swimming, playing pool.

BIOGRAPHY

[From the author: Linus doesn't have a formal biography. When I asked him for one, his reply was quite endearing. With Linus's permission, I've included it here.] Heh. I don't have one. I've never really needed one, and I have no idea what to write. I've spent two-thirds of my life programming and almost half writing and maintaining Linux, and it's what people who know me know me for. I suspect Wikipedia probably has a better bio than anything I could write, unless you want to go whole hog and just get *Just for Fun*, the book I wrote with David Diamond about being a geek.

"When I needed something, I'd just write it myself"

How did you get started in software?

My maternal grandfather got a VIC-20 (the lesser-known predecessor to the Commodore 64) that he used for his statistical calculations and introduced me to computers that way. I think I was 11 at the time, and I ended up helping him type in his programs that he wrote on paper.

Eventually, I started doing my own—this was back when you could buy computer magazines with program listings you could type in to make them do something and then modify them for your own amusement. I never really got into the whole "buying games" thing that a lot of teenage boys ended up doing, partly because I didn't have the money and partly because, unlike the Commodore 64 that came later, the VIC-20 was never that great of a game machine. I just wrote my own instead. The coding was more interesting than playing the games, which probably says more about my skills in game design than anything else. When I needed something, I'd just write it myself, and that's how Linux got started, too.

What do you consider your greatest accomplishments or contributions to software?

While I'm really proud of all the work and technical decisions that have gone into Linux, what ended up being much more important and far-reaching was the social side of it and the development model. A lot of that was just being in the right time and place, of course, but I also believe that Linux was one of the first and biggest projects to so aggressively do development in the open, with a rather pragmatic approach.

Most other bigger open source projects happened within the confines of some particular organization. Perhaps because Helsinki wasn't as centrally located as some other traditional open source projects, or perhaps because I was more interested in communicating over email than face-to-face, Linux never had much of a geographic center or even a strong central group of people; it became much more far-flung and virtual than other projects before it.

Also, Linux was basically the first big project that successfully balanced the idealism of the Free Software movement and pragmatism. So instead of becoming radicalized, we were being realistic and pragmatic and concentrating on actual technology. I think this was a big reason why commercial ventures had a much easier time growing up around Linux. That, in turn, resulted in a healthy balance between the purely technical issues and the issues that

Linus Torvalds

need to be solved for anything that becomes a real "product." It's a balance I think we've been very successful at.

Do you have a pet peeve in any aspect of the software world?

My personal pet peeve is how many people think the hard part is in the "big and hard problems" or in some fluffy but important-sounding thing like "innovation." In fact, all the real work is in getting the details right. It's that "1% inspiration, 99% perspiration" thing. People seem to think that inspiration is the much bigger and important part of the two, but I've come to believe that while it's important to have inspiration, where people actually stumble is when they can't execute on that inspiration. Inspiration isn't that rare in the end, but people who have it and then actually follow through... that's rare.

"I just work better if I enjoy what I'm doing"

What makes you feel successful about your work in software?

I absolutely love the fact that I still enjoy my work. I personally don't really set goals or have any other way of "measuring" whether I have lived up to some particular level of success. Just the fact that I enjoy walking downstairs to my office and can do my job, and would probably be bored out of my skull if I didn't do it...that's my personal measure of success.

It's what I hope my kids will have; something that they care about and really enjoy doing. The fact that I feel like I have made a difference and work on a project that is meaningful to others is obviously likely to be a large reason why I enjoy doing it, but I don't try to even analyze it too much.

I believe that I just work better if I enjoy what I'm doing. I suspect that if anybody wants to be "the best" at whatever they do, they have to realize that it takes decades of hard work. And the main way to actually keep doing decades of hard work is to simply enjoy it so much that you don't want to stop. I doubt that has anything to do with software—or even jobs, of course. It's probably equally true of sports or anything else.

What's the secret of your success? Have you approached your work differently from others?

I don't know if this counts as an anecdote, but one thing I personally find interesting in how all my personal successful projects have come about is that I have not actually aimed very high—or aimed for even being hugely successful. Both of these are apparently involved in how you're *not* supposed to do successful projects.

I've had two personal projects I'm very proud of: the Linux kernel, and the (much smaller) project that I use to manage the source code, called git. Both have been technically successful and are being used pretty widely—and both of them started out as much less ambitious projects than they eventually became. Linux itself literally started when I was playing around with some low-level hardware details and writing myself a terminal emulator—and it just kept growing. It took several months before I even realized that it was really becoming an operating system kernel, not just a terminal emulator. The same was true of git—it started with fairly modest goals as a stop-gap measure until something better came around. Now three years later, it's still what I use, and I don't expect anything better to come around anymore.

In fact, I've come to believe that the whole "Aim high" and "Have a big idea" talk is all just claptrap (see the pet peeve discussion). You don't leap tall buildings in single bounds; you walk up the stairs one at a time—and if you think about walking a hundred stories before you'll even get anywhere interesting, you'll just never bother. Or you'll keep your eyes on the far-away target and totally stumble because you cannot even see the individual steps.

"My work does dominate everything"

How do you stay on top of technology trends and innovation?

The flippant but somewhat true answer is that I have a hard enough time staying on top of my own work. I don't want to then worry about keeping up-to-date on other trends. But seriously, this is an area where open source simply means that I don't have to worry about it because if it's a trend I'm not seeing (and I do end up being involved with companies doing things that matter for the kernel), it's still going to be picked up by somebody else. And even if I'm personally doubtful and might not take it seriously, by the time the trend is in full bloom, those other people who did care and worry about it will just be able to say, "Ha, ha, see what we told you—and, by the way, here's the stuff we worked on again."

Technical leaders and executives are famous for being time-strapped. What strategies do you use to stay sane and use your time effectively?

I'm a total disaster area when it comes to managing my time in any kind of "organized" manner, so I've taken a different approach: I simply don't do things that don't matter deeply to me. I very actively rely on others in areas that aren't that high on my personal interest level. An example of this is public speaking; I did it for a while, but I realized that I just could never get

Linus Torvalds

interested enough in it for me to want to do it—and it was taking a lot of my time (not the speaking itself, of course, but the travel, along with the mental load of having things like that hang over me). So I got very good at just saying, "No, I'm not doing that."

The same goes for email. I try to read everything I get, but quite frankly, if somebody sends me an email that doesn't make me think that I personally am the only one who can answer that email, I won't even send a reply back to say so. I simply drop it. Rude? Probably. After too many years of too much email, I simply don't care.

I also totally refuse to do things by phone, and I've long eschewed meetings. I hate the synchronous nature of it, and how I have to make room for those kinds of things even while I'm in the middle of my work day (or in the middle of just wanting to relax, for that matter).

How do you achieve a work-life balance? How do you keep your professional life from dominating everything?

My work does dominate everything. I work weekdays, I work weekends. I shuffle down to my office when I wake up (often in my bathrobe—ahh, the joys of working from home), and I stay there most of the day. But on the other hand, one of the nice parts is the flexibility. I can take a break anytime, ranging from a few hours to take the kids to gymnastics or something, to a week because we just want to go on a vacation. And when I take a vacation, I usually just leave the laptops and everything behind.

That's one of the nice parts of having a real community and not being a "boss" that tells people what to do. I'm fairly central, and I really, really like what I do, and I'm pretty good at it, but it's still more of a big social group than any strict hierarchy where everybody needs to be in their assigned places.

"Realistic short-term goals at all points— not a pie-in-the-sky dream"

What do you see as the coming changes in the software field over the next 10–15 years that will impact career opportunities either positively or negatively?

One of the things I'm personally interested in (for obvious reasons) is how raising the level of the ubiquitous, and basically free, software we take for granted changes what people and commercial software companies do.

I think the current batch of open source companies may look fairly radical today because people compare them to traditional software companies.

But what happens when there really isn't any point in making a big deal about all the basic stuff that everybody needs—OS, browser, office tools, you name it—simply because everybody has access to it?

Do traditional pure software companies largely go away (and become more of the service and support houses like IBM), or do they retreat into very particular niches where customization is the big deal? Everybody may have all the basics, but you still will always have specialized needs. The actual software engineers won't go away—it's not like the software stops being important, quite the reverse—but I think the places they work for will need to adapt.

Of course, most programmers already don't actually work for "software companies"—they work for companies that do other things but require software to do so, so maybe this isn't actually a very big change in the end.

What suggestions do you have for others on being successful in software (either R&D or business)?

I suspect that the previous answers answered that for me. I don't think there is a "formula" or some particular strategy, but you'd better have a passion for your work. You want to have some reachable and realistic short-term goals at all points—not a pie-in-the-sky dream. We may all want to change the world, but if you start out with "I want to totally change how people do 'xyz,'" you're probably already on your way to failure.

Of course, part of that involves the fact that you'll never know beforehand whether you really will make a big difference or whether the short-term goals are just a dead end. And some of it may be luck, but some of it may well be that some people are just better at starting projects that have room to grow.

What final words of wisdom or caution do you have for people entering the field?

I have a hard time really giving much advice. I never saw this as a "profession"; it has always been a hobby to me—just one that happens to pay well. And I've been very lucky in that pretty much all the people I work with have been in that same situation (and that very much includes my non-open source work). That has made me appreciate my coworkers so much more, too. And I have this nagging suspicion that it's not a good profession to be in if you don't have that kind of passion about it. You wouldn't enjoy it as much, you wouldn't spend as much of your time (both paid and unpaid) doing it, and, as a result, you'd probably never be as good at it as the ones who do. So while I think it's a great profession, I also have this suspicion that it's one of those things where you really want to see it as more than just a job and a career. That's obviously true of any area of endeavor, but I think more so when it comes to software than most other areas.

Linus Torvalds

CHAPTER 11

Career Advancement

"Space isn't remote at all. It's only an hour's drive away if your car could go straight upwards."
—Fred Hoyle (1915–2001)

In any reasonable company, the most important steps you can take to help advance your career are to do good work, be a team player, innovate, and make a modest and constant effort to ensure that your manager and a reasonable circle of others are aware of your contributions. If corporations had a way to effectively monitor and accurately evaluate their staff, perhaps that would be enough. Unfortunately, the real world is so far from that ideal that it's shocking. I can honestly say without any hesitation that over the past 20 years in the software development, I've seen every manager I know work extremely hard to be as fair as possible to their employees and make sure that every employee had both opportunities for advancement and the fairest evaluation possible. No matter how hard we all tried across the industry, we never succeeded in transforming evaluations and promotional assessment beyond the murky waters of approximation and expert judgment. That's where you come in: Knowing just how unscientific the process is, and with a bit of insight on the process used to produce your evaluation or candidacy for promotion, you can take a few steps to bias the process in your favor. That bias can help you get the best evaluation you deserve (but unlikely one that is better), which is a huge improvement over something better described as random.

Why Evaluations and Advancements Are So Unscientific

Evaluations are always relative statements on an employee's contribution compared to those of his or her peers. Evaluations need to be relative, not absolute because no organization can afford to give every single employee a high evaluation or promote employees too rapidly. The number of promotions, top-rated evaluations, and large bonuses every year is usually tightly controlled. This generates both competition for the top evaluations and the need to start comparing employees with each other. Although daily work life is about co-opetition, performance reviews are pure competition. The challenge in honestly evaluating employees is manifold across several dimensions. First, when comparing people who do similar kinds of work, such as two programmers or two customer support personnel, both might do similar kinds of work, but the specifics of their tasks over the course of the year vary dramatically. One programmer might have done a brilliant job on a small but highly complex piece of code, whereas the other programmer was given tasks of lower complexity but blasted through them with sensational productivity. Which is more impressive, productivity or sophistication? Next we have the problem of varied personalities. When employees get evaluated, organizations generally factor in, either explicitly or implicitly, both what employees accomplished and how they accomplished it. A highly productive programmer who works alone, fails to support the team, and is generally a grouch will not get points for collaborative teamwork. Those are just the easy problems...after all, so far we're talking about pair-wise comparison of employees who do similar though not identical kinds of work. The problem becomes completely intractable when you expand this to a comparison of people who do radically different jobs, such as a department manager versus an architect, or a salesperson versus a customer support professional.

Evaluations are far from an exact science, and if you one day receive an evaluation you don't feel is fair, you can take some comfort in knowing that the process is far from perfect. Even so, despite the flaws in the process, you can take some steps to improve your odds and position you for the best possible evaluation. Over time, a string of good evaluations generally translates into more rapid promotions.

Track Record Is Credibility—Credibility Is Everything

For more than 30 years, Alan Cooper has been a pioneer of the modern computing era. He's best known as the father of Visual Basic, which remains one of the most important and popular programming languages in the world. Cooper once said, "You won't become a better marksman by enlarging the target." Your track record for accomplishment is the single greatest indicator of your talent. It gives you credibility that no other metric can offer. Naysayers might have their doubts when you do a fantastic job on one project, but string together a list of successes on hard problems, and nobody will doubt your talent and contribution. In any career, success feeds on itself, and it takes just a small effort on your part to make your successes known and translate them into new and more exciting prospects. Consider what Ray Tomlinson had to say in his interview with me:

> But you have to work yourself into that position; you're not going to get those opportunities up front. You have to prove that you can do what you need to do, and then you can start spotting opportunities and saying, "Well, I did a great job on this—I should be able to do a great job on that. Why don't you give me a chance on it?" It's not so much advice as much as recognizing your abilities and recognizing what you like, and looking for places where they overlap and pursuing that as your goal.

Don't expect your management team to keep a record of what you've done over the years—it might exist in a file somewhere, but nobody is reading that. All you need to do is gently remind them in a polite, quiet, and very occasional way. If you keep your eyes open about upcoming projects and give some thought to what you want to work on, you'll be well positioned to approach your management team and politely ask, as Tomlinson suggests, "Why don't you give me a chance on it?" They might not be able to accommodate your request every time, but you'll do your career a world of good by having asked. You'll be indicating that you're interested in getting bigger or more interesting work, you'll be indirectly reminding them of your track record, and you'll be showing some very important and significant initiative. If they like you, even if they can't accommodate your request, they will give deeper thought to what you'll work on next. That's a healthy and appropriate relationship to have.

Communicate Your Accomplishments

Can you get recognition, raises, and promotions by doing good work and consistently exceeding everything your management has asked you to do? Of course not—that would make way too much sense. Here's why not:

Your boss probably doesn't even remember all the things he's asked you to, whether they were easy, hard, or virtually impossible. You're one of many people in the group, and your manager, however talented and brilliant, is still only human. Software is a very complex business, and your manager has a lot on the go.

You've done outstanding work, but how will anyone know about it? Your code might be ten times higher quality that everyone else's, but there's no way to measure and prove that in the short term (a defect analysis over the next decade would show your modules have dramatically lower defect occurrence rates under test and in the field, but your next promotion isn't going to wait for that). Your algorithms are more ingenious. Your teamwork is more generous and helpful. You might be the perfect employee, but is anybody really measuring these qualities in a quantifiable way? Of course not.

So where does it leave you when your boss can't remember and nobody is watching? The answer lies in constant and appropriate communication. The best strategy includes near-real-time and *post-factum* communication. You need both to maximize the impact.

Near-real-time communication means that when you've accomplished good things, you make an effort to let your manager, and a reasonable set of others who will have a natural interest in the news, know about it. No chest pounding or self-aggrandizement required—just the good news. Smart people will connect the dots and attribute the source of the success back to the people who were driving the work. Boasting just looks bad and is truly uncalled for. People love good news at work (because there's always more than enough bad news to go around), so help satisfy their need by giving them some good news about your work in a polite, modest, and appropriate way. If you're working hard and are passionate about your work, you should have some kind of good news to share every two to six weeks. That's a reasonable frequency for sharing some upbeat information with interested parties.

Sometimes you'll find that a certain piece of good news is more interesting to others than you first thought. Other teams will want to start collaborating or referencing what you've done. For example, let's say you make a design change in your product's print function that allows PostScript data to be generated and spooled 35% faster. Suddenly the system verification team is very interested because their upcoming test cycle calls for extensive testing of the print function, and your new code will shave a week off their testing time. The marketing team finds out and determines that the improved print function could be the magic bullet they've been looking for against your company's major competition. When these things happen, it's time to start giving something for nothing. Think of ways you can help the marketing team generate collateral from your news or how you can help the test team get the new code sooner. It's a beautiful opportunity to build some emotional cache with others.

Whenever you accomplish something good, be sure to write it down in a book, a file, or a spreadsheet. As your performance evaluation draws near (in most companies, once per year), you'll want to be able to remind your manager a month or two in advance of all the good you've done. Most people don't bother to keep track of what they've done throughout the year; as a result, when asked, they remember only a partial story. You don't need to keep track of every little thing you've done—just the big stuff, the work that had high impact. Some accomplishments are special, though, and a distinguishing item, even if it was small, is worth tracking. Fixing a small defect in the code that helps save the day at a major customer account is one example. The code fix might have taken only an afternoon, but the effect might have saved the company millions—that's definitely worth noting. Write down your accomplishments so you're certain to have a list. This is the *post-factum* communication.

Don't expect your manager and peers to remember all your great accomplishments. Be cognizant of the fact that they'll remember impressions more than facts. Help them get the good news facts at the right times by communicating frequently in a business-appropriate and reasonably humble manner.

Goal-Oriented Careers

If you don't know where you're going, you're unlikely to get there. If you ever do get there, it'll take you a lot longer than if you had taken a straight path. Here's an analogy I've used that seems to resonate with many people. Imagine you wake up one morning and find yourself in a canoe, on a silent lake surrounded by glaciers and majestic arctic mountains. The sun is shining, and you are awestruck by the majesty that surrounds you. You have absolutely no idea how you got into this boat or where you are, but before you can even stop to contemplate the problem, a voice from Heaven calls out to you and says, "Go. Time is running out. You need to get there quickly." Then silence. You sit up in the boat and call out to the disembodied voice, crying, "Where? *Where?* Where am I supposed to get to?" There's no reply—just silence. You're alone on the lake with the mountains, the breathtaking scenery, and the canoe. You begin to wonder, "What are the odds of my getting wherever I'm supposed to be if I head *thataway?*" Pretty soon you realize that all directions are equally unlikely, and you're stuck in a completely impossible situation.

Of course, the story a metaphor and the lake is your career (or perhaps your life). Your mission, really, is to *know* where you want to go because without that knowledge, you'll be drifting on the water. Careers take a lot of time and effort, but if you have a clear vision of where you want to end up, you'll be much more successful traveling the shortest path to get there. Your goals don't need to be as specific as "I want to become the director of engineering for product X by the time I'm 40, with an office on the third floor overlooking the lawn." Having a goal of becoming the director of engineering is probably a reasonably specific goal that can help you focus your career planning. How long it will take to get there, or what product it will be, are parts that you can leave unspecified.

In the following figures, you can see a very talented person on a canoe trying to navigate his career path. In Figure 11.1, we see his path as he stays focused on his goal to become the CTO of a midsize software corporation with a few hundred software developers. He has a clear idea of where he wants to go and takes deliberate steps throughout his career to take positions that lead toward that goal. With the job of CTO in mind, he stays with purely technical responsibilities and invests time and energy in working outside the normal parameters of his job requirements, building up a portfolio of publications, patents, standards work, and industrial leadership. Through his work as chief architect, director, and vice president, he will naturally end up doing considerable customer and partner engagements that familiarize him with the business aspects a CTO needs fluency in. Over 20 years, with talent and grit, he has a good chance of realizing his dream.

In Figure 11.2, we see a more typical career path for the same person—same talent, same education, but no clear personal objective, such as becoming a CTO. In this case, although he still wants to become the CTO, his focus on that goal isn't as deliberate.

Through his career, he takes some senior jobs that are interesting and exciting but that don't contribute to his ultimate goal of reaching the CTO position. For example, switching to a different product for a period slows down his development of technical depth and expertise on the core product that defines his career. Stints as a second-line manager and support manager do not contribute to his goal of reaching CTO. Without the focus on reaching CTO, he fails to invest time in building a portfolio of technically visible external contributions in the form of patents, publications, industrial standards, and industrial leadership. He ends up with a very successful and varied career, but he never achieves a specific goal and, in general, his career achievements tend to be lower. His career is more haphazard, wavering across many more areas and career distractions.

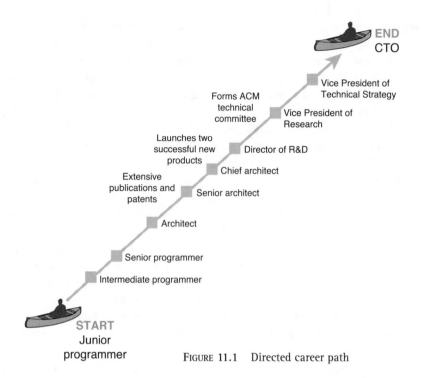

FIGURE 11.1   Directed career path

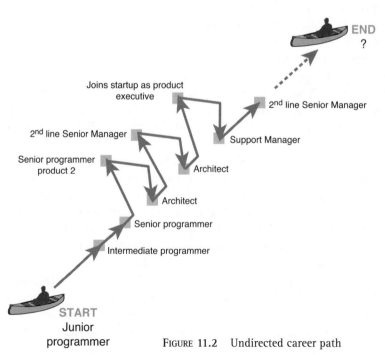

FIGURE 11.2   Undirected career path

This discussion is extreme, and a few career distractions and some exploration is healthy. There's something to be said for sampling areas and trying things off the beaten track to distinguish yourself. Trying different jobs helps you not only refine your career goals, but also round out your skills. But sampling and exploring without a final purpose leads to haphazard career development, so the key is to moderate the exploration and keep your career goals crisp. Looking through the interviews in this book, you'll see that, without exception, every one of the great seminal thinkers and contributors I interviewed was goal-oriented in the approach they took to their careers. Some had a deliberate goal to start a new company (Diane Greene, Marc Benioff) or to become an executive (John Schwarz, David Vaskevitch). Others had a personal mission concerning software methodology (Linus Torvalds, Richard Stallman, Grady Booch). Others knew early on that they wanted to be technical leaders whose role was to solve the hardest problems they could apply themselves to (Steve Wozniak, Peter Norvig, James Gosling). A final group wanted to master a specific technology (Ray Tomlinson, Robert Kahn, Mark Russinovich). They all knew relatively early in their careers what they wanted to do, and that pursuit defined their careers. This focus on where you want to go can come only from within—nobody else can tell you what you want to do, what you enjoy, or what your goals and aspirations should be. Knowing your destination helps you filter career choices, avoiding opportunities that take you adrift from your objectives.

Finally, it's worth pointing out that the importance of having a career goal doesn't mean you can't change your mind. Many people—in fact, probably most of us—have career aspirations in their 30s and 40s that were unimaginable to them in their 20s. We all change with time. Sensitive to the realities of changing interests and humbled by the vagaries of atavism, changing your goals can be healthy and commendable—but you are always served best at every stage of your career by having goals.

If you don't yet know where you want to get to, there are some good places to start. First, keep an open mind and try to expand your awareness of the possibilities. It's a broad and bold software world out there, and few people have experienced the complete breadth of roles. A great place to start is to speak to as many senior people as you can about their work and see which roles resonate with you. Goal-oriented people begin with the end in mind—they identify the goal and work backward. That's why you should start at the top and see which senior positions have the most long-term appeal to you. When you find out as much as you can about different roles, ask yourself the following questions:

▶ What kinds of technical work do I enjoy most?

▶ What kinds of management tasks do I enjoy most?

▶ Do I prefer breadth or depth?

▶ What do I do better than most of my peers?

▶ Am I more comfortable leading or following?

▶ Am I more comfortable working in a group and leveraging and contributing to the collective talent of the group, or do I prefer the single-minded focus and efficiency that a project of one provides?

▶ When I'm really honest with myself, what's my tolerance and interest in constant learning and flux? All jobs require constant learning, but some are more intense than others.

John Schwarz is the CEO of Business Objects, one of the world's leading software companies. In his interview with me, he shared a defining story of his career that helped him become a CEO. Early in his career, he had a meeting with a senior IBM executive who told him that if he wanted to be the CEO of IBM one day, he would need to take a set of steps to climb the corporate ladder to even have a chance. That got Schwarz thinking about the importance of building a career plan. He shared with me the retrospective thought that if he hadn't built a deliberate career plan, "it would have taken me so long to figure this out that I might have never made it."

Some people stumble upon success because they are in the right place at the right time with an immense portfolio of talent. For most of us, hoping to be in the right place at the right time by mere chance is just irresponsible. Instead, we can simply proffer words from Louis Pasteur: Fortune favors the prepared mind. When you've decided what your career goals are, the next step is to "do a Schwarz." In other words, work backward from that goal and build a career plan. You'll have a career plan, and if you've been realistic about thinking it through in chunks of two to four years, it will probably be a very good plan. Over time, your goals and interests might change, and your career plan should adapt accordingly.

Your Manager's Influence on Your Career

Aside from you, your boss has more impact on your career success than any other person in your company. It's completely impossible to get a promotion, salary increase, bonus, or good evaluation unless your manager believes you deserve it. These are just some of the direct ways you manager influences your success. Indirectly, you manager has very high influence on recommending you for new opportunities and coaching you in your professional development. Moreover, your manager can make your life at work great fun or pure pain, depending on his or her management style and impressions of your work. If you want to advance, it's vital that your boss believe you're deserving. Naturally, the most important thing you can do is work hard and make sure your manager knows about it. But aside from elbow grease and back-breaking labor, a few other tricks can help improve your posture.

It's worth noting that a new class of companies is emerging that approaches promotions and recognition differently. For instance, at Google and other companies that copy it, it's much less important than at traditional companies to have a manager support an employee's promotion. Of course, your manager is one voice in many, and the input of your peers often counts much more heavily. Even so, it's hard to get promoted in any organization if your manager opposes it.

Help Your Boss Look Good

Remember, your manager indirectly gets credit for all the good work you do and is always looking to showcase the contributions of the department. Getting work done might be what you were asked to do, but having demonstrable results in the form of demos, performance metrics, or customer testimonials can go a long way toward making your results tangible and visible for your manager in a medium that can be shown to others.

Look for Ways to Help

Your manager has an agenda. After all, managers don't get to where they are without having some ambition. However, managers aren't always aware of everything they need to do to achieve their own goals—and sometimes, even when they are, they might not want to burden their staff with the work. By looking for ways to help your manager both technically and organizationally, you can help advance the needs of the department and the aims of the one person (after you) who most directly impacts your career success. Like any sidebar, it's important not to spend too much time on these kinds of things— 10–20% would be a maximum because the main thing you'll be evaluated on is the core tasks you've been assigned, not the volunteerism you've proactively engaged in.

Have a Career Discussion with Your Boss At Least Once a Year

I believe all employees have the right to know where they stand in the organization relative to their peers and know what's required and expected to get to the next level. Any manager worth their salt should be willing, perhaps with some notice, to give you a straight answer to these two questions. Getting that feedback can absolutely help you direct your career planning and improve your chances of getting to the next big thing. Jack Welch was the CEO of GE for more than two decades, and under his leadership, the company became a leader in management effectiveness. GE increased in revenue from $28 billion to $130 billion, and the company's stock increased from $1.16 to nearly $60 a share. Identifying and growing leaders was a cornerstone of Welch's management style, and he emphasized how critical it is for managers to communicate clearly to their employees where they stand and what they need to do to advance. There's a beautiful interview with Welch published on YouTube by McGrawHill,[1] and the following snippet is worth recapping:

> You want to make sure that everyone knows where they stand in the organization. It's a leader's obligation. In most companies, the leaders hold back, and people don't know where they stand. In this case, where you praise the top 20 [percent], the middle 70 knows how they can improve to get higher (and you never forget them because they're the critical part of the organization), and the bottom 10 you tell... "Hey, it's time for you to move on." It's not firing; it's telling them to move on, and find something...and they do it themselves. You don't [have to] fire anyone when you do that, maybe 20% of them, but most of them leave on their own because who wants to be in a place where they aren't wanted? Nobody does .... You should always be appraising them. They've gotta know where they stand. If you've got any

---

[1] You can see the full video interview with Jack Welch at www.youtube.com/watch?v=F4R3D-Lu6_Q.

manager watching this show and they aren't thinking about "Do my people know where they stand? Have I told them candidly how I feel about them, what I like about them, and what they need to improve?" then they shouldn't be a manager. Because once you're a manager, it's about them, not about you.

In my experience, these kinds of conversations don't happen enough, and too few employees understand clearly where they stand in the organization and what's required to get to the next level. In the years I've spent coaching software developers I've been amazed at how many people thought these kinds of questions are inappropriate. "Really? I can ask that?" You bet you can. When the conversations do happen, employees are often surprised to learn that, to get to the next level, they're expected to take on tasks, responsibilities, and initiatives they never realized. So once a year, and maybe a little more often than that, it's a conversation well worth having. You might not be able to reach your next career goal without it.

The Secret Impact of Management Peers

It's a little-appreciated fact, but your manager can't decide your future independently. Any organization has a limit on the number of people who can be promoted and given raises, the size of bonuses, and the number of major leadership opportunities available. Obviously, business success drives a lot of this, and greater success creates a wealth of opportunities, but even in the most lucrative environments, not everybody can be rewarded. Even if your manager loves you and wants to give you opportunities, rewards, increases, bonuses, and more, the reality of organizational constraints means you'll be competing with others that your manager might not have direct responsibility for. This problem doesn't really exist in startups, where your manager might also be the CEO and president, but for the rest of the world, it's a reality: You'll be competing with people on other teams. At some point, you manager will have to make the case that you deserve something more than someone else. When that day comes, the most important ally on your side will be the image that your manager's peers and your manager's manager have of you and their awareness of your accomplishments. When in doubt, the nod will almost always go to the employee who is more widely known. Consider this short scenario to illustrate the process:

Five managers meet to discuss who should be promoted to manage the new Artificial Intelligence R&D team. The director of R&D is hoping his management team will have some impressive candidates to recommend.

Manager 1: "Moe is a great candidate to be promoted to manager of the new Artificial Intelligence Group. He has a background in AI, displays great people and programming skills, and always delivers for us. His graduate studies were in neural nets and genetic algorithms."

Manager 2: "I really recommend Curly. Curly's also got a background in AI, and she's a top-notch programmer with great people skills. Curly also has a graduate degree in genetic algorithms and did AI development at NASA before she joined us."

Director: "Can anyone else in the room comment on Moe and Curly?"

Manager 3: "I've worked a lot with Curly. I can't say enough good things about her. Her work on the last release of our product was outstanding, both technically and organizationally."

Manager 4: "We had a major problem last month in debugging a complex algorithm in the kernel. Curly definitely showed leadership there in getting us to a fix quickly."

Manager 5: "I know both Moe and Curly, but I confess I've had a lot more exposure to Curly's work. She's definitely a great candidate for this role."

Moe and Curly might be comparable in talent, or Moe might even eclipse her, but the managers making the decisions clearly have more exposure to Curly's work. Unquestionably, Curly will get the nod for this role unless Moe's manager makes a superhuman effort to gather additional argumentation and proof points. It's not impossible, but Moe's chances are now slim. These kinds of conversations happen within management teams every day in companies around the world, and the impact of cross-team exposure is dramatic. In fact, virtually every conversation your manager will ever have in order to recommend you for a raise, a promotion, a bonus, or a new position will end up in a conversation like this unless you are a hands-down winner or a clear loser, neither of which are very common. As a manager, one of the most important things you can do is help your employees get exposure for their work outside your own group. As an employee, you should take the initiative to politely and reasonably expose other teams to your work so that your manager will have a much easier time with these kinds of conversations. Honestly, the powerful influence of management peers is a very big deal, and leveraging it effectively is one of the biggest things you can do to advance your career in any organization.

Promoting Others Sincerely

Building emotional caches with others is done only partly by helping them in material ways, such as assisting with code reviews or helping to run test cases when a test cycle is running late. One of the most powerful and effective things you can do to build emotional cache with others is to sing their praises publicly. When you are sincerely appreciative of others and make a point of sharing that respect in a public way, you directly help them and build emotional cache with them. You're helping them both by advancing their career and by building up their ego, both things that all mere mortals need. That emotional cache will snowball in unexpected ways, not only when you need to call in favors, but in career development as well. The more you sincerely show respect and admiration for others, the less likely it is that people will invest energy saying negative things about you, and the more likely it is that they'll spend time returning the favor. We all understand that a world in which hallway conversation is dotted with positive references to your work will be a very different career development environment than one in which your name is invariably heard with specious references to your mistakes and character flaws.

Promoting the good work of others is neighborly behavior and good business sense because its echo is a positive environment for your career success. It's important to keep it honest and sincere. Everyone hates sycophants and self-serving suck-ups. But if you're like most people, you really appreciate and admire a lot of work that your colleagues do throughout the year, but you haven't felt the need to vocalize it. Getting to that expression, both verbally and in writing, is the right way to sincerely promote others.

The Secret of Promotibility Inversion

Most promotions recognize extended contribution over a period of time. They provide a means for employers to get even more productivity from their best employees, while engendering a little more loyalty to the firm and a means for the employees to advance to higher salary levels and accept new challenges and responsibilities. Three major categories of accomplishment factor into any promotion consideration. The secret of promotibility inversion is that the following qualities affect your possibility for promotion in the opposite order that you'd expect:

Contributions to the business are the work you actually produce over the course of years. You can loosely consider this to be the sum of the tasks you've been charged with. In theory, your contributions to the business should be the most important factor in your promotibility. *Professional contributions* is a category I use to refer to a wide range of largely optional tasks that software professionals frequently engage in, such as publishing trade or scientific papers, filing patents, public speaking engagements (for example, speaking at trade conferences about the latest features in your product), and engaging in customer advocacy. The tasks in this category are largely optional and generally can be regarded as "brownie points" on your list of annual accomplishments. Being optional, few, if any, of these could be categorized as actual commitments you are expected to deliver. *Expertise* is a definition of how well you know your professional domain and its tradecraft. For software professionals, this covers your knowledge of software fundamentals, software engineering methodology, and domain knowledge for the specific technical areas you have mastered for the products you work on. For example, you may have world-class expertise in an important technical area, such as web rendering, human computer interfaces, databases, AI, and so on.

In theory, the quality that should matter most in career evaluation and promotion consideration is your contribution to the business. What have you produced directly for the company that helped advance the team's business goals? Unfortunately, management teams have a very hard time assessing business contribution because it is so sensationally hard to quantify in software development. It's extraordinarily difficult to compare people with different challenges and responsibilities. So although almost everyone agrees that this is the most important, in a moment of candid honesty, they'll also agree that it's difficult to assess in a quantifiable way.

Professional contributions probably matter the least. The acquisition of patents, the publication of most papers, and other collateral rarely provide major forward momentum in achieving business goals (although notable exceptions exist). However, these kinds of tasks are noteworthy because they are literally notable. They're easy to list and enumerate. Few employees take the initiative to engage in these tasks, and those who do have (pardon the pun) a notable advantage.

Finally, expertise sounds like a valuable commodity, and indeed it is. But surely its true value is defined by the way it can be leveraged to create benefit to the business. A person with high expertise should be able to translate that skill into positive product impact. If he or she can't, it raises serious questions about the real value of the expertise the employee has or his or her skill in leveraging that expertise for the benefit of the business. That's why, again, if we're honest, contribution to the business is the primary quality we would want to measure to fairly assess promotibility. However, expertise tends to be a quality that is easily identified. Among any group of professionals, it's fairly clear who knows the most about certain topics. Get any group of software developers together for a few months, and they'll sort out pretty quickly who's best at AI, who knows the most about database systems or web interfacing, who's the most prolific programmer, who has the most sensitive soul toward development methodologies, and so on. It's more than easy; it's downright obvious. And this isn't unique to programmers. For example, if you get a group of musicians together, they'll quickly realize which is the most talented virtuoso, even though lay onlookers would have a hard time distinguishing them. Put simply, within a group of experts, expertise is obvious.

We're left with an uncomfortable reality that I call the *promotibility inversion*. The qualities that should most highly impact our promotibility are contribution to the business, followed by professional contributions, and then expertise. In reality, promotibility often correlates highly with expertise and professional contributions, followed by contribution to the business. That doesn't mean you'll get your next promotion without producing solid work; the system is approximate, but it's not blind. It does mean that, among a group of highly productive people who all contribute significantly to the business, the ones with higher expertise and a longer list of professional contributions will advance faster. You can accelerate your promotions by understanding the promotibility inversion and investing a bit more time (not the majority of it) on developing your expertise and professional contributions than you otherwise might. Your contributions to the business, a measure of your total work done, need to be formidable and impressive, but they do not need to be astronomical. People who invest 40 hours a week on contributions to the business and a further 10 on professional contributions and expertise will generally have more successful careers than if they had invested 50 hours a week on contributions to the business alone.

Career advancement requires hard work and repeated accomplishment. Aside from that, it helps to work the system a bit to ensure that your accomplishments are known—and not only by your manager. Having specific goals (even subject to change) will help focus your energies at any stage of your career and develop a strong track record and a compelling array of expertise. All of these will make you the clear choice for working on the next big thing and advancing to higher levels of influence and compensation.

An Interview with Mark Russinovich

Windows Guru, Microsoft Technical Fellow

CURRENT POSITION
Microsoft Technical Fellow and a Windows Architect in the Platform and Services Division

CLAIM TO FAME
The world's leading Windows guru, speaker, and author and creator of the indispensable Sysinternals tools

A prolific writer, Mark's blog (http://blogs.technet.com/markrussinovich/) is the #1 most-read TechNet blog, with 3.5 million readers per month. His Sysinternals web site is the most-trafficked and highest-rated TechNet web site, with around 2 million downloads each month.

DATE OF BIRTH
December 22, 1966

EDUCATION
Ph.D. in Computer Engineering, Carnegie Melon University, 1994

M.Sc. in Computer Engineering, Rensselaer Polytechnical Institute, 1990

B.Sc. in Computer Engineering, Carnegie Melon University, 1989

FAVORITE PASTIMES & HOBBIES
Playing video games (favorite: Battlefield series of online first-person shooters), biking, writing and speaking about Windows

BIOGRAPHY
Mark is a Technical Fellow working in Microsoft's Platform and Services division. He is a widely recognized expert in Windows operating system internals

and operating architecture and design. His discovery of a rootkit on popular Sony audio CDs led to industry reforms in the area of computer privacy.

Mark joined Microsoft when it acquired Winternals Software, the company he cofounded in 1996 and where he worked as Chief Software Architect. He is also the co-founder of Sysinternals.com, where he writes and publishes dozens of popular Windows administration and diagnostic utilities, including Process Monitor, Process Explorer, and Autoruns. He previously worked at IBM's Thomas J. Watson Research Center, researching operating system support for Web server acceleration and serving as an operating systems expert.

Mark is the coauthor of the Windows Internals book series from Microsoft Press (starting with *Inside Windows 2000*). He is the Senior Contributing Editor for *Windows IT Pro Magazine* and a contributing editor for *TechNet* magazine, and he has written dozens of articles on Windows internals. Mark has been a featured speaker at major industry conferences around the world, including Microsoft's TechEd, WinHEC, Professional Developer's Conference, Windows Connections, and TechMentor. He has taught Windows internals, troubleshooting, and file system and device driver development to companies worldwide, including Microsoft, the CIA, and the FBI.

"Hey, we can make some money here!"

How did you get started in software?

I got started I guess somewhere around 6th or 7th grade, when a friend of mine's Dad who worked at the University of Alabama got an Apple II computer. I went over my friend's house, and we started playing on it and writing programs: an editor, assembler, and disassembler. Later I started writing utilities, like a program that would print posters from the high-res Apple display, and started publishing those in computer magazines. That's been a theme running through my life from when I first got started, writing tools and utilities. So that's where I changed my career path from aeronautical engineering (which is what I had decided what I wanted to be back in 2nd grade) to computers.

Winternals helped put you on the map. Can you tell me how you got it started?

I met Bryce Cogswell in graduate school—he got his Ph.D. at CMU, and we had the same Ph.D. supervisor. We started writing computer articles together, and we started Sysinternals (at the time, it was NTinternals) together, providing freeware tools. I viewed that as a hobby outlet and would probably have continued operating that way indefinitely, but he said, "Hey, we can make some money here." One of the tools we wrote we decided to start selling, so we launched the Winternals site, connecting Sysinternals to Winternals. That started generating a little bit of side income that we kept on feeding with new updates and new tools. That ended up becoming an 85-person software company when we sold it. So it was Bryce pushing us to sell instead of give stuff away.

Why were you content to just give it away?

When we started writing tools like Regmon and Filemon, some of our most popular tools ever (and which have now been included in a tool called Process Monitor), and I started giving those away, I figured if I sold them, they would never have nearly the reach that they would if I gave them away for free. Even at the time, I gave away the source for them. I think giving away those tools and getting the exposure for them that it enabled is really part of what made Sysinternals great and contributed to my reputation, which fed into other things, like the launch of Winternals. If we'd been selling those kinds of utilities, which were more aimed at troubleshooting rather than providing utility type value, we wouldn't have gotten to where we got.

One of the other people I interviewed for this book was Richard Stallman, father of the Free Software movement. He actually thinks that much of what you and I do for a living is highly unethical for that very reason: We ship proprietary software, making it impossible for our customers to debug and modify its behavior. Your thoughts?

I think there's a place for his model and for the proprietary model. The fact is that you need to have people who care and are willing to fix the problems. Only a few high-profile projects have really benefited from that kind of model. Back when open source became the hip thing to do, lots of people turned their code out to open source, saying, "Oh, we're now going to benefit from the community contributions," and then there's nothing.

"It's that aspect of solving problems that excites me."

You mentioned that you moved from Chief Architect of the company you founded, an 85-person firm, to a Microsoft Technical Fellow. It's pretty astounding that Microsoft recruited you from a small company into its highest technical position. Is there a story to how you went straight to being a Technical Fellow?

I think a few things contributed to that leveling:

1. I had written many tools that were used throughout the kernel team, Microsoft support services, and Microsoft application developers.

2. I had been working closely with Windows kernel developers since 1995, both in reporting bugs in Windows and in working on the Windows Internals books. I had established personal and professional relationships with everyone from Dave Cutler to Jim Allchin, to the engineers around the Windows group.

3. I taught Windows Internals on Microsoft's campus to Windows developers for several years.

4. I consulted on various Microsoft projects, including serving as the technical due diligence agent for the Connectix acquisition.

5. Winternals bootstrapped from me and Bryce to 85 people, totally self-funded with positive revenue and income growth every quarter of its existence, with products that won industry awards and customer satisfaction far ahead of industry averages.

6. I proved myself as a great public speaker at Microsoft conferences, where I consistently rated as the top or one of the top few speakers out of several hundred.

That said, I am honored to have received this recognition at Microsoft!

What do you consider your greatest accomplishments and/or contributions to software?

The Sysinternals tools have been a significant contribution to the life of Windows administrators and developers all over the world. The Sysinternals web site today has around 2 million unique visitors per month, on average. The most popular tool, Process Explorer, is downloaded about 300,000 times a month. I get emails all the time. I think the way those tools have enabled people to understand the system better and to help their own software development has been beyond what I had ever imagined, especially if you look over the 10 years Sysinternals been around.

Have any of your tools been incorporated in the Windows images?

No. Many have asked why Windows doesn't just take in tools like Process Explorer, Process Monitor, or AutoRuns. Even I'm not in favor of taking those tools in wholesale because the audience really is a niche audience. When you

Mark Russinovich

look at the customers for Windows, just a tiny fraction of them really understand or find the information presented by those tools useful. So on the other hand, there is some functionality in those tools that is accessible—not to the majority of people, but still to a larger subset. Ever since I joined Microsoft, I've been working with the Fundamentals team, the team that's responsible for the in-box diagnostics and tools, to incorporate into the existing Windows tools. Look for some of that in Windows 7.

What makes you feel successful about your work in software?

That's kind of an interesting question, too. I've been entering into areas I can't talk openly about. I've been focusing on long-term Windows architecture, beyond Windows 7. There is a vision I've been driving at for how Windows should evolve, given Microsoft's organizational structure and the need for other groups in Microsoft outside of the Windows group to participate in that vision. It's been really challenging. On paper, a lot of people have bought into it. So I'm excited to try to get that vision to happen, but at the same time it's had its frustration in getting people to buy into it as a future strategy for the company, which is really what's required to execute something like this.

I think it's more the engineering thrill. When I look at the problem—and this is what has guided me my whole software career—I'm not just doing something for the sake of doing it. But looking and saying, "Hey, there's a problem—given the tools at hand and the technologies at hand, what's the best solution for that problem?" ...that's kind of what this vision has come out of. Looking at the landscape of how operating systems and computer usage is evolving poses challenges for Windows today in its current form. What does Microsoft have at its disposal to address those challenges? And that leads to the vision. The aspect of solving problems excites me.

"It's a constant struggle"

Time management ... technical leaders and executives are famous for being time-strapped. What strategies do you use to stay sane and use your time effectively?

It's a constant struggle. I basically have compartmentalized the different work items that I've got and keep track of when they're going to become problems as far as being late. I'm not successful 100% of the time in not missing deadlines, but I try to do it on a daily basis and on a weekly basis. I'm not totally rigorous about this, but I'll write down on a piece of paper the things I want to address or accomplish that day. Half the time I don't accomplish all the things, so they spill over to the next day, but it lets me keep track of things I need to do in priority order.

How do you achieve a work-life balance? How do you keep your professional life from dominating everything?

I've gotten a lot better at balance over time. In the early 1990s, especially during the early days of Winternals, when I was working at IBM and writing a book, I'd come home from work, pull out the laptop, and sit down with my wife in front of the TV, still working on the laptop. I'd even take the laptop to bed sometimes. I stopped doing that after a while and have now gotten to the point that, when I come home from work, I'm basically not at work anymore. I still check email after dinner, but I'm not doing any active work in the evenings anymore unless there's something really critical. On the weekends I do work, but the work for me, whether it's writing magazine articles, working on a presentation, working on Sysinternals tools, or working on something for Windows, is a hobby as well. That's what's great—my career is a lot of fun. I don't view it as work. Computers have always been my hobby. The fact that I get to go to work and work on my hobby and get paid for it is just fantastic. Whereas a lot of husbands on the weekends spend the afternoon playing golf or watching sports, I use that personal time to do stuff that other people consider work.

I get up at 5:30 or 6:00 and work between 30 and 60 minutes catching up on emails and miscellaneous things. I get to the office around 9:00, after exercising in the morning. I leave the office around 6:00. I guess I don't really add up the hours, but that's a typical day for me.

How do you stay on top of technology trends and innovation?

What I've always done is every day I read the main technology web sites. I've bookmarked some of the pages. Techme.com is a great aggregator of technology news. That site is kind of an indicator of the leading-edge trends, or what the tech community gets excited about. More mundane things I read are sites like OSNews, Slashdot, *Infoweek, Infoworld, PC Week, PC Magazine, PC World* ... those kinds of publications I've been reading constantly since I got into the PC world in the early 1990s, to keep on top of all that stuff. I read *Windows IP Pro Magazine* and *TechNet* magazine to keep on top of Microsoft and Windows technologies, including products from other companies. I definitely take a look at software when it's an area I'm interested in learning more about. I do have a network of people who have similar interests in following certain aspects of technology, and some of those overlap. Something will happen or somebody will hear about something, and they'll send it to me.

But a lot of times what drives me to go deeper on something is that I'm in a meeting and somebody mentions something, and I'll have no idea what they're talking about. This is one of the most frustrating things for me, to sit there and feel like I'm clueless. The next thing I do is go research what that is. I don't let it drop—if somebody mentions something, I have to go figure it out.

"But it's all interconnected in the end"

What suggestions do you have for others on being successful in software (either R&D or business)?

You need to be as broad as you can. This gets harder all the time because the space technology continues to explode. Keep on top of the current trends and the hot technology growth areas. For example, I'm in Windows working on the core operating system. In the core operating system group, I'm following what's going on in the world of Ajax and web standards, Perl, Ruby on Rails, and other technologies that a lot of people in my same shoes would probably look at and say "Well, I don't have the time for that kind of stuff—it's not relevant to me, anyway." But it's all interconnected in the end, even if it's on a small scale of understanding Windows as a whole, which is what I've driven myself to do. That has resulted in pushing myself to work on the Windows Internals book series, to give talks on how Windows works, to understand what's going on outside of Windows as well... I think that has really enabled me to be successful as well: to have a big picture instead of an isolated view.

I think that my path has been unique because until I was acquired by Microsoft, I'd never had a boss. Even when I worked at IBM, I was fairly independent with what I could do. It was more about working on a team where my boss was acting like a peer. It was almost as a volunteer basis that I was there because Winternals was already underway. It's not like I've had to work on something and go up the ranks. I've kinda been at the top of the ranks from the start, whether it was starting a tiny company with Bryce, to now being a Technical Fellow at Microsoft, which is the highest technical position there is in the company.

My perspective on working within an organization is really recognizing that even if you are at the top, you can't just order people to do things. You can't just say, "You're going to do this. You're going to write this code. Marketing team, you're going to do things this way." Nobody is really a total boss or a total dictator. You need to get people to believe in what they are doing. That means selling ideas. As the chief software architect of Winternals, there were products I thought we should do, but just because I was the chief software architect didn't mean I didn't have to go to the marketing people and the salespeople, and Bryce, and the CEO we hired. I still had to pitch the idea and sell them on it as something we should actually do.

What do you see as the coming changes in the software field over the next 10–15 years that will impact either the technology we work on or career opportunities either positively or negatively?

Career opportunities come about from changes in technology. We're on the cusp of a new wave of computing, which is mobile computing. I mean, we've heard the term "PC in your pocket," but that statement hasn't meant anything until just recently. I think we're entering this whole new wave of people carrying around PCs in their pockets and being able to connect them to things when they walk around and travel. I think there are huge opportunities. You can already see the Apple AppStore for the iPhone creating opportunities for people. The other big thing we see going on is the rich application runtimes moving on the browser and becoming cross-platform. While that poses challenges for companies like Microsoft that have operating systems where people are writing software specifically for those OSes and Apple as well, it's another great opportunity. That space and the richness of the browser are evolving rapidly at this point.

Do you have a pet peeve in any aspect of the software world?

It's probably not politically correct for me to tell you because it has to do with Microsoft software. But I think that just the fragility of software is something I find annoying. As a software user, there are so many cases of this. Usability is one example, but in some cases the software just falls on its face. In many cases I've needed my own tools to figure out why something was failing and how to fix it (or work around it). When that happens, I can't comprehend how the average computer user keeps from throwing the computer out the widow!

You have two graduate degrees in Computer Engineering. Do you think graduate degrees are professionally valuable? Do you see them as a substantial benefit to a candidate when recruiting?

That's a really good question—I've been asked that numerous times. My answer is that, for me personally, I didn't really view it as a choice. My father had an M.D., and one of the things he drilled into me when I was very young was to go and get the most education you can. Pick whatever career you want—he didn't try to direct me down a particular path—and whatever you pick, get the highest degree you can because you're going to be opening more doors than you're closing. If you stop, you'll never have a chance to go back. It's very rare and very difficult to go out to work and then decide to go back and get more education. So from the very start, I knew that I wanted to go through for myself and get a Ph.D. For other people, I would say that a Ph.D. probably isn't necessary unless you want to go down a career path that requires one, such as teaching in higher education or working in a research laboratory. But a master's degree is definitely worth it. In some senses, a Ph.D. could close doors because for certain jobs, people might consider you to be overqualified and might be afraid that you won't be stimulated enough. But a master's degree probably won't have that same kind of effect and can differentiate you from other people, not just in terms of the degree, but in terms of getting a little deeper knowledge in an area that you are interested in and want to pursue in the industry.

What final words of wisdom or caution do you have for people entering the field?

Try to differentiate yourself. For example, when Java exploded in the mid-1990s, everybody became a Java programmer, and the market became flooded with cookie-cutter Java programmers. It's really hard for people to stand out as something that isn't easily replaceable in that world. My whole career I have tried to stay away from that. Operating system internals, while not considered particularly sexy or part of the mainstream, have allowed me to stand out because of the relatively few people who go into that and the perception "Wow, that's really hard." Stay away from the mainstream and the crowds, and find something that is gonna be stable—not just flash-in-the-plan technology. I think there are great opportunities to have fun, to have a good career, and to make good money in software. Again, just when people think things are mature, along comes the Apple AppStore and shows us that a few people in their garage can still make apps, make a lot of money, and get high profile. There are spaces that haven't been fully explored. Look at the social networking sites that have come up, like Facebook and MySpace, that were started by just a few people to have fun and make money. Those are the kind of jackpot things. There's no end of need for people in the software business, so there are plenty of opportunities for somebody who really has a passion for it.

CHAPTER 12

Time Management

"Hard work never killed anybody, but why take a chance?"
—Edgar Bergen (1903–1978)

If you read only one chapter in this book, this should probably be the one. Organizing your time at work means organizing what you produce and how you develop as a professional. No other skill will help propel your career forward as much as this because it's the skill that leads to all other skills. I've seen employees get fired or repositioned to the most hideously unpleasant positions because they had such poor time management skills that they found it impossible to be productive for more than three hours a day. Other high-performing employees get stalled in their careers at the "career journeyman" level (a position that has different titles in different companies, but what I will call "just short of a manager") because they fail to consistently spend time to extend their skills (sharpen the saw), a key dimension in time management. Conversely, virtually all high-ranking executive and technical leaders get to where they are by having some strong skills in time management, whether they achieve this through formal study or come by the talents intuitively.

Time management in the 1950s–1980s was dominated by the idea of task prioritization: efficiently organizing your tasks so you could rack, stack, and pack as much productivity into your day as possible. The 1990s rejected task prioritization in favor of goal-oriented time management. The theory was that if you could just organize your time around your larger goals, everything else would follow. Experts reasoned that anything that doesn't directly contribute to your goals is probably a waste of time, a distraction from what's truly important. At a macro level, it really does work (and that's why goal-directed career paths are so effective, as I discussed in the previous chapter).

The new millennium brought with it the sober realization that to truly manage your time effectively, you need a healthy and balanced dose of both strategies. That's because jobs aren't just about macro-level, large-scale activities. They include lots of itty, bitty responsibilities along the way.

Goal-Centric Time Management

Goal-centric time management begins with deliberately taking the time to understand your professional goals and then reflecting on what's required to achieve them. There's a beautiful little story that's been told myriad ways in myriad venues. The details change, but the essence stays the same. Here's my version:

> A professor walks into a room and places a large clear glass bowl on a table. He asks his students whether the bowl is empty or full. The students sense a trick question but generally agree that the bowl is empty. The professor then pulls out a large box of rocks and begins placing blocks in the bowl until there's absolutely no way to add anymore. He then asks the students whether the bowl is full. The students didn't get admitted to college for being completely dim, and they quickly point out that there's some space between the rocks. The professor pulls out a large sack of sand and pours sand into the bowl, which fills the crevices between the rocks. Then he takes out a pitcher of water and pours water into the bowls, until the bowl fills to the brim and overflows with water. He asks the students whether the bowl is full, and everyone now agrees that the bowl is truly full. The professor then asks his students, "Assuming that the bowl is a metaphor for time management, what was the purpose of my little demonstration?" A keen student, certain that he had the answer, replied "Even when you think there's no more time, if you're efficient, you can eke out a little more time to get things done." The professor shook his head in dismay. "Quite the opposite. The point is that if I had put the water and the sand into the bowl first, there never would have been room for the rocks. The rocks, the big items, represent the most important things that need doing."

The secret of goal-centric time management is fundamentally to understand your goals and the tasks you need to complete to achieve those goals. If you don't develop that clarity, little things, urgent things, will always fill your time at work and distract you from what's truly important. Many people develop this awareness deliberately, by producing a physical list of goals they want to achieve. After you've defined that list, you'll probably find that it's much too large and daunting for you to ever complete in full, so you'll have to prioritize the goals and protect the time for completing the tasks that lead to achieving your goals. In the official language of time management, these tasks that lead specifically to the achievement of longer-term goals are called *critical success factors,* or CSFs, for short.

For example, if you have a goal to establish a successful restaurant that's profitable within three years, you might have CSFs such as hiring a top chef, developing efficient kitchen protocol, and securing a high-traffic location. In a software group, a project manager might have a goal of delivering a software product successfully, and some CSFs might include staffing the team with talent and critical mass, instituting a development process, establishing a scalable build environment, developing a platform for automated regression testing, building a process to collect key performance measurements for the team so he can track progress, and so on. When you understand your goals and the CSFs associated with them, you can prioritize your time. The CSFs associated with the most critical goals, usually defined in annual and multi-year objectives, trump everything else on your calendar. Everything else that needs doing should get relegated to the small chunks of time that fit between the critical tasks.

The greatest leaders and most successful software engineers and architects are goal-oriented. For the lucky ones, it's a natural art built into their DNA. For the rest of us, goal setting and brutal prioritization is a learned behavior. Goal-centric time management is a magic potion of sorts that has transformed the way many individuals approach their work, but it has some failings. It gloriously succeeds in helping us filter the important from the incidental, but it sometimes fails to help us differentiate between the important and the also important. That's where good old-fashioned task-centric time management still plays a role.

Task-Centric Time Management

Task-centric time management is about understanding the set of tasks you need to complete over the course of days and weeks, and prioritizing them on a daily basis. In my interviews with Mark Russinovich and Marissa Mayer, you'll see that they both use task-centric time management heavily to help structure their day and their week. Task-centric time management helps people prioritize their days and their weeks, but it might not help organize longer-term objectives over the course of a career. That's why twenty-first-century time management has largely evolved into a blend of the two strategies.

Goal-centric time management is necessary at the macro level over months and years, to keep you focused on the critical success factors that are necessary to achieve your most important goals. Task-centric time management helps you get through your week. An obvious example where task-centric time management falls down is marriage. Finding the right person you want to settle down with is never an urgent task on any given week of the year, but for many people, it's a very important goal to achieve in their lives. If we guided our lives by task-centric time management, organizing our time exclusively by the things that are important over the next few days, almost nobody would ever carve out time to engage in serious relationships and pursue marriage. For many a harried executive and overly ambitious workaholic, this sad reality has played out to their ultimate disappointment. They find themselves in their 40s and 50s without having pursued serious relationships because it was never an immediate priority.

On the flip side, managing your time throughout the day is important, and that's where task-centric management helps. Listing the items that need doing and completing them in priority order is a tried-and-true method for getting things done. Prioritizing your work is an unnatural process, and it's not something most of us do on the fly. For example, senior executives often sit down with their administrative assistants each week or each day and organize their calendars to ensure that the important tasks are prioritized high. Check out the interviews with Mark Russinovitch, Diane Greene, and Marissa Mayer to see how they depend on this process.

Consider a final point related to task-centric time management and software development. Software development is complex and requires considerable chunks of concentrated time. Managers, project planners, and marketing types can schedule their time in 30-minute chunks because the work they do often requires a mental transition of just a few minutes. In terms of both software design and software coding, software development is a highly complex process that blurs the line between art and math. If you're like most people, the complexity of the process requires at least a 15- to 20-minute context switch to get your head back in the game. That means if you're switching tasks every 30 minutes, you're going to get almost nothing done throughout the day. Folks who work in software design and coding need to schedule their time very differently from others, allocating large multihour chunks for design and coding activities. You'll see similar comments to these in the interviews with Ray Tomlinson, Linus Torvalds, and Bjarne Stroustrup. When it comes to software design and programming, Stroustrup nailed it when he said, "Multitasking is not for serious work."

Circles of Influence and Concern

We all have a broad range of things we are concerned about at work, at home, and beyond. These topics of concern define the scope of our interest and our emotional focus, as well as where we spend our mental energy throughout the day. The domains of all the things you care about and think about is the Circle of Concern. However, within that scope are many things that we have little or no control over, even though we might be deeply concerned about them. For example most of us have very little control over the stock market, the economy, international affairs, whether people close to us will contract a serious illness, and who the current or next CEO of our company will be. Unless you are very senior in your company, you probably have little control over the corporation's business strategy or who gets hired in all parts of the organization.

Within each of our Circles of Concern is a subset called the Circle of Influence. This circle includes the areas that we can personally control or at least influence by our actions. The time we spend thinking and worrying about things that we can't influence or control is almost always negative energy—time spent worrying. Not only does it generate negative emotions, but because we can do nothing about these things, it's largely time wasted. One of the key strategies in personal effectiveness is to sensitize yourself to which things are really in your circle of influence and focus your time heavily there. The more time you spend applying your mental and emotional energy to things you can control, the more effective you will become—because you are applying yourself to things you can impact, and more time spent on things you can impact necessarily translates to higher impact.

However, another, more subtle dynamic is at play. Time spent outside your Circle of Influence is time spent on things that will usually generate negative emotions. In one extreme case, a senior architect at one of the world's leading software companies told me he no longer reads the news because virtually all of it is outside his Circle of Influence! Although I don't advocate disengaging from the world completely (staying abreast of world affairs and local news certainly has some merit), there's no question that the more each of us focuses on our Circle of Influence and avoids time in the Circle of Concern, the more we can reduce negative emotions that distract us. Figure 12.1 illustrates this point well.

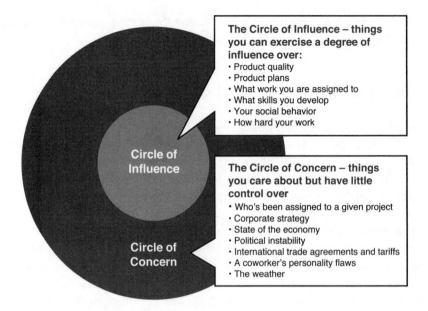

The Circle of Influence – things you can exercise a degree of influence over:
- Product quality
- Product plans
- What work you are assigned to
- What skills you develop
- Your social behavior
- How hard your work

The Circle of Concern – things you care about but have little control over
- Who's been assigned to a given project
- Corporate strategy
- State of the economy
- Political instability
- International trade agreements and tariffs
- A coworker's personality flaws
- The weather

Circle of Influence

Circle of Concern

FIGURE 12.1   Circles of Influence and Concern (From *The 7 Habits of Highly Effective People,* by Stephen R. Covey. New York: FreePress, 2004, reprinted with permission from Franklin Covey Co.)

One of the common missteps of new employees is their unbridled enthusiasm to effect change. New employees often join a large company such as Microsoft, IBM, Sun Microsystems, or Google full of energy, opinions, and an eagerness to change the world. Within a few months of joining the corporation, they've got a new proposal to entirely revamp the corporate business strategy, expand the company's use of open source, and invest in radical new artificial intelligence projects. Of course, they've set themselves up for failure because they don't yet have the business connections, corporate schlep, or process understanding to pull off a large-scale corporate makeover. In short, they're operating outside their Circle of Influence. By staying focused on what you can influence, you'll improve your use of time, increase your impact, and increase the amount of positive emotion you generate throughout the day. The net result is not just better use of time; through increased effectiveness you will also, over time, expand your circle of influence because the more effective you are, the more you can affect.

Indecision May or May Not Be Your Problem

Gen. George Patton Jr. was a leading American general in World War II, leading battalions in North Africa, Sicily, and the European Theater of Operations, and commander of the U.S. Third Army. He famously said, "A good plan executed today is better than a perfect plan executed at some indefinite point in the future."

General Patton's advice is good for software developers and project managers to take to heart. Software design is a very complex task. Software is as much art as science, and it's easy to get so bogged down in figuring out what to do that you spend more time deciding than you have time for—in many cases, the benefits of the better decision are far outweighed by the time delays. Many a software project has been delayed for six months or more to produce a benefit so small that the end user will never see or measure it. We call this paralysis by analysis.[1]

The larger the organization, the more senior people there are who might need to agree to a particular design or strategy decision. Many times, a truly perfect decision doesn't actually exist because the strategic decisions and design choices are both characterized by the trade-offs between simplicity and efficiency versus reliability, completeness, and sophistication. There may not be a right answer—just the right trade-off. Or at least a reasonable one. While engineering teams haggle over the pros and cons, the clock ticks away; it's easy for weeks to slip by. In the end, a highly developed software design or business strategy that took five months to refine might be only marginally (and perhaps not measurably) better than an alternative design the team came up within a day. Protracted designs are the bane of software engineering teams. They can massacre project development schedules and place the development team under impossible time constraints. There's an appropriate amount of time for every task in the software development cycle, and specification and design (including their reviews) should collectively account for about a third of the total software. Don't let tough decisions paralyze you into inaction. Set a timeline for decisions and stick to it, within reason.

---

[1] Sometimes also phrased "analysis paralysis."

Act with a Sense of Urgency

Consider this ancient African proverb:

> Every morning in Africa, a gazelle wakes up. It knows it must run
> faster than the fastest lion, or it will be killed. Every morning a lion
> wakes up. It knows it must outrun the slowest gazelle, or it will starve
> to death. It doesn't matter whether you are a lion or a gazelle: When
> the sun comes up, you'd better be running.

The greatest leaders in any organization are doers. As one executive told
me years ago, "It's hard to argue with people who get things done." What
makes someone a doer? Attacking all important problems with a sense of
urgency. Urgency is a collection of qualities, but I think the most important
are proactiveness and tenacity. Proactiveness is important because when you
perceive a problem or an opportunity as urgent, you don't delay in acting.
You don't wait for someone else, particularly your boss or your senior management team, to tell you it needs doing. The issue is at hand, and urgency
demands action. Tenacity is important because when you recognize that
something is truly important, you don't allow the normal roadblocks of life
to stand in your way.

Urgency = Proactiveness + Tenacity

The power of urgency is profound, and it can enable you to get twice as
much done in a day with far greater odds of success. People who act with a
sense of urgency are busier, more effective, and also more reliable. They make
far more effective use of their time. You can count on them because you know
they treat assignments as urgent, and they blast through obstacles and roadblocks as if their life depended on it. When Lou Gestner took the helm of IBM
in 1993, the company was flagging and inefficient, the stock had tumbled,
and one of the world's greatest technology companies was in serious trouble.
One of the company-wide principles Gerstner instituted and constantly
repeated to every IBM employee was for IBM employees to "act and think
with a sense of urgency in everything we do."

The personal quality of urgency can help turn run-of-the-mill employees
into leaders, and low producers into superstars, but it comes with professional
perils. First, people who develop the quality of acting with urgency also run
the risk that it will spills over and affect their impressions of others and their
life outside of work. They risk becoming deeply frustrated with everyone else

who doesn't–especially when they depend on those people for project deliverables. In any organization of significant size, some people will fail to act with a sense of urgency (or prefer not to), and it's unreasonable to expect otherwise. Second, people who act with a sense of urgency run the highest risk of becoming workaholics, taking work home, working the longest hours, and generally fouling up their work-life balance.

So the great challenge of acting with a sense of urgency is first to develop the quality and, second, to control it. If you can't do the latter, you're probably better off without the former. Urgency as a personality trait is a tricky balancing act. I have three pieces of advice. First, act with a sense of urgency but don't expect or demand that everyone around you do the same. Second, try to limit your sense of urgency to your work life. Being a considerate and polite bulldozer at work can be useful, but you might not want it to define all aspects of life. Finally, don't let urgency serve as an excuse to be a jerk. Acting with urgency is not an excuse to be rude to anyone. On the flip side, if you can master the art of acting with urgency while maintaining courtesy and sensitivity to the people around you, you will truly have become the master of your own domain.

How Much Time Wasting Is Reasonable?

Time wasting, which I define as spending time on anything not related to your job description, is a fact of life and a completely taboo topic. You will never find a human resources executive publicly state that time wasting is allowed at work. After all, we don't pay people to goof off...or do we?

Time wasting can be categorized into two types: socializing/networking and total goofing off. Socializing and networking represent a professional gray zone in corporate America today. On one hand, schmoozing over politics and sports might not appear to be job-related or contributing to the bottom line. On the flip side, we all realize that forming positive relationships and networking are a key part of professional life–even requirements for success. How many business deals have been closed on the golf course? How many technology acquisitions have been made because two techie buddies were chatting over lunch about a hot new company? Building your social network is not an optional side venture; it's a critical success factor in your long-term career that requires constant nurturing and fostering, especially with the folks you work with on a daily basis.

Work life has enough stress and conflict, and some effort on everyone's part to stay friends and get along is neighborly behavior at the office and also conducive to operational efficiency. You're probably thinking now, "Okay, I'll buy that—but there's no way you're going to convince me that goofing off is reasonable at the office." Believe it or not, even total goofing off is reasonable in moderation. By total goofing off, I mean activities like surfing the Web for the latest world news, checking your investment portfolio, calling a friend to say hello, or even taking some time to play a video game. The reason is simple: Software development and design is a mentally intensive operation that few people can do effectively in a nine- or ten-hour stretch. To keep the work efficient, the human mind needs mental breaks that allow the inventive and analytic processes to regroup.

Goofing off is good—it actually makes you efficient and productive. Obviously, there's a catch (or two). The first rule of thumb is that the total amount of time you spend in time-wasting activities (both in social networking and in total goofing off) should rarely exceed 75 minutes per day. Include in this sum any time you typically take for lunch or other breaks. The second point is that although time wasting is valuable in moderation, it looks really bad to all possible observers. It looks bad to your underlings, your peers, and your superiors. It looks bad even though everybody does some amount of it and everyone understands that some amount of it is needed and useful. The art of time wasting is, therefore, to constrain it in time to not more than 75 minutes per day and to ensure that it's a fairly invisible process to all around you.

The Scourge of Email

If you have a career goal to "make it big" in software, you probably are on track to have a career that is also packed with email. If one correlation holds true throughout the software industry, it's the one between email volume and career success. After all, email is just too easy to distribute, and everybody wants to keep the big shots in the loop. Why is that? Partly because it's the right thing to do, partly because people want to show off that they are taking care of business, and partly because it has become our industrial culture to behave that way. Because software teams are typically hierarchical, as in any tree structure, the higher up you are in the hierarchy, the more people below you think they need to communicate with you. In any significantly sized organization, senior people can expect to receive between 200 and 400 emails every day (by 2010 standards—who knows what the future will hold?).

Email is an emotional addiction, and many of us are addicts. We all probably need some therapy. As an industry and a society, we've advanced from desktop email; to laptop (portable) email that travels with us to meetings; and now to BlackBerry-based email that travels with us into our homes, bedrooms, and vacations. If you allow it to, hundreds of emails a day will dominate your time, work, and life. You will become nothing more than a glorified email server, and each year as you look back on your accomplishments, you will proudly reflect on little more than the sheer mass of email you have processed.

James Hamilton is one of the great visionaries and energetic personalities of the software industry. I met him when he was the Chief Architect of the DB2 development team at IBM in the mid-1990s. Hamilton went on to be a product architect in databases and then data centers at Microsoft before moving to Amazon as their Distinguished Engineer and Vice President of web application services in December 2008. In his February 22, 2008, blog entry, Hamilton shares some valuable thoughts on taming the email beast:[2]

> I get several hundred emails a day, some absolutely vital and needing prompt action, and some about the closest thing to corporate spam. I know I'm not alone. I've developed my own systems on managing the traffic load and, on different days, have varying degrees of success in sticking to my systems. In my view, it's important not to confuse "processing email" with what we actually get paid to do. Email is often the delivery vehicle for work needing to be done and work that has been done, but email isn't what we "do."
>
> We all need to find ways of coping with all the email while still getting real work done and having a shot at a life outside of work. My approach is fairly simple:
>
> Don't process email in real time or it'll become your job. When I'm super busy, I process email twice a day: early in the morning and again in the evening. When I'm less heavily booked, I'll try to process email in micro bursts rather than in real time. It's more efficient and allows more time to focus on other things.
>
> Shut off email arrival sounds and the "new mail" toast, or you'll end up with 100 interruptions an hour and get nothing done but email.
>
> I get up early and try to get my email down to under 10 each morning. I typically fail but get close. And I hold firm on that number once a week. Each weekend I do get down to less than 10 messages. If I enter the weekend with hundreds of email items, I get to work all weekend.

---

[2] Reprinted here with permission of the author.

This is a great motivator to not take a huge number of unprocessed email messages into the weekend.

Do everything you can to process a message fully in one touch. I work hard to process email once. As I work through it, I delete or respond to everything I can quickly. Those that really do require more work I divide into two groups: 1) Those I will do today or, at the very latest, by end of week, I flag with a priority and leave in my inbox for processing later in the day (many argue these should be moved to a separate folder, and they may be right). The longer-lived items go into my to-do list and I remove them from my inbox. Because I get my email down to under 10 each week and spend as much of my weekend as needed to do this, I'm VERY motivated to not have many emails hanging around waiting to be processed. Consequently, most email is handled up front as I see them and the big things are moved to the to-do list. Very few are prioritized for handling later in the day.

I chose not to use rules to auto-file email. Primarily I found that if I sent email directly to another folder, I almost never looked at it. So I let everything come into my inbox, and I deal with them very quickly—and, for the vast majority, they will only be touched once. If I really don't even want to see them once, I just don't subscribe or ask not to get them.

Set your draft folder to be your inbox. With email systems that use a separate folder for unsent mail, there is risk that you'll get a message 90% written and ready to be sent, get interrupted, and then forget to send it. I set my draft folder to be my inbox so I don't lose unsent email. Since my email is worked down to under 10 daily, I'll find it there for sure before end of day.

Don't bother with complicated folder hierarchies—they are time-consuming to manage. If you want to save something, save it in a single folder or simple folder hierarchy and let desktop search find it when you need it. Don't waste time filing in complex ways.

Finally, be realistic: If you can't process at the incoming rate, it'll just keep backing up indefinitely. If you aren't REALLY going to read it, then delete it or file it on the first touch. Filing it has some value, in that, should you start to care more in the future, you can find it via full text search and read it then.

One more point I'll add to this list: Avoid the urge to do email during meetings. Laptops and BlackBerries have made it possible to do email almost anywhere and anytime. While it may seem like an efficient use of time, doing email (obviously) distracts you from what brought you into the room in the first place: the meeting! All too often, hard-working people schedule meetings to present important updates or proposals, or to review and discuss key issues, while the audience is clearly heads down in their laptops doing email. The speaker is literally alone in a crowded room. Not only is this extremely rude, but from a business process model, if you consistently do email during meetings, you will effectively not be present in most of the meetings you attend. As a senior person in an organization (or one aspiring to be), your attention at meetings is, believe it or not, frequently required. The optics on this kind of behavior are also pretty bad. To build an image of yourself as a person who is informed, engaged, and engaging, keep yourself focused on the meeting, not on the email.

You can also find some great tips on managing the email tsunami in my interviews with Grady Booch, Diane Greene, and Linus Torvalds.

In this chapter, I discussed time management for each of us as individuals. Software projects are usually developed by teams of people working against tight financial and schedule constraints. In the next chapter, I discuss the macro aspects of time management as they relate to project teams and software overruns. If you've struggled with software project overruns, you're in good company. Most large software projects run late, but there are some secrets to minimizing the risks and dealing with the consequences.

An Interview with David Vaskevitch

Microsoft CTO (a.k.a. Mr. Big)

CURRENT POSITION

Chief Technical Officer, Microsoft Corp.

CLAIM TO FAME

Microsoft's architect for unified strategy and architecture of future platforms

DATE OF BIRTH

December 3, 1952

EDUCATION

M.Sc. in Computer Science, University of Toronto

B.Sc. in Math, Computer Science, and Philosophy, University of Toronto

FAVORITE PASTIMES & HOBBIES

Digital photography, competitive equestrian riding, time with family

BIOGRAPHY

David's career as visionary software architect, business innovator, and author spans more than 30 years. As Senior Vice President, Chief Technical Officer at Microsoft Corp., he works with Microsoft's Chief Software Architect Ray Ozzie to develop a focused and unified strategy and architecture for future Microsoft platforms.

Before this role David was Senior Vice President of the Business Applications Division, responsible for driving Microsoft's entry into the small and medium-size business software market through the creation of new software that changes the way businesses operate. As a central part of that strategy, he championed the acquisition of Great Plains Software, Inc., in December 2000.

David joined Microsoft in 1986 as its first director of U.S. marketing, and applied business planning and market research techniques to revamp distribution, sales, and broad-based channel marketing strategies. His four-year tenure in that position culminated in the launch of the popular Microsoft Windows 3.0 operating system and Microsoft Office products.

David went from U.S. marketing to propose and found Microsoft Consulting Services (MCS) to help enterprise customers transition their businesses to client/server computing. He served as chief technologist at MCS for two years.

In 1992 David became the General Manager of Enterprise Computing, undertaking the broad mission of defining an enterprise architecture and a 10-year road map for Microsoft and its enterprise partners. He built the teams that developed Microsoft SQL Server, Microsoft Transaction Services (MTS), AppCenter Server, and Microsoft .NET Platform and drove the evolution of Microsoft's COM+ and Windows DNA initiatives. He served as the chief architect for Microsoft from 1998 to 1999, while driving the definition and release of the first iteration of Windows DNA. He then moved to the helm of the new Microsoft Business Applications Division.

When digital photography emerged in the mid-1990s, David recognized that this was going to be a transformational technology for the computer industry. He then saw that his personal passion for photography had a direct connection to his work at Microsoft. He used his position to influence and further the digital imaging agenda at Microsoft, culminating in 2004 with the creation of the Rich Media Group (RMG). Under David's stewardship, RMG has grown to significant size and is starting to fulfill his vision.

Before joining Microsoft, David started up the software division of 3Com Corp., planning and building the business for EtherMail and other software products.

David began his career as a young entrepreneur, launching business planning and software ventures before the age of 30. The first, PlanDesign, was a Toronto-based strategic planning consultancy advising Canada's largest corporations on business processes and change management (later known as business process re-engineering). The second, Standard Software, was one of the earliest venture-capital-funded software companies in North America. David designed and marketed its TP monitoring product to Fortune 500 companies.

David is the author of *Client/Server Strategies: A Survival Guide for Corporate Re-engineers* (IDG Books Worldwide, 1993). The book explains client/server computing to general audiences, demystifying the technical, business, and cultural forces driving the distributed computing trend.

David Vaskevitch

While at the university in the 1970s, David invented a typewriter terminal-based communications messaging network that predated PC-based email systems by a decade.

"Quite often it finds you—you don't find it"

How did you get started in software?

I read a lot about computers in science fiction books, and I taught myself to program when I was about 13. I was programming on an IBM 1130 at the high school I went to.

Was there an event in your life that was pivotal in your career?

This IBM 1130 was a really big computer, but today we would think it was nothing. Physically, it was really large. It had a card reader and a printer. For the first year I used it, I fed cards into the card reader and things came out of the printer, and then I would change my program. On the main console, it had a keyboard and typewriter. One day I realized that I could write a program that would allow me to type things into the keyboard and type things out on the printer: I could speak directly to the computer. Today we take this for granted, but for me, this was a real eye-opener. That and all the science fiction I read spurred me to think about computers in a new way. Really, a lot of the things authors like Arthur Clark, Isaac Asimov, Ray Bradbury, and all the rest of the early science fiction writers were writing in the 1950s and '60s, computers still can't do today.

What suggestions do you have for others on being successful in software (either R&D or business)?

Do something you're excited about. Try lots of different things. There isn't any straight-forward answer to that. Quite often it finds you—you don't find it.

"It's a complicated question"

You have an M.Sc. in computer science from University of Toronto. Do you think graduate degrees are valuable in the software industry?

In our discipline, I don't think an advanced degree is directly useful. It's a complicated question. But you know, a lot of the benefit of university education comes from learning to think, along with the reading you get to do and the time you get to explore yourself and the world and people around you. Certainly, one of the main things I gained from my thesis was learning how to write really well. My Masters advisor was a really good editor!

How do you stay on top of technology trends and innovation?

I do a lot of reading, I talk to people a lot, and I try to use a lot of the technology. These all provide different values. Reading gives you first a lot of breadth; then it gets you breadth in selected topics you don't have more opportunity to drill into yourself. A lot of other topics, like understanding digital photography, or understanding how an electronic reader works, or understanding the power of the Internet ... if you don't experience those things directly, no amount of reading is going to help you know what they are about. In speaking with people, you get to ask questions; it's way more interactive. It takes you down unexpected directions because it's not entirely self-directed.

Do you have a pet peeve in any aspect of the software world?

It's still too hard to write code!

Technical leaders and executives are famous for being time-strapped. What strategies do you use to stay sane and use your time effectively?

I'm pretty careful about prioritizing what I work on, and I surround myself with good people. Those are the two primary strategies.

How do you achieve a work-life balance? How do you keep your professional life from dominating everything?

I just made a very conscious decision about 15 years ago that I was going to do both and compartmentalize so the two didn't interfere with each other. And that's one of the reasons I'm still working! It's not a fixed model. There are days I'll work 18 hours, and then lots of days I'm on vacation and I'll work zero hours; some days I don't work very much because I need to do other things.

What do you see as the coming changes in the software field over the next 10–15 years that will impact either career opportunities or the way we develop software?

I think computers are going to continue to be used in more different ways, so there will be more different areas for opportunities... Somebody could be at a car company writing software or be in the entertainment business writing

David Vaskevitch

software. That wasn't true in the past. I think there will be a lot more diversity. And I think in some ways there will be fewer opportunities to write core software like operating systems. In many ways software development will move up a level, and a lot of it will be expressing our intent to the computer, as opposed to writing programs in a low-level language. I think you'll see that change coming in the next five years.

"You need to be happy to be successful, not successful to be happy"

What makes you feel successful about your work in software?

I'd say there are two things: seeing things I have designed, or influenced the design of, being used in the world and working with great people and being able to create something together that is more interesting than what either of us could have come up with alone.

What final words of wisdom or caution do you have for people entering the field?

Same advice that I gave earlier in terms of thinking about a job: If you are entering the field, find something that you really love doing and get excited about doing so that you almost feel as if you should be paying them to come to work. I think you need to be happy to be successful, not successful to be happy.

CHAPTER 13

Avoiding Software Development Overruns

"Hofstadter's Law: It always takes longer than you expect, even when you take into account Hofstadter's Law."
—Douglas Hofstadter, from Gödel, Escher, Bach: An Eternal Golden Braid

Few things will damage a software developer's career more than consistently being late with what he or she is asked to produce. It's not just that completing work late fosters an image of the developer being tardy or underproductive. Most software projects are designed and implemented by teams of people. When a single programmer is late, there's a massive ripple effect on the entire team and a cascading effect that can propagate to marketing and sales and, ultimately, customers. The financial impact can be serious. In this chapter, I discuss the reasons software projects are so often late and explore what teams can do to prevent it.

Don't Be Moe

Let's rejoin our heroes, Larry, Moe and Curly, at SuperDuperTech Inc. In this scenario, Larry is the Director of Engineering, and Moe is a hot young programmer still waiting for a big break to show what he can do. His big break materializes in the next version of SuperDuperTech's leading product when his pointy-haired boss, Larry, asks him to lead the design and development of the product's most important new feature. The project, codenamed Gazoo, will introduce a dramatic new compression algorithm as a plug-in to MySQL databases. This story is fictional, but if you change the names of the characters, the dates, and the features, I guarantee this scenario has played out thousands of times in software projects around the world over the past decade:

September 6	Moe, anxious to show his stuff, tells Larry he can develop the compression features single-handedly in six months. The executives like what they hear and plan a February beta program and a May 15 product launch.
October 20	Moe's prototyping is going well. Initial results look promising using "toy data." But Moe feels his implementation is not "real" enough to draw conclusions, and his test data is too small and "well behaved."
November 25	Moe reports that the prototype code is nearly complete and working well. No more than two weeks are required. He's a week or so behind schedule, but given Moe's amazing results so far, management agrees to the two additional weeks because, they say, "We want to do this right."
December 17	Work begins to slow as the holidays approach: office parties, email jokes, people leaving on vacation. Good times.
January 11	Back at work, Moe realizes he is running significantly late with his work. The prototype, while impressive, needs a rewrite to make it a real product. It's the opportunity of his career so far, and he doesn't want to mess it up; he's more than willing to go the extra mile to make sure this project is a success.
January 27	Desperate to finish the code sometime close to the target, Moe locks himself inside his cubicle and focuses on Gazoo 14 hours a day. He's too busy coding to document the specification and design or to perform formal unit testing.
	[Dozens of empty Coke cans pile up on Moe's desk, and the single luxury he allows himself during the day is a ten-minute break to organize these into new geometric structures and fractal replicas.]
February 20	Moe admits that the Gazoo project is running a bit late. A week or two. The code isn't going to be ready for a Beta release in February. Larry has been around the block a few times and immediately translates "a week or two" into "months." Moe is in trouble; he hasn't shaved, has barely slept in eight weeks, and shows clear signs of exhaustion.
	An executive decision is made to cut two other features from the product plan so Curly can join Moe full-time to salvage the Gazoo feature. With Curly working for him Moe is now a "team leader" and feels that his hard work has earned him an indirect promotion of sorts.
March 17	Moe's productivity has dropped to a half of its former level, as he has spent much of his time over the past month mentoring Curly.

April 24	The rushed pace and the lack of design documentation and reviews has resulted in the late discovery of a design problem that requires 25% of the code to be entirely redesigned.
May 20	The feature is nearly functionally complete, and the six-week testing cycle can finally begin. Due to the rushed pace of the development, defects are being found at more than twice the normal rate. The code is "buggy."
July 15	Defect arrival rates have slowed only slightly. The engineering team is buoyed by this happy news and has renewed confidence in their ability to finish the test cycle shortly.
August 5	Larry agrees to ship the product for open beta trials. Since they are now almost six months late, there's an urgent need for market visibility. Marketing is certain that the IT magazines, bloggers, and consultants will go gaga for Gazoo.
September 17	Early results from beta show that the Gazoo feature is buggy and hasn't fully addressed customer requirements. A short causal analysis review finds that the problem would have been caught in advance had there been the normal functional specification review for Gazoo. Unfortunately, Moe delayed authoring the specification document, preferring to focus his initial energy on "prototyping," and was just too damned busy to return to it.
October 31	The product eventually ships to market fully seven months late, without strong confidence in product reliability or its value.

Moe's Perception

I am the senior technical leader on the project, a high-profile leader well-known to executives and the entire software engineering team. As "team leader," I led a small team including Curly and myself, to deliver one of the most important and complex features of the product. I'm also the most productive and dedicated person in the company, for only I have developed the master skill of working nonstop for 14 hours a day on core product development. My superiors love me and will soon reward me.

Executive Perception

Larry is a failed project manager. We need to put him somewhere where he can't pretend to know the art of software development. Moe is an idiot and a menace. He developed a buggy feature that failed to meet customer needs. Thanks to him, we shipped the product seven months late, costing us half a year of revenue. Curly had to bail out the incompetent goof, causing other important features to be cut from the product. Moe not only flubbed his own work, but he disrupted the entire engineering team. Moe has single-handedly ruined us. If it was legal to shoot him, we probably would.

Curly's Perception

Moe's a jerk. I had to bail him out, and my projects get canned as a result. I was forced to work on Moe's chaotic mess that was poorly documented, poorly scheduled, and based on his incomprehensible spaghetti-code prototype. As for Larry, there's plenty more blame to go around. When he saw that Moe was clearly running late, why didn't he intervene and enforce some software engineering process and required monitoring? Moe may be a jerk, but Larry is just plain incompetent.

Conclusion

Moe will probably survive the experience, but it will take both Moe and his manager several years and a necessary string of subsequent successes to outgrow the stigma of this debacle. This will set Moe's career back at least three years. He may even need to switch companies. Larry has lost credibility with his employees, and his ineptness in handling the Gazoo project will be very public, with ripple effects across the broader staff. It could be a long time before he's trusted to manage a development team with an important mission. As Director of Engineering, he probably had several projects running. How badly Larry is affected depends on what other project successes he has that can compensate.

How Common Are Software Project Overruns?

The Standish Group has been studying this for over a decade, with striking results. Figure 13-1 shows the Standish data between 1994 and 2004. The group's 2004 data showed that the average IT project overran its schedule by 84%, and only about a third delivered within 20% of the planned scheduled release date. The trends are improving, but as an industry, we remain far from predictable in cost and schedule estimations. The impact is dramatic because the study data also shows that schedule overruns are highly correlated with cost overruns. If it takes a group twice as long to deliver a project, the total project will also cost about twice as much. The reason is simple: In the software business, people are the dominating costs. The cost of the tools, servers, and development computers are all small next to the personnel costs of salaries and benefits. Capital costs for servers, computers, and software are often amortized over years, further reducing the burden. People, however, are paid based on the calendar. The longer they work on a project, the more paychecks they receive that are associated with that work (instead of moving on to the next big thing).

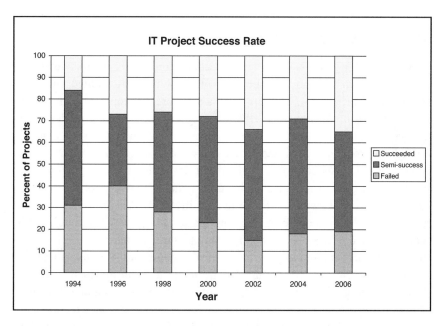

Figure 13.1   Average IT project schedule overrun

With more than $450 billion spent each year in North America on software development, the cost of schedule overruns is staggering. These overruns have potentially serious human consequences in the form of project failures, layoffs, and bankruptcies. From an industry viewpoint, the primary issues with schedule and cost overruns are the opportunity cost incurred by the loss in market mindshare, cash flow (delivering late to market means the product will start generating money later), and reduced competitive advantage (you're giving your competitors time to catch up). Schedule overruns are an epidemic of sorts in the software world. Few things are more common, and few things can have such a detrimental impact on your career, as being the person responsible for a major project overrun. Whatever you do, don't be Moe!

Why Software Project Overrun Occurs

Software is essentially all about people—their talent, their motivation, and the processes they use to develop and deliver software products. Following are the top 11 major causes of software development schedule overrun and what to do about them. As you'll see, most of them have people factors at their source.

#1: Scope Creep Happens

Order a door for your closet, and it begs a lot of questions. A solid wood door or a hollow one? A flat door or one with moldings? A painted door or a stained and varnished one? Even when a software development team understands the requirements of a software project clearly, levels of detail can always be added. This leads to a phenomenon in which features are continuously being extended to provide more completeness and robustness. It's easy to convince yourself that the product will be at risk without plugging one more use case or dealing with one more scalability issue. As the function expands, the development effort for specification, design, code, and test grows with it and schedules get compromised. This is known throughout the industry as scope creep, or creeping featurism (and sometimes "feeping creaturism"). It's not enough to ensure that the development team understands the functional requirements for what they're building; team members also need to understand the boundary of what's sufficient, or "good enough for now." Many organizations do a reasonably good job of defining what's required, but a poor job of articulating what's good enough. As a result, software developers worry unnecessarily about use cases of minimal (or nonexistent) importance, leading to scope creep and blown schedules.

#2: People Aren't Interchangeable

Human performance is hard to model because of the large performance variance between teams and between individuals. In their 1968 *CACM* paper[1] Sackman, Erikson, and Grant studied productivity differences between programmers and between programming environments and reported a difference in the productivity of high- and low-performing programmers as high as 28

---

[1] H. Sackman, W. J. Erikson, E. E. Grant, "Exploratory Experimental Studies Comparing Online and Offline Programming Performance," *Communications of the ACM (CACM)* 11, no. 1 (January 1968): 3–11.

times. A later study by Barry Boehm in 1975[2] reported a difference closer to 5 times. It doesn't really matter whether the difference is 5 times or 28 times— the difference is huge. Everyone who has managed a software development team has seen this in action. Top programmers produce several times what the weaker ones do. Add to this the fact that people skilled in a technology area (a programmer who has been working on existing code modules for a decade ... yes, such people do exist) can design and code to it much faster than people who are learning the domain and the existing code base, and you end up with a huge productivity variation. Modeling effort in person-months is misleading because it all depends on who's doing the work, how good they are, and how well they know the space. It's also why, if you want to be a star project manager, the no. 1 thing you can do to succeed is to hire the best and brightest. It's not just about productivity; the best and brightest produce better designs and more profound innovations. When you add up the benefits of productivity, innovation, and superior quality I believe 5 great programmers are better than 50 average ones (not just 50 weak ones). Costs vary as the product of your employees and the number of months they work, but project progress is far less linear.

#3: Adding Manpower to a Late Software Project Makes It Later

When projects are behind schedule, an obvious strategy is to try adding either people from other parts of the organization or brand-new staff to help buttress the effort. In theory, with more people, the work should get done sooner. Frederick Brooks famously managed the development of the System 360 operating system. The project ran late and over budget. Brooks studied the causes for the project overruns and authored his seminal book *The Mythical Man Month,* which became one of the most famous software engineering books of the past 30 years. Counterintuitively, Brooks found that exactly the opposite had occurred in the OS/360 project: Adding people had added person-months of capacity, but it hadn't necessarily added talent or productivity. Just look at what happened to poor Moe when Curly was added to his project. Moe's productivity was slashed as he began spending all his time training Curly. Instead of accelerating progress, Curly just sucked time away from Moe. The initial effect of adding people to a project is a steep increase in transaction costs as new personnel develop skills and make demands on existing staff. In the case of large, complex software projects, that overhead

---

[2] B. Boehm, *The High Cost of Software: Practical Strategies for Developing Large Software Systems* (Reading, MA, Addison-Wesley, 1975).

can last for months. As Brooks said, "It is a very humbling experience to make a multimillion-dollar mistake, but it is also very memorable." The idea that adding people to a software project can make it later was profoundly unexpected, and it's known today simply as Brooks's Law. It wasn't all bad news for Brooks. He was awarded the 1999 ACM Turing Award for his contributions to "computer architecture, operating systems, and software engineering."

#4: Goals Aren't Clear to the Development Team

A lot of "broken telephone" happens from the time a requirement comes as a suggestion from the marketing team, as a direct request from customers, or as a recommendation from executives until a programmer starts working on it. In larger companies, this happens so frequently that these companies institute formal requirements-tracking systems and detailed plan reviews to keep the engineering team clear about what's really needed. Conversely, in smaller companies, the CEO may be on a first-name basis with every employee, and the apparent intimacy of communication can lead to a false sense of expected clarity. Everybody thinks they know exactly what's needed, so reviews, tracking systems, and checks and balances are dispensed with. When the goals aren't clear, the engineering team will likely set down a course of building something that is useful but doesn't exactly satisfy requirements. If the company is lucky, the misunderstanding will be caught in time to make some course corrections, and the only negative result will be delays while the design is adjusted. If they're unlucky, the feature will be delivered to market, and they'll find out the hard way (from disgruntled customers and analysts) that they've missed the mark. Strive for clarity in requirements and delivery dates early in the development cycle. Just making sure that the engineering team unambiguously understands both of these will go a long way.

One more point: Keeping the engineering team clear about what they need to do isn't quite enough. They need to believe in it—they need to know "why." That means explaining to them the business context, what the competitors are doing, and why the timing is what it is. Consider this insight from James Hamilton, Vice President and Distinguished Engineer with Amazon.com:

> I've seen projects where the leadership falls down in not communicating the reasoning behind schedules, the target audience for the software product, how this product fits into the companies' overall business strategy, motivating everyone to know exactly what the competitors are doing, and sharing the business model for the product and how it works. As a consequence some decisions and some schedules have low credibility with the engineering team and, as a

consequence, the team isn't real motivated to find a way to make it happen on time (which translates to, within a small factor, making it happen within budget).

Once the engineering team clearly understands what they need to do, by when, and why, you're in much better position for them to deliver a successful project. Agile techniques combined with aggressive beta programs can help immensely in driving continuous definition and feedback to the development team.

#5: Dependency Management: Feature Estimates Can't Be Summed

When software projects are planned, the total effort for a software release is usually assumed to be the sum of the effort for the individual projects in the release. Software features normally need to touch common components. The more the development of multiple new features overlaps on common components, the more programmers will be tripping over each other's code and, more important, over each other's design assumptions. I call this Lightstone's Convolution Principle:

> The concurrent development of multiple features operating on intersecting componentry will take longer to complete than the sum of the schedule estimations for each.

Okay, when you think about it, it's obvious. But the reality is that nobody seems to give this much thought when they're planning software projects. The usual practice is to size up each line item independently and then add up the estimates for each to determine the total effort of the project plan. By identifying the line items that have co-dependent code sections, you can identify the areas that will need an additional wedge of time for completion and get a much better estimate of the project effort.

#6: Bad Estimates Come In (Watch the Ratio!)

Software developers are notoriously poor judges on how long things will take. Brooks found that the following rule of thumb allocates time for software development with reasonable accuracy: 1/3 specification and design, 1/6 programming, 1/4 function and integration testing, and 1/4 system test. Over the past 30 years those ratios have held true. However, in most cases, few project schedules allocate the required 50% for testing. Over the past 10 years, our industry has finally come to terms with the reality that testing is half the effort of a software development cycle, and that's probably the biggest reason project success rates have been improving. We still have major problems on the front end, and these are the areas that most significantly damage individual careers. For a wide range of emotional reasons, software developers refuse to believe that coding represents only 1/6 of the software development cycle. They refuse to believe this because software programming is fun, and it's what they want to spend their time on. It's just too depressing to believe that the very thing they jump out of bed excited to do, the very thing they planned to spend their professional careers on, represents so little of what they will actually be doing.

Software programmers also like to believe that programming is relatively hard (which it is) and that other tasks, such as testing and writing, are comparatively easy (highly questionable). So when you ask developers how long a piece of work will take, they are thinking predominantly about the coding effort. However, you need an estimate for the total effort, including specification, design, and testing. One tactic to avoid these issues is to never let a programmer estimate anything other than the coding effort. The ratios are well-known and hold true across a wide range of projects. If you can get a reasonable estimate on the coding effort from the engineering team, you can extrapolate easily to determine the time for design, specification and testing.

Design and spec	= 2 × coding estimate
Function and integration test	= 1.5 × coding estimate
System test	= 1.5 × coding estimate

These guidelines are simplistic, and, of course, well-known exceptions exist. Features that add performance value (speed) but otherwise leave externals unchanged require performance quality assurance but functionally may require little testing beyond regression testing (to ensure that what used to work still works). Dependencies between features under development always add delays as teams spend more time collaborating to understand a broader set of requirements. Although I don't recommend applying these guidelines naïvely to all projects, they make a good starting point for most. Then you can revise the estimates for the outliers as a (sometimes major) refinement.

#7: Aggressive Estimates Come In

Aggressive estimates are a little different from bad estimates. Aggressive estimates make development costs appear small during the planning phases and make development teams appear superhumanly efficient. When bidding for a project to get formally accepted into the official plans, justifying a project to senior executives or requesting initial project investment, management teams and programmers tend to provide aggressive estimates so the price tag looks as appealing as possible. Every project has uncertainty, and every project estimate is really a range (for example, this project will take between 6 and 12 months). Aggressive estimates aren't really lies or inaccuracies; they are simply the far end of optimistic. Savvy project managers and executives see these aggressive estimates coming from a mile away and implicitly assume some cost expansion over what they're told. But to an inexperienced eye—perhaps someone new to the domain—it's easy to be fooled. Once committed, the team is on the hook to deliver the project on an impossible timeline, and the project is on a collision course for an overrun before it even starts.

#8: The "I'm Not the Critical Path" Problem Arises

In 1999, I was Release Manager for the delivery of DB2 version 7. It was a large-scale development project with more than 200 software developers across three different development sites. I learned a lot about the software release cycle in that job, but even more about software developers and how they manage their time. One very surprising observation for me was the social dynamics of schedule overrun. I found that a significant number of programmers were running late only because they thought others were running late. As long as a software developer didn't believed he or she was the reason for the entire project missing the deadline, that developer was comfortable running late, adding small features that weren't in the original project plan, or doing work more slowly and carefully than normal.

Not only was it taking more time for everyone to finish their work, but people weren't coming free to lend a hand where needed. Every programmer was comfortable using the "extra time" for the betterment of their own work. Provided that they were on track to finish their work at least two weeks ahead of the slowest teams, they all felt they'd be so completely inconspicuous that nobody in senior management would worry about their lateness. After all, they weren't the so-called *critical path*. Adding to the hemorrhage, these developers evolved a group-think that led them to believe that the slowest line item in the product release was actually the typical line item in the release. The failed reasoning went something like this:

1. The worst laggard of the line items under development is running eight weeks late.

2. Rumor begins that the entire product release is eight weeks late.

3. Development team group-think translates the rumor to "Most line items are running eight weeks late."

4. Individual programmers and testers begin to believe that if they personally are not eight weeks late, then they are way ahead of the average, with time to spare for refinements.

Parkinson's Law says that work expands to fill the time allotted for its completion, but my own observation is this:

In software development, the average feature expands to the date of the feature with the latest greatest slippage.

My solution to this was to casually and politely remind developers that most of the line items were not running as late as the slowest one, and their lateness was actually quite conspicuous (which it was, to me). DB2 version 7 was the first release of DB2 to deliver its beta release one day ahead of schedule—and I firmly believe that the psychological management of the staff in understanding the deadlines and their personal position on the product development timeline went a long way in contributing to that result.

#9: Someone Decided to Throw Software Engineering out the Door

"Process? We don't need no stinking process." Just look at how that mentality helped Larry, Moe, and Curly. Software development processes are needed, and there are many to choose from (agile development, rapid prototyping, waterfall process, and more). I talk more about them in Chapter 15, "Secret Insights on Software Project Management," but if you're trying to get things done faster and leaner by getting rid of process and its red tape, you're in for a nasty surprise. It's critical to have a process that clarifies and verifies the requirements and objectives the development team is charged with fulfilling. Whether it happens through a formal specification process or an agile process that involves constant customer feedback, this step is crucial. Designs are important, so you need to do them. Nobody is perfect, so you need reviews for design, specifications, code, and test plans. Software is buggy; come to terms with it, and make sure you're doing well-planned and rigorous code reviews and testing. The people writing your code might not be around forever, so you'd better be sure other mere mortals can understand the code they write. If it's all spaghetti code, you'll be completely dependent on the few original authors and you won't easily be able to scale the team in the future. If you bypass the fundamentals of software engineering, the result will be longer development cycles and much lower quality and usability. Things will seem to take off quickly at the front end, but you'll pay for it later in the cycle, in extended testing (which takes much longer when there are more bugs) and when you go to market (with lots more bugs and poorly considered usability and internal design).

#10: You Forget to Count the Other Stuff Employees Do

Every software developer spends time on the job doing bona fide work that has nothing to do with programming the latest project deliverable. There are meetings to attend about project status, or a special lunch for a colleague going on maternity leave, or a pep talk from a visiting executive, and so on. And, of course, there's vacation time to factor in as well. Staff may get sick or quit. Servers may crash. A bug in a compiler or another important development tool can broadly impact the engineering team. For a wide range of reasons, people will be consumed with tasks and distractions beyond the sum of the work of the initial project estimate. Careful planning up front will minimize some of these risks, but not all of them. A reactive manager looks at each of these as a surprise, but experienced managers acknowledge at the outset that some of these issues will crop up and build some buffer into their product plans to mitigate the risks. You name it, there's a lot of stuff people spend time on that takes time away from project deliverables. The percentage of your time spent on work outside the initial project definition tends to rise with your seniority, but software developers and testers in most companies spend about 25% of their week on matters others than the design, development, and testing of their next product release. Management teams that forget to model this are 25% behind schedule on the day they start.

#11: Winds Change

Even if you're doing everything right, things can go awry: Requirements get clarified, prompting changes; market shifts (such as a new competitive threat) cause a scope change; you're proceeding with a dependency on another team (or vendor) that flounders; a change in executive leadership leads to reprioritizing the effort. These bends in the road happen all the time and are impossible to predict. Some companies, such as Apple, have managed to plan large-scale and successful—even visionary—projects with remarkable repeatability. Their secret sauce remains a mystery to most, and the overwhelming consensus in the industry is that large-scale "big bang" projects in which the engineering team starts out on a vision planning to deliver a masterpiece two years later usually represent unreasonable risk.

The fact of the matter is that large-scale engineering projects take years, and in an industry where literally everything can change in a two-year period, it's hard to make those kinds of bets pay off consistently. Instead, modern companies have adopted the mantra of "Ship early, ship often." The idea, related in style to agile development, is to get an initial version of products out early, building embryonic traction, garnering invaluable feedback and requirements, and mitigating risk. Shipping early with lower function costs less and gives you a chance to test the waters. Google mastered this with its Google Labs products, providing early versions of products to market where they can assess their quality, global interest, and potential for monetization. Shipping often, such as on a six-month of even four-month cycle, gives the engineering team a constant feeling of accomplishment and momentum. When strategic changes occur, the team may have only a few weeks or months of labor at risk. Shipping early and often is a win–win strategy. Not all products can be developed this way, but a large proportion of teams are adopting this approach whenever possible.

We're Late—Now What?

When a project runs late the most important thing to do is to take a deep breath and remember this is normal. This is a complex area that often involves tradeoffs between delivering value, jockeying for political position, maintaining commitments to other teams, and doing what you think is technically the right thing for the long term. You'll still need to deal with the problem, and, fortunately, the options are pretty limited. Here's a summary of the basics, and then we'll see how Larry, Moe, and Curly can leverage these methods to get Gazoo out of the gutter.

1. **Cut function.** Most software products are a collection of several features (or solutions). Different people work on the different components, so to salvage an important feature under development that's running late, you can cut other features and divert the developers who were working on those features to the more critical item. We saw how well that worked for Moe and Curly when Curly's features were cut in an attempt to salvage Moe's. It didn't help Moe much, and Curly got a raw deal. Cutting function is an act of desperation; if you have to do it, do it early. If they join early enough, the new staff will be part of the evolution of design ideas rather than a skills drain. The closer to completion the features are, the harder it will be to cut them, both emotionally and financially.

2. **Split function.** Splitting function means that you continue development on every planned feature while decommitting a subset of them from your next release. Work on the decommitted features continues, but with a new release date. In the hope of minimizing the opportunity cost of the decommitted features getting to market late, you can also opt to "prep the market" with early glimpses of the coming technology rather than completed products. For example, instead of delivering the fully functional feature on the original expected date, you can deliver an unsupported beta version.

3. **Renegotiate the dates.** Renegotiate the schedule and budget for the project. In many cases, this may be possible without compromising the project goals. Huge risks come in delaying projects, including scope creep (developers perceive that they have more time and begin adding "useful" extensions to the features and function), opportunity cost in the market, increased development cost of the release, and so on. All that said, delaying a project to get it done right is often a better choice than delivering garbage to market on time. Every technical leader knows it, but the pressure on business leaders to deliver on the originally planned calendar dates can be immense. Hopefully, the tension between business needs for urgent delivery and technical wisdom is a healthy one. There's never a perfect answer—just the healthy effort to find a wise tradeoff.

Let's see how some of these ideas could have helped Larry, Moe, and Curly avoid their Gazoo grief.

September 6   Moe, anxious to "show his stuff," tells Larry he can develop the compression features single-handedly in six months. The executives like what they hear and plan a February beta program and a May 15 product launch. Larry asks to see a project plan for review next week.

September 13   *Bad estimates:* Larry and Moe sit down to review the work, and Larry notices immediately that Moe hasn't budgeted much time for design, specification, or reviews. In addition, he sees that Moe plans to go straight from prototype to code completion in a few weeks, which suggests he's planning to reuse the prototype code in the product. Larry points out the issues and Moe agrees that Gazoo will be a two-person project. He's happy as long as he can lead it.

               Cut functions: Curly is assigned to the project—and she's delighted to be working on Gazoo. She hadn't been assigned anything else yet, so there aren't any hard feelings.

November 25	No one decided to throw software engineering out the door. During the design review, Curly points out that Moe's design for compressing structured data types is excellent but won't extend well to binary objects. With an increasing volume of data coming from unstructured sources, such as video and image data, it's critical to augment the design.
December 17	Work begins to slow as the holidays approach: office parties, email jokes, people leaving on vacation. Good times.
January 11	*Split function:* Larry has been monitoring the team's progress regularly. To get a beta out in February, he meets with Moe and Curly, and they agree to focus on English-language characters and image data. Other character sets and binary data are deemed less important for beta.
January 27	Moe and Curly finish the prototype and will spend the next few weeks readying for a beta launch in February.
	[Moe notices that he hasn't collected many Coke cans on his desk this year, but he pays it little mind.]
February 20	The beta ships, and the team begins to focus on production engineering of the code.
March 22	*Changing winds:* Beta feedback highlights 79% of users require Unicode and 15% require image support. The Unicode requirement is a big surprise. The team had assumed that because MySQL 3.*x* and MySQL 4.0.*x* don't support Unicode, few MySQL users would need it. Apparently, they were wrong. JPEG images are already compressed, so the overwhelming requirement for image data is to compress BMP data.
	Split function: Larry, Moe, and Curly meet and decide to defer all the binary object requirements except for BMP compression to a future product release and refocus all the engineering effort on Unicode support.
April 9	*Renegotiated dates:* Given the new pressures on Unicode, the team agrees that moving the product ship date from May 15 to July 15 is worth it.
May 20	Moe is finishing code and is adding trace and other diagnostics; Curly has function verification testing well underway. A second beta is launched.
July 15	SuperDuperTech delivers its SuperDuperCompression plug-in for MySQL (formerly codenamed Gazoo). Analysts are amazed that they knew exactly how to prioritize the delivery.

Final Thoughts on Software Development Overruns

When you look at the list of 11 causes in this chapter, you'll see that over-runs are dominated by people factors. Your ability to hire the right people is linked to your company's capability to avoid overruns. You want top people to work for you, and if you are a winner, the top people will want to work for you. Talented people generally prefer to work for a winning and profitable company that delivers on time. Talented people like to work on winning projects that make money, contribute to a company's overall bottom line, meet real customer requirements, and give them an opportunity to innovate and learn. Software developers like to work for managers and executives who "get it," who know how to succeed in the industry, understand what is easy and what is hard, and can make good engineering decisions. By being a winning company, or at least a winning project manager, you can attract the best and brightest. In doing so, you dramatically increase your odds of continued success and eliminating overruns.

I share further thoughts on management leadership in Chapters 15 and 16, but I didn't want to leave this discussion on overruns without mentioning it. Leadership and *esprit de corps* are critical factors in the capability of project teams to complete tasks without overrun. Leaders inspire, focus, and motivate teams to achieve goals and avoid overruns. Leaders help build the can-do, proactive, cooperative *esprit de corps* that distinguishes successful project teams. Motivated teams staffed with talented people, with a clear vision of goals and priorities, are always far better positioned to deliver on time. Junior (and sometimes not-so-junior) programmers often wonder what's so important about leadership. Let's not forget that these folks will make the most important decision of all: the decision to hire *you*. As Bill Gates once said, "Be nice to nerds. Chances are, you'll end up working for one."

Avoiding software development overruns is hard to do. If it were easy, the statistics on late software projects wouldn't be so glum. Still, some teams have managed to get quite good at delivering on time and on budget, through careful management, adaptation, and implementation of the ideas in this chapter. Every day around the world, dedicated professionals work long and hard to ensure their projects deliver on time and on quality, sacrificing their personal time for the good of the team. All work and no play makes Jack a dull boy and can lead to a serious long-term personal lack of fulfillment. In the next chapter, I talk about the necessity of work-life balance and how to achieve it.

An Interview with Grady Booch

The Sage of Software Architecture

CURRENT POSITION

IBM Fellow and Chief Scientist for Software Engineering, IBM Research

CLAIMS TO FAME

One of the founders of the Unified Modeling Language (UML), a thought leader in object-oriented design, and one of the original developers of Rational's product suite

DATE OF BIRTH

February 27, 1955

EDUCATION

B.Sc., United States Air Force Academy, 1977

M.Sc. in Electrical Engineering, University of California at Santa Barbara, 1979

FAVORITE PASTIMES & HOBBIES

Reading, traveling, kayaking, singing, playing the Celtic harp

BIOGRAPHY

Grady is recognized internationally for his innovative work on software architecture, collaborative development environments, and software engineering. A renowned visionary, he has devoted his life's work to improving the art and science of software development. Grady served as Chief Scientist of Rational Software Corporation since its founding in 1981 and through its acquisition by IBM in 2003. He now is part of the IBM Thomas J. Watson Research Center, where he serves as Chief Scientist for Software Engineering. There he continues his work on the *Handbook of Software Architecture* but also mentors and leads various software engineering projects that are beyond the constraints of immediate product horizons. Grady continues to engage with real customers working on very real problems and is working to build deep relationships with academia and other research organizations around the world. Grady is one of the original authors of the Unified Modeling Language (UML) and is also one of the original developers of several of Rational's products. Grady has served as architect and architectural mentor for numerous complex software-intensive systems around the world in just about every domain imaginable.

Grady is the author of six best-selling books, including the *Unified Modeling Language Users Guide* (Addison-Wesley Professional, 2005) and the seminal *Object-Oriented Analysis and Design with Applications* (3rd edition, Addison-Wesley Professional, 2007). He writes a regular column on architecture for *IEEE Software*. Grady has published several hundred articles on software engineering, including papers published in the early 1980s that originated the term and practice of object-oriented design (OOD), plus papers published in the early 2000s that originated the term and practice of collaborative development environments (CDE).

"I dreamed of making a difference"

How did you get started in software?

In 1967, at the age of 12, I dreamed of making a difference in the field of computer science. I went off to the local IBM office, literally knocked on their door, and said, "I will do anything for the summer—empty trash cans, you name it." They said, "Go away kid." But there was a sales guy who took pity upon me and threw me a nice Fortran IV [IBM Mathematical Formula Translating System] manual, with the expectation that I'd probably read it and get bored and never come back. But much to his surprise, I came back the following Monday and said, "Hey, this is cool! I just wrote a program and I want to run it." The sales guy was so impressed that he found me an open computer to work on where I could teach myself how to keypunch, program, and debug for what I still recall as a delightful summer. I have to admit that perhaps I took every 12-year-old boy's dream of building robots a little to the geeky extreme.

Another thing that inspired me was an article that was published in *Life Magazine* that same year, about a robot named Shakey that was being created at SRI[1] in conjunction with some work that Marvin Minsky[2] was doing. Shakey was one of the first goal-oriented robots. It was called Shakey because it took forever to navigate its room, and when it moved about, it shook quite a bit. That work introduced me to the really cool things you could do with computers. To wrap this story back around, when I was working with the Computer History Museum a few years ago, convincing them to become a museum of software as well as hardware, I was walking around with then-CEO John Toole and told him this story. He said, "Look in the box behind you"—and it was the original Shakey. That was pretty exciting to see.

What do you consider your greatest accomplishments or contributions to software?

Probably I would put that in the area of four things that I have contributed to. One is probably the general concepts behind object-oriented analysis and design. Some of the earliest papers that I wrote were on that topic, and I coined that term. So just bringing people from structured analysis and design to object-oriented analysis and design is one of my claims to fame. Working with Jim Rumbaugh to produce UML was the second. The third is my contributions in the area of software architecture, just working on the issues of how one represents architecture, architectural process, architectural transformation, and archeological digs. The fourth are my contributions in the area of collaboration. In a paper that Allan Brown and I wrote in 2003, we coined the term *collaborative development environment,* discussing the evolution of the development environment. Where I'm working a lot these days is ringing virtual worlds together with software development.

Tell me how you hooked up with Paul Levy and Mike Devlin in the foundational days of Rational Software, which grew to an $850 million company with 4,000 employees, with you as its chief scientist.

My first assignment as a fledgling lieutenant was at Vandenberg Air Force Base in central California. My early computing experience made it possible for me be one of the youngest project managers for a number of technological defense acquisitions. Toward the end of my assignment, I caught wind of the work Academy classmates Paul Levy and Mike Devlin were doing with a new programming language to be used for satellite control. It ended up being a perfect opportunity to collaborate. When I returned to the United States Air Force Academy, I was directed to find out how this new language, which would eventually comprise Ada, could be used for software engineering. This was a program that was intended to be quite important for the DoD at large, and I found myself teaching less and less and spending more time on travel assignments to a variety of projects around the world, helping them figure out their processes and methods for using Ada. Shortly after that, just when

I was deciding whether to make a career in the Air Force, I got a call from Paul and Mike saying they'd caught the "entrepreneurial bug" and wanted me to join them in a startup company. That's the story of how Rational Software was formed in 1982.

What makes you feel successful about your work in software?

Two things. The first is that I'm simply having a whole lot of fun. I enjoy solving hard problems that haven't been solved. I also enjoy seeking simplicity and elegance in the things I do. And I enjoy being a rainmaker—getting people with like-minded interests together and creating something bigger than the individuals involved. That makes me feel good because I'm contributing and I'm enjoying the process. The second is seeing where so many people have used my work in so many ways and in so many projects around the world. It's very satisfying to see so many organizations actually applying these ideas and being successful with them.

"There are different ways of thinking about things"

How do you stay on top of technology trends and innovation?

I'm a voracious reader. I subscribe to about a dozen refereed technical journals and probably as many trade journals, and I read those on a weekly basis. I also stay in touch with a variety of web sites; Slashdot.org, in particular, is a good source of information for me. I also read a lot of books in domains outside of where I'm normally in, like physics, chemistry, and engineering, as well as domains within software itself.

How do you see knowledge in these other domains helping you as a software engineer?

I see two ways. One is that there are different ways of thinking about things in these engineering domains, especially the engineering disciplines with true hard science behind them; those ways of thinking help me attack hard problems in the software space. Second is that this increases my knowledge of what can be automated. As we push the limits of software systems, many of these domains outside of the software space equally don't get out much and don't understand what's outside their domain [and how software can help] so there are some opportunities for cross-fertilization that I think are possible.

Grady Booch

Do you have a pet peeve in any aspect of the software world?

Probably what bothers me the most is a lack of recognition of what's gone on in the past. We seem to always be worried about the latest shiny thing, yet there are some fundamentals that that people and organizations tend to ignore as they push forward to the next greatest thing. So I think not building upon accomplishments from the past annoys me the most. Look at many of the existing languages today—you've got the classical languages of C++ and Java, and you've got the scripting languages of PHP and Perl. In many ways, the things that are in these languages look a lot like what was in Ada. In fact, Java and C++ are morphing more and more to the features that Ada itself had in terms of generics and exception and tasking handling. The way people design with these systems today, we tend to hack away with these little scripting kinds of things and often ignore the problem of architecture. As you get bigger things, people often don't think about the problems of that legacy architecture as they start building. Another aspect is that, in a number of cases in the software space, the U.S. Patent office has issued patents for software that has clear prior art.[3] While I respect what IBM is doing in this space, in many cases, software patents are not well understood or well managed by international patenting organizations because they often fail to appreciate the prior art.

"I don't sleep"

Technical leaders and executives are famous for being time-strapped. What strategies do you use to stay sane and use your time effectively?

I don't sleep. It is the case that I don't need much sleep. I need only five to six hours of sleep a day, and it does help. I don't use SameTime or instant messaging much because it's just another way to be interrupted. I intentionally stay off email for periods of time during the day because it's just too much of a drug to draw me to it. And I intentionally delete lots of email. I will respond to every meaningful email sent to me, but I tend to purge my email down close to nothing. As I look at my email now, I've got three email messages in it because I purged it over the weekend. Keeping control of my email is an important element. So is educating the people who want to connect with me, to say, "If you want to reach me, do so in this way." I've also rented an office outside of my home office so that a couple of days per week, I can pretty much unplug myself from the Internet so I can work on the handbook I'm working on.

How do you achieve a work-life balance? How do you keep your professional life from dominating everything?

That's a great question, and I'm not sure I have any great answers to that one, other than that because I am enjoying what I'm doing, I don't draw a line between my work and my personal life. But it's not that I just work–more than anything, I have a following, a passion, that defines what I do in the software space. That's very much a part of me, yet I also value very much the people I love in my life, so I have a rich life outside that. It's a matter of honoring that and making time choices about it. Last year I was asked to speak at the keynote of the Rational User Conference, and I said no because it was my 30th anniversary. Saying no is an important thing to do. It's a matter of setting priorities.

There are many things I love to do and get involved in. At the moment, I'm a Chief Scientist, a Fellow, a software architect, a project manager, a programmer, and a researcher. I'm also a mentor, lecturer, consultant, software archeologist, theorist, methodologist, developer, pragmatist, pioneer, mediator, historian, and visionary. In my working career, I've been a mower of lawns, a scooper of ice cream, and a singer of songs. By an act of Congress, I was once even an officer and a gentleman. I'm a good friend and confidant, a godfather, and a loving husband. I listen well and play well with others. More abstractly, I'm a child at heart, a warrior, a servant, a leader, a dreamer, a lover, a believer, a philosopher, and, most of all, an awe-struck seeker. In short, I believe in living a life of "ands," a life that is defined not by what I do at the moment, but rather by living fully in the moment. I will be the first to admit that I'm most imperfect when it comes to being fully present in every moment or living fully in integrity with my values, but such are the consequence of being fully human.

"We are moving quickly to the day where there is unlimited storage, unlimited bandwidth, and unlimited computational cycles"

What do you see as the coming changes in the software field over the next 10–15 years that will impact career opportunities either positively or negatively?

It's much easier to predict the past than it is the future. If we look over the history of software engineering, it has been one of growing levels of abstraction–and, thus, it's reasonable to presume that the future will entail rising levels of abstraction as well. We already see this with the advent of domain-specific frameworks and patterns. As for languages, I don't see any new, interesting languages on the horizon that will achieve the penetration that any one of many contemporary languages has. I held high hopes for aspect-oriented programming, but that domain seems to have reached a plateau. There is tremendous need to for better languages to support massive concurrency, but therein I don't see any new, potentially dominant languages forthcoming. Rather, the action seems to be in the area of patterns (which raise the level of abstraction).

Software developing has been, is, and will remain fundamentally hard. Mashup architectures, fueled by AJAX and SOA in the enterprise domain, are taking root, but these are less fundamental and more pragmatically expeditious than anything.

I want to add something I said at the Rational User Conference. We are moving quickly to the day where there is unlimited storage, unlimited bandwidth, and unlimited computational cycles. On the storage side, we can put about 200MB per square inch on magnetic media. With things like racetrack memory, we can probably have better than two orders of magnitude improvement over that, and the cost declines. On the computational side, as we move toward multicore systems, having today's supercomputer capabilities on our desktop or in our hand is very possible. And in terms of bandwidth, as we see the move toward even gigabyte rates across copper (and though this will be in various bumpiness around the world), it means that we can be connected in a very high-bandwidth way. That leads to some very interesting questions of what kinds of applications we might see in that case and how one can make any money where there is such abundance. In storage, if we can store everything, meaning nothing in our life is ever forgotten, what does that have to do with privacy issues? If we have multicore systems, we have really limited ways we know of in software to deal with that intimate concurrency. And on the bandwidth side, this creates new opportunities for security attacks on our data and on our networks if bandwidth and openness is so pervasive around the world. So there is an upside and a downside to any future we might consider. Yet, that being said, no matter how bold a vision we can imagine, it's still going to require software that is yet unwritten—which is why I think this field is such an exciting one to be in.

What suggestions do you have for others on being successful in software (either R&D or business)?

First, don't be afraid to fail. Don't be afraid to speak truth to power. It takes a while to get the confidence to do so, but ultimately, you'll win in the end. Second, read and get out of your box more. Many people get so tied up in the particular domain they're in that they forget to put their heads up and look around them. Those two are the biggest suggestions I'd offer to folks.

What final words of wisdom or caution do you have for people entering the field?

Even though what we're doing is deeply technical stuff, there are ethical, moral implications about what we do. And it's not just in our sciences—look at the struggles the physicists of the 1940s and 1950s had in dealing with their ability to unlock the secrets of the universe. As software developers, we collectively and literally change the world. Being a software developer is both a privilege and a responsibility. In this field, there are so many places to grow and contribute. Learn by studying the work of others; follow your passion. Most of all, be sure you have fun in the process. I can't think of any other industry that has impacted every other business in the way that we as humans and civilizations connect. What a cool business to be in. It is a privilege to be a software developer because we have done things that have changed the way individuals work, organizations run, and civilizations collaborate with one another. It's an incredible privilege to be able to be in a place where you are able to do that. At the same time, it's an amazing responsibility because we do change the world. What other industry can we imagine that you can change the world?

Notes

1 SRI International is an independent, nonprofit research institute in operation since 1946. According to SRI, Shakey was the first mobile robot to reason about its actions. Shakey was developed by SRI's Artificial Intelligence Center from 1966 through 1972. [Source: www.sri.com]

2 Marvin Minsky is Toshiba Professor of Media Arts and Sciences and Professor of Electrical Engineering and Computer Science, at the Massachusetts Institute of Technology. He is generally considered the father of artificial intelligence, having made a prolific impact on that field. He was winner of the 1970 ACM Turing Award, the 1990 Japan Prize, and the 1995 IEEE Computer Society Computer Pioneer Award, among many other distinctions. I recommend a review of his biography at http://web.media.mit.edu/~minsky/minskybiog.html.

3 The term "prior art" is commonly used in patent law to refer to information (about technology and inventions) that were previously made public. When a patent application is submitted to a patent office, it is evaluated for its novelty by comparing it against prior art. Only truly innovative inventions not described in the prior art should be granted patent status.

Grady Booch

CHAPTER 14

Zen and the Critical Art of Balance

"Most of the time I don't have much fun.
The rest of the time I don't have any fun at all."
—*Woody Allen (1935–)*

Careers span decades, so you should really make sure you're doing something you enjoy. Fortunately for us, software is a fun. Of course, no matter how much fun you're having at work, some degree of work-life balance absolutely is required. As the old saying goes, "How many people on their deathbed wish they'd spent more time at work?" The grand challenge for many of us is that the years we most want to spend time with our families and enjoy life outside of work are also the same career-building foundational years—in our 20s, 30s, and 40s. The split between work and life is a very personal one, but as personal as it is, I'll go out on a limb and make three statements that I think are generally true for most of us:

1. Left to its own devices, work in software development has the power to consume all of my time. If I don't want to allow myself to be consumed by my work, then it's important to make a personal decision about how I want to split my time between work and personal interests.

2. I am not defined by my work. Work is what I do, but it's not who I am. I don't want my tombstone to read "Software Guy." My work is part of who I am—perhaps a large part—but it doesn't define me as a human being.

3. While I'm at work, I work harder, do more, and feel better about myself when the work I'm doing is enjoyable and important to me.

Work-life balance is really about two balancing points. First, you have a balance between the fun and not-so-fun work you do professionally. It's critical that your time at work have the right balance of good old-fashioned elbow grease and hard work on one hand, and fun-filled excitement that really makes you happy to be there on the other. Second, you have a balance between work and the rest of life that allows you to carve off time for your family, friends, community, and nonprofessional interests. In this chapter, I offer some insights on honing both these balancing points. Unfortunately, there's no silver bullet—finding the right balance is hard. Very hard.

Work-Life Balance

No matter how much fun you're having at work, if you're like the majority of people, you won't be really happy unless you achieve a balance between your professional life and your life goals outside work. None of us should be defined entirely by our professional life. If you are defined exclusively by your work, then your role as a parent, spouse, lover, sibling, hobbyist, or community member means nothing. First and foremost, work-life balance requires that you define for yourself who you want to be to your family, in your spiritual life, in your hobbies and interests, and, of course, in your professional life as well. It's all about beginning with the end in mind: If you know who you want to be, you can work backward to achieve that vision and the balance it requires. Your emotions are your most sensitive barometer. If you find yourself frustrated by an inability to get to things that are important to you, that's a signal that your work-life balance might be out of whack.

What then? Repartition your time to allocate more of it to what's missing. The trick to the repartitioning process is that it needs to be sustainable. When push comes to shove, any of us can adjust our time temporarily, for a day or a week, to do things differently. If it's just for a day or a week, it's little more than fleeting shadow play. The time you make available for the luxury of fitting in an extra fitness session, taking in a movie, or spending more time with your family gets just as quickly counterbalanced the next week when the work you didn't get to as a result of the fun stuff reaches a boiling point in subsequent weeks. Temporarily fitting things in is a desperate measure, and it's not sustainable. To make a qualitative change in your work-life balance, you need to repartition you time in a sustainable way, and that's very hard to do. Almost all the senior software personalities we interviewed for this book confessed it's a struggle for them. Some of them required major life trauma to force them to take life outside of work more seriously. Consider these tricks:

- ▶ Don't assume you can use your time more efficiently or get less sleep.

- ▶ Making more time for yourself usually means having less time for work. Concentrate on how you will adjust work pressures to constrain your professional work hours to a limit you can live with. (for example, 48 hours instead of 60).

- ▶ Increase delegation to others, if you can. If you are in a leadership position (either as a technical leader or in a managerial role), keep in mind that delegating to others is a huge part of what you should be doing anyway and a way to help grow the next generation of leaders.

- ▶ Expand the time allotted to long-running tasks. No need to get everything done all at once.

- ▶ Process information in bulk. Bulk processing is generally more efficient for computers and for human beings alike. For example, do email in blocks two or three times a day instead of checking every few minutes.

- ▶ Block meetings in chunks instead of randomly throughout the week.

- ▶ Scale back your responsibilities. It's better to do fewer things exceptionally well than to commit and fail to conquer a vast range of responsibilities. You might think that scaling back will hurt your career, but the excellence it will allow you to achieve will propel you forward.

- ▶ Examine which of your work tasks and responsibilities have little impact on your career success or job satisfaction, and purge them. Use goal-centric time management to eliminate the waste.

Organizational Culture Affects Balance

Companies have personalities, just as people do. Software companies are particularly sensitive to the cultural barometer because software has so little to it aside from people and because software development has evolved out of a culture of bohemian startups and basement buddy innovators where innovation and solid code trump corporate formality. Software companies take liberties with corporate culture that other professions won't or can't. Another, more subtle balance problem comes from hating your work, and that's where corporate culture may be playing a dominant role. Some people are so miserable at work that very little outside their life can compensate. If you're in that situation, it might feel like you've gone down the wrong career path, but the root of the problem might have more to do with the culture of your organization than your profession. Some companies are notorious for creating highly competitive cultures that thrive on intensity. Microsoft is one extreme, where it's all about the career advancement and competition. Google is at the other extreme: Career advancement is important, but the company has gone to great lengths to create a grad school feeling to the work environment. Work environment is an important aspect of corporate culture. Some companies expect their employees to work in cubicles and behave professionally for a solid eight-hour day. Other companies provide an open-concept work environment and encourage software developers to have the occasional Nerf gun battle (or other similar distractions) in the hallways, provided they clock a solid 10 to 12 hours a day. Nerf gun wars aren't for everyone, and neither are cubicles. If there's a significant mismatch, it commonly manifests as grief outside of work, disrupting our energy for other life interests. Trying to compensate for the mismatch, some people will spend two to four hours a day unwinding and recouping their emotional balance before they feel ready to get on with their nonwork (life) agenda. If you experience a serious cultural mismatch, you might improve your career and your work-life balance by finding a different kind of company to work for. Conversely, many people are largely unenthusiastic about their work duties but so enjoy the social relationships they have at the office and corporate culture they work in, that their enjoyment of the cultural dynamics dominates their experience.

Life Impacts Work

If you're happy and contented in your personal life, you'll be able to focus and be more productive while you're working. Nothing impacts productivity more seriously than pieces of anxiety rattling around our heads throughout the day. That's why you can often tell when people are going through some kind of tragedy or upheaval in their lives long before they tell you, simply by noticing a marked reduction in their work contribution. It's hard to focus 8–10 hours a day on software if you're going through a divorce or dealing with treatment for a life-threatening illness. Those are extreme examples to highlight the point, but the effect happens in increments with smaller pressures, too. Some examples of top stressors that negatively impact our ability to focus are the death of a spouse, divorce or separation, death of a close family member, personal injury or illness, marriage, health problems of a close family member, pregnancy or birth, a move (to a new home), sex difficulties, and fitness concerns. Many of these aren't issues you have control over. And although several in the list are downright negative, some, such as marriage, the birth of a child, or a move to a new home, are wonderful life-cycle events to pursue and cherish. Even the good stuff causes stress and distraction because it's so overwhelming; it consumes most of us in both time and mental focus. A fair body of literature suggests that taking certain steps can counterbalance stress. The most commonly cited activities include physical exercise, yoga, meditation, and music (particularly playing rather than listening).

Patterns, Possibilities, and Defining Yourself

If you're feeling overworked (or underlifed), you might have good reason. The statistics are sobering—just look at the current state of affairs in the United States:

Of an estimated 304 million Americans, 115 million are in school, and 87.9 million are retired. That leaves 101.1 million people available for the work force. Breaking this down by sector, 51.2 million Americans work for some level of federal, state, or municipal government, and an additional 32.8 million are stay-at-home spouses. That leaves 17.1 million people available for the nongovernment workforce. At the current unemployment rates, 11.4 million people are out of work, and 2.9 million are working in some level of national security, leaving a remaining workforce of 2.8 million. However, 2.7 million are in jail, and there are 99,998 people in the hospital on any average day. That leaves only two people remaining in the workforce—you and me. And you're reading a book!

Work-life balance is a very personal thing, so the answer is different for everyone. That means you can't just copy someone else's recipe for successfully balancing work life and home life. I know many people for whom work is simply a means to retrieve a paycheck, and they're more than delighted to spend as little time at the office as possible. That might not be a winning strategy for career achievement, but it's a perfectly valid approach to life, and for some folks, it's the ideal approach. Other people love their work so much that they really have little interest in much else, and as long as they're happy, who are we to tell them otherwise? Most of us fall somewhere in between. How do you know if your work-life balance is out of whack? You won't generally be able to answer that question by looking at your current state. Too many business and family pressures and emotional issues are brought to bear making an honest assessment of the *now* muddied and unreliable. Instead, to figure out your own answer, I recommend working backward. Ignore how things are today and simply explore your own vision of how you want things to be. Figure 14.1 shows a simplified version of how to leverage the idea.

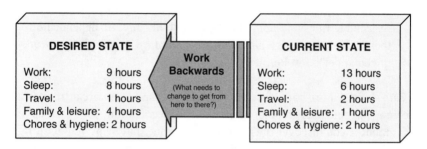

FIGURE 14.1 Working backward from a desired state

Keep that vision realistic, not fantastical, and then work backward from that ideal state to help define where you want the balance to be. With the balance defined, you can continuously evaluate and adapt your life in an attempt to achieve true balance. Most people find it effective to work backward through a process of time-boxing, by allocating an approximate amount of time every day for different kinds of activities. It takes rigor and discipline to stick to the time-boxing, but it's needed because work-life balance is a zero-sum game: Wherever you take extra time for an activity, you necessarily give away time somewhere else. Sleep and family time almost always lose out. High-profile professionals have the highest risk for working themselves into serious health issues, marital disintegration, and disenfranchisement from their children. Microsoft CTO David Vaskevitch and *Programming Pearls* author Jon Bentley shared some powerful observations with me:

> I just made a very conscious decision about 15 years ago that I was going to do both and compartmentalize so the two didn't interfere with each other. And that's one of the reasons I'm still working!
> —David Vaskevitch

> Set inviolable rules (the easy part) and then don't violate them (always much harder). In the mid-1990s, I was simultaneously involved in

rushing a product to market and being the full-time single dad of a middle-school son. I made a point to take my son to school every morning, to pick him up most afternoons, and to have dinner with him and lots of other "quality time" every evening. At the slight expense of my pulling all-nighters on a weekly-or-more basis, everything worked out okay: We shipped the product without delay, it won national recognition, and my kid turned out okay (except, of course, for becoming a software engineer). A few months after the product was shipped, my company cancelled it, and a few years later, I had a heart attack at age 46. Since then, I've been willing to draw much more reasonable rules and abide by them, well, like my life depended on them. Think very, very hard about the word *life* in the phrase "work-life balance!"–Jon Bentley

Careers do require hard work and enthusiasm, and those are attributes that encourage people to spend more time at the office. Finding your own balance is hard, but if you discover the Philosopher's Stone that helps you get it right, you'll have done the best possible service to your career and your life. No other tactic or vice will serve you better. With only one life to lead, it's definitely worth the effort.

An Interview with Tom Malloy

Adobe Chief Software Architect

CURRENT POSITION

Senior Vice President and Chief Software Architect, Advanced Technology Labs, Adobe Systems, Inc.

CLAIM TO FAME

During his 22 years at Adobe, Tom has developed or led the development of breakthrough Adobe publishing, graphic design, and digital imaging technologies, including Adobe Type Manager, multibyte type technology, font substitution technology and multiple master fonts, the first version of Adobe Illustrator for Windows (he subsequently led the Illustrator engineering team), and the design and prototype of the security system for Acrobat that underlies its digital signature and document security features.

DATE OF BIRTH

July 23, 1952

EDUCATION

M.S.c. in Computer Science, Stanford University, 1976–1978

B.S.c. in Mathematical Sciences, Stanford University, 1970–1974

FAVORITE PASTIMES & HOBBIES

Hiking, swimming, spending time with his family, and building a new house (once in a lifetime, hopefully)

BIOGRAPHY

As Senior Vice President and Chief Software Architect, Tom leads Adobe's Advanced Technology Labs. Spearheading Adobe's long-term research and development initiatives, he leads a team of computer scientists who are delivering the next generations of Adobe software innovation.

Tom Malloy

Tom plays a key role in defining Adobe's technology strategy, as well as overseeing multiple R&D focus areas, including Adobe's Visual Computing Lab, Creative Technology Lab, Systems Technology Lab, and Document and Applications Technology Lab. His organization also takes a leading role in incubating new products, championing industry standards, and facilitating collaboration with universities.

Before joining Adobe in 1986, Tom worked for Apple Computer, where he helped drive software development for the Lisa computer, the precursor to the Macintosh. Tom began his technology career at Xerox Palo Alto Research Center (PARC), where he was the lead engineer of the Bravo document processing system for the Alto computer.

Tom sits on the board of Aklara, an electronic auction firm, and is a member of ACM and IEEE. He holds three patents, as well as bachelor's and master's degrees in computer science from Stanford University.

"Most of my accomplishments are really team accomplishments"

How did you get started in software?

I learned to program in Fortran on an IBM 360 at a National Science Foundation summer program for high school students in 1969. There was no undergraduate program in computer science when I attended Stanford, but I took quite a few CS classes as a Math Science major. My big "break" came when Charles Simonyi hired me at PARC with only a B.S. degree. It was a lucky break for me. The other career option I was considering at the time was to become an actuary. While that may have involved some fun math, I think it would have made for a much duller career than being at ground zero for the beginning of the personal computer revolution.

What do you consider your greatest accomplishment or contribution to software?

Most of my accomplishments are really team accomplishments, both teams I led and teams I was a member of. This is true of the Bravo project at Xerox, where I was considered the lead programmer but where Charles Simonyi provided overall leadership. It is also true of the Adobe Type Manager project. There were a number of fun things about that project. As a team, we solved a hard problem: rasterizing scalable type to the screen. We did it very rapidly: 6 months from concept to shipping product. We dropped the solution into existing Mac and Windows systems; it involved finding the "choke points" in the system for font handling and injecting our rasterizer into that system in the field.

More recently, my personal contributions have been exclusively of a management nature. I am most proud of the model of advanced technology development and research we have established at Adobe. So far, we have managed to balance the need to be relevant to corporate priorities while having enough freedom to produce cutting-edge results.

I am also proud of a few personal projects. About 10 years ago, I personally prototyped the digital signature and document security features of Acrobat. And, finally, way back in my youth at Xerox, I personally built a suite of developer tools for the Mesa language, code-named DeSoto. The result was ahead of its time. It had the rudiments of a version control system, a make system, and a recompilation optimizer for high performance. That last component was considered particularly innovative at the time (1978).

"Don't be afraid to back out of career 'cul-de-sacs'"

Leaders have to take risks and make tough decisions. Was there a risk-taking decision in your career that had broad impact? How did you make your decision?

File it under "Don't be afraid to back out of career 'cul-de-sacs.'" Back in the mid-1990s, I was a director of the typeface group at Adobe. I had broad management responsibility for three areas: type engineering, type design, and type production. Type technology was a hot area from the mid-'80s to mid-'90s, but the really interesting technological innovation was on the wane. Typeface technology is over 500 years old, but there have only been a small handful of periods of disruptive innovation during that half-millennium. I was fortunate to participate in one of those periods: the period of scalable, digital, hinted outline fonts. But by the mid-'90s, my estimation was that we were moving back toward the 500-year status quo—namely, a business driven by design and production, not technology. The production and design stuff was important and valuable, but not my area of expertise. I wasn't as passionate about it, either. I decided to give up my management responsibility and join the Advanced Technology Group as an individual contributor. It was a risky career move. I went from being a senior manager to an individual contributor. I did some of my best work in the next few years, including the Acrobat digital signature and secure document technology I mentioned earlier. From that work came the opportunity to lead the Advanced Technology

Tom Malloy

Group (now Labs). It was not directly related to my Acrobat work, but without that success, I am not sure John Warnock, Adobe's founder and then-CEO, would have made me the offer. I followed my passion and was rewarded in the end in a conventional career sense. In my opinion, that is the kind of risk worth taking.

What makes you feel successful/accomplished about your work in software?

I have always derived the most satisfaction from seeing my work and that of my team in the hands of customers, making them more productive and creative. There are ancillary gratifications—contributing to the success of a company, solving hard technical problems—but having an impact on users is in a category of its own.

What does your role as chief software architect mean both in daily practice and to you personally?

I think it's not nearly as interesting a place to probe as you might think. It's a nice title to have, but in terms of the impact I have on Adobe, and whomever else I have impact on, you really have to go to the heart of what my job is: leading the Advanced Technology labs, which is our research group. I could do that with the title I have, which is Chief Software Architect, and I could do that with any number of other titles, including a more traditional title like Director of the Labs, but that wouldn't change what I do on a day-to-day basis. My responsibility is to husband and champion computer science advanced technology and research at Adobe, and create innovative technologies that we then transfer into our products and, with luck, have an impact on our businesses.

I don't believe someone at my level can really have the deep understanding of all the different technical areas that are being explored within organizations. And if there are such people in the world, I am not one of them. Because of my background, there are areas that I still consider myself relatively well informed on, but my job is much more about finding the right people with the right skills and giving them the right environment and the right context to explore science and technology problems that are liable to have an impact on Adobe's business. So selecting the people and creating the environment for them to explore is critical to my job. I do provide focus, especially in the case of more junior people, but for more seasoned team members, I exercise a "bubble up" philosophy of project selection and personnel management. By that, I mean that we create context about what's happening in the field, in the community, and in Adobe, From there, the expectation is that the researcher will internalize that context and then envision and execute projects that are liable to be relevant to Adobe. So it's not a very directed process at all.

"Hire people who are smarter than you"

How do you stay on top of technology trends and innovation?

This is a favorite question to ask CTOs or other senior technology executives. The simple answer is, "You don't." There is just too much to know to stay on top of everything relevant to a diverse enterprise like Adobe. For that, you need to rely on the talent and insight of the people who work for you. Hire people who are smarter than you. They will guide you to the next trend, breakthrough, or disruption.

Having said that, I still enjoy reading about technology. I try to read all the papers that are published by my team, even if I don't understand them in detail. I usually have one or two fairly technical books on the go. Right now, I am reading a book on multiple view geometry, the mathematical underpinnings of some fascinating computer vision techniques. Next up on my reading list is a book on wireless sensor networks. I want to see what has changed in network architecture and protocols since I implemented Ethernet and TCP/IP protocols back in the 1970s and '80s.

You have a master's degree from Stanford. Do you think graduate degrees are professionally valuable? Do you see them as a substantial benefit to a candidate when recruiting?

They're very useful but not absolutely essential. Don't forget, when I went to Stanford, there was no undergraduate degree in computer science. Getting a master's degree really rounded out my education. On the other hand, I learned as much, if not more, at the feet of the masters themselves at Xerox PARC as I did from my graduate classes. I also received unexpected benefits from my graduate education that really would not become apparent for years after I graduated. For instance, it was in a graduate seminar that I quite serendipitously came across Diffie and Hellman's seminal early work in public key cryptography. That was in the late 1970s. In the mid-'90s, I invented digital signatures and secure documents for Acrobat based on public key technology. Were it not for that chance encounter in the seminar, I don't think I would have had the context to pursue that interesting path.

Tom Malloy

"I am not a harried executive"

Time management ... technical leaders and executives are famous for being time-strapped. What strategies do you use to stay sane and use your time effectively?

I know only three ways to manage time:

1. Prioritize

2. Delegate

3. Work harder

I'm going to challenge you on your very brief answer because I'm sure there's more to it than that. It sounds like you have it all nailed up!

Quite the contrary! If you look at the three things I listed, learning how to prioritize and learning how to delegate are two skills that are not at all obvious. Most people aren't born with those talents. They are not absolutely essential to individual contributors, but they become so as you get wider and deeper areas of responsibility and as you move into a management track or a leadership track of some other kind. It is succinct, but I think those words are pretty well defined. I really do think those are the key.

I am actually pretty successful at it. I judge that by the amount of free time I have at work. I am not a harried executive. For better or for worse, I have time to read, I have time to study things, and I have time to reflect. I don't want to give myself total credit for that ... I have the luxury of running a very talented, self-directed organization whose priorities are driven by a multiyear vision. Most of the people I know who are harried are so because their time horizon is very short, and they feel like they have to become informed and make decisions in incredibly short periods of time.

Does it follow directly that your work-life balance is pretty good? Do you find yourself working long hours?

It depends on what you consider long hours. For Silicon Valley, I don't work long hours. Someplace else in the world, maybe I do. I don't work 80-hour weeks, but I don't work 40-hour weeks, either. I would say it's between 50 and 60. I think of myself as working five days a week 10 hours a day, and then rarely there's stuff to do outside of that.

"It wasn't totally luck-driven"

When you look back on your career and think about "Why me?" was it maturity, intellect, or just being in the right place at the right time?

There certainly was a fair amount of luck involved, but I'm immodest enough to believe that it wasn't totally luck driven. One of the luckiest parts of my career was getting the opportunity to work at PARC. That was pure luck. I happened to know somebody who knew somebody who needed somebody who was of a totally different profile than what they typically hired at PARC. So I got what amounted to a graduate education in an industrial setting, basically for free. Apart from that, I'm a pretty smart guy and I don't like to fail. That's a driving force for anybody. I think I bring a certain amount of creativity to my work. I don't think the successes that I've had in my career are totally a result of luck—there was skill and hard work involved.

How much was technical accomplishment versus business acumen or social interactions, maturity, kindness, and so on?

The majority were technical accomplishments. I'm a technologist with business sense. The business sense does count. You can apply your technical acumen to things that don't have an impact, and I think my business sense did help me to focus on things that had potential impact, and some percentage did have impact. I consider myself a top-flight technologist; I don't consider myself a top-flight administrator or a top-flight coach. If you think about all the other realms of skills that you want to have as an executive, it's the technical skills that I value most and that others value most. My administrative skills are good, but they are nothing exceptional. My interpersonal skills are good, but I wouldn't consider them exceptional. I really think my technical skills and insights have gotten me to where I am today.

What suggestions do you have for others on being successful in software (either R&D or business)?

Any career is a marathon race, not a sprint. For it to be rewarding over years and decades, it has to be something you like to do. As you consider career decisions, listen to your heart as well as your head. Your head will tell you how to succeed in a traditional sense. Your heart will tell you what fulfills you, what you find fun. Here is a simple metric: Ask yourself how fast the time passes at work. If you "lose yourself" in your work—that is, if time passes quickly—that is a powerful, positive message. If, on the other hand, you find it difficult to concentrate on the work at hand or watch the clock, then it is time to think about a change. Another important element to think about in planning your career is how you like to work. Software development has traditionally been a fairly solitary pursuit. This is changing, of course, as we embrace new methodology, but there remains a strong individual component. If you are an extrovert who wants fairly constant interaction with people on the job, some roles are better than others, such as program management or product marketing.

Don't be afraid! Don't be afraid to change within the context of what you like and what you are good at. Some of the most successful people I know deliberately take a new career path every 5–10 years. In a similar vein, don't be afraid to experiment, take risks, and ultimately fail. The lessons from those experiments and failures will stick with you longer and more vividly than your successes. The successes that build on those experiments and failures are that much sweeter than the easy ones. Don't be afraid to challenge the status quo. The company you work for needs change as much as you do personally. Positive change comes from examining the reasons things are the way they are and finding solutions outside the box of the status quo.

"Software engineering is a great field!"

What do you see as the coming changes in the software field over the next 10–15 years that will impact career opportunities either positively or negatively?

The mix between pure software companies and hardware or services companies that have core competence in software will shift. Consequently, a software engineer is more likely to work for one of the latter type of companies.

As the educational systems of lower-cost geographies produce more and more qualified engineers, opportunities for software engineers in those geographies will increase.

As a community, we are going to solve some hard long-standing problems in computer science. The general category of understanding—understanding speech/audio, images, video, and so on—comes immediately to mind.

Hopefully, the tools we use to create software in 15 years will be unrecognizable to those of us who practice in the field today—unrecognizable because they will be an order of magnitude more productive, allowing engineers to operate at much higher levels of abstraction.

Do you have a pet peeve in any aspect of the software world?

I worry that the value of software has peaked in the eyes of the customer. I have been lucky enough for my career to span a real heyday of the software business. It is extremely gratifying to have customers pay directly for your work product: the software. I worry that in the future our work will recede from the customer's view and go back to being perceived as simply an enabler for some other product (such as hardware) or service.

What final words of wisdom or caution do you have for people entering the field?

Software engineering is a great field! The last 35 years have been extraordinary, but there is plenty of room for creativity, invention, and innovation for those just entering the field.

Tom Malloy

CHAPTER 15

Secret Insights on Software Project Management

"Become a fixer, not just a fixture."
—Anthony J. D'Angelo

This chapter is a collection of some little-known insights and techniques on effective software project management. It includes hidden gems that you might not find in traditional sources. I assume that you have already learned, or will learn when the time is needed, the basics of software project management:

- Assembling a team

- Collecting requirements and building a project plan

- Setting delivery milestones

- Establishing source code and document controls, and development processes

- Managing and tracking risk

- Managing employees

- Managing the schedule and the delivery dependencies

- Instituting quality assurance processes for unit test, functional verification, acceptance test, system verification, and performance quality assurance

- Running early release programs, such as alphas and betas

- Building marketing and publicity collateral

- ▶ Executing defect tracking, monitoring, projecting, and take-down

- ▶ Handling packaging and delivery

- ▶ Performing causal analysis

Once you've got all that under your belt, some little-known gems can help turn a good project into a great one. They group into ideas around managing people, process, and quality. Adding these tips and insights to your portfolio of skills can help you manage teams with the alacrity of a seasoned Fortune 500 executive.

Goal-Oriented Project Management: Lessons from Space

In the 1960s, the world witnessed an international space race between super-powers while the Union of Soviet Socialist Republics (USSR) and the United States went head-to-head for dominance. The USSR struck first with the unmanned orbit of Earth by the Soviet Sputnik satellite on October 4, 1957. The USSR had the next big win as well, with the first-ever manned orbit by 27-year-old Russian cosmonaut Yuri Gagarin on April 12, 1961. The USSR seemed firmly ahead in the race for space when President Kennedy declared a massive investment in the American space program. In his May 25, 1961, speech to the U.S. Congress, President Kennedy made an urgent appeal for support of the NASA space initiative that would send a man to the moon. The speech was impassioned and eloquent, and it illustrates some remarkable qualities of effective goal-oriented project management:

> First, I believe that this nation should commit itself to achieving the goal, before this decade is out, of landing a man on the moon and returning him safely to the Earth. No single space project in this period will be more impressive to mankind, or more important for the long-range exploration of space; and none will be so difficult or expensive to accomplish. We propose to accelerate the development of the appropriate lunar space craft. We propose to develop alternate liquid and solid fuel boosters, much larger than any now being developed, until certain which is superior. We propose additional funds for other engine development and for unmanned explorations—explorations which are particularly important for one purpose which this nation will never overlook: the survival of the man who first makes this

daring flight. But in a very real sense, it will not be one man going to the moon—if we make this judgment affirmatively, it will be an entire nation. For all of us must work to put him there.

Looking just at this small extract, you can see how the speech defines a specific goal that was clear to all listeners. The project has a defined timeline for completion and engages not only its direct participants (NASA), but a very broad community, the American public, for support. Most important, the goal of sending a man to the moon, while extremely difficult, was, in fact, achievable. Table 15.1 summarizes how these qualities are expressed in the text.

TABLE 15.1   Space Program's Project Management Qualities

The goal is extremely specific and clear to everyone involved.	"... before this decade is out, landing a man on the Moon and returning him safely to the Earth"
The goal is measurable.	"... landing a man on the moon and returning him safely to the Earth"
The goal was attainable.	At 4:18 p.m. EDT July 20, 1969, Apollo 11's Lunar Module touched down on the moon at Tranquility Base. Mission leader Neil Armstrong reported back, "The eagle has landed." At 10:56 p.m. EDT, Armstrong touched one foot to the moon's surface.
The goal was realistic.	"We propose additional funds for other engine development and for unmanned explorations ..." [acknowledging that additional research and experimentation was required and would be provided for].
The timeline is specific from the outset.	"... before this decade is out ...."

These qualities are not accidental, and Kennedy's speech writers clearly were also experienced project managers. In the vernacular of project management, the acronym SMART is used to refer to these principles: specific, measurable, attainable, realistic, timely. Fortunately for all of us, SMART is also easy to remember.

Why is having a specific goal always so important? It has to do with boys and their toys. Given an unlimited amount of time to deliver leading-edge research in a broad domain, a team of engineers can be trusted to flit the time away on a broad array of fascinating projects that don't add up to a collective whole. A specific goal helps focus the team on a target, and that focus has immeasurable value. Imagine if the teams at NASA hadn't been focused on the single-minded goal of getting a man to the moon and returning him safely to Earth, but instead were given the same level of funding to "advance American capabilities in space exploration." You would have ended up with dozens of interesting scientific projects surrounding jet fuel, satellite technology, and self-sustaining colonization on remote planets, most of which would have incrementally advanced the boundaries of scientific knowledge, but collectively they wouldn't have produced a major result.

Similarly, goals need to be very clear to everybody involved. Ambiguity causes inefficiencies as people within the team exert energy on ideas that aren't focused on the target. Funding can get compromised, and there is a downward spiral. Kennedy and his advisors knew that clarity of purpose was critical to their success.

Kennedy also set a very specific timeline for the project, insisting that the goal be accomplished by the end of the decade. Presumably, he was advised by NASA and their scientists that this goal was achievable. Placing a realistic stake in the ground for when a project has to be completed helps the execution team organize around the schedule and focus on delivering. It improves efficiency and clarifies team objectives. When there's a specific timeline, there no time for sidebars or delay. The date is the goal, and the team organizes itself around it.

Aside from defining project goals that were SMART, Kennedy engaged a broad community at an emotional and inspirational level. He alit the curiosity and dreams of a nation to stand behind the program and support it. Imagine what that must have meant for the scientists, technicians, managers, and politicians who were engaged on the project—the spring it would have put into their step, the renewed enthusiasm they would bring to their work. For most software projects, public engagements during early R&D aren't possible—but you don't need to engage the hearts and minds of an entire nation to help your team get jazzed. Engage the organization and the executive levels of your company. Engage the broadest community you can that is appropriate for the project, and that will be enough to get your team excited. Why should it matter? After all, if a project has huge potential and exciting technology, what difference should it make whether executives or a broader internal community are engaged at the outset? Call it human nature, but people care. Having an organization and its executives jazzed up about a project always does wonders to inspire the execution team and secure funding.

Finally, Kennedy knew that the political future of all leaders depends on their ability to deliver. Promise without delivery always crushes credibility.

The larger the investment, the larger the scandal if it fails. He carefully chose a goal that he felt the nation could achieve with adequate funding and political will.

Ultimately, software projects are just like space missions.

Managing Human Nature

If everyone did what they were supposed to do, we wouldn't need project managers or team leaders. If programmers would just write bug-free code, we wouldn't need software test teams, either. Yet the reality of our industry is that teams need leaders and managers, and code needs testing. As a project manager, you will find yourself tempted to blame the team members when they write buggy code or fail to deliver on project commitments—that's a natural reaction, but a flawed one. If the team was perfect, you wouldn't need to be there. Your role, to a large degree, is to help the team overcome its own human nature. Here are some expressions of the software team's human condition that you can expect: Software developers will write code that is far from flawless, using designs that are more expedient than strategic. Team members will engage in sad, pointless, and altogether childish squabbles over the most trivial things. Work will expand to accommodate the time allotted for its completion (and then some), and projects will run late. Left to their own devices, the team will jettison some tasks in favor of others based on their own creative assessments of right and wrong (rationalizing to work on what's fun rather than what's necessary). The team will do all these things, not because they are evil, spoiled or childish, but simply because they are human.

Managing a project means managing human nature. Keep in mind these three ideas, and it can take you far:

1. **Make 'em feel loved.** People fight with each other often because they are anxious about their own sense of achievement and perceptions about their work. When employees feel their own contributions are limited or are being perceived that way, it's common for their frustration to be directed at their coworkers (and their boss). Psychologists call this "projection." They begin to see their own faults in others, or blame others for their own failings. The number one thing a manager can do to avoid this kind of destructive dynamic is to make everyone on the team feel appreciated—even if they really aren't the cat's meow

in software development productivity. Make 'em feel good to be at work, and make 'em feel appreciated. This isn't hard to do. Make a point of complimenting your employees, individually, a few times a week. Let them know that other managers, other groups, and executives are very supportive of their work. This will work magic in keeping the team happy and focused.

2. **Status makes the world go 'round.** It's sad but true. When you ask for a status update on project deliverables, employees feel compelled to deliver a good message. Collecting status reports regularly keeps the members of the team constantly interested in producing good news messages for their management. Be careful with this because you can overdo it. Although status updates do make the world go 'round, too much of it reeks of micromanagement, and people hate that. Status is a Zen-like entity—it requires balance. Junior staff and poor performers can tolerate it more because they need it. Senior staff and superstars require it less and resent it more. Use status reporting as a device to keep individuals on track and focused, but demand it carefully with a sharp eye on who you're asking it from and how they will perceive it.

3. **Provide a face-saving exit.** Sometimes you need to point out to people that they blew it or are on a path to. They need to change their ways or fix a problem. As a people or project manager, you can't escape that. That being said, you want the person receiving the message to leave the room motivated to change and to continue working with enthusiasm. If someone leaves feeling dejected, depressed, or defensive, things could spiral into ever-worsening results. To avoid that, make sure every harsh conversation provides the recipient a face-saving exit, a way to leave the room with a smile. It's not that hard to do. Conceding a few points, or partial points, about past causes usually deflates much of the tension. Second, despite the problems that are in flight, provide an optimistic outlook for the future if things can be turned around. For example, consider a case in which software programmer Moe is two weeks late on a component. Moe claims that a bug in the compiler was the reason. Although the bug in the compiler did exist and cause problems, it doesn't explain most of the delay. As his manager, you want to give him a strong message but also keep him motivated:

"Moe, I know the compiler bug slowed you down. There might have been other things causing delays as well. The reality is that this component you are working on is super important. We've got another three weeks until the test cycle begins. I need you to pick up the pace now. You know, our executives heard about the compiler bug and the delays, and they're watching this carefully now. I think if you can deliver this on time despite the past delays, it's going to make a really good impression."

This little blurb tells Moe that you acknowledge the delays from the compiler bug, but it also hints that there have been other causes. If he's not a complete idiot, he'll realize you're just being polite, and you and he both know he's not working hard enough. Depending on how socially aware Moe is, you might need to be more explicit than "there might have been other things." But you made him feel special because his work is particularly important and suggested to him that he has a chance to redeem himself by picking up the pace. In essence, you gave Moe a face-saving exit, a way to leave the room and still feel good about what he needs to do next. At the same time, you added the pressure that his work is being scrutinized more closely than might be comfortable. The pressure is on, but with the possibility for a happy ending.

Making Use of Students

Students are cheap labor, often very productive, and a great low-risk way to identify star talent. Even better, they're usually happy to do all the grunt work that your high-paid superstar employees won't. I've always felt strongly that internship students (8- to 16-month work terms) trump coop students (4- to 8-month work terms) for value because the complexity of software positions generally means that the first few months on any software job are pure learning. For most coop positions, the work term is only a few months, so the effective time you can get out of the student is pretty minimal—and, in some cases, coop students drain more resources than they provide. Internship student are usually placed for 8–16 months, and you can get significant value out of them during that time. It's a low-risk process for identifying talent. Think of student placements as your opportunity to "try and buy." If the students are superstars, you'll find out quickly through the course of their work term. Whether the students turn out great or not, the work term experience will give a far more profound understanding of their capabilities than a short interview or aptitude test ever could. If a student is a dud, there's not much harm done, and you have no obligation to hire him or her back once the student term is over. Students are a fantastic way to recruit the best and brightest with little risk, while buttressing some of the low-end tasks you'd rather not spend your high-cost, experienced talent on.

In addition to regular student terms, many companies have begun doing joint collaboration with graduate students by helping to fund the graduate research, in return for the research being directed toward your corporate business goals. Funding graduate students is cheap compared to building your own research laboratory, so this strategy can help you get doctoral-level research into your organization at a fraction of the price. Although it's certainly not the same as having a research division the likes of Microsoft, IBM, and Google, it's a great low-cost alternative with all the associated "try and buy" benefits for subsequent recruiting.

The Value of Measuring Value

One of the hardest things for a development team to do, and also one of the most powerful, is to measure the value of the software it creates. It's sensational how measuring value itself creates value. One of the great things about measurement is that it lends itself to imagery. You can illustrate a number in the form of a line graph, a bar chart, or another form. Consider a couple examples from my own experiences at IBM. In 1995, I was the technical lead on a project to rearchitect our high-speed data loader in DB2 to exploit symmetric multiprocessors (SMPs). SMPs were the new emerging class of data servers that had multiple CPUs within a single server. Bulk data load processing was seen as a good opportunity for exploiting an SMP server because the load process is CPU-intensive. For customers trying to load several gigabytes or even terabytes of data en masse the capability to easily complete these jobs several times faster by leveraging the parallelism of SMP systems would be very valuable. In a few months, we had the new parallel-processing code running, including a fair bit of fancy footwork to preserve the cluster sequence of data and some fancy tricks to keep the cache lines unpolluted. Everyone could see that the utility was running faster, and there were general nods of approval for things going well. I partnered with some folks at Sun Microsystems to run experiments of the new load performance across varying numbers of CPUs, and I sent the result to my manager. The results showed near-linear scalability from 2 up through 12 CPUs, an even better result than expected. The next morning my boss left a note on my desk saying, "Great job!" and the graph showing the result got merged into some of our dominant customer-facing presentation materials that year.

If IBM hadn't run the tests with Sun Microsystems, the perception of the parallel-processing technology would have been good but nowhere near as strong. We would have seen occasional performance results from customers and improvement on some internal tests, but it would have stayed anecdotal in nature. By measuring the performance as CPUs were added we were able to quantify the scalability across a number of CPUs and present that data visually. The net result was better awareness inside IBM of the scalability we achieved and how it would help and, more important, far better articulation of the benefit to customers. In 2009, the DB2 team introduced technology to natively support a number of nonstandard language elements and data types that had become de facto popular usage in the database community. The new support made it profoundly easier for companies that were using these nonstandard interfaces to move their applications to DB2 if they so wanted. With the interfaces being natively supported in DB2, moving an application meant dealing with exceptions rather than a complete rewrite of both the application and database layers.

The project went well, but we decided that to really show potential customers, it would be useful to create a utility that could scan database source code (procedural logic, triggers, functions, data definition, and so on) from the non-IBM database, and report back to users the level of native support they could expect from the new version of DB2. For example, you can imagine the benefit to a sales conversation when you can run a small utility and, within seconds, say with confidence that DB2 would support 99.4% of the database source code without modification. In fact, we found the utility had that benefit and a number of other fairly profound ones we hadn't expected:

1. **Quantifying our success.** Measuring what we supported for each customer and partner database we studied allowed us, over a short period to start making general statements about our support, not just point out statements about a single customer experience.

2. **Demystifying our product planning.** Measuring what we supported also allowed us to analyze information about the frequency of occurrence of the things we didn't support. We easily constructed a histogram of how often the unsupported items were popping up at real customer accounts. That dramatically demystified the product planning cycle for the next few releases of DB2.

3. **Marketing impact.** After running a few dozen analyses with real customer and ISV systems, our marketing team became extremely excited about the results. Within days of producing the numbers for the first 18 experiences, the charted results had been converted to marketing

material, polished and shined, and were then included in every single customer-facing presentation and technical training program.

4. **Team morale.** The quantified results were a sensational morale boost to the engineering team. Although the members knew they were doing good work, nobody knew just how well this technology would scale across a range of customer environments. The initial results arrived during the beta cycle and seriously buoyed a tired and still striving engineering team.

Measuring value has sensational impact. It helps you understand where you have really succeeded and where you still have a distance to travel. When the results are good, they will buoy the development team's spirits, provide hard data for marketing efforts, improve the planning process of following work, deepen the credibility of your claims from anecdotal experiences to broad statements, and help your management chain fully appreciate at a glance the business value your software has provided. Not only will you get better visibility for the good work you've done, but you'll also be helping sales, marketing, and product planning. With some luck, those benefits will reflect back on you as well.

Of Mice, Men, and Project Plans

Software project plans always have business components (who our audience is, what advantages and benefits we hope to bring to them, how we will bring our technology to market, how it will be monetized), engineering ones (feature definitions and specifications, design, code, unit test, function test, integration and acceptance testing, and system testing), and the associated project management ones (dependency analysis, staffing, and development scheduling). In an industry as dynamic as ours, it's virtually impossible to plan all aspects of a project up front and execute without needing to vary the plan. Helmuth von Moltke was the chief of staff for the Prussian army starting in 1857, a position he held for 30 years. He was famous for his detailed battle plans that included thousands of planning factors. Despite his extreme dedication to detail in planning, he was famous for saying, "No battle plan survives contact with the enemy." In fact, only the early engagement of a battle can be truly planned at all (and only if you are planning the first strike). If there is a truism of software project planning, it's that the plan you end up with can't be the plan you started with. If it is, one of the following has happened:

▶ You are a soothsayer and have predicted the future with ease.

▶ You are working on a really simple project, and you probably didn't need anything sophisticated enough to call a plan.

▶ You have failed to react to the changing environment around you, and you are about to deliver a software project that has seriously failed to reach its objectives.

Project plans change because, in any project with moderate complexity, certain parameters can't be known at the outset. From the time you start until the time the project completes, parts will be in motion, such as improved understanding of requirements; line items that run ahead of schedule (few) and others that overrun (several); competitors introduce leapfrog technology that forces you to modify your strategy; and people who move, change, or disappear. Iterative development strategies have helped make that adaptation more natural, but changing a business plan is never easy.

Development leaders can take two constructive actions to mitigate the risks associated with plan change. The first is to build a team culture that is mature enough to acknowledge from the outset that not all the original project goals are likely to be achieved, and new ones invariably will be added. A team that enters a project expecting change and adaptation will be far less frustrated by it. The second point is to adapt the development process (waterfall, agile, or other) to include enough checkpoints and moments of pause when the senior leaders in the development organization can review and rethink the plan, making changes as required. Iterative development models are better suited to that, but this can be done with waterfall and rapid prototyping models as well. A culture of change matched with a process of review and evaluation creates a dynamic and constantly course-correcting model for software development teams to bring the right software to users with the right features at the right time. These qualities of adaptive planning and constant renewal have brought agile development to the fore in recent years. It's an idea I touched on in Chapter 13, "Avoiding Software Development Overruns": Ship early, ship often. Agile methods are particularly well-suited to this philosophy, but you can apply it to waterfall methods as well.

Assessing Your Development Maturity

The most important point about software development methodologies is to have a methodology and make sure the team is using it. If you're cranking out code without an established process for doing so, you're going to burn more time and generate more bugs on the back end. The net result will be schedule and budget overruns, lower quality, and probably missed requirements. The major methodologies widely in use today include agile development methods, waterfall software development process, and rapid prototyping. It's worth knowing what each of these really is.

Iterative Development

What it is: A methodology for software development that emphasizes building software in waves of function. Each wave must be fully functional before proceeding to the next. Teams commonly evolve from a waterfall process to an iterative one and then to more agile processes.

Advantages: This methodology trends toward a more stable development environment because subsequent features are built on a stable base. Early stages generate learning to improve the next. Problems are discovered earlier. Features developed in some of the earliest iterations get longer exposure to testing and usability analysis.

Disadvantages: Late cycle features get squeezed for time, placing them at high risk for low quality or failure to deliver. Mature teams will cut function to maintain quality and schedule high-risk features early and low-risk (or low-importance) items toward the end, minimizing this pitfall.

Scrum

What it is: A strategy for organizing people in a development team for highly efficient and collaborative work. A scrum is a group of people working on a project, each with specific roles, including a product owner and a scrum master. Scrums meet regularly (daily) for fixed time (such as 15 minutes) and organize themselves around "sprints," time periods of a few weeks with specific goals defined by the scrum. Scrum also emphasizes demos and early user feedback. In addition to the daily meetings, meetings are scheduled to help plan the sprints and review the completed sprints.

Advantages: This method is effective in forcing/encouraging collaboration, achieving early feedback, and maintaining pace. Scrum is a simple, great place to start as a foray into agile methods. Scrum/agile methodology spreads the planning and management throughout the development cycle in priority order.

Disadvantages: Although the daily scrum meetings encourage collaboration and progress, some people might start treating the relentless press for updates and status flippantly. Second, scrum isn't a complete development process, so it's best applied as part of a larger iterative/agile process. It doesn't cover any technology/development practices, nor does it address starting a project or releasing into production.

Agile Development Process

What it is: Also known as the Disciplined Agile Delivery Process, this is an expansion of the iterative development model into a full-blown software development methodology. It adds the notion of daily scrum, multidisciplinary teams (development, testing, usability, beta and packaging, marketing, and so on), and fully complete testing cycles for each iteration. Agile development emphasizes adapting to the knowledge learned in each iteration.

Advantages: Agile development adds significant quality improvements over the basic iterative development model through more extensive testing of each iteration. The daily scrums keep the entire team coordinated, and the multidisciplinary teams ensure that the work is more than a coding fest. Agile development captures the desired business value (with a particular focus on user stories to flesh out traditional problem definitions) and seeks constant feedback that the goals are being addressed.

Disadvantages: Exhaustion. Agile development is incredibly effective, but it keeps intense pressure on the teams as they move from iteration to iteration. The intensity is far higher than iterative development alone because the methodology includes several additional aspects of the development process aside from design and code. Second, as with any iterative model, the late-cycle features get squeezed for time. Third, the willingness to adapt product plans based on new understanding from each iteration means that team members (and business leaders) might not know with certainty what will be delivered until quite late. A major stumbling point occurs when leadership teams try to apply agile methods to deliver fixed-scope projects on a fixed timeline. Agile lends itself to adaptation and the willingness to compromise either content or schedule as the iterations refine the team's understanding of requirements and priorities. Fourth, unlike the waterfall methodology, which for years has advocated that code be tested by people who didn't author it, agile development encourages author-based testing as a method to accelerate the test cycle. This adds efficiency to testing but also presents considerable risk because any misunderstanding of the project requirements that the programmer had while authoring the code will likely permeate the test effort.

XP: Extreme Programming

What it is: This variation of agile development places high emphasis on pair programming, test-driven development (TDD), on-site customer requirements, design refactoring, and intense code reviews.

Advantages: XP takes the benefits of software engineering's best features to an extreme. It enforces the idea that two heads are better than one on any design and coding effort, and the emphasis on code reviews leads to notably higher code quality as code reviews remain the industry's single most effective method for defect detection and removal.

Disadvantages: Extremes are rarely healthy in any aspect of life, and usually this model fails to scale to large teams. Through TDD, test cases are written before product code, which defines the intended function of the yet to be written product. Because test cases themselves are code, XP advocates writing code that defines code (instead of writing a natural language specification), an approach that some have argued is both uncomfortable and discourages effective requirement reviews.

Lean Development

What it is: This project management methodology is closely related to iterative development. It favors late cycle decisions, where more knowledge and understanding is available: "Commit as late as possible." Emphasis is on reducing waste and process overhead; it's all about cutting red tape. Lean development also emphasizes delivering products to market as fast as possible. The mantra of lean development speaks volumes to its philosophy: "Think big, act small, fail fast; learn rapidly."

Advantages: This methodology improves organizational efficiency by eliminating waste. Lean methodology emphasizes continuous evaluation, ideally through measurement, to eliminate waste. It explains why agile development works, providing the foundational philosophies behind it. Requirements and code that don't contribute to customer value are dropped. Product plans are not considered commitments until as late in the schedule as possible.

Disadvantages: Lean development is more about principles than process. It's the methodology for leaders to help implement agile development efficiently and integrate the agile development process with business thinking. Lean development is high on ideals but a bit less specific on the prescriptive steps for execution. It is indeed more conceptual, and it takes more effort to apply than, for example, plugging in scrum. Junior programmers often miss the value.

Waterfall Development Process

What it is: This is the classic model for software development, where development progresses in a linear sequence from requirements to specification, design, code, unit test, functional verification test, integration test, acceptance/beta test, system verification test, and product release.

Advantages: Software developers know what they need to do up front. Business planners, marketing, and sales teams all understand the product content and target release date from early on.

Disadvantages: Fully understanding the requirements and complexities to produce a solution that you'll deliver in 9–18 months is usually close to impossible to do up front. The waterfall process almost guarantees a need for plan change midcycle, but it's not well designed to accommodate it. Second, a fixed scope and schedule squeezes quality as schedule pressure mounts at the back end of the cycle, where all the testing and defect correction occurs. Up-front plans are brittle and break easily. Changing market, customer needs, acquisitions, competitors, and similar considerations continually break the plan.

Rapid Prototyping

What it is: This is the notion that any complex software design should be prototyped quickly as a proof of concept, to fully understand its strengths and weaknesses before committing to it. This model is often used as an early phase of the waterfall development model.

Advantages: Rapid prototyping takes a lot of the risk out of the waterfall development process. The early prototype helps explore the limits of a proposed design early in the cycle.

Disadvantages: Prototype code is usually pretty hacky and limited. Following a successful prototype, the prototype code should be thrown away, and the team should continue fleshing out the project using classic waterfall methodology. However, teams have ubiquitously found it almost impossible to resist using the prototype code as the starting point for product development. The net result is a final product built at its core on top of low-quality unreliable code.

Modern development organizations are increasingly tending toward agile methods (see the left side of Figure 15.1), but agile methods are not without their problems. Whether you choose an agile strategy or a more classical model, you can apply these methods to run a first-class software organization and develop high-quality software.

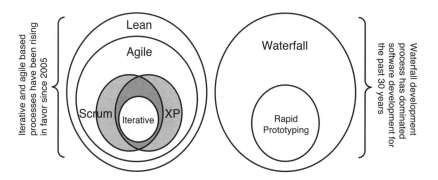

FIGURE 15.1   Software development processes

How do you know if your team is successfully applying a professional amount of discipline in its software development process? Table 15.2 shows a test I've found very helpful in uncovering the truth; it's a simple but sufficiently accurate test I've developed over time.

TABLE 15.2   Testing Maturity

QUESTION	YES?	POINTS
1. Does your team historically deliver projects with the highest-priority features, with excellent quality, and within 20% of the original planned delivery date?		10
2. Does your team use a defect-tracking system?		10
3. Does your team use a source code control system?		10
4. Is every architect, programmer, and tester clear on the process they should be using for requirements, specification, code management, testing, and defect tracking?		10
5. Do your teams author and review test plans that define the tests they intend to execute?		10
6. Does your project management team track defect rates for new arrival rates and backlog size?		10
7. Does everyone working on the product have a clear and unanimous definition for "done?"		5
8. Do you run field tests (alpha and beta programs) and/or usability studies to get early feedback?		5
9. Do your developers clearly understand the short-term business goals for the product they are working on, including clarity on what the major market segments are for the product?		5
10. Does your in-house testing scale to the size and intensity of your largest number of expected users?		5

TABLE 15.2 Testing Maturity (continued)

QUESTION	YES?	POINTS
11. Does the development organization have clarity on both the completion date for the project and a series of interim milestones?		5
12. Does your team author and complete reviews of product specifications before they are more than 30% finished with the coding phase?		5
13. Does your team have written description of the project requirements, in the form of either a specification, problem statements, or user scenarios?		5
14. Are at least 80% of your test cases automated and executed periodically?		5
Total		(Maximum score: 100)

If you score lower than 70 on this test, you've got a serious problem with the maturity of your software organization. At a personal level, this is an opportunity for you to show leadership and influence your organization for the better. If you score higher than 90, congratulations; in my opinion, you're working in a group that's in the top tenth percentile of companies worldwide for software development maturity.

Software Defects and Costs and Efficiencies

Study after study has confirmed what every software executive knows as plainly as the speed dial to their travel agent: The later you find a defect in the code, the more it's gonna cost ya. There's a huge cost differential, with late-cycle defects dominating by orders of magnitude. Early-cycle defects can be found and fixed by a single developer while working on the code. The cost might be only a couple person-hours of labor. Conversely, a defect that a customer finds after the product ships could involve multiple account representatives, telephone support specialists, costly back-and-forth with the customer to understand the customer's environment that you have no physical access to, and, ultimately, a team of developers (who might not have originally written the code and are much less familiar with it) who need to reproduce the problem, develop a fix, and work to integrate the new code outside the product development cycle. Depending on how urgent the problem is and how important the customer is, the team might need to develop a special new version of the product to urgently deploy and might have to go through a special cycle of testing. When all the effort is added, a late-cycle post-availability defect might cost hundreds of person-hours of labor when the time and effort of all the people involved are considered.

In the pressure to achieve product release schedules, software developers notoriously and recklessly cut corners on software quality, reviews, testing, coding standards, and boundary conditions. Even worse, the more pressure they are under, the more a software development team will rationalize that certain bits of time-consuming code yet to be completed are needed only for rare scenarios that almost nobody will be interested in. Sometimes these rationalizations are true, and only a small percentage of the expected user base (say, 1%) will encounter an affected scenario. The problem, of course, is that any single large-scale product includes many thousands of features. If each major feature has one or two of these unlikely-to-be-found defects, the multiplicative effect is disastrous: Virtually every customer will run into one of these. Sometimes the rationalizations border on comical. As a leader, you need to be sensitive to what your executives know: In plain dollars and sense (let alone market optics and customer satisfaction), low-quality products mean finding and fixing problems later in the cycle, often after the products ship, with dramatically higher costs. The weight of these costs can crush an organization.

For junior and intermediate developers, the facts are more subtle. Most developers don't fully appreciate that defects are dramatically more expensive to fix in post-production, so they make the personal unilateral decision on behalf of the entire team to defer known problems to a later fixpak or release, hoping that a problem "won't be too bad" in the meantime. Who put them in charge of the product's future? As a leader, helping to educate your team to internalize the reality of deferred defect costs is one of the best things you can do. Deferring the cost means multiplying it, and that multiplication can seriously damage your business, limit your ability to develop new code quickly, and cause your happy developers (who are currently busy doing fun design and development) to spend a much larger swath of their time doing painful support and bug fixing. It's a downward spiral:

▶ More cost on support means less money for new development.

▶ Grumpier software developers mean a less motivated and efficient development team.

▶ Late-cycle defects heavily impact the team's ability to wrap up the project, leading to schedule overruns.

▶ Lower quality in the shipped product leads to reduced customer satisfaction and product success. The low quality translates quickly to reduced revenue.

Figure 15.2 contrasts a mature development organization and an emerging one. Note that the cost of defect removal by phase is the same in both cases. The figures illustrate the percentage of defects found by phase. Not shown is that fact that the software produced under the immature development cycle will have significantly more defects over its lifetime.

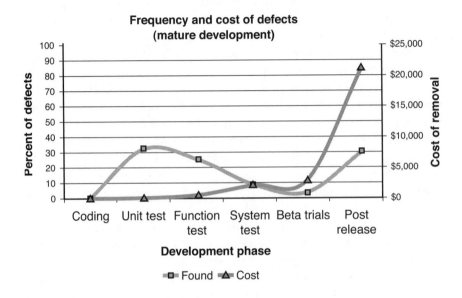

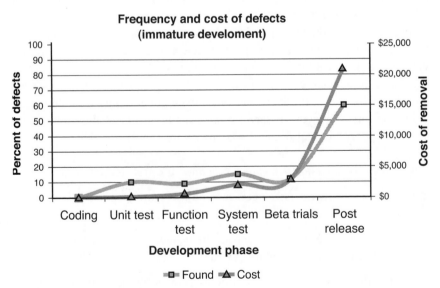

FIGURE 15.2   Defect frequency and correction costs by phase found (top, a mature development organization; bottom, an emerging one).

Mature development teams inject fewer defects into their code in the first place and find a higher percentage of their defects during unit and function testing. The net result is relatively high code quality, usually in the range of 1-6 defects per thousand lines of code (KLOC). Immature teams, low in development process and quality control, will ship code with as much as 8-20 defects per KLOC. Treating late cycle defects as being no more dangerous or expensive than defects found early is a perilous position fraught with high risk and dramatic cost increases.

Armed with the understanding that late-cycle quality effort costs dramatically more and produces less, how should an aspiring project manager avoid the pitfalls and quagmires of late-cycle detection?

▶ Design, specification, and code reviews remain the most effective method for early defect detection.

▶ Use an iterative development methodology so that testing is performed in waves throughout the development cycle, not as a mass back-end process.

▶ Build in testability by adding extensive trace points, assertions, and programmatic hooks that can force test conditions (such as simulating a memory constraint or device failure when none exists).

You Can't Test In Quality

Some would like to believe that more testing means higher quality. I'd like to believe that, too—but, sadly, it's not the case. Although testing certainly helps identify defects, you can never find all the defects in a section of code through testing alone. When you come to the admission that no matter how hard you test, a significant percentage of defects will always remain, an uncomfortable reality begins to appear. If testing finds a percentage of the existing defects (say, 65%), then the more defects you find through testing, the more defects likely remain in the code. The more defects you find through testing, the more defects there will be in the delivered product—not less. That might seem counterintuitive, unless you view testing as a statistical measurement of quality rather than a process of trying to find all the bugs. That's why, within software engineering literature, function and system testing are actually called "function verification testing" and "system verification testing." The people who have studied software engineering scientifically have come to view these test efforts as a verification process more than a fixing process.

If more testing means finding more bugs, and more bugs found means lower ship quality, perhaps product quality will improve with reduced testing! Not so again. Better testing improves the percentage of defects found. A weak testing process might detect only 30% of the existing code defects, whereas a solid test effort could find 50%, and a very robust process could find as much as 65%. A significant number of defects will always remain, but a better test effort both reduces the number and, more important, provides better fidelity on the likely ship quality. Unfortunately, nobody has yet figured out how to develop bug-free software. (If you do, you'll definitely be up for a Nobel Prize—the contribution to society would be immeasurable.) Because you can't find all the bugs through testing, you'll never generate the highest-quality code through testing alone. Many companies have tried and failed. Historically, the single best method for improving code quality and removing bugs has been code reviews. That said, the highest-quality code is developed without cutting corners on design and specification review, code reviews, formal inline assertion (runtime) testing, instrumented code, and, finally, robust testing.

Software project management is about managing people, process, and quality. The previous ideas can help you leapfrog traditional thinking about project management in ways you won't find in management courses. These tools complement modern software project management methods, but they don't replace them.

An Interview with James Gosling

Inventor of the Java Programming Language

CURRENT POSITION

CTO Client Software Group and Sun Fellow, Sun Microsystems, Inc.

CLAIMS TO FAME

Inventor of Java, the world's most popular programming language; originator of UNIX Emacs

DATE OF BIRTH

May 19, 1955

EDUCATION

Ph.D. in Computer Science, Carnegie Melon University, 1983

M.Sc. in Computer Science, Carnegie Melon University, 1982

B.Sc. in Computer Science, University of Calgary, 1977

FAVORITE PASTIMES & HOBBIES

3D modeling, hiking, and skiing

BIOGRAPHY

James' doctoral thesis was "The Algebraic Manipulation of Constraints." He has built satellite data acquisition systems, a multiprocessor version of UNIX, several compilers, mail systems, and window managers. He also built a WYSIWYG text editor, a constraint-based drawing editor, and a text editor called Emacs for UNIX systems. At Sun, his early activity was as lead engineer of the NeWS window system. He did the original design of the Java programming language and implemented its original compiler and virtual machine. In February 2007, James was named an officer of the Order of Canada. He was also elected to the United States National Academy of Engineering.

James Gosling

"So many gizmos completely enthralled me"

How did you get started in software?

I always liked to build stuff. When I was a kid, I was banging pieces of wood together or playing in my grandfather's shop. He had a full blacksmith's forge, where you could shoe horses and all the rest of it. I just have this inclination to bang things together. But when I was 14, a friend of my dad's took my dad and me on a tour of the computer center at the University of Calgary. I was instantaneously hooked—it was absolutely love at first site. So many gizmos completely enthralled me. We lived about 2 miles from the university, so I started walking over there. At 14, I was tall enough to look like a university student, so people didn't really take much mind of me. I just had to figure out how this worked, how this happened. I spent a lot of time reading in the library and a long time dumpster diving for account passwords, and I got a little too good at breaking combination locks and such. I literally taught myself by breaking into the computer science department during the summer. All the doors had these dumb combination locks with a keypad on the door. People would come up and punch in the combination and go in. All you had to do was stand around looking natural, and you could see the sequence they would punch in. That's where the dumpster diving comes in [to salvage user IDs and passwords], and a lot of the machines didn't even have user IDs and passwords.

I did a lot on a time-sharing PDP-8 running an operating system called TSS8, which I used a certain amount. I started on a PDP-8 that was very barebones. It was in an odd corner of one lab that nobody was using. So I taught myself. The first programming language I learned was Focal5, which stands for FOrmula CALculator. It was a pretty simple language for doing Fortran-ish kind of stuff. I did things that plotted curves, and did the usual blackjack games and solitaire games; somewhere in there, I also taught myself assembly [language] because Focal was pretty limited. So I started writing assembly on the PDP-8. At about the same time, I was also playing around—the university had some IBM machines (IBM 360s, 50s, and 40s) that were used for courses. So I started writing Fortran programs and PL1 programs. Then they started getting some CDC machines in, so I taught myself how to do CDC Fortran. At some point, I started meeting university students. They had all kinda figured out that I was this kid who was just barely in high school. They were cool with it, for the most part. Most of the teaching assistants had it figured it out, too. They were perfectly happy to have me around, as long as I wasn't breaking anything. Two of the professors knew and were mostly just amused. At some point, one of the professors had a job in the physics department, needed some help writing software, and asked me. I started working in the physics department then—I might have turned 15 by the time I started working there. Ever since then, it seems like I've been on this straight-line vector.

What inspired you guys to start Java?

We had this other project called the Green Project. We were asked to go off and explore what was happening in the computer world that might affect Sun in the future. We spent a certain amount of time noodling about it. Pretty quickly we hit up all the places where people were using digital systems outside of the computer industry. So we did a bunch of surveying. We visited people in consumer electronics companies, people who were building early cell phones, and people who built elevators and locomotives and all kinds of weird stuff. We also tried to understand what was going on with digital systems. It was an interesting exercise because a whole universe of people were using the same tools as people in the computer business, but they came at it from a fairly different direction. On one hand, they were reinventing stuff that had been done 20 years before in computer research and remaking a lot of the same boneheaded mistakes. But on the other hand, they had a very different attitude toward things like reliability and safety. They understood what it takes to build something that lives with people, rather than living in a raised-floor, air-conditioned room. That was a pretty interesting collision of mindsets. Being a bunch of engineers instead of paper writers, we built a prototype based on some ideas from the people we visited. As we were working on that, we realized a bunch of the issues we kept having ended up being about software methodology. My part of the project was dealing with that problem. It started out as fixing some of the problems in C++ and turned into something completely different. It wasn't as though I woke up one morning and said, "Gotta do a new programming language!"

We were working with Mitsubishi and their consumer electronics folks. They were the folks we had the most interesting conversations with. They had problems with how to build consumer electronics devices like VCRs and TVs. The way they did their software architecture was all messed up. They had a number of issues surrounding how to evolve from one platform to the next. They wanted to be able to treat CPUs as commodities and put one CPU in this TV and another CPU in that. They were in a world where software reuse was almost completely unknown. That was driven by the fact that their platforms were so radically different. Yet they could see the way things were going. The software costs were spiraling out of control because the things they were trying to build were getting so sophisticated, yet because they had to build everything from the ground up for every last device, it was a nightmare. Plus, everything was getting connected with everything else.

James Gosling

James Gosling

Some of the goals would have centered on code reuse, platform independence, networking, and so on?

Our goal was to deal with the reliability issues they had. You'll find a lot of stuff in Java about things like fault containment. Then as we worked with other people, around other issues, that forced me to spend a lot of time on issues like security and reliability.

"Most of the smart cards on the planet are Java"

What makes you feel successful about your work in software?

Having people use it. I get a tremendous amount of satisfaction from talking to people who use the stuff I built. I get a huge rush seeing the places Java is used. For example, the fact that most of the control software for the Large Hadron Collider—all the above-ground consoles—is big bags of Java code ... I get a big rush out of that. I get a big rush out of the fact that most of the smart cards on the planet are Java. Those are really simple, but you just can't beat 'em for volume.

To what do you attribute your own success? How did you get to be you?

I've been pretty lucky at building systems that people found interesting kinda at the right time. Certainly, the whole success of Java was 10% technology and 90% just dumb-assed lucky timing.

Do you have a pet peeve in any aspect of the software world?

Things that break in the tools that I use. If I'm using somebody's library and it's broken, that's really annoying—especially if it's a library you can't get the source for. Even if it is a library you can get the source for, I tend to just rewrite it.

How do you stay on top of technology trends and innovation?

I read all the time. These days, it's almost exclusively stuff on the Web. I do read *The Economist* religiously. I also tend to read *Science*. But other than that, it's roving the news sites on the Web, like Slashdot and SFGate. People also send me emails saying, "Hey, this is cool—why don't you look at this?" That's actually one of the best filter functions out there. The social network is often one of the most powerful.

"At some level, you just have to accept that you are doomed."

Technical leaders and executives are famous for being time-strapped. What strategies do you use to stay sane and use your time effectively?

This is a hard one because I don't think I've ever been particularly good at it. I've gotten myself in bad medical situations just from being overstressed about time management. I think I have learned two important things about time management: First, say "no." I generally have a hard time with "no." I don't mind if someone says to me, "No, I can't do it," but I have a hard time telling somebody, "No, I can't do that for you." Second, no matter what, you end up with way more stuff on your plate than you can possibly do. Even after you have delegated stuff to other people and said "no" as much as possible, you'll still be swamped. At some level, you just have to accept that you are doomed. You're going to fail at some fraction of things that you think of as things you ought to be doing. Be comfortable with a certain amount of failure. Learn how to triage the things in your life that you need to do.

How do you achieve a work-life balance? How do you keep your professional life from dominating everything?

I have a wife and kids who won't let me get away with it. They're pretty militant about it, and I'm okay with that. For me, after going through the wringer a few times, you figure out that spending more time on stuff actually makes you less effective, and the only way you can think clearly is to back off for a while. Once you accept the fact that going off and clearing your head with your family is really a positive thing; that deals with a lot of the guilt issues. When I was a grad student, CMU was right next to a really big art gallery. I used to go the art gallery several times a week, to look at paintings as a mechanism to clear the head and restore life balance. It's really hard to beat that.

What do you see as the coming changes in the software field over the next 10–15 years that will impact either career opportunities or the way we develop software?

Hundreds of issues are swirling around in there. Some of these are really cycling, and it's hard to know how they're going to settle.

One of the issues has been, "What is a team and how does a team work together?" If you wind the clock back a decade, if you wanted to be in

James Gosling

a software team, you pretty much had to all be together. These days, it's starting be common for software teams to be dispersed; nobody shows up at the office—they all come in through the Internet. But there are all kinds of strains in that model. People end up feeling disconnected. The teams don't bond very well. The worst part is very little mentoring: Mentoring just doesn't work as well over email or Skype, especially when there is a big time zone difference. So we've been edging around trying to make sure projects are localized at least around a time zone, if not geographically. I honestly don't know how it's going to turn out. It's a social experiment, and I think it's going to be somewhat variable. In some ways, we've over-rotated on the dispersed team thing. I would guess there's going be a little more coming together over the next few years. I would love to think there's going to be more work on tools for teams to work together. Lots of people have done work on tools like these over the past ten years, but they've never really taken off. Nobody has found anything that really makes a difference, other than distributed source code management—but that seems somewhat inadequate.

One of the other big ones out there has been the implication of multicore and multithreading. Most folks come out of college having never written a parallel program. Java has all kinds of facilities in it for doing aggressive parallel programming, but it's still tricky. In some domains, writing a multicore program is easy, like writing standard web applications. But the more tied-together scientific algorithms become very difficult, and there are a lot of issues in figuring out how to do that as the core count on the machines increases. A lot of issues also surround the ever-spiraling complexity of the systems people are building. In the Java world, million-line systems are a dime a dozen. Systems that are north of 10 million lines are remarkably common. These are systems that nobody can wrap their head around. It's an area where there are dozens, if not hundreds, of Ph.D. theses that have yet to be written—simple things like how to refactor on a 10-million line program.

"A lot of times, it's too easy to give up too early"

What suggestions do you have for others on being successful in software (either R&D or business)?

I've had such a weird career, it's hard for me to believe that I have a valid viewpoint. For me, the biggest thing is to make sure I always have fun. I can't do a good job of anything unless I find it interesting.

Most people who are good at software engineering also tend to be fairly introverted. Working in groups in an organization is somewhat tough. I don't think I'm terribly functional ... I'm just a horrible manager. Me doing management is a really bad thing. But one good management trick I use is that I tend to not tell people what to do. If somebody comes to me with some design they've done, and I think there's something wrong with it, I usually won't say, "Oh, there's something wrong with it," because that just gets people defensive. My favorite technique is to start asking people questions about it and then have them realize, "Oh, yeah, that's kinda broken."

You have a Master's and a Ph.D. You've been working for many years since then. Do you think graduate degrees are valuable in the software industry? Do you see them as a benefit when you are recruiting someone?

Yes. We definitely look at someone with a Bachelor's differently than we look at someone with a Ph.D., especially at a company like Sun, where very deep expertise is essential for just about every job. But lots of jobs aren't that way—they don't require the same kind of depth. And I think for me, even considering the pay I get for my job, I had more fun working on my Ph.D. and being a grad student than anything I have ever done. I would go back to being a grad student in a heartbeat. Some of my friends actually have, and I'm jealous!

It tends to be a combination of depth and breadth. Most people who have gone through a Bachelor's degree know things like algorithms fairly superficially. If you've got a graduate degree on analysis of algorithms, you're going to know a lot more, especially if you've had a really good professor.

What final words of wisdom or caution do you have for people entering the field?

My number one piece of advice is to have fun. Number two is to be really stubborn. A lot of these things are really easy to give up on. Whether it's organizations that you give up, or APIs, or software, a lot of times, it's too easy to give up too early.

James Gosling

CHAPTER 16

The Big Leagues: From Medium-Shot to Big-Shot

*"Leadership is communicating to people their worth and potential
so clearly that they come to see it in themselves."*
—Stephen Covey

Leadership is defined more than anything by the quality of inspiring and directing improvement. When your actions and vision inspire others to improve individually or as a group, you are a leader. Some people seem born to lead. Most of us have to learn about it. What many people don't realize is that leadership is a skill. As with learning to play piano or to cook a great pot roast, leadership might take practice, but most people can learn it if they apply themselves. Leadership in software requires many of the same qualities needed in other fields, including a vision for change, a dash of charisma, an outstanding track record, and a heavy dose of trustworthiness. In this chapter I discuss what makes a leader, explore different leadership styles and when to use them, cover how to pick a new course for a team, and detail how to lead people to get there.

Leading Versus Managing

Many people think of leadership and management as synonyms, but the two are very different. Managers appear to be our leaders; they run the show and decide who does what. It's a common perception—and an incorrect one. Management is about making sure things get done. Leadership is about defining new paths and empowering others to make things happen. Change always requires leadership, whether you are changing strategy, changing a process, or inspiring people to change for the better. Execution requires management. Funnily enough, some people are great at one and lousy at the other. Of course, being great at both is ideal.

As an individual working in a software organization, through a process of hard work, skill building, and effective time management, you hope to carry more than your weight in the organization. If all works well and you can effectively communicate your contributions, your efforts are visible to others. You have done more, and it shows.

When you become a manager of a group, your responsibilities change, and you spend more of your time helping your team stay on course and work through the process of getting *their* work done. Your own time is significantly spent helping the team, and you have less time for individual contributions to the project. At the end of the project, the team members will have gotten to the finish line successfully largely because of your solid management. In this scenario, you've carried your weight in the organization, and hopefully it will show accordingly. You'll get the much deserved recognition for managing the entire team through the process. As a top-flight manager, you can achieve a larger impact than a talented individual contributor.

As a leader of people, you help direct the team to change and improve as individuals and as a collective team. To do that, you'll spend more of your time on them and less of your time making personal contributions. However, if you are a good leader, you'll empower the members of your team both as individuals and as a group, so the group will carry more weight. You'll help create a more powerful team. You'll legitimately achieve a larger impact and project a larger image because you've helped a set of people to all be more effective. Leaders are people who foster improvements. In doing so, they have an exponentially positive impact far beyond what they might have accomplished as an individual or as a manager of a well-established process.

In Figure 16.1, the height of the people in the team represents the perception that others have of their value to the organization. A top producer certainly appears to have greater value than other average members of the team. Although exceptions exist, the manager of a team generally gets considerable credit for the accomplishments of the entire team and thus garners more credit and perceived value than a single individual member of team, including prolific producers. Leaders, however, not only get credit for the accomplishments of the team, but they also raise the perception of the team because they drive improvements to people, organization, and process. What's more, not only do leaders have higher perceived value than good managers or prolific individual contributors, but the individuals they lead have greater perceived value and accomplishment than people on more average teams. Of course, this is approximate, and wide variation exists across individuals and teams, but this phenomenon is generally true in most organizations.

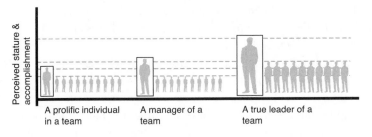

FIGURE 16.1   Contributions in a team

Leadership Styles

Research by Hay and McBer (summarized and published by Goleman) in the mid- and late 1990s studied 3,871 executives[1] and found that their leadership styles could be categorized into six major types. Each style has its place, although the best leaders use a mix. The choice of style can have a major impact on the atmosphere and effectiveness of the team, its ability to perform and innovate, and, ultimately, its financial results. To become an effective leader, you should take on the following challenges:

▶ Understand the six leaderships styles and their relative virtues

▶ Reflect on your own style and understand your own natural tendencies

▶ Recognize that each style has benefit in different situations and set a path of self-improvement to develop your own leadership style that includes the best attributes of multiple styles

---

[1] D. Goleman, "Leadership That Gets Results," *Harvard Business Review* (March/April 2000): 78–90.

Table 16.1 summarizes the six styles.

TABLE 16.1   Leadership Styles

Style	Summary	Goleman's Description in a Phrase
Coercive	Coercive leaders encourage their teams to do what they are told. These leaders are decisive and exude confidence and efficiency.	"Do what I tell you"
Authoritative	Authoritative leaders inspire others through their mastery of domain and their personal charisma. They motivate others to follow.	"Come with me"
Affiliative	Affiliative leaders place people's needs and interests above all else. They build dedication and loyalty through the constant creation of emotional caches.	"People come first"
Democratic	Democratic leaders lead by inclusion. They empower the team to participate strategically, and they create a sense of shared purpose and joint responsibility.	"What do you think?"
Pacesetting	Pacesetting leaders lead by example. They set a bar of excellence and encourage others to be just as professional, expert, and hard working. Through their example, they set a clear standard for commitment and impact.	"Do as I do, now"
Coaching	Coaching leaders focus on the constant renewal and growth of the team. By developing others, they improve performance and develop the long-term capacity of an organization.	"Try this"

Although each style has its pros and cons, Goleman's article citing the Hay and McBer research found that the coercive and pacesetting styles have the most negative impact on an organizations. Nobody likes to be bullied, and the hallmark of a coercive style is a dictatorial approach. Pacesetting styles force employees to run at a pace that might not be comfortable or sustainable for them. As a general-purpose leadership style, the authoritative style is usually the most versatile and effective. But it's naive to think that any single style is enough to create a good leader. Different business environments and different personalities that you work with require different leadership. Every style has a time and a place where it's suitable—even the coercive style. Let's take a look at when to use each style:

▶ **Coercive.** Nobody likes to be bullied, and long-term exposure to this style leads teams to feel resented, abused, and underappreciated. Still, this dictatorial style delivers huge operational efficiencies. As a result, it's useful during crisis situations when there's little time for discussion and the inefficiencies it brings. A good plan today is better than a perfect plan in the future, and coercive leaders produce rapid, if far from perfect, results. In a crisis, a highly effective get-things-done dictator is often just what's needed.

▶ **Authoritative.** The authoritative style is really about vision from the top. It's the most effective style when charting a new course or strategy. An authoritative leader needs to truly command respect. This style has the highest overall impact on an organization; people want to work for leaders who know their stuff and can make clear, intelligent decisions.

▶ **Affiliative.** This style places people interests first, so it proves the most effective style in healing a team undergoing any kind of social tension, such as intense business pressure to meet a deadline or past grievances over a previous manager, unfair compensation, or unmet personal needs.

▶ **Democratic.** This style promotes collaboration. It's effective with teams of senior staff who don't necessarily expect to be told what to do, and probably have far-reaching and insightful ideas of their own to contribute.

▶ **Pacesetting.** This style promotes speed, efficiency, and hard work. The pacesetting style isn't about standards, recognition, or clarity of purpose; it's about sprinting. Not everybody wants to come into work every day and get on the treadmill, of course, so this style can be effective for short-term projects and for getting more from teams that are underperforming and need to raise their level.

▶ **Coaching.** This style promotes employee improvement. It's the best style to use with employees who are underperforming on any front aside from raw productivity, and for new teams (or new employees) that require development and nurturing.

The best leaders apply styles selectively, depending on the nature of the teams they're leading, the project circumstances, and the personal needs of individuals. You might need to use an authoritative style with some employees and a democratic style with others. Deciding which requires you to tap into your emotional intelligence (EI). Good leaders deploy one or two effective styles, but great leaders master most of them.

Be an Authority

Be an authority, not an authority figure. In business, a certain relatively small amount of respect comes from your title and your position. However, to really command the respect of others, you need deeper and more compelling insights and leadership qualities than most people you work with. In a discipline of highly skilled and intelligent professionals such as software, if you don't clearly have leadership or innovation skills that set you apart, no title or job description will garner you respect and influence over others. You won't be able to leverage the multiplying effects of leadership. Titles and job description do help, but they provide a temporary veneer that casts you as an authority figure, not as an authority. People quickly see through the layers to the quality and character beneath. The best strategy is to become an expert in a domain before you rise to any official position of leadership or authority that depends on it. The obvious places to acquire domain authority are technical topics (expertise in a programming language; a development methodology; or a specific technology such as e-business, cloud computing, or database architecture), but nontechnical domains can be just as compelling. For example, managers and business leaders can become authorities in people management, team processes, crisis management, customer presentations, and so on.

If you suddenly find authority and leadership thrust upon you in a domain where you aren't an expert, make it your primary focus over the first six weeks to become as expert as possible. During your first few weeks in the role, the organization will be forgiving if you aren't yet a clear authority figure. Months into the work, it will be expected of you.

How long does it take to become an authority? You want to reach a level of proficiency that makes you a go-to person for expertise within your organization. For technical topics, it's usually two to four years of intense participation; for soft skills of business and management practice, it probably falls closer to five to seven years.

It doesn't take people too long to figure out who the real experts are. If they come to you and you don't have answers or, even worse, you know less about the topic than the people looking for answers, they'll quickly paint a picture of you as a nonauthority on the topic. One valuable strategy to avoid this: When posed with a problem you can't answer, take the time to study and develop an answer instead of just redirecting the asker to someone else. Not only will you truly have become more knowledgeable (now you know the actual answer, plus most likely a number of new, related things you picked up during your search for truth), but the questioner will perceive you as an authority. Of course, people can't always wait for an answer (whether five minutes or five days), but usually they can, which makes this tactic a winner.

Shoot First, Take Questions Later

The larger an organization, the more decision makers it has and the more red tape is involved in getting things done. Many times it's just impossible to make headway on an initiative through formal channels. Smaller organizations are more nimble, flexible, and adaptive. Ironically, most small organizations wish they could become bigger ones! A tried-and-true strategy for getting things done in the face of certain objection is to proceed without asking. Ask for formal support only when you have some initial success in hand. After all, success is hard to argue against. This approach requires some careful handling, however, to be pulled off successfully.

1. Know the rules before you break them. In some organizations, this kind of behavior is revered; in others, it's despised. Understand the risks clearly before you engage.

2. The only way to get things done without formal approval is either to do it yourself or to have staff you can influence spend time on the initiative. Like any skunkworks project, be careful not to let it dominate the time of people working on it. That would seriously compromise work that is more formally committed.

3. The higher the risk, the more you should try to keep your side effort quiet. If it shows signs of failure, shut it down quietly. If it blooms as you expected, start advocating for it and showcasing its success in ways that are culturally appropriate in your organization.

4. Practice moderation. No matter how successful you are, if you are constantly running projects below the radar, you're going to incur the ire and resentment of many. People will see themselves suffering in a morass of red tape and urgent business needs while you appear to do whatever you want. So use the "shoot first" tactic sparingly. The frequency with which you try this should correlate with your success rate.

Building Teams and Recruiting the Best

As a leader in an organization, you will be evaluated partly by what you know and do, but much more by what the teams you lead achieve. Sometimes these are teams you manage directly, but they can also be teams managed by others in the human resources aspects (evaluation, salary, benefits discussions) but who take technical leadership from you either directly or indirectly. The best leaders understand the value of strong teams.

In Chapter 13, "Avoiding Software Development Overruns," I cited research in the 1960s and '70s that found huge differences between the best and worst programmers, often by an order of magnitude. A 1990 study[2] by Hunter, Schmidt, and Judiesch found a similar result: The best people produce 12 times what the lower producers do. That measurement factors into productivity, but it doesn't include all the other benefits top performers bring. The best and brightest employees are also the people who act as agents of change, innovating the next wave of new technology or process improvements that are absolutely critical to software companies. They don't just produce more output; they produce higher-quality output with more elegant approaches. The net effect is that a team of superstar programmers will run circles around average teams. If you're going to be evaluated by the impact of your team, then, given the choice, you want one stacked with superstars. Remember this and sear it into your memory forever:

Five great programmers are better than fifty average ones.

How do you build a team of superstars? It's a four-step process: attracting, selecting, recruiting, and keeping.

Attracting Candidates

You'll always be looking for both people inside your company and external recruits. If you're recruiting from within, you'll know some of the best people in your area already (but in a large firm, you can't know everyone); the challenge will be to attract them without "poaching." If their current managers get the impression that you are stealing the best people, you'll be in trouble.

---

[2] J. E. Hunter, F. L. Schmidt, and M. K. Judiesch, "Individual Differences in Output Variability as a Function of Job Complexity," *Journal of Applied Psychology* 75 (1990): 28–42.

Rule #1: Don't burn bridges. To attract these people, you need to put the word out about the exciting new project team you're building and hope that the best and brightest people in your company approach you. The only way this has a happy ending is if they come to you. Recruiting from outside should involve all the usual tactics of posting to the best universities; speaking to friends, family, and professional contacts to identify top talent; possibly posting in the want ads; or using a professional search agency—especially if you are looking for experienced people. One other tactic that I've found useful is posting to grad school forums at universities you have a connection with. When reaching out to graduate students, make sure your job description sounds cool, scientific, and innovative and that your team sounds fun and freewheeling. In medium to large companies, the Human Resources group will do most of the legwork collecting applications and doing an initial filtering.

Selecting the Best: The Initial Filtering

Now you've got a pile a resumés to look at—what next? Chances are, most of them look fairly similar, especially those submitted by recent graduates. When hiring new graduates for programming positions, I recommend looking for differentiators such as these:

▶ Participation in ACM programming contents, math contests, and so on

▶ Awards, academic or otherwise

▶ Highly proactive activities, such as starting their own business or volunteering large amounts of their time to any worthy cause (coaching, tutoring, first aid, and so on)

If a candidate shows high academic achievement and serious time spent in extracurricular activities, it's a good indicator. Why? Because high grades can be achieved through large time investment, but getting high grades while spending a lot of time doing other things outside of school is a real talent.

Also, if candidates have super-high grades and some musical/artistic or athletic accomplishment, it indicates a range of skill and talent that is valuable inside a team. These are all just "indicators," of course, and exceptions do exist.

Recruiting the Best People

When you've narrowed the field a bit to roughly ten resumés for each position you have available, it's good to do a quick screening phone call of 20–30 minutes (assuming your company's HR practices allow for this). You'll be pretty amazed by how people with such similar paper credentials are so blatantly different when you speak to them for a brief conversation. Narrow the field to four people per position you are recruiting for and start the interviews.

Interviews are a bidirectional process. You want to find the best possible candidate to join your team. If you're especially impressed with a candidate, you'll want to sell this person a little bit on your organization and the work involved. You want the best candidates to leave the interview thinking "Wow, this job looks great! I hope I get it."

Consider some tips for successful interviewing:

▶ **Look for a spark of genius.** Your goal should always be to recruit the best and brightest. You don't have to worry too much about ending up with a team of superstars. First, that's a problem you want to have. Second, the interview process, however rigorous, just isn't foolproof enough. Even if you think you've recruited a team of superstars, some usually turn out to be a little more mortal than they first appeared. Work ethic and organizational skills, in particular, are hard to judge during the interview process.

▶ **Personality and character fit.** One of the most important qualities of any programmer is his or her ability to work within a team. This means candidates need to be half-decent communicators, be humble enough to willingly accept constructive criticism, and generally have enough sense of humor that they'll be able to roll with the punches. Figuring this out in an interview is hard, and it will have a lot to do with your own EI, your sensitivity to character and emotions of others. Spend some time during the interview having a relaxed conversation, perhaps about your company and the candidate's background; drop a few small jokes and try to ascertain the candidate's emotional style. Remember that you want superstars, not prima donnas.

▶ **Ask skill-testing questions.** Usually a few questions will help you get a sense of how the person thinks. I recommend asking a mix of some that are highly algorithmic and others that are more common sense-oriented. By seeing how candidates work through the problems, how quickly and accurately they do so, and how well they communicate verbally, you will learn a lot. These should be questions that they can answer in three minutes or less. It's also worthwhile to slip in a starter question that's fairly easy so that every candidate will leave without a complete sense of humiliation. Your goal is to identify talent, but you should be as sensitive and generous to candidates as possible. When you see that a candidate is struggling, don't proceed with harder questions; that will just frustrate the person more and waste everyone's time.

▶ **Teach candidates something about your work.** This will garner you some points as a mentor they would like to work with, but will also help you judge their willingness and ability to learn. Did they understand you? Did they ask sensible questions?

▶ **If the candidate looks strong, sell the job and yourself.** Talented people want to work with smart people on important projects for executives who understand the business. Have a prepared description of the job you're offering and of yourself that highlights those qualities. Remember that the most talented candidates are usually being courted by several suitors, so you've got to make a pitch that's more exciting and more compelling than the others.

Keeping the Best People Happy

Keeping the best people happy can be hard. Up-and-comers know who they are, and they expect to climb the professional ladder and entertain opportunities at a swift clip. The interesting thing is that everybody is a little different, so keeping them all happy takes a varied approach. You'll need a bit of a candy store with different kinds of treats to make sure you've got something for everyone. Here are some effective tactics:

▶ Truly care for the interests and careers of everyone who reports to you. People value sincerity; if you look after people's professional needs, they will value that more than anything else you can do for them through technical leadership, mentoring, or project management. Besides, it's the right thing to do!

▶ Racehorses need to run. Try to have projects that are worthy of the best employees. Okay, that's easier said than done, but it's a worthwhile goal.

▶ Encourage your team to publish in trade publications and academic venues (scientific conferences and journals).

▶ Encourage your team to patent good ideas.

▶ Make travel and public speaking opportunities available. Some people loathe these; others adore them.

▶ Constantly praise and recognize your people at a personal and team level.

▶ Give your team some time off in the form of extra vacations days as a token of their hard work. This is particularly suitable after a crunch period.

▶ Wine and dine them. A team outing, with a good meal and some other activity a couple times each year does wonders for team morale. Make sure it's something they'll really enjoy, not just "a company thing" they feel obligated to attend.

▶ Spend some of your own money on them. Spending the corporation's money is nice, but if you invite people over for a BBQ or buy them a book as a gift once a year as a token of appreciation, the personal effort won't go unnoticed.

▶ Have the courage and decency to let a top employee move on to bigger and better things in another group when that's really in his or her best interests. Never compromise a person's professional interests for your own. In the end, it will backfire, and all the time and energy you've invested to develop an emotional cache with them will be instantly depleted. By supporting your employees when they choose to move on, you garner their continued loyalty and gain an ally in another organization (within your company or beyond).

Team Mix

As in assembling a sports team, a software team needs people who can play different positions. If everybody is an innovative software developer but nobody can test or document what they do, you're going to have a problem. The recruiting process needs to be thought of as a team-building activity in which you're trying to fill playing positions. A high-efficiency team needs people who are innovative, who are massively productive, who pay attention to detail, and who can help manage and document the process. Unfortunately, few people have the full mix of skills required. If you make the common mistake of hiring the smartest people you can find without attention to their skill mix, you'll be lacking some critical skills leading to execution problems. This isn't intended as a contradiction to the advice I've given throughout this book to hire and work with the best and brightest. Rather, it's a qualifier that, in addition to hiring the best and brightest, you need to balance the skills they bring with them.

Superstars or Prima Donnas?

Not all jobs call for superstar performance and intellect. I've worked with many hiring managers who strongly believe it's a mistake to recruit only the best and brightest. There's some truth in that. You don't want a team of prima donnas who collectively refuse to do the important but less exciting work (such as testing or customer support). This goes back to making sure you have the right mix of skills in the team. I've found the recruiting process so imprecise that if I try to recruit only the best and brightest, I will invariably still end up with a subset of people who are high performers but aren't in the superstar category. That model, coupled with leveraging students for some of the least pleasant roles, has served me well. If your recruiting skills are more accurate than mine, you should consider making a deliberate choice to recruit some professional journeymen who are suitable for long-terms roles in midtier positions to balance the team.

Follow the Money

The 1976 film *All the President's Men* tells the story of two reporters, Woodward and Bernstein, who uncover the details of the Watergate scandal that leads to President Nixon's resignation. Here's a memorable quote from the film:

> **Bob Woodward:** Hunt's come in from the cold. Supposedly he's got a lawyer with $25,000 in a brown paper bag.
>
> **Deep Throat:** Follow the money.
>
> **Bob Woodward:** What do you mean? Where?
>
> **Deep Throat:** Oh, I can't tell you that.
>
> **Bob Woodward:** But you could tell me that.
>
> **Deep Throat:** No, I have to do this my way. You tell me what you know, and I'll confirm. I'll keep you in the right direction if I can, but that's all. Just ... follow the money.

There's no question that part of your success in software is related to working on the right project or the right accounts. The trick is figuring out how to be at the right place at the right time. In most organizations, a few people are tracking this, but they're rarely the majority. That's bad, because to achieve the maximum business value, your organization really needs all eyes to be looking for the big catch. If you make the effort, you probably won't have a lot of competition. Two tactics will help you be in the right place at the right time, and they both involve following the money.

The first tactic is to watch is where your executives are investing. Pay more attention to where money is being spent than what's being said. If an executive tells you he thinks multimedia editing software is the big strategic play for your company but then spends 65% of his budget on cloud computing for social networking, you should probably stay far away from multimedia.

The second tactic is to watch what other companies are investing in, both in purchasing and in R&D spending. Again, let the marketplace be the telltale measure. If advertisers are diverting spending to SaS web sites, what should that change imply? Does it open new frontiers for disruptive or competitive software that your company can produce?

Spending is the truest and most honest representation of what a corporation feels is important and what the market believes in. The highest-paid employees are generally the most valued. The highest-cost R&D projects are projected to generate the most revenue. Yes, there are exceptions, but they are rare. Follow the money (both inside your company and in the market), and you'll quickly discover what's hot and what's not.

You Get What You Reward

What does your organization want from its employees, and what does it reward? By "rewards," I mean only that you offer some benefit for a certain behavior. Rewards can be as inexpensive as a public thank you to a colleague, or as dramatic as a large corporate financial bonus. Rewards are an emotional influence on the behavior of individuals, and emotions are powerful. It's a tool used throughout society—for example, macroeconomics is based entirely on getting what we reward. The monetary system rewards investment in new ventures by lowering interest rates and, conversely, encourages savings and discourages credit by increasing the interest rate. We reward people for investing by making it cheaper for them to get access to investment capital by lowering interest rates, and we reward people who save money by raising interest rates. Does it work? You bet. When it comes to individual behavior, people are skeptics. It's hard to believe that individuals would behave differently in their work on professional matters because of small rewards and minor biases in the system. We all want to believe that software developers, doctors, and teachers alike will do their jobs with total professionalism, regardless of the reward system. Right or wrong, it seems we're all human.

Our ability to be influenced by rewards is partly due to human vagaries, but another force is at play. Rewarding people for a behavior doesn't just satisfy selfish needs and personal desires; it's also the truest form of communicating what the organization really values. If you pay your staff $3 each to eat a bowl of ice cream once a day, you can expect the consumption of ice cream to rise dramatically. Now it's not only yummy, but it pays. If in addition to paying people a $3 bonus to eat ice cream you also gave a weekly lecture about the health risks of high-sugar, fattening foods; posted health-watch notes around the building; and distributed these by email periodically, would ice-cream consumption still be up? Chances are, the consumption of ice cream would go down a bit, but it would still be much higher than when people had to pay for it. The problem is, you've told people in one medium that ice cream is unhealthy for them, but you've paid them cold, hard cash to keep eating it. Which is the more credible indicator of what you value, the propaganda or the cash? Organizations constantly behave in this fashion, declaring certain business behaviors unwanted but rewarding them. For example, organizations often ask for teamwork but reward individual effort, demand high quality but reward productivity without concomitant reliability, and plead for innovation but invest only in established technology. The problem isn't just the mixed message; it's that, at a group level, we believe the reward more than the intangible messages. In short, talk is cheap.

The idea that you get what you reward is one of the pillars of effective management, and it's probably one of the most poorly used. To help improve the management of your own organization, align the attributes and behaviors you want from the group with the things you reward. This works for both ice cream and macroeconomics, and it works for software development, too.

Creating Shared Values

In their 1981 book *The Art of Japanese Management*, Pascale and Athos studied 34 Japanese companies operating in the United States over 6 years. They found that one of the distinguishing factors that set these companies apart and increased their ability to deliver product excellence was the attention they gave to *shared values*. Management guru Tom Peters developed and expounded on the same point in *In Search of Excellence*. Similarly, in their classic 1961 work *The Management of Innovation*, Burns and Stalker identified shared values as a pillar of effective organizations. *Shared values* provide a corporate framework that fosters teamwork and focus, yielding a dividend in efficient and motivated employees and, consequently, overrun avoidance. In Chapter 15, "Secret Insights on Software Project Management," I gave the example of the 1960s moon landing initiative. One of the reasons the NASA project was so successful was that it created a shared and very specific vision for the moon landing project and for the entire nation.

Motivating groups of people to work in a common direction requires the ability to clearly and convincingly communicate goals, schedules, and business vision. A classic mistake in project management is to define central values around operational style, ethics, and goals, but communicate them only to the senior staff, hoping for trickle-down communications. It's a poor strategy because the trickle-down might never happen—and even if it does, it won't be coming from the leaders. If you want to inspire others and establish a clear, common vision for the team, do it yourself and then make sure the message is repeated by every level of management and technical leadership. There's a time and place for delegating, but this isn't it. Set the vision and communicate it broadly to everyone. Then watch with amazement as the team rallies around the shared values.

Effective Delegation

Good leaders realize that, no matter how talented they are, as long as they're doing the work, they are an army of one. As a leader, the only way you can scale your talents is to delegate to others. The more you delegate, the more time you'll have to mentor, direct others, and spend time on the important but not urgent things that will lead to skills growth and strategic development. When in doubt, delegate. A pretty reasonable strategy is to delegate almost everything except for strategy and tracking. Delegation is easy. Follow-up and support for what you've delegated are hard. Perhaps more important, the more you delegate to others, the more you are pushing down responsibility and giving others a chance to learn and grow professionally. Good delegation is central to building the next generation of leaders; fundamentally, the role of leaders is to produce more leaders, not more followers.

Directing Others

Coercive leaders tell other people what to do and how to do it, while authoritative, affiliative, democratic, and coaching leaders rarely do. When you tell people how to do something, you rob them of the creative opportunity to figure things out on their own, make their own mistakes, and perhaps even improve on your vision. Directing others in the style of true leadership comes down to two qualities:

1. Directing them toward a goal without coercing them into any specific path to get there

2. Successfully redirecting them when they choose poorly

As the old saying goes, "Never tell people how to do things. Tell them what to do, and they will surprise you with their ingenuity."

Sometimes left to their own devices, people will come up with some pretty bad ideas. You need to point out the deficiencies in their thinking, but how can you do that without making them feel like underappreciated idiots? A classic tactic is to direct people into seeing the weaknesses of their ideas on their own, without directly criticizing them, by politely asking some probing questions. This takes a little more time than just blurting out that you disagree with them, but it helps them save face and more deeply realize their errors. It's a technique that James Gosling uses all the time; here's how he described it in his interview with me:

> One good management style I use is that I tend to not tell people what to do. If somebody comes to me with some design they've done, and I think there's something wrong with it, I usually won't say, "Oh, there's something wrong with it," because that just gets people defensive. My favorite technique is to start asking people questions about it and then have them realize, "Oh, yeah, that's kinda broken."
> —James Gosling, inventor of Java, Sun vice president, and Fellow

Taking a subtle approach that helps people see the limitations of their ideas for themselves takes more time and patience. In truth, you don't have time to deal with every issue that way. That's where emotional cache comes in. The more you have an emotional cache with people, the more liberty you can take to draw from that cache, to give them the straight talk and tell them the bad news bluntly.

PART III

Greatness

CHAPTER 17

Leadership in Software Innovation

"If I'd listened to customers, I'd have given them a faster horse."
—Henry Ford

Making it big in software has always been characterized by innovation. Innovation is the point where science and the art of software meet to create value. The greatest names in software have been defined by their mastery of innovation; some by their creation of a single dramatic technology that changed the world, and many others by their ability to continuously dream up innovations year after year. It's easy to believe that some people are simply geniuses and that it's all in the DNA. While most people would agree that genius is a helpful attribute for any aspiring inventor, it's less about intellectual prowess than it appears. There are ways to better your "innovation odds" and compose teams that collectively and frequently push the envelope of technology.

Why Innovate?

From a career perspective, it's a well-known phenomenon that technology leaders are also leaders in innovation. There are always exceptions; individuals and companies have done very well financially by performing routine tasks or providing services to legacy systems. For example, many people have built great consulting careers around services for VM, z/OS, and IMS, just as examples. Computer Associates (CA) has several lucrative products that provide features and functions for administering legacy systems and so on. Yet at a macro level, innovation drives new business and improves business efficiency. The people who drive the innovation that drives business advantage are rewarded. In every software segment, from the tiniest basement startups to the largest multinational conglomerates, the innovators earn more money and have more advanced positions, on average, by a large margin.

In 2006, the IBM Institute of Business Value surveyed 968 CEOs, with the goal of understanding CEO priorities. The survey clearly called out that growth through innovation that matters is a dominant consideration. Eighty-seven percent recognized that their organizations needed to make fundamental changes to respond to external forces in the next two years. Seventy-eight of the CEOs surveyed felt the innovation they needed would require changes to both their business models and their technology, "creating new opportunity for IT to participate directly with business in driving the innovation agenda." Similarly, a March 2005 study published in the *McKinsey Quarterly* surveyed 9,345 global executives and found that ability to innovate overwhelmingly topped executive opinion as the critical capability required for business growth. Figure 17.1 shows a summary of their findings, with the ability to innovate clearly dominating other important concerns.

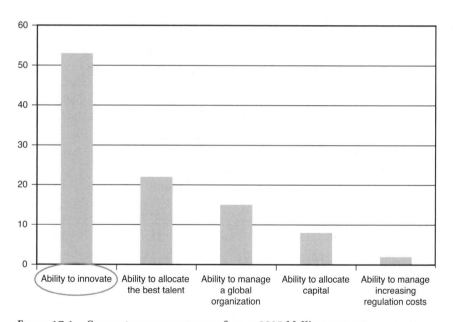

FIGURE 17.1   Corporate success concerns from a 2005 McKinsey report

It's clear from these findings that companies around the world are looking to innovate by adopting cutting-edge technology, including cutting-edge software. The results are striking but perhaps not unexpected. For companies that buy and leverage technology, it's really about winning the technology arms race that will propel them ahead of their competitors and drive ever-increasing efficiencies. For the companies that produce technology, it's about building the more compelling armaments. In a global marketplace, companies (both software companies and others) are looking to gain business advantage in three ways:

▶ Differentiating themselves by producing cutting-edge technology that will help improve their market positions against competitors

▶ Delivering new technology to market so they can establish a beach-head as the market leader

▶ Improving organizational efficiency throughout their R&D, manufacturing, logistics, marketing, sales, and support groups through process innovation and the adoption of new technology

Each of these three goals is achieved through innovation, whether it is product innovation or process innovation. Software companies commonly hold this belief:

In a business that redefines itself every few years, only the innovative survive.

It's only a half-truth, and many companies do extremely well with tried-and-true products and services that aren't defined by cutting-edge innovation. Even so, there's more than just a speck of veracity in this idea. Ask ten people you know who work in software, and you'll find that the majority are working on something new and innovative (or are working to support or integrate something that is). Innovation is the wind in the sails behind every successful software organization. It propels software companies to success and brings new capabilities to customers and end users. Of course, not all innovation is valuable, regardless of how brilliant it is. The key to successful innovation is to create something that is both new and useful. Novelty without business value is bad engineering.

Software Innovations That Succeed

Successful software innovations get implemented and have perceptible value to an organization or a market segment.

Follow these guidelines for identifying innovation that really matters. If any one of the following rings true, you have a winning innovation worth pursuing:

- ▶ In many or most cases, users will prefer the innovation over the current leading alternative.

- ▶ The innovation will measurably improve organizational efficiency (for my organization or the organizations of our customers).

- ▶ The innovation will measurably improve product reliability.

- ▶ The innovation will measurably improve product serviceability. (For example, it will radically reduce the time to detect and resolve product defects.)

- ▶ The innovation will be marketable to customers (either as a key new feature of an existing product or through the introduction of a new product).

- ▶ The innovation will solve a problem my executives are focused on.

- ▶ The innovation will get implemented because someone in my management chain feels strongly enough about the idea that they will authorize people to spend time working on it, even if only as a skunkworks/after-hours project.

Again, the value doesn't have to materialize in flashy marketing material to be of major value. On the contrary, the connection between innovation that matters and innovation that is valuable to marketing in pretty tenuous. In fact whether the value is flashy enough to motivate marketing commentary and artifacts might be secondary to whether the innovation is important and can help propel your career. Why is that? After all, if marketing is about presenting the greatest attributes of a product to the world to inspire further sales and revenue, and innovation is about improved efficiency and generated excitement, it should be a marriage made in silicon heaven. Consider a few reasons why marketing and sales might not key off really valuable innovation with a product.

Marketing and sales rarely promote more than two or three key messages to customers. In a product with many features and innovative ideas, only two or three that are more meaningful to the market will be hyped. That leaves lots of great innovation left unmentioned for customers to discover through other means.

A product might have a number of innovations, but in the interest of limiting its message to two or three key ideas, the marketing teams typically aggregate ideas into higher-level messages. In this case, the technology gets marketed, but only indirectly. For example, several new patented ideas relating to the performance (speed) of a product might get rolled up into a single marketing message about "speed" or "efficiency."

Internal innovations related to how a product is tested, compiled, or managed will (almost) never be discussed externally in marketing material, but will have major value to the efficiency-hungry dollar-watching executives managing the profit-to-expense ratios of the development team.

We can learn a lot from past flops and successes. Two notable ones were the fall of OS/2 and the phenomenal success of the Apple iPhone. Both products offered significant technical benefits over their competition. In 1982, IBM and Microsoft began joint development of OS/2, a new Intel-based operating system that would drive the personal computer industry. OS/2 had many revolutionary qualities, including exploitation of the Intel x86 protected mode processing that allowed virtual memory addressing, paging, and multitasking, and a high-performance file system called HPFS. In 1992, OS/2 was quick to support 32-bit addressing that was emerging with the Intel 386 processors, which resulted in huge memory-management efficiencies for both the computer and the programmers writing to it. By comparison, Windows was a toy system.

By 1990, the relationship between Microsoft and IBM began to unravel, and Microsoft moved to dominate the personal computing operating system market with Windows 3.0. Despite the technical advantages of OS/2, some obvious (in hindsight) factors allowed Windows to dominate. First, OS/2 shipped with a limited set of device drivers. This made it particularly difficult to use OS/2 with any peripheral device, particularly printers. Windows, in contrast, shipped with a huge array of device drivers, making it user friendly and versatile for home and business use. Second, Windows gained traction with a set of killer apps, including Word, Publisher, and PowerPoint. These programs also ran in emulation mode on OS/2, but they showed a clear difference in robustness and flow when running natively on Windows. With applications and device support in hand Microsoft successfully arranged for most new computers to sell with Windows 3.0 installed, catapulting the operating system to worldwide success. Windows sold nearly 10 million copies between 1990 and 1992. OS/2 offered better engineering, better memory management, and multitasking, but without device drivers and core applications, people just didn't want it.

The iPhone was introduced in the United States on June 29, 2007, along with wide speculation on whether it could live up to its marketing hype. It was an instant success, outselling all forecasts. In fact, in the first three months of 2009, during the worst economic recession of the past 50 years, Apple sold 3.8 million iPhones, generating $1.5 billion in revenue.[1] Simply put, the iPhone did everything that OS/2 didn't. Instead of making it difficult for the device to connect and interact, the iPhone exemplified the integration of phone, music, video, and Internet. To improve its appeal, the iPhone introduced a number of usability features, such as improved resolution video, simplified graphical navigation, and integration with Google Maps. Instead of lacking a base of core applications, Apple supplemented its own iPhone development with the Apple App Store, allowing a worldwide community of application developers to develop and sell applications using the iPhone SDK—unlimited developers, unlimited ideas, and centrally sold, with 70% of the revenue going to the application sellers. Whereas consumers and businesses considering OS/2 had to choose between performance and multitasking benefits, and printer hassles (device drivers) and missing applications, iPhone users gained much and sacrificed little, compared to users of other mobile phones on the market.

The Opportunity to Innovate

The rewards are evident; perhaps the biggest question software developers have is where they can find opportunities to be innovative. I contend that most jobs in high-tech, particularly programming jobs, offer golden opportunities for innovation. True, some have more potential than others, but the opportunities for innovation have more to do with how software developers view their jobs than what opportunities come their way. Innovation can be the introduction of radical new technology that generates new industries (such as the introduction of the relational database, or social networking sites) or technology that improves many industries through broad, sweeping impact (such as the introduction of hypertext links by Tim Berners-Lee). The industry needs these massive-scale innovations to succeed and grow, but your career absolutely doesn't. Innovations can come in the form of much more modest improvements to product features or product efficiencies or in the form of software tools and processes that companies use for purely internal purposes. Few people are assigned the job responsibility of being professional

---

[1] Michelle Megna, "What's Behind the iPhone Success Story?" www.internetnews.com/bus-news/article.php/3817276.

innovators. You'll find that the opportunities to innovate usually come from two avenues:

1. Most innovation comes through the day-to-day projects people work on when they stop and ask, "Can this be improved?" Whether you're working in customer support, testing a system, or developing a new feature for a product, that's always a fair question that can lead to innovation.

2. Outside of your own job, consider what your team or organization does that can be improved through new technology, such as test automation, automatic product upgrades, or new or improved product features.

Hope to succeed but plan to fail. Good ideas are hard to come by and even harder to bring to fruition. Always keep in mind that your latest innovation ideas might not pan out. It's not only expected, but healthy. (Then again, if all your innovations fail, you are probably doing something wrong—time to reassess how you are going about things!) The trick to healthy innovation is quickly realizing the failures so you can cut your losses and press on to more valuable projects. Every failure has learning value, so fail fast, fail often. Fortunately in software, the opportunities to innovate are so plentiful that you can fail often and still have an impressive set of additional projects to drive to success.

Brainstorming

Most people have heard the term *brainstorming* and have an approximate idea of what it is: something about getting people together to rapidly consider ideas, right? That's mostly correct. Brainstorming is about getting people together to quickly consider ideas, but there are a few rules on how to do it effectively. One of the hardest parts of brainstorming is the idea of feeling free enough and comfortable enough to make suggestions that you haven't had time to think through completely, suggestions that, on second thought, are probably completely idiotic. Effective brainstorming requires people to have that freedom and use it. The second major principle of brainstorming follows from the first: "Don't jump on the idiot." Because effective brainstorming requires people to suggest ideas quickly, even if they haven't been fully thought out, it requires the receivers of those ideas to be encouraging and polite. If the first time someone in the room says something stupid everybody jumps on him or her, it immediately kills the brainstorming for the rest of the meeting.

> You idiot—the tiny little problem with that genius idea is that it will require 4,000 programmers and a galactic-scale nuclear power plant to supply the necessary server grid. [sigh]. Does anybody else have an idea that's at least in the realm of reasonable?

Aside from being rude and cruel (the most important reasons not to speak that way), a single negative comment like that will immediately kill everyone's willingness to offer up new ideas. Instead, people will start thinking more carefully, wanting to rethink ideas several times before they suggest them, and the dynamic pace that characterizes brainstorming will evaporate. Brainstorming is about a group of people getting into a mental and social groove to rapidly explore dozens of ideas over the course of an hour. It cannot thrive without trust that the participants have the freedom to proffer the stupid along with the sublime. Instead, turn dumb ideas into a good-natured joke and press on quickly to the next idea. The more lighthearted you can keep the mood, the more people will relax and let ideas flow—that's the essence of brainstorming.

The Value Perception Cycle

Virtually all innovative ideas pass through a cycle of relative excitement, lowered expectations, and maturity. New ideas begin with a technology trigger in which market demand and a new technology come together. Initially, people grow excited about a new idea, usually beyond the true potential of the technology. The excitement is always exaggerated because the initial focus is on the benefits and capabilities of the technology, and the limitations are rarely understood or discussed in full. You can think of the height of this phase as "the promise." It represents the ultimate vision of everything the technology could theoretically bring, most of which is completely beyond near-term possibility. As new technology begins to mature, the warts and limitations begin to surface, and the excitement that came with the promise declines precipitously to a new low I'll call the point of crushed expectations. Finally, as the bugs get sorted out and the market begins to better understand what the new technology can and can't do, it takes hold and matures in a more stable way. The marketplace then realizes its value. Figure 17.2 depicts a typical maturation cycle.

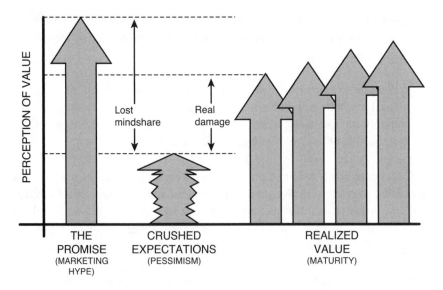

FIGURE 17.2   Technology value perception

Consider any technology you know. In most cases, you'll see that it has gone through a similar cycle. Global positioning systems (GPS) were expected to revolutionize our ability to navigate, know where our children are, and even help us locate our keys. Those were the early days of GPS, the height of the promise. We soon realized that satellite connectivity was spotty, that GPS didn't work indoors, and that GPS devices were too expensive and bulky for many consumer uses. We sank quickly to the point of crushed expectations. GPS continued to improve; newer and more satellites were launched, greatly improving reception; and the market came to understand the places were GPS could be trusted (navigation). The technology matured and created realized value. Similarly, when speech recognition entered the market, with the promise of replacing the keyboard, it quickly crashed to the point of crushed expectations when it struggled with punctuation, background noise, poor enunciation, the nuances between similar words, and accents. It later matured as a technique that was valuable to specific limited domains when aided by the notion of voice training. Expectations were adjusted to position the technology as a way to reduce the need for human typing and editing rather than a tool to replace them, and a modicum of business value was realized.

A key to success in innovation is knowing that your technology innovations will pass through this curve and striving to minimize the slope and depth of the point of crushed expectations. That's best done by correctly positioning the technology for what it can and can't do up front. This has the side effect of dampening inflated expectations, which can limit initial enthusiasm and funding. The larger the gap is between the promise and the point of crushed expectations, the more you have lost credibility and mindshare. The larger the gap is between the point of crushed expectations and the point of realized value, the more real business damage you've done by sustaining unwarranted negativity about your software. You've got a bad rap where it wasn't deserved. There's no silver bullet as you strive to strike the balance between keeping enthusiasm high and keeping expectations realistic. If the fall toward the point of crushed expectations is too steep, too fast, and too far down, it can kill a worthy innovation. The best innovators generate excitement around the promise of their technology while repeating ad infinitum the current limits of its use. Dampening the expectations to a realistic level and being honest about the limitations of use (as best as they are known early on) builds credibility and engenders support.

The Innovator's Twelve: Fostering Successful Innovation

Apple, IBM, Google, Microsoft, and others are well-known as innovative companies that have brought breakthrough software technology to market. What is truly remarkable about these companies is not just that they've had some good ideas, but also that they seem to have created corporate cultures and strategies that allow them to churn out innovations year after year. They've managed to find a formula to maintain and extend the pulse of innovation as their product portfolios have grown. Google started with a great search engine, thanks to breakthrough ideas from Larry Page and Sergey Brin, but Google has expanded its market presence dramatically beyond simple search and continues to do so with products related to mapping, video, image search, news, data analytics, hosted services, and many others.

Microsoft pioneered personal desktop computing and was the master of desktop operating systems. Although dominance in desktop operating systems remains the company's forte, Microsoft has continued to churn out top-notch technology in myriad new domains in professional productivity applications (Office, Microsoft Project), databases, cloud computing, speech recognition, gaming, application and web development, and more. Twenty years ago, IBM was predominantly a hardware company that happened to make software to support its vast hardware product array. Today IBM is a $22 billion software company (with total revenues from all divisions approaching $104 billion), with leading technology in databases, collaboration software, middleware, system administration, data analytics, and application development, as well as one of the world's largest software patent strategies. Apple began the personal computer revolution with the introduction of the Apple computer in July 1976, but it expanded to graphics leadership with the Macintosh, and then introduced brave new innovation for personal computing with products like the iPhone, iPod, and iPad.

These companies, and others like them, have clearly latched onto effective models to develop not only innovative software, but also recipes to keep doing it year after year with alarming consistency. From my own experiences in the IBM Software Group, and knowing many of the senior architects at each of these companies personally, here are some of the key tactics I've found these companies use to keep the ball of innovation constantly rolling.

1. Surround Yourself with the Best People You Can Find

I said earlier that 5 great programmers are better than 50 average ones. In the context of innovative thinking, I'm going to recast that a little: "Five great innovators are better than 500 average ones." In terms of pure innovation power, the best people can create what average ones cannot. Innovation isn't just about writing code. Aside from intellectual potential, the best people are often more ambitious and driven to tackle harder problems. The best people do something else: They raise the bar on each other and across an entire organization. Within a team, some will have qualities the others do not; as a team, they can accomplish more than their sum as individuals. Their impact is multiplicative, and that's why you should want to work with them. Pound for pound, the best people will produce more innovation (and spur others to do the same) than any other single catalyst or tactic you could inject into an organization. One final thought: Be mindful that "best" isn't quite the same as "smart," and it isn't limited to programming skills alone. "Best" is multidimensional, with qualities in technical skill, street smarts, business savvy, ambition, and drive. Remember that the best people are smart but also highly motivated and ambitious, qualities independent of their intelligence.

2. Reward Innovation

In Chapter 16, "The Big Leagues: From Medium-Shot to Big-Shot," I discussed the powerful idea that organizations get what they reward not only because people seek the reward, but because tangible rewards (especially rewards that cost the company something) are the truest form of communicating what the company really values. When you reward innovation and the teams that produce it, you send a powerful message that you value and encourage innovation. You do something else as well because if you're fair about it and consistently reward your best innovators, then you're encouraging the most innovative people to stay in the game.

3. Kill Territorialism

We are taught in school that accomplishing an assignment on your own is ideal, and it seems like common sense. After all, if one person completes what would normally take a few other people to do so, isn't that an impressive accomplishment? Strangely, in organizations, the opposite is generally true. First, however wonderfully you could have created, accomplished, or designed something on your own, it will be better with others to review and refine with. Two heads are better than one. Second, for truly complicated problems, no single person really understands all the bits and pieces required to solve the entire problem, because no single person is a guru in every relevant field of computer science (graphics, Internet, GUIs, database processing, event handling, performance optimization, mathematics, control theory, artificial intelligence, and so on). When experts from different fields work together, they can accomplish more than a single expert working alone. Finally, and perhaps more important from a career perspective, when you work as a team, more people know of your accomplishments and can praise the work of the team. For example, if five people worked together on a new invention, then all five of the coinventors become advocates and advertisers for the team's accomplishments. Collaboration not only leads to better results, but it also helps make your results visible to a much wider audience. Better results, happier colleagues, improved visibility—there's no downside.

The challenge for leaders is to successfully build software teams that live and breathe the idea of working as a team, where territorialism is anathema to the organizational culture. Remember, you get what you reward: If you reward team efforts and inclusiveness, and eschew the accomplishments of the one, you'll be sending a strong message to the team about the behavior you want to see and truly respect. It's a difficult challenge because, at the end of the day, you do want to reward your stars and keep them happy. I don't know that anyone has really found a perfect solution. One strategy I've seen work well is to reward team efforts modestly and reward the leading innovators within the team generously. That model allows the people who contributed in minor ways to get recognition and shows that you value the team effort, while providing some latitude to give special recognition to the rainmakers who made it happen.

4. Iterate

Agile development grew out of the realization that getting things right up front in a single organizational burst is just too hard and is fraught with risk. By iterating over a design space, refining a clearer understanding of the problem, the market needs, and the solution you are building, you will evolve better designs and generate early feedback about what you're doing. Innovation can be about a "Eureka!" moment, but often it's about carving, polishing, and refining a good idea into a truly elegant one through iteration. Central to leveraging the benefits of iteration is the need to generate real feedback that helps you improve over the iterations. Iteration without feedback is just another programming model. The wonderful thing about iteration is that it also frees you from the fear of making mistakes—and everything we know about the history of innovation in technology bolsters the idea that great ideas come from mistakes.

5. Give People Problems, Not Solutions

You've got really talented people working for you, or perhaps with you, on a problem, and you want to leverage their talents to develop the most elegant solution possible. Elegance in software refers to the simplicity and value of the technology. If you try to impress others with the profundity of your insight and genius by dictating up front how a problem should be solved, you're robbing them of the opportunity to make a contribution of their own. If you're lucky enough to be smarter than the entire team combined, at least you'll be providing some efficiency in giving them a proposal that is better than anything they could collectively dream up. That's an unfortunate situation for you to be in. Hopefully, if you've recruited well, you've got talented people who have good ideas of their own, and you want to give them a model for leveraging their talents and creativity. Stay far away from dictating solutions; instead, give the team the problem statement and see what they come up with. Direct them by asking questions and clarifying the nature of the requirements instead of by suggesting solutions. It takes a bit more time than just telling the team what to do, but a good team will surprise you frequently with innovative approaches you'd never have conjured up on your own.

6. Remember That Data Is Apolitical

Group opinions are biased heavily by the charisma and authority of the people pushing a viewpoint. People can be swayed. But raw data is pure and unadulterated. Arguing a point is a precarious tactic in the absence of real data. The more you can base decisions on cold, hard math, the more you clear a path for advancing ideas and projects that is largely void of politics and the personal charisma of antagonists. Decisions made in corporate America today are often based on approximate data and anecdotal evidence. Business cases are commonly compiled with minimal science behind the forecasting. In that world, charisma, charm, and a strong track record are necessary to create and be trusted with the development of real innovation. Driving decisions through analytic data-centric discussions creates a meritocracy where ideas are fairly evaluated on their value. With data behind them, good ideas more readily get approval, attract funding, and have a much higher likelihood of success.

7. Think Inside the Box

Creativity loves constraint. In 2006, I had the pleasure to attend then–Disney CEO Michael Eisner's keynote address at the Information on Demand Conference in Las Vegas. Too often, software teams invest unreasonable amounts of money on the development of bad ideas. Eisner's philosophy at Disney, which helped focus the design and production efforts of numerous blockbuster hits, including software-intensive projects such as *Pirates of the Caribbean,* was for innovators and leaders to spend more time thinking "inside the box." It might seem like counterintuitive advice, but Eisner isn't actually recommending against innovation. His point is that if you want teams to be innovative and deliver on time and on budget, you need to be serious about constraining both the time and money they have at their disposal for any project. Time and financial constraints—what Eisner calls "the box"—help teams stay focused on the possible and deliver innovative results on time. Time and resource constraints force innovation. An unconstrained amount of time and money leads only to excess, as teams fuddle with ever more elaborate choices; constrained time and resources, on the other hand, force the teams to get creative. The key is to define the constraints early and stick to them.

8. Affinitize

Affinity is the natural attraction and connection between bodies. In chemistry, it refers to the attraction of chemicals to each other. In operating systems, it often refers to the time scheduling of threads and processes to specific CPU cores. In software innovation, powerful opportunities for affinity can help good ideas bloom into great successes, by connecting people with one another. There are two important ways to affinitize for software innovation, specifically:

- ▶ R&D affinity

- ▶ Business affinity

When I talk about affinitizing, I mean seeking out and bringing together people who can help each other. Affinitizing people connect thinkers and doers who can collaborate on a project, to create something greater than any of them working alone. Affinitizing people isn't just about adding people to a project; it's more about crossing organizational boundaries and connecting people in different groups or even different companies (such as a connecting a corporate R&D team with a university research team). Getting people together with different perspectives and deep skills helps propel new technology efforts and foster innovation in dramatically positive ways. R&D affinitizing means connecting the programmers and designers who will share a passion and bring new ideas and skills to the project. Business affinity helps connect the intellectual innovators with the businesspeople who care and can help foster and direct the business aspects of an idea to bring it to market. When you bring the right mix of people and skills together, what they can accomplish together is truly more than the sum of their parts.

9. Avoid Catching "Not Invented Here" Syndrome

One of the most limiting and ubiquitous organizational attitudes among software teams is the idea that they can't and shouldn't trust any idea, strategy, algorithm, or code implementation they haven't personally developed from scratch, unless it has been canonized for more than a decade and deployed by at least a thousand production users. Sound crazy? Believe it. The vast majority of engineers will roll every new solution and every new feature from scratch. The problem with doing so isn't just limited to the obvious "time to value" problem. Obviously, an engineering team can produce a result faster if they leverage precrafted components from open source or commercially available components (COTS), but they have a valid argument that using these components limits their control over quality and serviceability of the combined solution. It's a very valid counterargument, but one that, taken to an extreme, will eliminate code reuse and drive scalability of the industry into the ground. However, the more distressing consequence of constructing every new software component from scratch is that it limits an engineering team to their own knowledge and expertise. By agreeing to reuse existing components from other teams, an engineering group can refocus its energies on the really hard problems that don't have existing solutions, where they are more likely to have the bigger breakthrough ideas.

10. Build Knowledge About Other Fields

You can learn a lot of creative approaches by studying topics that are not directly related to your own. For example, in recent years, software innovations related to self-managing software systems have drawn heavily from software techniques in control theory, economics, cybernetics, and artificial intelligence. Cross-disciplinary skills give you incredible power to innovate. You don't need to become a guru in all possible fields, but a general awareness gives you enough knowledge to know which disciplines to delve into deeply when the time comes.

11. Understand the Current State of the Art

Start every "hard" software project by studying what others have done (so-called "prior art"). Although this might seem obvious, only the best software innovators take the time to study the published literature, their competitors' technology (to the degree this is available through published papers, patents, and so on), and related strategies from other fields. You need to understand the current state of the art before you can expand it. In the process, you can turn yourself into the local "guru" on the topic because you'll be the most current on the latest techniques and literature in the domain. Gurus are the domain experts who are almost always better positioned to innovate beyond the limits of today's technology.

12. Don't Allow Users and Markets to Dictate How to Do Things

Steve Jobs once said it, and truer words were never spoken: "It's really hard to design products by focus groups. A lot of times, people don't know what they want until you show it to them." Markets aren't about innovation; they're about creating demand and passing judgment. The good news is that the market is a profound judge, and a good product brought to market with the right amount of marketing and publicity can rely on the market to provide demand and acceptance. Markets can never predict or request innovation. As long as you are looking to the market for innovative ideas, you'll always be relegated to the rank of the followers. "Follow the money" to understand business requirements and trends, but don't use the market as a source of innovation.

99% Perspiration

A lot of people have good ideas, but few have the fortitude to carry them through to completion. I loved what Linus Torvalds had to say about it during his interview with me—not just because I agree with him, but because something about his open source cultural perspective eschews so much of the corporate necessities the rest of us have to embrace:

> My personal pet peeve is how many people think the hard part is in the "big and hard problems" or in some fluffy but important-sounding thing like "innovation." In fact, all the real work is in getting the details right. It's that "1% inspiration, 99% perspiration" thing. People seem to think that inspiration is the much bigger and important part of the two, but I've come to believe that while it's important to have inspiration, where people actually stumble is when they can't execute on that inspiration. Inspiration isn't that rare in the end, but people who have it and then actually follow through...that's rare.

Innovation is sensationally important to the industry and can be a catalyst in your career, but only if you carry it through to a meaningful result. Someone will always tell you that it can't be done or that there isn't enough time or resources. You'll always encounter unforeseen technical challenges and moments of personal doubt. When you carry innovation through to creation, you change it from something "fluffy" and "important-sounding" to a thing of great value.

An Interview with Dr. Robert Kahn

Co-inventor of the Internet

CURRENT POSITION
Chairman, CEO, and President of the Corporation for National Research Initiatives (CNRI)

CLAIM TO FAME
Co-inventor of the Internet

DATE OF BIRTH
December 23, 1938

EDUCATION
Ph.D., Princeton University, 1964

M.A., Princeton University, 1962

B.E.E., City College of New York, 1960

Honorary degrees from Princeton University, University of Pavia, ETH Zurich, University of Maryland, George Mason University, the University of Central Florida, and the University of Pisa. Honorary fellowship from University College, London.

FAVORITE PASTIMES & HOBBIES
Golf, skiing, squash, tennis, figure skating, crossword puzzles, cooking, and traveling

BIOGRAPHY
Robert E. Kahn is Chairman, CEO and President of the Corporation for National Research Initiatives (CNRI), which he founded in 1986 after a 13-year term at the U.S. Defense Advanced Research Projects Agency

(DARPA). CNRI was created as a not-for-profit organization to provide leadership and funding for research and development of the National Information Infrastructure.

After earning his Ph.D. in 1964, Dr. Kahn worked on the Technical Staff at Bell Laboratories and then became an Assistant Professor of Electrical Engineering at MIT. He took a leave of absence from MIT to join Bolt, Beranek & Newman, where he was responsible for the system design of the ARPANET, the first packet-switched network. In 1972, he moved to DARPA and subsequently became Director of DARPA's Information Processing Techniques Office (IPTO). While there, he initiated the United States government's billion dollar Strategic Computing Program, the largest computer research and development program ever undertaken by the federal government. Dr. Kahn conceived the idea of open-architecture networking. He is a co-inventor of the TCP/IP protocols and was responsible for originating DARPA's Internet Program. Until 2005, CNRI provided the Secretariat for the Internet Engineering Task Force (IETF). Dr. Kahn also coined the term National Information Infrastructure (NII) in the mid 1980s, which later became more popularly known as the Information Super Highway.

In his recent work, Dr. Kahn is developing the concept of digital object architecture as a key middleware component of the NII. This notion is providing a framework for interoperability of heterogeneous information systems and is being used in many applications such as the Digital Object Identifier (DOI). He is a co-inventor of Knowbot programs, mobile software agents in the network environment.

Dr. Kahn is a member of the National Academy of Engineering, a Fellow of the IEEE, a Fellow of AAAI, a Fellow of ACM and a Fellow of the Computer History Museum. He is a member of the State Department's Advisory Committee on International Communications and Information Policy, a former member of the President's Information Technology Advisory Committee, and a former member of both the Board of Regents of the National Library of Medicine and the President's Advisory Council on the National Information Infrastructure.

He is a recipient of the AFIPS Harry Goode Memorial Award, the Marconi Award, the ACM SIGCOMM Award, the President's Award from ACM, the IEEE Koji Kobayashi Computer and Communications Award, the IEEE Alexander Graham Bell Medal, the IEEE Third Millennium Medal, the ACM Software Systems Award, the Computerworld/Smithsonian Award, the ASIS Special Award, and the Public Service Award from the Computing Research Board. Twice, he received the Secretary of Defense Civilian Service Award. He is a recipient of the 1997 National Medal of Technology, the 2001 Charles Stark Draper Prize from the National Academy of Engineering, the 2002

Prince of Asturias Award, the 2004 A.M. Turing Award from the Association for Computing Machinery, and the Presidential Medal of Freedom. Dr. Kahn received the 2003 Digital ID World award for the Digital Object Architecture as a significant contribution (technology, policy or social) to the digital identity industry. In 2005, he was awarded the Townsend Harris Medal from the Alumni Association of the City College of New York and the C & C Prize in Tokyo, Japan. He was inducted into the National Inventors Hall of Fame in May 2006 and awarded the Japan Prize for his work in "Information Communication Theory and Technology" in 2008.

"It has changed everything"

How did you get started in software?

I wouldn't argue that I'm a software person. When I started my career, I was an applied mathematician working at Bell Laboratories and ended up teaching communications and systems courses after joining the faculty at MIT. In late 1966, I took a leave of absence from MIT and joined Bolt, Beranek & Newman (BBN), a small local consulting firm, where I started working on the design of computer networks. Based on that work, we wrote a proposal that led to a contract to build the very first computer network, the ARPANET. We had a team of people at BBN who were engineers trained in building real systems. They actually took the lead in building the ARPANET; my main role was systems designer/architect.

I wrote some code when I started my career at Bell Laboratories—mainly simulation software and the like. For the most part, I would say my role in recent years has been that of a systems architect and designer, with software written by others.

What do you consider your greatest accomplishments and/or contributions to software?

Well, I know people generally cite the work I did on computer networking and the Internet, but I would say my greatest contribution to the field was through the work that we did when I was running the information processing techniques office at DARPA. We established the strategic computing program, which was the first large-scale computing program in the federal government. It was planned as a billion dollar program, which included computer architecture, software for parallel machines, artificial intelligence, and a variety of different application areas. It helped to make the Internet happen by funding network connections and computer workstations, as well as by fostering applications of that technology.

Robert Kahn

Robert Kahn

I view the work I did on computer networking and the Internet as being quite different. The work on the ARPANET focused on creating one specific packet network, as was the work I did on packet radio, creating a packetized radio net. Some of the work I did on the satellite net, helping to create a kind of a broadcast satellite net, also falls into the category of specific network developments. As a global information system, the Internet was more about architecture and protocols for allowing all those different networks to work together. I think if you put those together, they probably represent the most important contributions.

How has your work on networking contributed to the field and to the world?

Packet switching was the basis of all the networking efforts, and it basically changed the way communications switching is done today. I wasn't the first to come up with the idea, but I think our group was the first to actually build a working computer network. The Internet enabled many different networks and computers to interoperate and has become the means of worldwide communication—so it has changed everything.

Do you have a pet peeve in any aspect of the software world?

I wish it were easier to develop software and that we had better techniques for specifying functional architectures so they could be compiled, as appropriate, more directly into software. But I don't think we're there yet. The fact that we don't actually know how a particular piece of software will work when it's actually deployed is another concern. That becomes especially important in areas that are critical to life and limb, whether it's aircraft-based, hospital-based, or financial-based software. In the future, it's going to have to be easier to actually create software and get it into the hands of individuals who are not coding experts.

"Get your hands dirty"

Was there a particular event pivotal in your career?

Perhaps the most important event on my career path was an input that I got when I was on the faculty at MIT. There were a lot of very good people on the faculty at the time; I viewed myself as one of them, but I was probably the only one who had no practical experience in building real systems or equipment. So the fellow who was running the group, Jack Wozencraft, basically provided me with some helpful advice. In essence, he said, "I don't know if it will be helpful, but if I were you I would think about working with someone who has actually worked on making things happen and get your hands dirty." That's what got me into networking soon thereafter. I took a leave of absence from MIT, thinking I would go back in a year or two, and ended up at BBN working on network design. At the time, I thought a paper design for building the real thing was "getting your hands dirty," but when we actually got the contract, I decided to stay on and help build it.

What makes you feel successful about your work in software?

Lots of different things. When I'm working on an intellectual challenge, it's coming to grips with the challenge—understanding it or solving the problem. If it's a system, it would be in the form of creating it and actually seeing it work. It's the challenge. If you get engrossed in solving a crossword puzzle, it's not the thrill of solving a puzzle. It's just an intellectually challenging thing to do. Making lots of money has never been a primary goal for me. I think I would have done lots of different things if that had been the main focus. Working on interesting problems has been what I wanted to do. For me, the Internet wasn't about impact because who knew what the Internet would become back in those days? Nobody had the problem for which the Internet was the solution. We were just exploring the possibilities for getting computers on different networks to talk to each other; a sub-problem was getting the different networks to intercommunicate. It was an interesting research challenge. And bit by bit over time, we could see it having a larger impact. This was especially true after the personal computer was created because then you could see that it would impact not just a few hundred organizations that could afford big time-sharing machines, but maybe thousands or tens of thousands or even hundreds of thousands of individuals. Of course, shortly thereafter it became clear that it could affect billions. But that's not how we started out.

Most software doesn't scale beyond what it's designed for. It's interesting that the Internet was designed for thousands and scaled to worldwide impact.

Well, there are always limitations. With the ARPANET we had a 16-bit address space, and that basically would have allowed us to interconnect about 64,000 different machines—but in practice, we connected only a few hundred machines on the ARPANET. When we developed the Internet architecture, we decided that we needed a different addressing scheme, so we invented the notion of an IP address. We made it 32 bits long and thought that was more than enough to cover all possible machines we would ever encounter. Remember, this was the early 1970s, so the personal computer had not been invented, and the micro computer had only just been introduced.

Robert Kahn

You would have had a really tough sell back then to convince anyone that there would be as many as a billion machines. If a typical machine cost 1 million USD in those days, a billion machines probably would have cost more than the GNP back then.

"The essence of hockey is knowing where to be!"

What suggestions do you have for others on being successful in software (either R&D or business)?

One of the projects I started was a gigabit testbed initiative to help put high-speed networking on the map in the U.S. The project was supported by NSF and DARPA and made the front page of the *NY Times* in the first week of June, 1990. In September, they ran a story about it on the front page of the business section. After that, I must have gotten thousands of inquiries from people just wanting to provide comments or wanting know how could they do something like that. That wasn't even the Internet—that was just high-speed networking. What do you tell them? I explained about writing a proposal to the National Science Foundation. What are the odds of something like that happening again? I don't know.

There's obviously more to it than that. First you have to become a world renowned scholar, and get that job at MIT, and then do world-leading work in networking. All those things obviously came into it.

They were all relevant. But I would not want to tell somebody who is very motivated that they can't. I mean, that would be the most off-putting message you could ever give to anybody. On the other hand, you can't tell them exactly how to succeed, either, because it's a function of many circumstances. Who is interested in funding what? You have to be at the right place at the right time. Things need to fall in place for you. The hockey player Wayne Gretzky is reputed to have said that the essence of hockey is knowing where to be! I think that's the best you can offer. You need to have a sense of where things are going. If you know where the puck is going to be, it prepares you to be in the right place to take the right shot.

If you try to change the world, it's so much harder than simply doing research because all the antibody forces are out there to try and prevent it. If you are affecting something that exists, and others don't want to see it go away, they will resist the change. Or perhaps they think there's something out there that is monetarily important, and therefore they want to go after it, too. So competition arises in that case.

How do you stay on top of technology trends and innovation?

I think the biggest source of insight for me is to have many friends and colleagues who are also aware of things and share their observations. Perhaps as much as 70%–80% of what I really take in comes from others who I trust. Someone might send me a note saying, "You ought to meet this guy. If he's in town, can I bring him over?" or "Here's a paper you should look at." Very little of this is just from rummaging. I don't do a whole lot of that because there's so much out there you could spend your whole life just going through published material. And if you try to do it by going through the net, not only is there so much more out there, but you can't always tell what you can rely on.

"It's kind of a seamless whole"

Time management. Technical leaders and executives are famous for being time-strapped. What strategies do you use to stay sane and use your time effectively?

I run an organization, so I have to parcel my time so that key people in the organization who need access to me can get it. Part of that is keeping your reporting chain within reason. I've never had a reporting chain of more than about 10 individuals, and probably about a third of that has been administrative. I think the real question you're asking is about the external inputs, and I get a lot of that; such as to talk at conferences. Occasionally, it's in the form of an award—for example, I recently won the Japan Prize with my colleague Vint Cerf. That event requires a week for all the festivities, which frankly, is really grand because they treat you like royalty. However, I've also received a lot of invitations over the years to give talks, chair sessions, and the like. If I can manage to leverage two or three things at a time, I prefer it— so if a trip half way around the world is useful for multiple things, that would be fine. Or if it's something like the Japan Prize, that would be sufficient in its own right. If I'm in a meeting in London, I might try to package another meeting in Paris or Geneva. Or if I have a meeting in San Diego, I'll try to arrange a meeting in LA or Seattle. But I usually limit the number of external things I do in a year to some manageable number, and once I get beyond that I say, "Too busy this year. Let's talk about it in the future maybe."

Robert Kahn

How do you achieve a work-life balance? How do you keep your professional life from dominating everything?

You think I don't get eight hours of sleep a night or something like that? Well, let me put it this way. If you are doing what you like to do, then it's hard to be troubled by work-life separation. If somebody who would rather be on a golf course seven days a week or sailing on the Atlantic has to take time out to go to work, then I can understand. It's a matter of strong prioritization–work ends at five o'clock, and then it's personal time. But when you are working on the problems you are fundamentally interested in solving–and that's been my life from the get-go–then it's kind of a seamless whole. As I said before, one of the things I like to do is play golf. I was on the golf team in high school and college. There are times when I say to myself, "Time to get out on the golf course." Fortunately, my wife also likes to play golf, and we just make time to do that. I'm fortunate that my wife has a field that is very compatible with my own–namely, intellectual property law. I've been working for the past 20 years on the issue of information management on the Internet. With my colleagues at CNRI, we've been trying to define a strategy that is a higher level than just moving bits. For example, if research results are put on the net in the form of electronic journals, you would like that information to be easily accessible in 100 or 1000 years. Users would still need to locate the information and access it. Although my wife has her own law firm, she does work with us and for us, and often times we'll get together to brainstorm. So business and personal matters often blend together and become a seamless whole. For example, this past weekend we were at a meeting in Woods Hole that was held at the National Academy facility there. When the meeting finished, we had a choice–should we get on a plane and go home? Instead, we thought, why not take a few days vacation and stay over the weekend. So we did.

"Trust your instincts"

What do you see as the coming changes in the software field over the next 10–15 years that will impact career opportunities either positively or negatively?

If you're asking me to predict what the next big breakthrough will be that nobody has yet thought of, I can't do that. Sometimes you don't even know until it's right on top of you! The Internet was deemed to be the product of the year in 1993–can you imagine? [Although the work to develop the Internet was done in the 1970s] it was a full 20 years before others in the media actually recognized it. The areas I'm working on now might very well be impactful in another 5, 10, or 20 years. It takes time for people to recognize these things. One of the more obvious things is that broadband networking is going to become ubiquitous; by "broadband," I mean whatever is beyond your current view of what data rate is sufficient. When I first started in networking, 50kbps was viewed as broadband because everybody else was at much lower speeds (for example, around 300 bps–2400 bps using dial-up modems). Today, I'm sitting at my desk with a 100Mbps connection to my laptop and external communications at 45Mbps. I can easily see all of that moving to Gbps range in the not-too-distant future. Second is wireless. Over the past 15 years, the growth of the wireless industry has been enormous. Who knows what mobile networking will enable, especially when you factor in higher speed mobile computing and GPS-related applications. When you are mobile, you can be found and you can communicate; you can know where you are and where you need to go. This whole area of information management is also just the tip of the iceberg. The Handle system (www. handle.net) provides a good example. Most scientific journals use this particular technology to uniquely and persistently identify their digital information and to resolve the identifiers. The IEEE, the ACM, and other scientific publishers (such as Elsevier, McGraw Hill, Springer-Verlag, and John Wiley & Sons) all use this basic underlying technology for identifying digital information because if they publish in an electronic journal today, they might like it to be accessible from the electronic bookshelf 100 or 1000 years from now and still have the clickable references work. That technology has been on the Internet now for more than 15 years, and 7x24 for more than a decade, and it is very powerful. Using the system, a party can save information about a digital object so that it can be verified and authenticated; you can find out terms and conditions for its use and do all kinds of things that otherwise would be much more difficult.

"Don't you want to convince people to make it is small in software?"

What final words of wisdom or caution do you have for people entering the field?

My first thought is to ask: What is it about the field that is interesting and motivating to them right now? I would try to encourage each individual to think about what causes him to be interested. If they are completely blank and are looking for what to go into—computers, law, medicine—that's a whole different situation. From that perspective, I would try to explain to them the important role that computing and computational devices can have for society as a whole, give a few examples of things where it has made a big difference in the past, and ask them to tap their imaginations of how it can affect things in the future. For people who have already made the selection, I presume they have some sense of that. Then my advice would be that if they have an idea they really believe in, trust their instincts, and go with what they believe is the right thing to do. Had I not done that, none of the things I am noted for having done in my career probably would have gotten done. Few people thought computer networking was a worthwhile field when I first went into it. Had I listened to what people were telling me at the time, I would have picked some other field.

When I was in DARPA trying to get the Internet program going, we were already building multiple nets. We were building a radio net, a satellite net, and I wanted to work on making them work together. Nobody in the rest of the DoD had yet encountered that problem! There were no personal computers, and local area nets hadn't been introduced yet. We were just working on an interesting technical challenge. I could see the potential, but few others could. To say when it would mature—who knew? But if you don't trust your instincts, you won't do those things.

What's the title of your book going to be?

The working title right now is Making it Big in Software

Don't you want to convince people to make it is small in software? If we can get the same thing done with less software, wouldn't we all be better off?

CHAPTER 18

The Big Leagues:
From Big-Shot to Visionary

"The best way to predict the future is to invent it."
—Alan Kay

Every company has leaders; few have visionaries. I'm going to define a visionary as a person of internationally renowned expertise and innovation. In software parlance, we call them gurus. Getting to the level of world-recognized guru takes a fair bit of skill, discipline, and more than a healthy dose of dumb luck. Some visionaries become household names, such as Steve Jobs or Bill Gates. Several people interviewed in this book are visionaries, and although they're perhaps not household names, they have acquired major fame within the industry for both their brilliance and their contribution. James Gosling, Linus Torvalds, and Robert Kahn are all examples. Nobody really needs to reach the level of a visionary to have had a successful career, but it's definitely good to know you can improve your odds of achieving guru status. Visionaries don't get where they are by luck and genius IQ levels alone. In this chapter, I explore some of the classic behaviors that people at the highest levels of the game almost always embody.

Be the Authority

Feeling some déjà vu? Didn't this topic just appear in Chapter 16, "The Big Leagues: From Medium-Shot to Big-Shot"? Earlier I spoke about the importance of being an authority. There's a huge difference between being *an* authority and being *the* authority. The single major qualitative differences between important people (aka big shots) and true visionaries is that the

333

visionaries are broadly recognized worldwide. When you think of Bjarne Stroustrup, James Gosling, Mark Russinovich, Diane Greene, or Grady Booch, what comes to mind are people who are world-class leaders in C++, Java, Windows, software virtualization, and software architecture. Some of these people truly are the world experts in their fields; others are clearly in the top ten list—plenty good enough. Being top ten in the world is good enough to open doors, take you places, and influence the industry in major ways.

How long does it take to become a world-class authority? In Malcolm Gladwell's book *Outliers,* he describes the 10,000-hour rule, which approximately defines the amount of practice most experts invest before reaching world-class status. That's about three hours a day for ten years. Unfortunately, a ten-year model doesn't work well in an industry prone to complete renewal every couple years. That's why the people we think of as world-leading experts tend to be those working in domains that lucked on to some longevity: for Stroustrup, C++; for Gosling, Java; for Greene, virtualization; for Russinovich, Windows operating system internals. A major exception arises when you're an expert in an emerging field. In a new field, even with two or three years of experience, you'll outshine all comers. That's not because you've reached the ultimate pinnacle of proficiency, but simply because you're at the top of a still fairly short pole. Facebook.com founder Mark Zuckerberg rose to international fame, becoming the youngest self-made billionaire, without 10,000 hours of expertise in social networking. Many founders of emerging technology startups followed a similar pattern.

Becoming recognized as the authority on a given topic takes passion, persistence, and a willingness to create a public platform for your work. Becoming the authority is nontrivial, but being an early pioneer in a field is usually a key factor, followed by some critical steps to gain notoriety: patenting, publishing, and public speaking. Each of these expands your credibility, grows your social network, and builds your fame.

Personal Breadth

School teaches us about the art and discipline of software, but the greatest breakthroughs often come from merging ideas from unrelated domains into technology. For example, genetic algorithms draw heavily on ideas from evolutionary theory, and many optimization algorithms draw on techniques and ideas from physics, economics, and control engineering. Greatness often comes from bringing disparate ideas together in powerful ways. Su Song, Aristotle, Leonardo Da Vinci, Isaac Newton, and Benjamin Franklin were polymaths, Renaissance men of the highest order. The common perception is that their extreme genius allowed them to excel across multiple fields such as art, mathematics, science, politics, and literature. Not to diminish their great genius, but I think it's also true that the great sense of curiosity that drove these men to study multiple fields helped them excel in each of the fields they studied. The cross-disciplinary understanding enabled them to draw from unexpected viewpoints in the pursuit of solutions within any single domain.

The same phenomenon is common among software innovators. I often wondered how the software industry became so expert in typography, with detailed skills in fonts, glyphs, character sets, serif and sans serif fonts, and proportional character spacing that emerged first with the Apple Macintosh. Apparently, much of this came from Steve Jobs, who surveyed a calligraphy course after he had formally dropped out of Reed College. "None of this had even a hope of any practical application in my life," he said. "But ten years later, when we were designing the first Macintosh computer, it all came back to me. And we designed it all into the Mac." If he'd had a classical computer science education, it never would have happened. As another example, Alan Kay and Richard Stallman are both voracious readers. Both men constantly read across disciplinary lines. Alan's study of biology was fundamental in shaping his breakthrough ideas in object-oriented software. Richard's ideas in Free Software are clearly based in political exegesis more than software skills. Jon Bentley told me, "Learn everything you can; it is all relevant to software, somewhere, someday, somehow." James Gosling told me he reads everything he can get his hands on and reads *The Economist* religiously. Grady Booch follows the latest trends in physics, chemistry, and engineering. When I asked him how that helps him, he explained it much as Leonardo might have if he'd only had software in his time:

> I see two ways. One is that there are different ways of thinking about things in these engineering domains, especially the engineering disciplines with true hard science behind them; those ways of thinking help me attack hard problems in the software space. Second is that this increases my knowledge of what can be automated. As we push the limits of software systems, many of these domains outside of the software space equally don't get out much and don't understand what's outside their domain [and how software can help]; so there are some opportunities for cross-fertilization that I think are possible.

None of us can be an expert on everything. Not even Leonardo and Isaac Newton managed that. But we can all aspire to be a bit more than just software professionals. Having a little Homo Universalis within you is an exceptionally healthy thing. By following a few fields outside software, you can aspire to a kind of greatness and depth of problem solving that pure software experts alone are unlikely to achieve.

Believe in Your Ability to Master New Ideas and Technology

One of the most fascinating and motivational stories in the history of computing is the story of Steve Wozniak and the development of the Apple computer. Steve built the first commercialized and broadly usable personal computer. The Apple computer included significant advancements in software and hardware, and Steve did it all without spending a day enrolled in a college-level course on computer architecture of software design. It's unique among technology stories because of the range of expertise it certainly required. I always wondered how Steve did it. A young guy with little formal training in what he was doing, he managed to outpace and out-engineer the major companies of the day. Every new technology or business idea requires somebody, somewhere who is thinking outside the box and is willing to become the expert in a field they may not have formal training in, or which may not have significantly existed before they dreamed it up.

> Be goal-oriented. Know what you're going to do. If you are smart enough to put together the pieces, and as much of them yourself as possible, then you can achieve that goal. You don't need to have learned them. You don't need to have had courses on them. You can do it if you're smart. You can pick up some books, start working on some papers, and figure out how you can solve a problem. Whatever it is, just trust yourself that you don't need a book—you can write the book. I'm saying that from personal experience. Also keep in mind that almost all the revolutionary great advances, the big home runs in technology, come from very young people in school or not so many years out of school. You've got the energy to follow it through and to work a lot of 20-hour days.
> —Steve Wozniak, inventor of the Apple computer

Industry leaders and revolutionaries such as Bill Gates and Larry Ellison have similar stories through their founding of Microsoft and Oracle, respectively. So does the world's youngest self-made billionaire, Mark Zuckerberg, who founded Facebook.com. These folks taught themselves what they needed to know to create revolutionary software. Our industry is filled with success stories of self-made innovators who invented the future with grit, perseverance, and a hefty dab or two of ego. A common thread in these stories is that, in every case, their heroes believed in their ability to conquer new ideas and master new domains. Most people are unwilling to believe that they can become an industry-recognized leader in a technology area, but everything we know about the history of software and the history of technology confirms that if you have the will, you can achieve it.

Business Fluency

Steve Jobs co-founded Apple computers with Steve Wozniak and built an empire. To do that, the two Steves needed to understand the technology they were building and also master many aspects of marketing, sales channels, and quality assurance. Jobs's ability to master a broader space set him apart from other leaders of Silicon Valley startups. The share price of Apple Corp's stock has grown under Jobs's leadership from $1.81 in August 1985 to $214.38 in January 2010, a growth of 118 times. Bill Gates became one of the most fearsome and respected men in business as the CEO of Microsoft, and his friendship with business luminary Warren Buffet is well-known. Gates started as a simple programmer with a BASIC interpreter for DOS, but he managed to do what few founders of startups have been able to: He grew with the company. He became an expert negotiator in trial-by-fire training when negotiating with IBM.

Under Gates's leadership, the Microsoft per-share stock price grew nearly 300 times between its initial public offering in 1986 and his departure in 2006. As Microsoft grew in value, Gates became a frequent public speaker, and despite his natural shyness, he learned to socialize and work a crowd. He developed a fiercely combative business strategy that led Microsoft to dominance in numerous technical areas, making Gates the richest man in the world. Jobs and Gates achieved as much as they did in part because they realized early in their careers that their success depended on having a significant and deep business acumen in addition to technical depth. Technical depth alone wasn't going to cut it. The balance between technical depth and business skills varies across the greatest leaders in the software industry, but virtually everyone who reaches the ranks of visionary does so with a healthy dose of both. Business skills for software professionals would be an entire book on its own, but some topics worth understanding include pricing, packaging, software marketing, business partner relations and contracts, services (consulting) models, acquisitions and mergers, global financing for IT, product support models, supply chain dynamics, and cost-benefit analysis (and

ROI) for software development projects. As with many things, most people can achieve a range of skills in both technical and business domains. It's not that most people can't do it, but simply that they don't. If you make a point of developing this range of skills, you can rise to positions that are out of reach for equally talented and intelligent colleagues simply because they chose a narrower path.

Patenting

Patents in software are contentious and it's fair to say that a significant percentage of software professionals don't believe in them. Politics aside, software patents are real, and having your name associated with a few (or several) key patents helps identify you as an innovator. Patents typically cost tends of thousands of dollars (easily $30,000 when legal fees for preparation and defense and filing costs are included), so before your company will spend that money, they'll want to be sure your invention is worth the trouble. After the patent application is filed, it gets reviewed by the patent office in the affected countries, where it is compared to other patents and prior art to establish whether it qualifies as a valid patent. The reviewers are looking for three qualities: new, useful, and non-obvious.

> ▶ New. Nobody has had the idea already and placed it into the public domain by means of implementation in a product, publication, or public discussion.

> ▶ Useful. The idea has some value to society and, ideally, commercial value.

> ▶ Non-obvious. The invention isn't obvious to people who work in the field. You can reasonably estimate whether an idea is non-obvious using the "computer science obviousness hypothesis test." Here's how this test works: Imagine yourself posing a problem to a class of second- or third-year computer science students. Consider whether the problem is one they could solve in less than 90 seconds. If the students can't dream up the basics of an approach that matches your idea within that time, then your invention is probably non-obvious.

If you are working in software development, as either a designer, programmer, or tester, you probably create innovative technology that is new, useful, and non-obvious from time to time without realizing it. The most subtle of the three is "non-obvious." Most software professionals believe that before an idea can be patentable (or, at least, worth patenting), it needs to be a sophisticated innovation, something worthy of graduate research. Nothing could be further from the truth. The best and strongest patents are the simplest ones. Remember that "non-obvious" doesn't mean "complex." Just take a look at U.S. patent 6,161,223 for style-mixing pants, shown in Figure 18.1. The idea is simple: The left and right sides of the pants can be separated by means of a zipper. This allows the wearer to mix and match left and right legs from different pairs of pants. You can wear your brown corduroy pants on the left and your blue jeans on the right. It's a simple idea, but it was awarded a patent because it was deemed to be new, useful, and non-obvious.

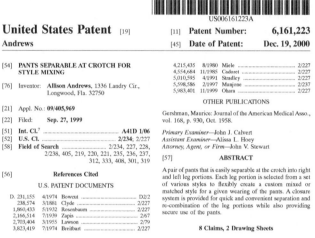

US006161223A

United States Patent [19]

Andrews

[11]   Patent Number: **6,161,223**

[45]   Date of Patent: **Dec. 19, 2000**

[54]   PANTS SEPARABLE AT CROTCH FOR
       STYLE MIXING

[76]   Inventor: **Allison Andrews,** 1336 Landry Cir.,
                   Longwood, Fla. 32750

[21]   Appl. No.: **09/405,969**

[22]   Filed: **Sep. 27, 1999**

[51]   Int. Cl.⁷ **A41D 1/06**
[52]   U.S. Cl. **2/234; 2/227**
[58]   Field of Search 2/234, 227, 228,
                   2/238, 405, 219, 220, 221, 235, 236, 237,
                   312, 333, 408, 301, 319

[56]   **References Cited**

U.S. PATENT DOCUMENTS

D. 231,155	4/1974	Bowcut D2/2
238,574	3/1881	Clyde 2/227
1,860,433	5/1932	Rosenbaum 2/227
2,166,514	7/1939	Zapis 2/67
2,703,404	3/1955	Lawson 2/79
3,823,419	7/1974	Breitbart 2/227

4,215,435	8/1980	Miele 2/227
4,554,684	11/1985	Cadoret 2/227
5,010,595	4/1991	Stradley 2/227
5,598,586	2/1997	Munjone 2/237
5,983,401	11/1999	Ohara 2/227

OTHER PUBLICATIONS

Gershman, Maurice: Journal of the American Medical Asso.,
vol. 168, p. 930, Oct. 1958.

Primary Examiner—John J. Calvert
Assistant Examiner—Alissa L. Hoey
Attorney, Agent, or Firm—John V. Stewart

[57]   **ABSTRACT**

A pair of pants that is easily separable at the crotch into right and left leg portions. Each leg portion is selected from a set of various styles to flexibly create a custom mixed or matched style for a given wearing of the pants. A closure system is provided for quick and convenient separation and re-combination of the leg portions while also providing secure use of the pants.

8 Claims, 2 Drawing Sheets

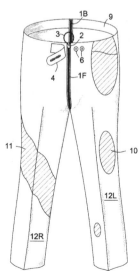

FIGURE 18.1   U.S. patent for style-mixing pants

Does it really achieve all three criteria for patentability? The first observation is that the technology for the idea has existed for hundreds of years (pre-zipper, you could accomplish the same with snaps, buttons, or strings). Is the idea useful? Sure, I can easily imagine this becoming a teenage fashion style—why not? It's certainly new because we haven't seen this before. How about non-obvious? Well, that's where it gets interesting. If you asked a group of reasonably intelligent and educated people how they would build style-mixing pants so that the left leg and the right leg could be swapped between different pairs of pants, clearly most people would figure out this solution or something sufficiently similar. What's not obvious is the question that motivates the invention because the notion of style-mixing pants is non-obvious. It's clearly non-obvious because nobody has thought to do it, even though the technology for it has existed for hundreds of years.

Some of the most powerful and creative ideas in software have been the simplest ones. Consider the idea of the graphical user interface. Today we take it for granted. The idea of representing each running program in a graphical box, like windows on a wall or pages scattered on a desk, seems natural enough. However, the idea took years to develop, and when it arrived for broad commercial use, it was revolutionary. Google's search engine is driven by the simple idea of page rank, a measure of a URL's usefulness that is measured by the frequency with which other pages link to it. Google's page rank model was simple but it instantly dominated existing search engines that were based on sophisticated content-analysis engines. Simple ideas can be powerful, and the simpler the idea is, usually the more powerful it is and the broader its utility.

Not all patentable ideas are worth patenting. More important than your inventions being patentable (that is, new, useful, and non-obvious) is that they must be compelling enough to make the decision to protect them with a patent an easy one—despite the tens of thousands of dollars of cold, hard cash this requires. When you have a patentable idea (new, useful, and non-obvious), try to determine whether an idea is worth patenting using the following two questions:

1. Will other companies want this innovation?

2. Could someone conceivably start a small company around this innovation?

If the answer to either of these is unabashedly and certainly yes, then you're on to a very strong and highly patentable idea. If the answer is yes to both questions, then it's a no-brainer.

The names on the patent should reflect the people who contributed to the invention, not the people who implemented it. So if programming an invention (even for the first time) doesn't qualify you as an inventor at the patent office, what does? Patents have a specific structure, and most of the front matter that describes the invention is informational. The core of a patent is a set of points at the back called claims. The claims are the aspects of the invention that the inventors feel are unique and innovative. The inventors of the patent should be the people who contributed to the ideas (not the code) described in one or more of the claims.

Patents are strongly correlated with career success, although some of the most notable and most highly successful people software have none, and some people with impressive patent portfolios to their credit haven't climbed very high on the ladder of career success against almost any metric. Even so, in 2008, I examined the correlation of career success and patent portfolio at IBM in one of their largest product teams. I examined the number of patents held by Senior Technical Staff Members, IBM's most senior non-executive technical position. From a population of 10 Senior Technical Staff Members in that group, 100% had patent filings, and 50% had more than 12 patent filings, earning them IBM's coveted title of Master Inventor. When I extended the analysis to include Distinguished Engineers, a technical executive role held by approximately 0.1% of IBM employees, the statistics for Master Inventors jumped to 63%. I don't believe the correlation is caused by IBM simply promoting people with a lot of patents. The reality is that people who are innovative thinkers and technical leaders also end up with more patents to their name. While innovation helped them establish successful careers, their patent portfolios helped both illustrate and disambiguate their history of innovation.

Publishing

Publishing gets your name out into the field and can garner you a dedicated group of committed readers who follow your work. The impact varies with the kind of publication. Research papers can influence the direction our industry takes over time. You can see the impact when other research groups begin to incorporate your ideas into their own projects. It's fairly easy to track by citations of your publications. Industrial and trade publications focus on a different space and are clearly more valuable in helping customers and field experts. There's no question that whitepapers and customer-facing technical articles have massively helped customers; they help your customers consume your technology, build larger and more committed technical communities around your products, and help maximize the value your customers can extract from your products. Finally, opinion columns and blogs can help establish you as a domain expert with valued opinions, a voice that investors and analysts trust. Your views as a well-known columnist or blogger can strongly influence the marketplace. A stroke from your pen can make or break the success of emerging products.

I started with failure. I submitted a couple papers to conferences and then waited on pins and needles for months, only to be rejected. It was disappointing and motivating at the same time. I realized there was something fundamentally wrong in my writing strategy. At the same time, some of my counterparts at Microsoft were publishing prolifically, and I asked myself, "What is it about their papers that gets them accepted so regularly?" I printed several of their papers looking for a pattern, and I found it. Every one of their papers used the same template and certain stylistic elements. I started using a similar formula and found my papers getting accepted almost immediately. My team submitted papers to some important venues—SIGMOD, VLDB, ICDE, and others—and had 90% of everything we submitted accepted, even in venues in which the acceptance rates were 1 in 6 or 1 in 9. Between 2001 and 2007, my team published more than 35 papers. We became incredibly efficient at it, authoring professional papers in just a few days, almost always using ideas and experimental results we had on hand from our regular line item development work. By splitting up the effort, we could compose a solid paper with each of us just doing a small fraction of the work.

Authoring a book was an entirely different experience, which came later in 2005 and then again in 2006. It's much harder, more profound, and more satisfying.

Here's a short list of reasons you should strongly consider publishing:

▶ It's a way to make a contribution to the industry that goes beyond your normal circle of influence in your company. Publications are read and reviewed by your competitors, your customers, and academics around the world. I remember sitting down to lunch at VLDB 2004 and, coincidentally, sitting beside a program manager from Microsoft SQL Server (one of my major competitors). He told me he had been reading my papers, and a few were circulating around Microsoft. I managed a forced, painful smile and thought, "Oh, no." Then I thought. "Cool!" It was a stark reminder to me that everything we publish as software professionals can be used against us, but at the same time, when we publish important ideas, our influence extends beyond the limited bounds of the company that employs us.

— Industrial publications such as whitepapers directly help your customers and your company's field staff (sales, support, and so on) maximize the value they get from your products. What can be more satisfying than realizing you've helped an entire organization do things better and more easily?

— In the case of professional and academic books, you can find a real sense of contributing to the computer science and user communities, including application and web developers, system administrators, DBAs, professors, and students.

▶ Most authors get a lot of satisfaction when their writing survives the peer review process. Particularly in the academic space, these publications are often reviewed by some of the biggest names in the industry; a real satisfaction comes from knowing that your ideas have been reviewed by that community and are still recommended for publication.

▶ Many of us in high-tech share the problem that the technical work we do can be hard to describe to our families and friends if they're not in one of the IT professions themselves. But even if they don't understand the content of the publications, they understand that a book or a paper has been published. Publishing helps your family and friends connect with your work life and share in it. Finally, yes, it's definitely nice to see your name in print!

▶ If you're a manager, you might find, as I have, that your team enjoys publishing, and although authoring papers doesn't require (relatively) much time, it's a fun and team-bonding experience. Everything we know about people and teams supports the ideas that happy and enthusiastic employees are far more productive than those who aren't. In my experience, the time we spend authoring we recoup tenfold in productivity gains across the team. Perhaps it's counterintuitive, but publishing is time well spent in building a high-efficiency organization.

The Value of Publishing to Your Career

First and foremost, publishing forces writers to learn things in a much deeper way than they otherwise would, and to grow professionally as a result. I've always been amazed by how many times I think I know a topic thoroughly, but once I start writing, I discover so many aspects I'm forced to learn more deeply. I feel I'm a significantly broader and better engineer, database expert, and computer scientist because of it.

Inside your company, promotion to higher levels along the technical track can come in many ways, and publishing helps. It's true that you can get promoted to positions such as Product Architect, Director of Engineering, Distinguished Engineer, and Technical Fellow without an extensive publication history. In most companies, you don't need to be a prolific author to reach these levels—but it helps. Publishing is one of the few things you can do that spreads your name outside your company. Although it's not as intimate as public speaking, where people can hear and see you, it has greater potential for scalability. Whereas a big room for a speaking engagement in computer science or commercial software might draw an audience in the hundreds, a well-written piece can reach tens of thousands.

Advice for New Writers

Here are some tips for software professionals who are new to writing.

- ▶ **Write what you know.** Even when writing about a topic you know very well, you'll have to do a lot of research to get little details right about syntax, semantics, competitors, and so on. This is true for professional and academic publications alike.

- ▶ **Focus on quality.** Ultimately, the quality of what you write will propel you, not the volume. Authoring frequently without quality in the content might get you a few more entries on your resume, but over time, it will work against you. Take particular care when writing for venues that don't use a strong, independent peer review process. In the absence of a critical review process, try to impose one on yourself by finding at least three skilled people to review what you've written.

- ▶ **Ask whether you'd bother to read it.** If you wouldn't, why should someone else? Use yourself as a guide post and try to focus on authoring things that you would personally feel compelled to read.

- ▶ **In general, collaborate with coauthors.** Collaboration almost always means less work and a much better publication. It's rare that any of us have the depth of skill and business understanding to cover all angles of a topic thoroughly and articulately.

- ▶ **Remember that style matters.** Writing involves more than just having something to write about. Study the styles and strategies others have used successfully.

- ▶ **Don't write to get rich.** Some companies offer a small financial incentive to employees when they publish—but most do not. Even if your company does pay some form of token award for publishing, it will be small; you won't pay off your next home with it. Book publishing (aside from authoring articles and papers) has the unique addition of author royalties, but most people don't understand how little these usually are, so consider some facts: Most technical books don't make it to a second printing, which means they sell less than 3,000 copies. Authors usually get a small percentage of the sales price (exact amount varies with the contract), which they divide among them if there are multiple authors. So the royalties are relatively small, and after taxes, there's not much to take home. You'll make a lot more money over time by spending just a few more hours a year managing your retirement investments! What about all those millionaire authors you read about? After all, isn't J. K. Rowling richer than the Queen of England? True, but she wasn't writing about databases or virtual reality algorithms. Here's an actual conversation I had with my wife recently:

> "All we have to do is sell a million copies of my book *Physical Database Design,* and then we can retire."
>
> "That's great, honey! How many more do you need to sell?"
>
> "About a million."

Consider the long-term benefits of publishing. In the short term, the ratio of benefit to time spent might not appear compelling. Writing can be a lot of work with little immediate return. But in the long run, writing pays off many times over and in unexpected ways. Help customers, influence the industry, broaden and deepen your skills, propel your career, produce something your friends and family can connect with and be proud of, and see your name in print. It's totally worth it.

Public Speaking

Public speaking is an absolute necessity for leaders in the software industry. If you aren't speaking to external audiences outside of your company, such as customers, analysts, and reporters, then you'll certainly be speaking to internal audiences such as executives, architects, and sales and marketing teams. Here are some tips for people performing for an audience as a public speaker in the software industry:

▶ **Understand your audience.** Who are they and what do they want to hear? Are you speaking to users, senior architects, salesmen, or business decision makers? Depending on who you're talking to, the messages you share will be radically different. For example, senior architects want to hear about how things work. They won't believe anything you say unless you can clearly articulate in technical terms what's going on under the hood. It's all about architecture and experimental proof points. Business decision makers usually care much less about how things work and care a lot about field-tested proof points (not just well-behaved laboratory tests). How has the software system performed for others? Make sure you always give the business folks the business case: market size, sales potential, expected costs, and project revenue. Even if you only have crude estimates, they'll appreciate seeing it. End users will always be captivated by facts about what the technology can do for them, the easiest path to most quickly experience those benefits, and, most significantly, the best practices to maximize their experience.

▶ **Adapt your style to the audience (not just your content).** A generous dose of humor is almost always appreciated, but a casual speaking style is better suited to some venues than others. In a formal setting, be more formal; in a college setting, be more young at heart; among techies, be a geek; and among business leaders, speak with forceful confidence and an accommodating ear.

▶ **Clarity and pace are key.** Public speaking is generally done at a slightly slower pace than conversational discussion. If you speak at a normal conversational pace, you're probably speaking a little too fast. Be clear and moderately slow in pace, while keeping the enthusiasm of your message high.

▶ **Keep the audience engaged.** Most of us have had the unfortunate experience of sitting through a lecture given by a monotone, unenthused presenter. A few jokes, some rhetorical questions along the way, and a bit of voice inflection do wonders for keeping people focused and awake. Drawing from other unlikely disciplines is a good tactic for adding color to your talk. For example, if you're discussing a normally unexciting topic such as Java Runtime Engine compatibility, pull in an anecdote about a NASA mission to Mars, or a JRE-related project at the Guggenheim Museum, to make a point or two in a colorful way. Not only will the particular point you're making be more memorable, but you'll have snapped the audience to attention and guaranteed their interest for the next 5–10 minutes.

▶ **Moderate your hand motions.** Waving your hands around like an overexcited salesman is almost the worst thing you can do as a public speaker. It's bested in damaging effects only by the opposite behavior of putting your hands in your pockets or clasping them together. Keep your hands in front of you, and move them moderately. How much? Go to YouTube and watch President Obama or President Clinton as they give public speeches, and you'll get a very good sense of appropriate use of your hands.

▶ **Smile.** Smiling always exudes a warm, positive, and upbeat emotion. When a public speaker smiles, it exudes that positive feeling to the audience and reflects positively on everything the speaker says in his or her talk. It shows confidence and removes tension.

▶ **Remember, you, not the charts, are the speaker.** Presentation charts support what you're saying, but they aren't intended to actually be the presentation. "Speaking to the charts" has become an epidemic in corporate America, particularly among software specialists. The curse of chartware is that the speaker packs all the useful information into the presentation charts and then, when presenting, simply reads the material off the chart. First, since the audience can read, reading the text you've projected to a large screen is neither appreciated nor impressive. Second, in the overwhelming majority of cases, the speaker is positioned between the screen and the audience. If you read the material off the screen, you end up turning your back to the audience. I've witnessed inexperienced speakers literally give their entire presentation with the backs to the people they are intending to present to. You are not there as a speaker to present the charts. You are there to speak, and the charts are there to add graphical material that supports your talk.

▶ **It's not about you.** Unless you are truly a celebrity, avoid excessively using the word *I*. Unless you're a household name in your field, your talk is never really about you, and your audience didn't attend your talk to learn more about your life, professional or otherwise. The one place it's okay to use the first person is when you're telling a story. Storytelling is an ancient art, and everyone loves a good one. Tell them some really good war stories about software, and they will love you for it.

▶ **So what?** Every chart you present and every message you convey should have a purpose. Be clear about the purpose of your messages and why your audience should want to hear them. If you don't think the audience will likely care about a certain point, don't include it just for completeness. Either remove it completely or move it to a backup section that contains supporting material. As you prepare a talk, constantly review the presentation material and your speaking plans, and ask yourself, "So what? What message do I want to convey with this chart, and why will my audience care?"

▶ **Create an antagonist.** One of Steve Jobs's stylistic tactics is that he uses his competitors as antagonists in his public speaking, with brilliant results. This creates a sense of melodrama that keeps the audience engaged. If you are the hero, who is the bad guy? In 1984 Jobs declared "IBM wants it all," and his Apple company would be the only corporation standing in their way. The masses ate it up. The hero versus villain presentation is particularly effective if you can position yourself as the underdog, and it makes for a gripping presentation. After all, everyone roots for the underdog. So introduce your antagonist and declare how you'll vanquish the enemy against all odds.

Success Is a Lousy Teacher

"Success is a lousy teacher. It seduces smart people into thinking they can't lose."
—Bill Gates

As much as success is a lousy teacher, failure is a brilliant one. Failures give you the opportunity to look back, understand what went wrong, and improve. Even better than the learning experience, most of us find the disappointment of a failed project so gut-wrenching and visceral that we're emotionally compelled to do everything we can to avoid its repetition. Look at all great leaders, and you'll see a series of failures that have helped them learn, grow, and improve to the leaders they became. The secret of turning your failures into brilliant growth experiences is in the causal analysis. Take the time after every project (failed or successful) to look back and study the mistakes. Most projects have some mistakes worth learning from, although failed projects have the zingers.

Frederick Brooks learned the hard way on the System 360 project, but the causal analysis he did not only propelled him to fame, but helped garner him the ACM Turing Award in 1999. More profoundly, the lessons Brooks learned from the event significantly improved the software industry worldwide through his publications and lectures. Unquestionably, the System 360 project was one heck of a teacher for the software industry. Of course, having too many failures in your professional history will have a deleterious impact on your career because track record is everything. Having a few rough spots is survivable and can help you grow to remarkable heights if you take the time to study and reflect on what went wrong. One benefit of reaching the highest levels of the industry is that it gives you the opportunity to have much broader scope, with potentially several projects on the go at any time. With that kind of range, you can afford a few failures and still keep your track record high.

Advanced Social Networking (Social Steroids for Nerds)

A key to becoming a great leader and visionary is to remember that even if you become the next Bill Gates or Steve Jobs, it's never really about you. Everyone is heads down trying to succeed with their own projects, paying their bills, and keeping their family stable and happy. Keeping yourself current and connected with an increasingly broad community that is focused on their own legitimate needs requires scalability. What you can offer others is always more important to them than what they can offer you. It comes down to the major ideas I discussed earlier about building emotional caches and social networks. The problem is that whereas an intermediate technical leader might have dozens of professional relationships, a senior leader could have hundreds, and a major personality will have thousands. It's impossible to have close relationships with thousands of people—how can any of us traverse the grand morass and maintain a true, vibrant, and real relationship with the people we need to?

> ▶ **Some relationships are more equal than others.** Some professional relationships are more valuable and important to keep strong because of the value their collaboration can offer. Figuring out which those are usually isn't hard. You can't build tight relationships with hundreds, let alone thousands, of business colleagues, but you should invest the time to stay close to the 10–20 people you feel you have

the most valuable relationships with. These might be a trusted mentor, a brilliant innovator, or a leading executive. When you've figured out your most important relationships, deliberately invest the time to keep them strong by staying in touch and building emotional cache over months and years.

▶ **Scale the dissemination of information.** You can stay in touch with a large range of people using email distribution lists. Although you might not be able to go out for lunch once a week with each of your thousand closest friends, you can drop them all a line to say hello, pass on a short joke (four times a year is plenty), ask them for their opinion on a professional matter, or let them know about interesting news.

▶ **Leverage social networking.** Facebook, Pulse, LinkedIn, and other emerging social networking platforms are allowing people to maintain relationships and scale their social interactions both personally ("I just got back from tennis.") and professionally ("We just released version 2.0 of our product. I had a blast working on the video feature. Check out the demo here: www.myproductdemo.com.").

▶ **Help people connect with one another.** As a leader, your role is more about the people you lead than about you, and the best leaders make a point of helping others succeed. You don't have to (and shouldn't) do other folks' jobs for them, but often one of the most important things you can do for your colleagues is to connect them with the right people and resources they need to accomplish their goals. It's not what you know but who you know, and the people with the broadest social networks are best positioned to become the powerful connectors that bring people and resources together.

Passion and Process for Your Art

If you're going to reach Gladwell's 10,000-hour rule honing your skills on a topic, whether it's computer science, sports, musical performance, or anything else, you'll need some passion and drive to get you there. While authoring this book, I contacted Alan Kay for some of his insights on professional growth. Alan is a wonderful example of a software visionary. He was one of the major forces behind the invention of Smalltalk and dynamic interpreted languages. He was one of the early pioneers in object-oriented programming, and he had a seminal impact on the development of graphical user interfaces. For his contributions, he was awarded the 2003 ACM Turing Award, among a long list of awards. For Alan, computer science is art. He has always viewed it that way, and his passion for the art drove much of his success in the 1960s and 1970s:

> Artists are people who are driven by inner senses of ideals to do their thing. They tend to be very focused and compulsive. Music of various kinds has been an "alternate art form," but I've been similarly compulsive about it (highly developed forms of music like classical and jazz require lots of thinking and lots of grinding, at least for me). For many such personalities, idealism pretty much sets up goals that are unlikely to be reached. Butler Lampson likes the Browning "reach should exceed grasp, else what's a heaven for?" quote, and he's a lot more balanced than I am (I think). I have a master glassblower friend who told me he would take a bite of the molten glass if he could. I know exactly what he meant. This is "happiness in art."

The greatest visionaries in software aren't just people who enjoy what they do—they love what they do. They're passionate about and driven to their art. Passion helps us work harder and be happier and frees us to dream. Passion and drive are necessary but insufficient on their own because the creativity that drives them is almost, by definition, too organic and unstructured. What distinguishes the visionary from the dreamer? I believe the difference is structure, or what software engineers like to call process. Process converts the seeds of creativity into impressive higher accomplishments. Passion wrapped with structure drives successful art and forms the engine of visionary thinking and results. The combination is rare because it requires the careful blending of the highly creative with the highly organized. In software terms, we call that structure software engineering. There's a time for dreaming and a time for building with attention to detail and process. In fact, I think some of the greatest software luminaries do these at different times of the day or dates on the calendar. When you discipline yourself to excel at both (perhaps by leveraging a team that supplements your talents and compensates for your weaknesses), you create an environment that's ideal for cultivating your own greatness.

An Interview with Steve Wozniak

Inventor of the Apple Computer
Co-founder of Apple Inc.
Pop Icon

CURRENT POSITION
Co-founder, Apple Computer; celebrity speaker

CLAIM TO FAME
Inventor of the first widely adopted personal computer, and co-founder of Apple Computer.

DATE OF BIRTH
August 11, 1950

EDUCATION
B.S. in Electrical Engineering and Computer Science, University of California, Berkeley, 1971–1986

FAVORITE PASTIMES & HOBBIES
Attending concerts, playing Segway Polo and Tetris on Gameboy, telling jokes/pulling pranks, and exploring gadgets

BIOGRAPHY
A Silicon Valley icon and philanthropist for the past three decades, Steve helped shape the computing industry with his design of Apple's first line of products, the Apple I and II, and influenced the popular Macintosh. In 1976, Steve co-founded Apple Computer with the Apple I computer. The next year, he introduced his Apple II personal computer, featuring a central processing unit, a keyboard, color graphics, and a floppy disk drive, and helped to launch the PC industry.

For his achievements at Apple Computer, Steve was awarded the National Medal of Technology by the President of the United States in 1985, the highest honor bestowed on America's leading innovators.

In 2000, Steve was inducted into the Inventors Hall of Fame and was awarded the prestigious Heinz Award for Technology, The Economy and Employment, for "single-handedly designing the first personal computer and for then redirecting his lifelong passion for mathematics and electronics toward lighting the fires of excitement for education in grade school students and their teachers."

After leaving Apple in 1985, Steve was involved in various business and philanthropic ventures, focusing primarily on computer capabilities in schools, stressing hands-on learning, and encouraging creativity for students. Making significant investments of both time and resources in education, Steve "adopted" the Los Gatos School District, providing students and teachers with hands-on teaching and donations of state-of-the-art technology equipment. He founded the Electronic Frontier Foundation and was the founding sponsor of the Tech Museum, the Silicon Valley Ballet, and the Children's Discovery Museum of San Jose.

Steve is also a published author, with the release of his *New York Times* best-selling autobiography, *iWoz: From Computer Geek to Cult Icon* (Norton Publishing, 2006).

"So it was, like, no tools, no money..."

You have a fascinating background that has had a massive influence in both software and hardware. Do you see yourself as a hardware or software guy?

I always saw myself as a hardware person first, chronologically and in life, but I was very goal-oriented, and I would take on projects. And to do a project, you had to [master the software aspects as well]. I was very independent. I didn't want to say, "Hey, I'll do this part and you do that part." No, all my life, I wanted to do my own design from start to finish. And although most of them were pure hardware, up to the Apple I computer I had taken software classes, and I loved software. If I saw computers that weren't running a program late at night, I wanted to sneak in with a purloined key and start running programs on them. And I did that! In college, I ran every program I could think of. I tried to do the most outstanding examples. If a teacher said, "Here's a program for you to write, and the fewest steps I've ever seen anyone do it in is 11," I would do it in 6. I would search every manual. I was the same way with hardware, and I applied that to software thinking. With low-level software, close to the registers of the machine—not like higher-level language, and not even like C that much—your thinking has to be how to use every little bit very efficiently. When I had to build a computer, I knew that Bill Gates had written a BASIC language for the Altair VM Intel microchips. I was using a different microprocessor because that was all I could afford—I had no money at all. I decided, "Hey, I'll write a BASIC!" I had never been trained in writing computer languages. But when you are goal-oriented, you have to get there. You have to think it out. It's almost like you are writing a book: Here is the logic; here is how you do a certain thing. You have to write the book in order to do it, and that's how I was. So I was able to do incredible software and hardware tasks all on my own because nobody else was involved to say, "Why don't you do that?"

If you wanted to write a computer program like the programs of the Apple II, you would write your program with another computer that would compile the code and turn it into 1s and 0s that my microprocessor could understand. Well, I couldn't afford this little program called a compiler. You could rent terminals and time-shared computer systems, and pay a certain amount of money per month, and you could actually write your programs. But since I couldn't afford that, either, I wrote my programs on one side of a piece of paper by hand. Then I wrote the 1s and 0s that they would translate into on the other side, figuring it out from little cards I had about how the microprocessors work. No other project that large has probably ever been done that way. I still have the whole handwritten manual. But that made me very intimate with the code. Every little line mattered a lot, and it was a representation of myself, too. It had to be so perfect that nobody else could have thought of a better way. If I ever thought of any little section of code that had a slightly better way, I would change it and go that way. The lack of money actually helped lead to that because the lack of money forced me to be very intimate with the code I was writing. Then I would have to type the 1s and 0s into my computer. For BASIC, it took me 40 minutes. I'd turn on the power, type it in for 40 minutes, test that there weren't any errors, and then go on debugging the next section. So it was like, no tools, no money—I did it all myself without tools, and that led to a very noticeable type of skill excellence. I've been that way my whole life.

It must have been incredibly difficult to debug the thing if you ever had a typo!

You know, I never found it that way. If I ever had a bug, I could go though it and examine all the 1s and 0s in memory, and look at them on my screen and see one little bit that was off. I was very good at typing; I really didn't make any mistakes. And when I wrote a new section of code that screwed it up, and it went somewhere and crashed the system, then I would reboot and go analyze memory. I would rewrite the code with little traps storing in certain locations what it was doing so I could go back and figure it out. So it was a very much about manual tools—skip the automated tools.

"So confusing for a human to use"

Do you have a pet peeve in any aspect of the software world?

Software that just isn't thought out to be perfect for a human to use—so confusing for a human to use. Confusing wording. Confusing buttons. Which steps you want to take. Now here's a word that sounds like it but implies something else. If you know a fact that you want to present to somebody else, you can make up a million different ways to say it, yet does the person who hears the way you've chosen to say it understand the fact that you're trying to get across? How do you make software intuitive? The early Macintosh days did such a good job. I was very oriented for the kind of thinking that machine was aimed at—making things really intuitive. I think that [today, as an industry] we've basically lost it. If a program has the function somewhere, it's called good. And it just doesn't feel like anything in computers is intuitive very often these days. Sometimes I'm wrong: The iPhone and the iPod were outstanding in that way. But software on both Windows and Macintosh is just too focused on getting out the next advance. Are there positions in the company for people to study what naturally works intuitively to humans? We don't have people like that with high authority. It's really just engineers, and engineers are noted for poor communications skills.

What do you consider your greatest accomplishments and/or contributions to software?

Well, software...wow. It's so difficult to say. Everything from even the little 256-byte monitor of the Apple, I was so critical to changing computers, because every computer before the Apple I had a front panel. Every computer since the Apple I had a keyboard and a display. And the key to it is that when you turn it on, there is a little program running these things. That little program that got rid of the front panel might have been the most important. The Apple II was so incredible, but many of the advances were hardware. And I did every piece of software from the ground up, through applications that you can't pin down for any one of them. The hardware was so interrelated that I can't really divide it into software and hardware alone. Those days were that way. Today, if you work on embedded processors, you put a little microprocessor into a small product. That's the job in the world that I would

Steve Wozniak

Steve Wozniak

love to this day! That's what I did back then; it mixed both hardware and software.

What makes you feel successful about your work in software?

For me, it's clear. I like when people look my actual engineering, the programs I wrote, step by step, and look at my circuits—we published all this in the open in the early days of Apple—and say, "Wow, the way his mind worked to put together these steps, these programs, and to do these clever things!" That means more to me than anything. Not changing the world or bringing personal computers to people—I'd much rather just be honored as having been a very gifted engineer with one-in-the-world skills. It was how the lines of code were chosen and how the routines were designed more than the 1s and 0s; people would look at it and think, "Oh my gosh, I couldn't have saved 1 byte of code."

"It was like I was made a superman"

Was there an event in your life that was pivotal in setting the course of your career?

There were so many little accidental things, any one of which would have tipped me where I went. I can't really answer that easily. My high school teacher in electronics, Mr. John C. McCollum, saw that I knew all the electronics in the school. I'd had a ham radio license since 6th grade; now I was in 10th or 11th. He arranged for me to go to a company in town and program a computer. Our high school couldn't afford a computer. I somehow was gonna be the only one who was privileged to learn how to touch a computer that could do a million things a second? It was like I was made a superman. What he found was that not all the solutions to education are in the school system. Not all of them are in the books for courses and teachers. Some people can get better education if you find connections for them in local industry. And I really always admired that, to this day. Some colleges have coop programs—I absolutely admire that because you can work and go to school. The work earns the money for school, and the work prepares you more for the real world. The world of engineering isn't what you think when you go to college. You go to college and learn this and that. Then you get out and find that engineering almost always involves checking carefully and making sure you don't have something you didn't think about—a little oversight or something that doesn't work in some little case. Over and over, it's a rigorous devotion to making things as perfect as you can.

What do you see as the coming changes in the software field over the next 10–15 years that will impact career opportunities either positively or negatively?

I think software is popping up in every little product and appliance. Almost every product today fails on me. A card looses its Bluetooth connection. Or my car window wipers don't work—so I stop the car, turn it off, and turn it on again, and it works. Everything today has a tendency to crash. In the old days, you couldn't build hardware that could crash that way. But we're building [software] into small little appliances all over the place. That's absolutely going to increase. Eventually, small little appliances throughout the house will be talking to each other. The communication media of various types of radios will possibly change over time.

What do you want to do with yourself in the future? Do you have as-yet-unaccomplished dreams?

Well, you know I have a game I play, and I want to get a certain score. I've had that dream for about 10 years, and I'm still working on it.

Can I ask what game it is?

Gameboy Tetris. I want to get 750,000. Little goals like that. Sometimes I achieve many of my goals years later. I have certain areas I would like to work on. I'm on boards of a few companies. In personal areas, I like to make light and optics do the functions of computer hardware that I grew up with—logic gates. So instead of electrons, photons are routing their way through the equivalent of chips. That way, we could have computers that are much faster, without heat. That might be possible, might not. I'd also like to build some devices for GPS tracking of important objects so you can easily find them, at a very low cost, small size, and no hassle. I started a company to do that—it didn't achieve it. But there isn't a day that I don't think that I want to find a way to do it.

"It's always gonna be a problem with me"

Technical leaders and executives are famous for being time-strapped. What strategies do you use to stay sane and use your time effectively?

It's always gonna be a problem with me. It was a problem when we started Apple. I'm always gonna be pretty much out of time. Constantly things and ideas push me, and there are things I want to do. And if I didn't have that,

Steve Wozniak

I'd have games. I'm poor at managing time. I had early philosophies—try to be accessible to everyone and spent a lot of time talking to fans and answering email. But it pretty much drags me down eight hours a day now. Being accessible really does get me. And I just say yes my whole life. Nowadays I have assistants, and their job is to say "no" and regulate my time. I just tell my assistant that whatever's on my calendar, I'll do it. I'm so busy that I don't even look a day ahead because I don't want to see, "Wow, it's so bad." We schedule things appropriately so I get a few days free here and there. But to get a whole week free is almost unheard of. Sometimes I'm home only a day or two a week. When I was younger, the problem was that I just had all these technical ideas—building things, soldering this and that. And it didn't take time—it was all fun. I was doing the one thing I wanted to do in life. It's wasn't like a requirement. The more you can merge what you want to do with your job, the better.

How do you stay on top of technology trends and innovation now?

I'm pretty much way behind. I'm just a reader of technology press and news releases for certain products that are out. I do look at certain chips—early building blocks of devices, which are going to suggest devices you can and should be working on building in the future. That's still true. But a lot of today's technology is manufacturing. Computers have become so big that you can't just hand-build something and sell it. It's much more into how things are manufactured, with all these chips on a board—the ways we make things small and compact also makes them more usable by people. If you're a software engineer you don't have to worry about that so much. It all fits in a pinhead, so it's a different software world.

"Believe that you are important"

What suggestions do you have for others on being successful in software (either R&D or business)?

I would start out with a bunch of questions—the Socratic method—as long as I could. I would ask them what they've been interested in, if they've had some pet projects at home or at school. What have they thought about, what have they read or seen in a movie? I'd try to get a feel for whether this person has a passion for a particular thing in life—it might be far from software—and try to keep them in touch with that. Don't forget what you are from a very young age, and what you want to do, as unimportant as people might think it seems. Keep looking for little insights that you can someday achieve. That's the critical thing: Be goal-oriented. Know what you're going to do. If you are smart enough to put together the pieces, and as much of them yourself as possible, then you can achieve that goal. You don't need to have learned them. You don't need to have had courses on them. You can do it if you're smart. You can pick up some books, start working on some papers, and figure out how you can solve a problem. Whatever it is, just trust yourself that you don't need a book—you can write the book. I'm saying that from personal experience. Also keep in mind that almost all the revolutionary great advances, the big home runs in technology, come from very young people in school or not so many years out of school. You've got the energy to follow it through and to work a lot of 20-hour days.

You can't feel like, "I'll always have time to do something." After a while, you develop interests you get from other people in your life. All of a sudden, so much of your life is consumed time-wise that you don't have as much time to really devote yourself to something you're passionate about.

What final words of wisdom or caution do you have for people entering the software field?

Know yourself. Believe that you are important for the future way humans will live their lives. And always try to do a better job than almost anyone around you would do. When you finish a project, large or small, go back and look over pieces of it and try to make extra improvements. As you do that on every single project, you'll find one thing here and one thing there; you'll develop a cadre of tricks. Think very deeply in your head—try to find something. What is an improvement? It means using less. If you're in software, it means using less code or making more straightforward code more understandable; replace a couple of approaches, and you'll remember that for life. All your work will start being absolute excellence—and excellence is what the world needs in our products.

I have one more answer to that, too. The human is more important than the technology. Put your work into satisfying and making things a little easier for the user—more natural, more correct. You can, of course, go infinitum; you could take a project and work for another year making tiny little improvement after improvement, so you have to stop somewhere. But that's more important than getting the user to bend to use your software products. Where are the buttons? Where are the menus? What do you drag from here to there? Try to think things out and make humans more important.

CHAPTER 19

If I Knew Then What I Know Now

"I am not young enough to know everything."
—Oscar Wilde (1854–1900)

There's so much they don't tell you at the beginning. I joined IBM as a student software developer in 1989. I was pretty good at programming, but my experiences were limited to the Pascal, Fortran, and BASIC languages using the DOS and Commodore operating systems. When I arrived at IBM, everyone was programming in C on hot new multithreaded, multitasking, GUI-based operating systems. To say the least, I was completely lost. I was absolutely certain that someone in the human resources group had accidentally placed my application in the "hired" pile instead of the "rejected" pile, where it belonged. For whatever reason, I was there, and as long as I had an official IBM badge to get me into the building, it was a decent gig. It's amazing I survived.

As a manager and senior manager at IBM since 1995, I've seen myriad new employees suffer through the same kinds of issues I experience during my early (and fairly clueless) years and have done my best to coach them through the experience. Some were new graduates; others were experienced employees joining a new team from another group or company. This chapter touches on some not-so-obvious bits you need to know up front. This is a chapter about starting something new, but it's also about what great managers can do to bring new staff on board, to junior and senior positions alike.

The First Few Months on Any Software Job

When I joined IBM as a student, I shared an office with another student I'll call Bob. Bob was an immensely talented programmer who was finishing a degree in engineering mathematics. He was one of the top students in the school and, from what I could gather, also one of the top students in the country. We joined IBM the same week and were assigned to work together. Bob was an expert in C programming, and I was amazed at his ability to pick up any manual and absorb new information. Every day I'd come into work, and there was Bob, a student from my university who had started the same time I did, pounding away at the keys doing advanced programming while I spent my days struggling to figure out pointer indirection and make files. It was brutal, and for the first couple of months I came to work thinking, "Today I will be fired."

The real risk of getting fired was nil, but I didn't know that. I just came to work and tried my darndest to build skills and get work done. Somewhere around four months on the job, I realized that I was starting to get comfortable with what I was doing at IBM. I'd become a pretty fair C programmer, the development process was no longer a complete mystery, and my role in the organization as a tester for the new image-processing API set was becoming clear. By the time I finished my 12-month internship at IBM, I knew that I was truly skilled at my craft. I was a powerful C programmer, with strong skills in image processing, parsing, graphical interfaces, and multithreaded programming.

The lessons were simple enough: The first few months on a software job are usually pretty painful, especially if you're joining an existing project that has a sizeable existing code base. Your time will be dominated by climbing the learning curve. While it might feel painful, it's completely normal. That was 1989, and it would be very rare today to land a job at a major firm as a C programmer without knowing C, but the analogy translates forward in time. Today people get hired all the time for jobs that require skills they lack, forcing them to develop those skills quickly while also learning the existing code base, absorbing the business domain, building a social network, and learning the organizational culture. Software is massively complex, and even the smartest people need time to wrap their heads around the complexity. This process is true for new hires, journeymen, and senior architects alike.

I know that my early success as a student at IBM was due in large part to my sharing an office with Bob. Bob taught me a huge amount about the C programming language and about programming practice. I'll never know how he picked it up before we joined IBM, but he seemed to walk in the first day knowing everything. In return, I shared my code with Bob, and he was able to improve the utilities he was building as a result. I also did a lot of the painful grunt work he really didn't want to—such as authoring our 400 page test plan. It was a win-win relationship. The experience taught me the value of a good mentor: A good mentor can teach you a lot and cover your rear.

As an experienced programmer, manager, or architect, you'll go through a similar cycle of climbing the learning curve when joining a new group. The big difference is that you'll have less time to show value. Your challenges are lower than the new grad's (you already know how professional-scale software is developed, you have a reasonable sense of the business of software, you understand typical office dynamics, you should be much better at schedule and effort estimation, and you have a more developed emotional intelligence). Even so, whether you're fresh out of school or bringing 20 years of experience, if you land in front of 200,000 lines of source code, it'll be months before you have component expertise. You can work around this temporarily by focusing on the higher-level architectural and process aspects of the job that are faster to assimilate. An initial focus on process and architecture allows you to make some strategic impact and bides some time for you to get deep into the lower-level components.

Since becoming a manager, it's been interesting for me to bring new people into an organization. I try to help new employees adapt to the organizational culture and become effective as quickly as possible. Times have changed a lot, but the old mantra still seems to hold true for new grads and experienced professions alike: The learning curve dominates the first few months on a software project. If you know that coming in, you won't be quite so anxious about getting a pink slip.

Who You Work For

Managers have a dual role of serving the needs of the organization and serving the needs of their employees. Ideally, these needs align. But reality never turns out that way. Your personal happiness and career success depend to a large degree on your managers placing a high value on helping and protecting their employees.

Sadly and disturbingly, too many managers do an excellent job at fulfilling the needs of the company while largely ignoring the needs of their employees. Their vision is upward only, and these are not people you are well-served to work for, regardless of how important or interesting the projects they offer you appear. Conversely, if you have a manager who is focused purely on employee needs but isn't paying attention to the needs of the business, the work environment for the team will be frustrating. They'll be working on a poorly managed project, surrounded with less-than-stellar colleagues. They'll pick up pretty quickly that although the manager is friendly, little strategic thought is going into the cold, hard business aspects that need attention.

Working under a talented manager who is motivated to work toward both the needs of the company and the needs of the employees is wondrous. It gives you the stability of a well-managed team environment staffed with talented people you'll respect and grow from (and whom you'll help grow), while giving you opportunity, professional growth, fair compensation, and a pleasant work environment. That's why happiness and fulfillment in your professional life depend heavily on who you work for—potentially more so than what you work on.

How do you figure this all out before you accept a position? Do some homework:

▶ **Meet the manager.** With every new position, whether it's joining a new company or making a change within your existing one, you'll generally have a chance to meet the manager of the team you'll be joining. Use that meeting to get a sense of the manager's priorities, strategic thinking, and awareness of employee needs. Some key questions to ask might include: What will my role will be? How will our next project help our customers? How will this role help me grow professionally? Who are the top people in the team? What has the turnover been and why?

▶ **Ask the current staff.** If the team has some existing staffing and you have access to those people, confidentially ask them about their work environment. For example, is this a manager who effectively handles project management, helps to drive strategy and innovation, and helps the team get through organizational roadblocks? Does this manager create good opportunities for staff members and ensure that they are well recognized and compensated for good work? While you're asking them, consider whether the current staff are people you want to work with, who have the talent to help raise your game.

▶ **Check out the manager's track record.** Unless this is your manager's first management assignment, he or she will have some history of managing teams and projects. By asking around the organization politely and confidentially, you can get a sense of how successful those projects and teams were.

Who You Work With

Surrounding yourself with people you can learn from and get along with is critical to enjoying your work and growing professionally. The most exciting project for the best boss will still be a professional horror show if your colleagues are jerks. You'll be hindered daily by an inability to depend on them for collaboration, and you won't have much social interaction with them because of the personality mismatch. A good manager works hard to staff the team with reasonable people with good teaming skills. When push comes to shove, most managers will recruit one or more superstars to the team on the basis of their prolific technical skills, even knowing that those employees lack teamwork and social skills needed in the broader team. A modicum of that kind of recruiting is unavoidable and normal, but doing it excessively results in a stilted team that is stacked with both IQ power and social dysfunction.

How do you figure all this out before you accept a position? Do some homework:

▶ **Existing staff.** If the team has some existing staff before you join, find out who's on the team and get a sense of whether these are people you will enjoy working with. Are they talented technically? Are they a reasonable bunch of folks who can take a joke?

▶ **Track record.** If the team you're joining has been around for a while, ask around about the track record of the team. Their track record is their history of delivering important projects successfully, on time, with good quality. It can also include their rate and consistency in successfully producing new innovations and driving strategy.

▶ **Your selection process.** Examine the selection process the manager used to identify you for the role; it might give you some insight into how the manager is selecting and recruiting people for the team. If you're confident that the process that picked you was a good one, it's a fair indicator that the other team members will be filtered and selected using a similarly successful method.

Managing Your Manager

The very best managers are passionate about fulfilling the needs of the business and the needs of their employees. They work tirelessly to keep their staff engaged, happy, fairly compensated, and efficient (block and tackle); they recruit the best and brightest; and they plan for the future. Despite all that, managers are mortal. Precisely because your boss isn't omniscient, there are steps you should take to help the management process along. Managing your manager is just as important as your manager managing you. The following key points will help you improve your employee-manager relationship:

▶ **Keep your boss in the loop.** Your manager should always have a handle on what you're working on and what you've accomplished. Make it your responsibility to ensure that your manager is getting that information.

▶ **Play to the referee.** The workplace is a competitive environment, and just like a sporting event, you need to play to the referee. Some referees call fouls more quickly than others. They see things differently, and they expect a different level of play. Your manager is no different, so it's important to spend some time discovering what your manager values (Does he/she value productivity over creativity?) and the rules they play by (How strict is he/she on business ethics? Does he/she shoot first and ask questions later, or do everything by the book?). Once you understand their values and rules, you're well-positioned to perform to their best expectations.

▶ **Workload.** Building software, supporting clients, and doing product planning and quality assurance are all highly complex tasks in the software lifecycle that are hard (that is, impossible) to estimate with accuracy. Managers try to distribute work across their staff based on volume and individual skills, but it's far from a perfect science. You can help this process by making sure your manager knows whether you are drowning in work or have some spare cycles to take on more. The worst thing you can do is allow yourself to be underloaded when your teammates are drowning in pressure and overtime. Even if nobody says a word to you about it, this will rear its head eventually. Keep yourself busy with important work at all times.

▶ **Constructive observations and suggestions about the team.** Because your manager isn't perfect, there will always be things to improve on in the team. By politely and constructively pointing these out to your manager, you can influence the way the team is managed and help create a more effective and more pleasant work environment. If your observations and suggestions are good, your manager will try to put some of them into effect. Some caution on this: You also need to show that you're willing to help with the solution. Just making a lot of suggestions, even good ones, can peg you as a "talker," not a "doer."

▶ **Your career aspirations.** Even a manager who wants the best for you can only help you reach your goals if he/she understands your professional aspirations. Most employees don't discuss their future goals and career aspirations with their managers; moreover, the vast majority of employees haven't completely thought through what they really want from their careers over the next two to five years. Figuring out what you want is the first step, and your manager can both help you understand your own objectives and help you build a career plan to achieve them.

▶ **What's needed for promotion.** This is often thought of as a taboo subject, but it's far from being so. Talk to your manager once or twice a year about what you need to do to get your next promotion. Also ask approximately how far you are from that goal, in your manager's estimation. Your manager should be able to give you specific information on the first question and approximate thoughts on the latter.

Creating Opportunities

Some projects are more exciting than others, and none of us can expect to work on the most exciting projects all the time. Even so, in a professional and thought-driven environment such as software, people can usually carve out some time (perhaps after hours) to work on interesting projects and proposals. What I didn't understand when I was younger is that this is how most projects get started. There is no guru at the top of the corporate hierarchy dreaming up all the project ideas. In fact, good ideas come from everyone and everywhere, and it takes the creative energy and tenacity of individuals to get projects going. The higher you are in an organization, the easier it is to launch your own projects. And if you find yourself with a good idea, but without the seniority to bring it to fruition, partnering with a senior established figure can be the ticket to making it happen. Some companies have institutionalized time for skunkworks projects. For example, since about 2000 Google instituted a policy that allows every engineer to spend 20% of their time working on side projects of their choice. Google News is a great example of a successful project that came from that policy. Krishna Bharat was an avid news reader, visiting 10 or 15 sites every day to keep himself abreast of the latest events. One day Krishna asked himself, "Why don't I write a program to do this?" Krishna applied his background in artificial intelligence and developed a web crawler to cluster articles on specific topics. Google News was born. Krishna made an opportunity for himself. Although perhaps less formally, many companies work this way, including IBM and Microsoft. Whether you're given a formal block of time or you carve out time from your workweek, spending some time outside your normal responsibilities is healthy for your career growth. It's worth discussing ideas with your manager, who can help you get access to resources and filter good ideas from bad.

Many ideas that came earlier in this book can help you turn skunkworks initiatives into big opportunities. I'll highlight just a few:

▶ **Spend time in the growth quadrant of important but not urgent tasks.** That's where creative thinking and professional growth happen. It's where the ideas for new projects are born.

▶ **Act with a sense of urgency.** Urgency is proactiveness and tenacity, two qualities that help bring a creative project into fruition.

▶ **Shoot first, ask questions later.** Depending on the organizational culture you find yourself (not all companies formally encourage employees to spend 20% of their time on pet projects), your superiors may frown on your initiative—that is, until they see it working. Then they'll praise you for it. Sometimes it's better to build it and ask for permission later.

▶ After the idea has some proof points (a working demo or some experimental runs), review and iterate with individual decision makers to help refine it before formalizing the project.

Waiting Until You're Ready Is Waiting Too Long

"... you should always do something that you're not ready to do. Doing something you're not ready to do means you're taking a step forward, you're going to learn something new, and you're going to grow."
—Marissa Mayer, Google VP

Everything in our lives from the time we enter kindergarten until we start our professional careers teaches us that when we succeed at what we're doing, society will conjure up future opportunities and challenges for us. During your school years, the education system pushes you to ever greater challenges. When you graduate from first-year college, the system rewards you with the challenge of entry into your second year. That's not so in the real world. The professional world isn't hard-wired to push you and force you to grow. When you find yourself completely comfortable in a job, with all the skills you need, it probably means you're coasting; the same feeling of confidence that makes you feel authoritative in your role may actually be silently hampering your advancement. Coasting isn't growth, it's flat-lining. That's why you should always be ready to push the limits and stretch yourself. We're better off knowing this early on: Left to our own devices, most of us will rise to a level of technical and professional competency and then coast. After you reach that point, growth will slow to a glacier's pace. Why let your career hit an early plateau when you can accelerate its progress through a little professional engineering? Be brave enough to take forward steps when they are a little uncomfortable, and you'll grow professionally at a much faster rate. Chances are, if your leadership team is willing to let you take on the role, and the fear factor scares you but doesn't terrify you, then you're ready. Take the leap.

An Interview with Marc Benioff

CEO, Salesforce.com

CURRENT POSITION

Chairman & CEO, Salesforce.com

EDUCATION

B.S. in Business Administration; University of Southern California, Marshall, School of Business; 1982–1986

FAVORITE PASTIMES & HOBBIES

Swimming with dolphins, practicing yoga, writing, listening to music, collecting ukuleles, spending time in Hawaii

CLAIM TO FAME

Founded Salesforce.com, the first enterprise cloud computing company to reach $1 billion in revenue; disrupted the enterprise software industry and created a 1/1/1 model (1% equity, 1% time, 1% profits/products) as a way to integrate philanthropy into a business model

BIOGRAPHY

Marc is chairman and CEO of Salesforce.com, the enterprise cloud computing company. He founded the company in 1999 with a vision to create an enterprise cloud computing service that would replace traditional enterprise software technology. He is regarded as the leader of what he has termed "The End of Software," the now-proven belief that multitenant cloud computing applications and platforms democratize information by delivering immediate benefits at reduced risks and costs.

Under Marc's direction, Salesforce.com has grown from a groundbreaking idea into a publicly traded company that is the market and technology leader in enterprise cloud computing. At end of fiscal 2009, Salesforce.com reported its first billion-dollar revenue year. For its revolutionary approach, Salesforce.com received a *Wall Street Journal* Technology Innovation Award, was lauded as one of *BusinessWeek*'s Top 100 Most Innovative Companies, was named no. 7 on The Wired 40, and was selected for the past two years as a Top Ten Disrupter by *Forbes*. Salesforce.com has won the Software & Information Industry Association Codie Award for Best CRM for the past six years, and the Codie Award for Best On-Demand Platform in 2007, as well as multiple Editor's Choice designations from *PC Magazine*. Marc has been widely recognized for pioneering innovation, with honors such as the 2007 Ernst & Young Entrepreneur of the Year, the SDForum Visionary Award, and Alumni Entrepreneur of the Year by the University of Southern California (USC) Marshall School of Business, and was ranked no. 7 on the Top 100 Most Influential People in IT survey by eWEEK.

Throughout his career, Marc has also been committed to using information technology to produce positive social change. In 2000, he launched the Salesforce.com Foundation—now a multimillion-dollar global organization—establishing the "1/1/1 model," whereby the company contributes 1% of product (donated or discounted service to nonprofits), 1% of equity, and 1% of employee hours back to the communities it serves. Marc authored *The Business of Changing the World* (McGraw-Hill, 2006), in which 20 great leaders reveal how businesses can go beyond writing a check and leverage the full scope of their resources to make a difference. Marc's other book, *Compassionate Capitalism* (ReadHowYouWant, 2009), is the first-ever best-practices guide for corporate philanthropy that illustrates the success of the integrated model. Acknowledging his commitment to building partnerships between business and society to improve the state of the world, the members of the World Economic Forum named Marc as one of its Young Global Leaders. In 2007, the Committee Encouraging Corporate Philanthropy presented his with the coveted Excellence in Corporate Philanthropy Award; a year later, they welcomed him to their distinguished board of directors.

Before launching Salesforce.com, Marc, a quarter-century veteran of the software industry, spent 13 years at Oracle Corporation, from 1986 to 1999. In 1984, he worked as an Assembly language programmer in Apple Computer's Macintosh Division. He founded entertainment software company Liberty Software in 1979 when he was 15 years old.

"We never stopped listening to the customer"

How did you get started in software?

My obsession with software began when I wandered into a computer lab in high school. I saved the income I earned at my after-school job (cleaning cases at a local jewelry store) to buy my own computer and wrote my first piece of software, How to Juggle (I sold it for $75.) That led me to start my own company, Liberty Software, which I founded when I was 15 with my friend Steve Fisher. We wrote adventure games like Crypt of the Undead for the Atari 800. The reviews that we received taught me about the importance of listening to the user. Although the car I bought with the proceeds is long gone, what I learned about customer success remains with me and reigns as the number one priority of Salesforce.com today. (That's not all that lasted from those early days; Steve remains a lifelong friend and is doing amazing work at Salesforce.com.)

What turned you on to software as a service?

In the late 1990s, I was looking at all these web "sites" (as we called them then), such as eBay, Amazon.com, and Google. I was amazed at their marriage of technical complexity and usability. They were rich data-driven applications that were constantly getting better, but as a user, I didn't have to do anything to make that happen. I never worried about whether I was on Amazon.com 5.13.2 or 5.13.3. I was always on the most current version, and the best part was that I never had to crack a manual to tell me how to use it. Although these sites opened up a new way of life for consumers, nothing exciting like this was happening in the enterprise world. None of my business applications performed this way—they were complex to install and maintain. Upgrading them was always a hassle. To make matters even worse, all of these burdens came at an exorbitant financial cost. I saw a huge opportunity to leverage the power of the Internet to approach enterprise software differently, and I started Salesforce.com to pursue it.

You founded one of the fastest-growing and most successful startups and grew it to a nearly billion-dollar company. What are a few of your key strategies that made that possible?

Actually, I detail the top 111 strategies we used to make Salesforce.com successful in my new book, *Behind the Cloud,* but if I had to select the most pivotal strategy, it would be recognizing the importance of customer success. Fairly early on, we discovered an opportunity to leverage the enthusiasm of our customers and make them a part of our marketing team. This idea came to really define the company, but it started organically.

From the very beginning, we enlisted the insight of the people who would use our service, and we listened to their advice. As a result, we built something customers loved, and they were eager to talk about their experience using the service. I had never seen this in the enterprise software world. Customers actually stood up at our events and talked about their experiences with our service. There was an evangelistic feel to it that was very positive

Marc Benioff

and very contagious. In that way, our customers taught us that the best way to sell the service was not by selling features, as most companies did, but by selling the customers' success with our unconventional model. We never stopped listening to the customer, and we used their feedback to evolve our service as well. Once customers were successful, they asked for more: more customization, more integrations, more applications. They pushed us. We created only what they wanted, not what we thought they wanted. This was different from the way the rest of the industry worked, but evolving by this sort of intelligent reaction evolved us from a service that customers adopted to a service to which they became addicted.

Many software startups fail to get traction and become profitable, despite having an innovative product or service offering. What are they doing wrong (or failing to do right)?

I think a big mistake that many entrepreneurs make is that they get too myopic. They fall in love with their product, and they ignore the voice of the customer. Deep customer engagement has been the key for us. Our subscription model keeps us close to the customer, and our technology model ensures that if big customers like Cisco or Dell request a feature, every customer benefits because we are working on a single code base. That's something that has never before happened in enterprise software. Another important aspect to recognize is that every business is different, and every customer deserves to have a system that is customizable to their unique processes.

In addition, I think our marketing has been instrumental in our success. Initially, we positioned our company against the market leader (startups should always go after Goliath, either the marker leader or the status quo), and we employed many tactics to differentiate ourselves. I am a firm believer in the dictum "Tactics dictate strategy." We found that many of the tactics we used to go after the competition were successful at garnering publicity and needling the competition, and this inspired our strategy.

"Experience and great relationships are critical"

Do you think being the CEO of a software company is different from being the CEO of other companies or even other high-tech companies? What makes software companies different to lead?

Our business and technology model requires that we are a very responsive organization. We release three major upgrades every year, which is very different from the one release every five years that is typical of the traditional software establishment. This fast pace requires a different management style in all aspects of the business, from marketing to finance. It is a challenge to constantly innovate, embrace change and, at the same time, remain completely aligned as an organization. We've found a way to do that, and I think it's one of the biggest secrets of our success.

I've had the pleasure of meeting some of your leadership team— Parker Harris, Jim Steele, Polly Sumner. You've attracted some impressive people, and it's clear you know what you're looking for. In your view, what makes a great software executive?

Experience and great relationships are critical. In many positions, I look for natural evangelists, people with not just the native skills, but the passion to communicate them. Most of all, I look for people who want to change the world.

How do you know one when you meet one?

It's often the questions that they ask. We have created a business that has challenged conventional wisdom in many ways, and I look for thinkers who demonstrate they can do that as well.

"Integrated corporate philanthropy"

You're well-known for having some distinctive business philosophies. One of these is your outlook on corporate philanthropy. Can you tell me about it?

We believe in a different approach, called integrated corporate philanthropy, which advocates going beyond writing a check and leverages a corporation's full assets. It's based on what we call the 1/1/1 model: 1% of our corporate equity was set aside in a separate charity, 1% of paid employee time is available for work on philanthropic work, and 1% of our product is available at little or no cost to charities. This model is catching on. Google has adopted pieces of it and now has a foundation valued at more than $2 billion that is making a real difference in addressing the world's most urgent problems. Other companies have embraced our model as well, and more companies are looking closer at it every day. It's very exciting because we can make a much deeper impact by working collectively. We call this idea the power of us, and we're passionate about encouraging others to join forces with us.

What's equally important about our commitment to integrated corporate philanthropy is that employees have positively responded to this new model,

Marc Benioff

Marc Benioff

and we find that it has been a key factor in recruiting and retention. This is especially true for people entering the workforce today. They are questioning the conventional wisdom that has told them that philanthropy is something done outside of work or at the end of their careers. Integrated corporate philanthropy puts an end to that false choice.

Do you see corporate philanthropy as a kind of social kindness to be applied when business conditions permit or something more fundamental—a moral obligation?

This is absolutely not something capricious to be applied only when business conditions permit. To be successful, it must be part of the fabric of an organization. I do think that corporate philanthropy is the right thing to do, but there is also a secondary gain. It gives employees a purpose beyond collecting a paycheck, and that makes them happier. People are no longer singularly commercially oriented. They want to contribute in many ways, and businesses must offer them these opportunities. I believe that this is a fundamental, generational change in employee expectations.

You've made "No software" the motto for Salesforce.com—the idea that the software your customers use is hosted and managed by you, so all they have to deal with is using the function. Companies like Salesforce.com made software as a service mainstream. How do you think SaaS will evolve? Will it become absolutely dominant?

I think that it already is the dominant paradigm, especially when you consider that there are no new traditional software companies being funded. Everyone's energy and resources are being invested in the cloud. That said, no one paradigm completely replaces another. We have customers who are still running mainframes, and they will for some time. However, it is fair to say that innovation on that platform stopped years ago.

Furthermore, the current economic climate has made cloud computing even more relevant and attractive. The choices one has to make when it comes to traditional software decisions have become too painful. Making a decision to upgrade to the latest technology is almost impossible because the capital and credit needed for large expenditures is hard to find. Enterprise customers are also questioning what they are receiving from the large maintenance fees they pay just to keep the client/server apps running. Cloud computing has really emerged as the right solution for right now. And with the ability to deliver constant innovation in real time with zero capital expenditure, I think it will continue to evolve as the best solution for any size of company and during any economic climate.

You've gone on record as saying that platform independence needs to be a key priority for the industry—"write once, run anywhere," in your words. This is the vision of languages like Java, HTML, PHP, Perl, and others. What more needs to be done to achieve this vision?

The reality is that, with the languages you mention, the "run" part of that equation remains dauntingly complex and expensive. You still need expensive hardware, software, and the data centers in which to run them. The exciting change is that now we are seeing new cloud platforms like Amazon Web Services, Google App Engine, and our Force.com, which are revolutionizing how software is developed by taking cost and complexity out of the equation by orders of magnitude. Nowadays, virtually any developer anywhere in the world has access to unlimited computing power. That's an incredible change, and what excites me most is the potential it unleashes for mass innovation. Because the cost of development is greatly reduced, application diversity will increase. Cloud computing stands to completely remake the economics of software development, and this will result in a huge win for customers.

"I aim to always stay connected"

What suggestions do you have for others on being successful in software (either R&D or business)?

The amount of innovation going on in cloud computing is really incredible. Almost every day we are seeing new apps and new companies that are taking advantage of this paradigm. I'm still in awe of how the economics of software development are completely different today than when I started in this business more than 25 years ago. It was rather painful then, but that pain is now a thing of the past. Today a developer can use our datacenters to build, test, deploy, and run enterprise applications—all without spending his or her own capital on hardware or software. Then when it comes time to sell their services, they can promise that their applications are as reliable as ours. It's incredible!

Today we have a completely different way of thinking about software development, and it makes this a better time than ever to be a software entrepreneur. Startup companies should investigate all the cloud computing platforms available and use them to build their businesses. They'll find that they can accomplish much more when they are not bogged down by infrastructure and can solely focus on innovation.

Marc Benioff

Marc Benioff

Do you think graduate degrees are professionally valuable? Do you see them as a substantial benefit to a candidate when recruiting?

I received my undergraduate degree from the Marshall School at USC, and I found it very valuable. I found the experiences working at companies such as Apple and Oracle to also be of tremendous value.

At Salesforce.com, we hire a number of MBAs every year, and a number of them have been very successful. Ultimately, though, a diploma is never enough; the ultimate test, of course, is how they apply their education. Although I do have a deep respect for education, overall, I don't believe that MBA programs have done a very good job of educating our corporations' CEOs because they don't look at the world in a broad view. If we could extend the consciousness of the school, we would produce more successful and inspired MBAs and more successful business leaders.

What would you change about grad schools if you could?

Very little is taught about corporate social responsibility, and I see this as a very big problem for the future. If business schools want to stay relevant, they have to catch up in this area. Young entrepreneurs have so many questions about CSR: What are the models that work? How do I start a business with a CSR program at the same time? What are the best structures for social enterprises? The fact is, today's top talent rejects the idea that work and social contribution have to remain separate. I'd like to see business schools recognize that and actively recruit more experts in this area—and even establish centers of excellence. In these days when we are collectively questioning much of our conventional wisdom about risk, regulation, and capitalism, business schools need to step up and lead the way so that the next generation of leaders does not repeat the mistakes of the last. I am not saying that CSR programs will magically make good corporate citizens of bad actors, but there is room and reason for more balance in business education.

How do you stay on top of technology trends and innovation?

A read a number of blogs that keep me up-to-date. Lately, I have been enjoying Vinnie Mirchandani's Deal Architect. I am also always talking with colleagues, peers, and friends about what's happening in technology and innovation. (This is not something I merely do for business; it's a personal passion.) Recently, I spoke at a TechCrunch conference and had the opportunity to see several demos of new cloud apps. I loved it, but the reality is that I don't have much time to go to conferences. (David Kirkpatrick's Brainstorm is an exception—it's very stimulating, and I always try to participate.)

"Work only on what is important"

Time management ... technical leaders and executives are famous for being time-strapped. What strategies do you use to stay sane and use your time effectively at the office?

I aim to always stay connected, and I make generous use of videoconferencing to do so. That technology helps my team and me avoid travel and save time. Overall, when it comes to time management, I use the 80/20 rule. I spend most of my time on the most critical things. In other words, my advice would be to work only on what is important.

How do you achieve a work-life balance? How do you keep your professional life from dominating everything?

I do make sure that I take breaks that are completely disconnected. At these times, only a couple of people can reach me. In addition, I exercise daily and am a big believer in yoga to reduce and manage stress.

What do you see as the coming changes in the software field over the next 10–15 years that will impact career opportunities either positively or negatively?

I think the biggest change comes from cloud computing, which has democratized the software development process and given rise to a new enormous population of developers. I believe that cloud computing will continue to unleash innovation.

Social networking has been an exciting recent change, and we are finding that it has been influencing our products, especially the Service Cloud, which allows call center agents to communicate with customers through every possible channel: phone, email, chat, Web, and social networks. I think these new ways of communicating will revolutionize the way customer service is done.

Part of what makes working in our industry so thrilling is that we have no idea right now what the next great devices will be and how they will be able to benefit from information technology. I see wonderful efforts happening in cleantech and imagine there will be a revolution in how energy is produced, transported, and stored. Health care is another area that is begging for better information technology, and I hope the current push for health care reform will result in new ways to partner on that effort.

Marc Benioff

Marc Benioff

What final words of wisdom or caution do you have for people entering the field?

The most successful people in business are driven by profits—and purpose. You have to find a way to integrate philanthropy into your daily work life. Steal our model or invent your own, but whatever you do, don't adopt the twentieth-century model of waiting until your retirement. You'll miss out on the best and most rewarding work of your life.

CHAPTER 20

Going Out on Your Own: The "Software Startup"

"I'm convinced that about half of what separates the successful entrepreneurs from the nonsuccessful ones is pure perseverance."
—Steve Jobs

Starting your own company is probably the shortest path to making it big, running your own show, and making heaps of money—if you can do it successfully. According to a study titled "2008 Compensation and Entrepreneurship Report in IT," published by CompStudy.com, 31% of all CEOs and CTOs were founders of their companies. The study covered 342 respondents and 1,600 executives. That result also matches fairly closely the cross-section of people interviewed for this book and the organizations they represent. In fact, of all the impressive people whose interviews you'll find between these covers, the only two who rose to senior executive levels by climbing the corporate ladder were John Schwarz (CEO of Business Objects) and James Gosling (Sun Microsystems Senior VP and Fellow). The conclusion is straightforward enough: The fastest way to the top is to be one of the founders of a successful company.

The pay gets better too (of course), with CEOs averaging $230,000, along with a significant share in the company, preferred stock or stock options, and lucrative bonuses tied to revenue and stock performance.

In this chapter, I discuss the difference between good technology and good business. I also touch on the big themes of product bootstrapping, financing and the phases of venture capital (VC) investment, how to move from startup to mainstream, the centrality of trials and demos, and plans for growth or acquisition.

Unfortunately, it's not easy. The early days of any startup are fraught with a relentless search for operational revenue and high employee turnover. After all the sweat and heartache, most software startups go out of business or fall into serious decline after about 30 months. This is not a path for the faint of heart.

Good Ideas Versus Good Business

The good news is that a few guys in a garage can still change the world. Look at Google or Facebook. Lots of disruptive hot technology is still yet to come, and founders of startups need one attribute more than anything else: They need to be believers. Your mission as a startup is challenging because you have the complex engineering hurdles of creating new technology, but also the daunting challenge of creating market demand and running a business. Unfortunately, good technology ideas aren't enough to make good business. Does anybody remember OS/2? By all technical standards, it was a far superior operating system to Windows in 1989. Beta Video was superior to VHS. RCA Laser Disk technology predated modern DVDs by several years. Every day throughout the world, startup companies with great technology are going out of business because they were unable to convert their intellectual capital into business momentum. The number one cause of startup company failure is that brilliant technologists think they're also savvy businessmen. In most cases, a good CTO does not make a good CEO. CTOs are product-focused instead of market-focused, which invariably leads to scope creep and poor execution on business elements such as marketing, publicity, demand generation, sales enablement, cash flow, contracts, and business controls. A good startup entrepreneur recognizes what he's good at and what he is not, and recruits people who complement him. Find a CEO who understands the business space and a competent marketing strategist who can put ideas into action. Take a cue from Larry Page and Sergey Brin, who founded Google in 1998. They were smart enough to see themselves as technical gurus, not businessmen. As Google's fortunes rose, they sought out an experienced executive who could help them go mainstream, recruiting Eric Schmidt as their CEO in 2001. Eric had been CTO of Sun Microsystems and CEO of Novell, so he brought an extraordinary history of high-tech growth to the fledgling company. If you really have only a few guys in a garage churning out code, approach a VC firm or an executive search company to connect you with the right people to flesh out your senior leadership.

The Plan and the Pitch

If you want anyone to take you seriously, the first thing you'll need is a description of your new technology and a business plan. The business plan summarizes your business idea, your market and financial goals, your strategy to getting to the first several milestones (technical milestones, such as the dates you'll have a beta or a first product; project milestones, such as the dates you'll have different aspects of the work staffed; and business milestones, such as the dates you expect to have sales channels in place or reach a target for initial customers, or your first few reference quotes), a review of competitors, and some market analysis and forecasting. Your business ideas are your competitive advantage, so be careful with whom and how you share them. It's common practice to sign a confidential disclosure agreement (CDA) or nondisclosure agreement (NDA) before sharing your detailed business plans with anyone outside your fledgling company. Not everyone will be willing to sign legal contracts, and in many cases you won't want to delay a key opportunity to discuss with an important investor or contact, so for better or worse, you'll need a slimmed-down version of the vision you are prepared to share with respectable people without having legal contracts in place. Having a few versions of the business vision is the norm, for use in different situations.

- ▶ **Elevator pitch.** A short description of the business idea, with just enough detail to make it compelling. The elevator pitch is useful to pique the interest of venture capitalists, private funders, potential customers, or strategic partners. It should be well-planned and rehearsed. It isn't called an elevator pitch for nothing: Most experts recommend keeping an elevator pitch around 60 seconds long, short enough that you can deliver it in an elevator while moving between the ground floor and the eighth floor.

- ▶ **Summary presentation.** A captivating presentation that has the same kind of summary information as the elevator pitch but also includes some facts and figures worthy of discussion. The summary presentation can be covered in 30–45 minutes. Interested parties will want to review the content and perhaps take a copy with them. The venues where this is presented should also include a product demo, if one is available. This should be highly visual; the charts are there to support your talk, not the other way around. Maximize use of graphics, video, and graphs. Keep the textual content minimal so the messages come from you, not the charts. As a general rule of thumb, assume that each chart represents 3–5 minutes of talking time, so this presentation should be 5–10 very visual (graphics intensive) charts.

▶ **External business plan.** A formal document (not charts) that includes the material from the summary presentation and the written context to understand it. It should be reasonably detailed and highly polished. The audience for this document is the venture capitalists, private funders, potential customers, or strategic partners who want to take their interest to the next level. This is where you go into the details of your product vision, staffing, rollout and milestones, startup costs and revenue projections, and so on. You need to demonstrate that you'll be using the investors' money responsibly. This means a solid, realistic cash-flow budget reflecting the uses of cash over the specified period. If you ask for a million dollars and it lasts only six months, investors will want to know where you're getting the rest of the money when that runs out. Why should I invest capital in your fledgling concern if the risk is so high? This document should be around 20 pages. If it's 5 pages, you probably don't have enough detail; if it's 60, nobody will read it.

▶ **Internal business plan.** This document is similar to the external business plan, except that it's for internal use. Because it's for internal use, it can include a lot more of the painful truths about where you are and what you need to accomplish to achieve success. It should be clearly labeled as internal and confidential. Make sure that every employee who sees this document understands the repercussions if they leak it. Ideally, only a small inner circle of people should have access to it.

Bootstrapping Your R&D

You're an aspiring entrepreneur with some creative new technology ideas. Unfortunately, writing code still takes talent and time. Writing quality code is even harder, and writing extensible code that will grow with your company is hardest of all. Most startups face the pressure to get to market quickly with little funding and few able-bodied programmers. Fortunately, new startups can use a few really good tricks to get to market quickly and without large initial investments in intranet infrastructure, source code control systems, and expensive scalable server infrastructure.

▶ **Make heavy use of open source.** Hundreds of millions of lines of source code are readily available for new startups to leverage. Why start from scratch? Using and modifying open source software can save you the time you would have spent writing tens of thousands of lines or more. Projects that would have taken several person-years can be completed in a person-month. Leveraging open source can be incredibly cost-effective and also a good way to attract motivated engineers who want to contribute to these projects.

▶ **Leverage cloud computing services.** For instance, Twitter doesn't run its own servers; it uses Google's cloud to scale up its demand as needed. Cloud computing is taking off, and numerous companies are now offering scalable virtual server resources on demand for a fee. It's a pay-as-you-grow model well suited for startups. Amazon, Google, or some other provider sets up the servers and the storage where your company software runs. You pay for the storage (and possible CPU cycles) you use.

▶ **Make use of remote workers.** I recommend keeping your core engineering team in one location, if possible. The locality of people brings great efficiencies in brainstorming, code sharing, and team *esprit de corps*. However, you might not be able to find all the talent you need in one location. That's okay—despite the disadvantages (you can't brainstorm around a whiteboard as easily), some unexpected benefits arise. It's easier than ever to work remotely, and small teams with remote workers can be very effective whether they're in another city or halfway around the world. First, staffing projects with skills from overseas locations such as India, China, or low tax geographies such as Ireland can significantly reduce your operational costs for salaries. Second, you can effectively achieve (or approach) 24-hour worldwide operations. Finally, as your company ramps up on the business side, having people in different parts of the world will make it a lot easier to become an international company with reach into remote geographies.

Financing

If you're really lucky, you can start your new idea in your spare time or while at school. Sergey Brin and Larry Page started Google during their graduate years at Stanford. Likewise, Mark Zuckerberg founded Facebook while at MIT. If your company requires more up-front investment, you'll need money.

Unless you have your own secret store of *dineros* to draw from, you'll need to go tin-cupping to raise the seed funding for your ideas. Funding for new companies is done in phases, but the hardest part is funding an idea that has nothing to show for it, so-called angel funding.

Emerging software startups pass through four stages, summarized in Figure 20.1, each with different funding models.

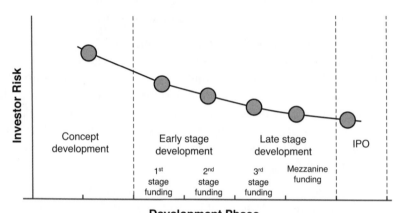

FIGURE 20.1 Startup phases and their risks

1. Angel funding is the term for the money that gets you your earliest start. It's called angel funding because you basically need a heavenly source to help you at this point. Once an idea takes shape and has indicators of success and perhaps a demonstration version, seed funding covers concept development and initial prototyping. To get to the next level, you generally need first-stage funding, also called the startup phase, which results in either a beta-level product or a first version of an actual product. Nearly two thirds of companies that start the seed funding process and more than 50% that reach the startup phase will eventually fail. Investors know it, so getting investor money at these early stages is rough. Try to get through these phases without asking anyone for money if you can.

2. Second-stage funding takes the product to market with a goal of gaining market share, getting to real revenue, and trying to generate enough revenue to cover operational expenses. This stage provides the necessary funding to establish the company infrastructure, including the management, marketing, and sales staff.

3. Third-stage funding is about expansion. This funding serves both to expand market share and to begin exploring additional products and services that can round out the company's portfolio. Companies that reach this stage have much lower financial risk for investors, and many VC firms are interested in engaging only at this stage.

4. Fourth-stage funding[1] is the final stage of VC funding that prepares the company for an initial public offering (IPO) and provides a possible exit for investors to achieve a return on their investments thus far.

These four stages are loosely applied. Many startups modify this template, for example, having a couple of seed rounds or only one VC round. Starting a business is anything but neat and linear. No hard-and-fast rules work, and in any specific situation you need to trade dilution of existing stockholders against the perceived benefit of additional investment.

Good ideas can almost always find funding, especially if they are presented with a compelling business case and demo. Before the dotcom bust in 2000, VC funding was easily had. Since then, a jaded investor community has become far more risk averse about software. Even so, plenty of VC funding is available for good ideas, particularly at second-stage funding and beyond.

Investment capital is fraught with its own share of issues, such as how to retain control of your company while finding the necessary capital and quality board of directors to help you through the startup phases. Importantly, the more financial help you accept, the more control you will be asked to relinquish. If the mantra of modern software organizations is "Ship early, ship often," the manta of software startups may well be "Start cheap."

Getting to Revenue

I asked Diane Greene, cofounder and CEO of VMware, how a bunch of engineers were able to bring a major success story like VMware to life. Her answer was simply that they focused on getting to revenue. Although many things are necessary to become successful, getting the money stream going is really the "do or die" factor for emerging companies:

> We were focused on getting to revenue. We knew we had to have revenue to be successful, and we were very pragmatic about it. We

---

[1] Both third-stage and fourth-stage funding are occasionally called mezzanine funding.

always had a fallback scenario in case the scenario we wanted didn't work out. We hoped for the best but planned for the worst, always. We had the big vision for all computing devices from the beginning, but we wanted to get a large early base. The first customers we targeted were software engineers. We knew what kind of product they would like. In terms of marketing the product, perhaps because of my technical background, I had a very direct and grounded approach. We were bringing this very complex software to market, and it had a number of huge and interesting applications... We were straightforward but passionate.

Perhaps the greatest dichotomy for successful startups is that they are founded on a bedrock of great vision and passion but are made successful through great perseverance and pragmatism. This steadfastness allows the founders to drive aggressively toward a stable revenue stream before the venture funding evaporates. Like VMWare, you're wise to focus on getting to revenue quickly. An initial flow of revenue keeps investors hopeful that the money floodgates will soon burst open.

Crossing the Chasm

Getting from the early adopters to the mainstream users is the hardest part of taking technology mainstream. Most users, whether they are end users or corporate consumers of IT infrastructure, are wary of fads, startups, and untested technology. Put simply, the mainstream has no interest in being a guinea pig. This creates a chasm in the market between the early adopters, who are willing to accept more risk, and the mainstream market, illustrated in Figure 20.2. It's a huge problem and the main topic of Geoffrey Moore's classic book *Crossing the Chasm*. Companies that fail to cross the chasm may survive but will never thrive. They live out their existence constantly on the verge of making it big, but success is always just out of reach. They are the walking wounded of high-tech, the almost-but-not-quite-there companies. They rise, stabilize, and then fade within five to ten years as their once-innovative technology is outpaced by technology from larger, more aggressive firms. Learning how to cross the chasm into the mainstream is less of an art than it appears, and I highly recommend Moore's book.

Companies need to take specific mechanical steps to get traction with new products:

1. **Establish a beachhead of customers to focus on, from whom you'll generate an impressive list of success stories and reference quotes.** With a few dozen starter customers, you can build a set of testimonials and reference accounts that spiral into mainstream activity. If your initial customers are passionate about your product, they'll form a community of evangelists to willingly spread the word about your products and service. Just listen to how Marc Benioff describes his experience turning Salesforce.com into a billion-dollar-a-year software giant:

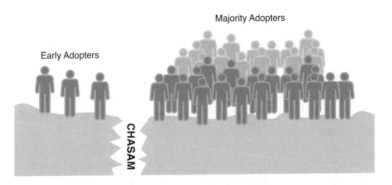

FIGURE 20.2   Crossing the chasm

From the very beginning, we enlisted the insight of the people who would use our service, and we listened to their advice. As a result, we built something customers loved, and they were eager to talk about their experience using the service. I had never seen this in the enterprise software world. Customers actually stood up at our events and talked about their experiences with our service. There was an evangelistic feel to it that was very positive and very contagious. In that way, our customers taught us that the best way to sell the service was not by selling features, as most companies did, but by selling the customers' success with our unconventional model. We never stopped listening to the customer, and we used their feedback to evolve our service as well. Once customers were successful, they asked for more: more customization, more integrations, more applications. They pushed us. We created only what they wanted, not what we thought they wanted. This was different from the way the rest of the industry worked, but evolving by this sort of intelligent reaction evolved us from a service that customers adopted to a service to which they became addicted.

When your initial users are passionate about your technology, they form an extended marketing team for you. They'll passionately extol the benefits of your product on user groups and blogs, and they'll attend your conferences and user group meetings. Passionate users will take you mainstream. Better than that, if you can generate passion for your technology, you'll find that it creates not only a virtual team of evangelists, but something even more powerful: technology bigots. Technology bigots are people who love a product so much they will defend it beyond reason. No other product can compete in their minds. Technology bigots do for software products what Heinz ketchup lovers do for condiments—there are no other kinds! Your technology bigots will defend the investment in your product to others and to their executives. They will create a groundswell of allegiance to your technology and encourage others to feel the same way. Of course, to create a loyal following of technology bigots, you need to have a product that is compelling and valuable; you have to become a clear leader in some aspect for long enough that they feel that every other competitive technology they try is simply inferior.

2. **Demo till you drop.** We live in a TV culture of 30-second commercials, instant communications, and on-demand programming. These are not patient times. Make it easy for people to see the value of your offering with an easy-to-run and easy-to-understand demo video or live demo. Each of these serves a different audience. The live demo will be more impressive, but the canned video will scale to a much larger audience. A good viral video never lasts more than 2 minutes. Apple's Mac versus PC ads became a cult classic on YouTube and run consistently at 30 seconds. If you're trying to show all the bells and whistles, you're on the wrong track. The most successful startups have consistently been the ones that have placed a premium on making it easy for new customers to see the value of their offering and quickly begin realizing that value for business gain. Microsoft, VMware, Google, Facebook, Nintendo, Adobe, Sage, Symantec, and Salesforce.com are notable examples.

3. **Leverage the worldwide reach of the Internet.** Use the Internet and the blogosphere to make it easy for people to hear what your company offers and try both your beta versions and your established

products. A common mistake of beta-stage deliverables is the focus on making the product a little more functional and a little less usable. As engineers, we rationalize that usability can come later, but during these early phases, usability should outweigh function by a significant margin. Your focus needs to be getting noticed and producing a happy trial experience. That means the trial code has to be easy to get to, easy to install and configure, and easy to test drive. Giving customers easy access to free downloads worked wonders for VMware, and it has become the fundamental path to market for many software products. Here's what Diane Greene had to say about how VMware leveraged the Internet:

> We gained viral marketing from the fully functional trial copy made available free over the Internet with a 30-day renewable license. These two approaches combined were how we introduced VMware to the world. We had that engineering spirit of being open and straightforward about things: 'Here is this great new product—try it, and if you like it, buy it.' The Web made it a lot easier to reach people; I don't think we could have done it without the Web. 75,000 people downloaded our first beta—we couldn't have reached that many people without the Internet.

4. **Look big.** The Internet allows small companies to have the same look and feel as larger ones. It's relatively easy today to create a professional Web presence that rivals that of much larger companies. IP telephony also enables you to create local telephone numbers in major geographies for a very low cost. Now you can have direct calling numbers in London, Paris, Tokyo, and New York while sitting in your living room anywhere in the world. Slick demos, professional Web presence, and international phone numbers help position your company as a player and reduce some of the risk that initial users feel in dealing with a startup.

Be Nimble, Be Quick

All companies need to be well-managed, but excessive dedication to a plan can lead to your company's demise. Business opportunities evolve in unexpected ways. Some market segments might find uses for your technology that you never dreamed of, allowing your technology to take off in unexpected ways. One example I heard of recently came from a company in Israel that developed night-vision digital video. Its first market? Not defense, espionage, or interdiction, as you might have thought. Instead, it was nighttime security for local junkyards. When steel prices shot up between mid-2007 and mid-2008, theft from junkyards leaped, and night-vision surveillance suddenly had a market the company had never anticipated.

Looking at VMware, the company fully expected its virtualization software to be adopted by IT shops (which it eventually was), but the initial flood of requests came heavily from the academic community, where students and professors were looking for reasonable ways to virtualize and divide shared server resources across different research projects or among a large population of students and professors. Reacting quickly to these opportunities takes more than just business agility; it takes engineering agility, too. Traditionally, software products have shipped on release cycles ranging from 12 to 24 months. When major requirements come up, you may be 12–18 months out before you can begin working on them and then another 12–24 months before delivering the required capabilities. Most products no longer have that luxury, and agile development methods combined with software as a service (SaaS) delivery models have made it possible and necessary for companies to ship new releases a few times a year or even a few times per month. That's a degree of responsiveness never before seen in software. It's now allowing companies to react and ship new features quickly, but it can mean that larger products need to divide their engineering teams to develop releases in parallel. For startups that are just building their niche, this kind of adaptability is crucial. Be nimble, be quick.

Growth Versus Acquisition

Most lay followers of technology have the impression that small companies become successful and get acquired by larger ones. This is actually rarer than most of us know. In reality, small businesses often have to decide early on (usually sooner than is comfortable) whether they want to grow into larger and even more successful companies or be acquired. Natural advantages and disadvantages accompany each (see Table 20.1). Whatever the decision—company growth or acquisition—it dramatically impacts the behavior of the company, its investment and R&D decisions, and its corporate structure and focus.

TABLE 20.1   Growth Versus Acquisition

	PROS	CONS
Company growth	Founders maintain control. Revenue can soar, eventually leading to larger profits for the founders and key employees.	The founders face great risk. The current owners might not succeed in taking the company to the next level. The time required to achieve the increased profitability could be uncomfortably long.
Acquisition	The founders and key personnel enjoy instant gratification, realizing financial benefits quickly. In the hands of a wise and qualified parent company, the acquired company might reach higher levels of success in both technology achievements and profit than it would in the hands of the original founders and VC investors.	Control will significantly change hands to new owners. The current leaders will need to share (or possibly lose) their control, both financially and strategically. If the company really has huge profit potential, the future profits will accrue to the parent company, not the original founders. Risk is involved. The new parent company could manage the newly acquired group poorly. The founders might have been better off on their own.

If your goal is corporate growth, you'll balance the need for revenue generation and a growing and delighted customer base with investment in growth activities. You'll spend significant energy and investment on new R&D to enhance existing products and services or create new ones. Your focus will be on revenue growth and much less on profit. Profit will come in time if the revenue is there, but every good businessperson knows that you have to invest today to achieve gains tomorrow.

By contrast, if your goal is acquisition, revenue growth is not a priority. Your focus will be on demonstrating profitability and successful channels to market. You'll want to make sure your financial metrics look good. As a result, you'll invest less energy and finances (but not zero) in R&D and you'll be less aggressive in how you financially extend the company.

Both strategies are valid, but the choice directly impacts your operational and strategic decisions pretty dramatically. Choose wisely, but perhaps more important, make a deliberate choice. Too many companies fail to make a deliberate decision. Their business strategy ends up convoluted, and they achieve neither the critical mass of investment in R&D and infrastructure to grow their revenue base nor the stable financial state, profitability, and well-established channels to market that make them attractive as an acquisition.

How to Get Acquired

New companies have their eyes on three business goals and usually make a deliberate choice to aggressively pursue one of these with gusto:

1. Staying independent and becoming profitable

2. Going public so the founders get a high return on their efforts

3. Getting bought

Getting acquired by another firm has some very appealing qualities. First, when it happens, the founders enjoy instant reward with minimal risk. Second, acquisition removes some of the burden from the founders on figuring out how to turn a small company with millions of dollars in revenue into a big company with tens of millions or hundreds of millions in revenue (or more). Expanding a new company to the big leagues of revenue generation often requires experience and infrastructure that the founders of a startup don't have. If you're a founder of a startup and you're looking to get acquired, it's helpful to know some of the steps and tricks to making it happen.

Large companies are always considering five categories of acquisition:

▶ **Segment leadership.** These companies are more established and already successful. An acquisition of a segment leader allows the buyer to instantly own a successful business that is a market leader. The price tag will be high, but the risks will be relatively low and the return on investment somewhat predictable.

▶ **Opportunistic consolidation.** This kind of acquisition is about garnering customers and market share. It can help collapse the number of vendors/competitors, and some companies have become famous for acquiring companies purely to remove a competitor from the market (apologies, but I'd better not name names). Usually the purchasing firm intends to retain the acquired company's customers while achieving cost/expense synergies. Opportunistic consolidation represents a small subset of all acquisitions.

► **Complementary gap filler.** Most acquisitions fall into this category, in which a larger company decides to acquire a smaller one to round out its existing portfolio. Although the larger company could probably develop the software itself, the benefits of acquisition are the time to market for the new components and access to its customer base and sales channels.

In many cases, the larger company is better suited to expanding and accelerating the acquired technology because of its existing marketing and sales infrastructure and more mature customer base. This kind of acquisition is more about acquiring technology than acquiring business.

► **New segment entry.** These companies are high profile (and might or might not be high revenue) and will provide a new segment for the acquiring firm. Segment leadership companies might fall into this category. For example, IBM's acquisition of Tivoli, Rational, and Lotus allowed IBM to leapfrog into systems management, application development, and operational communications with robust and mature portfolios.

► **Skill acquisition.** Another big motivator driving corporate acquisitions is the opportunity to rapidly acquire talent. The acquiring company might not even care about the startup's technology or product. When a large company wants to branch into a new field or grow a fledgling engineering team, the first thing it needs is skill. With learning curves to develop deep expertise in a domain typically running at two to four years, recruiting experienced staff with domain-specific knowledge provides a massive catalyst for bootstrapping deep technology. Companies that haven't crossed the chasm are easy targets. They might have lots of skill at lower valuation that larger companies view as a kind of fire sale for great talent.

The buying company has one or more of these objectives in mind as it looks for new acquisitions. If you're about to put your company on the selling block, you'll want to have a clear ideas of which firms might be interested in acquiring your company and for which of the previously mentioned five reasons. But how can you get the word out that you want to be acquired without scaring off your current customers and investors? You don't want to take out an ad in the *New York Times* because it will kill your existing business. Acquisitions require some subtlety and stealth. If you want to get acquired, consider these tips:

- ▶ **Establish relationships with key companies so you're a known quantity.** Where possible, don't just form relationships—form business partnerships in which you can work on some joint accounts. This dramatically improves your odds for acquisition down the road because large companies like to buy entities they already know. Make sure you're speaking with the right folks. The people you do business with can be an excellent entry point, but they might not be the people who work on acquisitions. Ask to set up an exploratory meeting with the company's business development team.

- ▶ **Reach out to a good VC (ideally, one that knows you).** VC firms can help approach potential suitors. A good VC usually has a stable of competent investment bankers who do the higher functions of acquisitions. The investment banker will be able to increase the visibility and demand of your technology to strategic acquirers. This can enable a bid-up on the value, and higher exit valuation for you and the current investors. It's helpful to produce a "sell package" that describes your firm, its technology offerings, its business stance, and its revenue and expense details; play up how you'll fit into one of the five acquisition objectives.

Once a potential buyer shows initial interest, you can expect an exploratory meeting where you'll have a chance to present yourself. Ask what they need to see and don't be surprised if they ask for some pretty detailed financial data. If the potential buyer is seriously interested, a due diligence phase is common. The buyer explores the legal status of the company, including Intellectual Property (IP) ownership; intercompany relationships; customer and vendor contracts; technical review of products and their architecture; and the size, skills, organizational culture, and locations of the staff.

Three major showstoppers can kill a promising acquisition:

1. **IP issues.** Problems with IP rights are one of the most painful and common ways for deals to die. A buying company will never knowingly incur the legal risk of acquiring a company that is built on IP that it doesn't have the rights to. You should always make sure you have legal rights to the IP your company uses, but before a due diligence phase begins, you really need to dot the i's and cross the t's.

2. **Untenable contracts.** For example, a reseller agreement might include terms that would prevent the acquiring company from selling products to a third party's customers. Such a limitation on what you can sell to whom might have been reasonable for a small startup firm, but often completely unreasonable for an acquiring company. You can't do much about this signed contract years later. As a shrewd executive, you need to keep the possibility of an acquisition in mind when you make deals with business partners, ensuring that these clauses are excluded or inserting an exit clause that allows you to void the contract—or, at least, the objectionable clauses—in the future.

3. **Hidden warts.** You might be tempted to dance around some of your company weaknesses to improve your leverage at the negotiating table. All financings and acquisitions are subject to due diligence; what's not said up front will probably be discovered and could turn out to be a deal breaker. Be careful of malicious omission.

Founding a startup (or getting in on the ground floor of one) is one of the tried-and-true ways of making it big. If the company is successful, you can rise to a position of influence along executive or technical paths and dramatic compensation. You'll also experience a range of life lessons that few of us can hope for. The risk is high, the road is long, and the challenges are immeasurable, but the successful few reap great rewards.

An Interview with Diane Greene

Co-founder and past CEO of VMware

CURRENT POSITION

Past CEO of VMware

CLAIM TO FAME

Co-founder, president, and CEO of VMware

DATE OF BIRTH

1955

EDUCATION

Master's in Computer Science, University of California, Berkeley, 1988

Master's in Naval Architecture, MIT, 1978

B.A. in Mechanical Engineering, University of Vermont, 1976

FAVORITE PASTIMES & HOBBIES

Family and friends, sailing and skiing, public service

BIOGRAPHY

Diane was the President and CEO of VMware, Inc. between 1998 and 2008. Under Diane's leadership, VMware created the market for mainstream virtualization and the resulting virtualization software industry. Diane has held technical leadership positions at Silicon Graphics, Sybase, and Tandem, and was CEO of VXtreme.

Before co-founding and leading VMware she founded VXtreme, a streaming video company purchased by Microsoft in 1997 and served as its CEO. Greene held technical leadership positions at Silicon Graphics, Tandem, and Sybase. She is a global leader in software for virtualized desktops, servers, storage, and networking. Diane has been an independent member of Intuit, Inc.'s Board of Directors since August 17, 2006, and is a member of the MIT Corporation.

"In college, I had a TI calculator"

How did you get started in software?

In college, I had a TI calculator and went from the slide-rule to the calculator that year. We were using both at the time. I played around on a computer, but it was really when I went to MIT in 1976 that I ended up becoming friends with a group of people who were part of MIT's artificial intelligence lab. I was excited by what they were doing. They had a large vision for what computers were going to enable for people. That was when I said, "This is really exciting. I want to learn more and get involved." I graduated from high school in 1972. My high school had no computer. I received a degree in mechanical engineering from the University of Vermont without needing to ever use a computer.

Your degree in naval architecture is interesting. What compelled you to do that?

I grew up sailing in Annapolis, Maryland, and we had a house on the water. I was very active racing sailboats. The head of my department in mechanical engineering at the University of Vermont had a Ph.D. in naval architecture and encouraged me to go to MIT; his Ph.D. was from MIT. It was really that and a love of being around the water in boats that got me there.

What do you consider your greatest accomplishments and/or contributions to software?

I led VMware in creating the modern virtualization industry and showing the power of a transparent and caring culture. Virtualization already existed, but we added many new inventions and made it mainstream. We built extremely high-quality software and took the company from 0 to a $1.8 billion run rate in 10 years. We created a value- and merit-based work environment where people did excellent work. In sum, we created the virtualization industry as we know it today, and we set a bar for very high-quality software and for a high level of openness and transparency.

Do you have a pet peeve in any aspect of the software world?

The paranoia of companies in the tech industry makes it difficult to realize the full potential of cross-company collaboration. Every company has

Diane Greene

concerns about their intellectual property. They have concerns that if they help another company, that company might get stronger and hurt them. When you go to partner with another company, it's very difficult because everyone is always thinking through the worst-case scenarios instead of the best-case scenarios. And we could do so much more if people were a little more optimistic about the outcome!

"We hoped for the best but planned for the worst"

You and a few others started VMware. Getting a good product idea together isn't new, but most fall over because engineers don't know how to bring a product to market. You guys seemed to figure it out. How did you know what to do?

We were focused on getting to revenue. We knew we had to have revenue to be successful, and we were very pragmatic about it. We always had a fallback scenario in case the scenario we wanted didn't work out. We hoped for the best but planned for the worst, always. We had the big vision for all computing devices from the beginning, but we wanted to get a large early base. The first customers we targeted were software engineers. We knew what kind of product they would like. In terms of marketing the product, perhaps because of my technical background, I had a very direct and grounded approach. We were bringing this very complex software to market, and it had a number of huge and interesting applications. I had met a phenomenal public relations person who had just sold her firm. She came in as our first Vice President of Marketing, and together we focused on taking our story to the press. We did no paid advertising, but we did take our story out to events, the Internet, and press meetings, and the press wrote about it. We were straightforward but passionate. We gained viral marketing from the fully functional trial copy made available free over the Internet with a 30-day renewable license. These two approaches combined were how we introduced VMware to the world. We had that engineering spirit of being open and straightforward about things: "Here is this great new product—try it, and if you like it, buy it." The Web made it a lot easier to reach people; I don't think we could have done it without the Web. 75,000 people downloaded our first beta—we couldn't have reached that many people without the Internet. First and foremost, we believed in the usefulness of what we had, were very passionate about it, and communicated that with every mechanism we could. We reached out to all the hardware vendors constantly to show them how useful this would be for them. IBM understood it immediately; virtualization originated at IBM, so they were our first partner and were wonderful to work with. They were instrumental in taking the products to market on the server side.

One interesting thing about our first downloads: The people we seemed to reach were college professors. A huge percentage was physics and chemistry professors. We had this little private joke at VMware: "VMware: It's not for everyone—you have to be really smart." We wanted to reach everyone, but something about the messages we were giving (or not), were causing the product to be picked up first by that group. They did have a real need to run windows and Linux, and they are generally a group that is continually trying new ways of doing things.

Did a certain event in your life have a pivotal effect on your career?

In the late 1970s, I saw the first mouse-based windows system at Xerox Park. It was the predecessor to the Alto computer. I remember looking at it, not completely understanding what was going on, but simultaneously realizing that it was going to change everything. It was a huge deal, but I wasn't confident enough to sit down and play with it—I would be today. It was a formative experience for me, seeing something when it was novel that is now second nature to anybody who uses a computer. I think that it helped me form a model for how new technology comes into the world. It gave me a sense of how to share new technology with the world and get people to incorporate it and use it. I had a similar experience with windsurfing. The first time I saw a windsurfer was in a newspaper photograph. It was just someone standing still in flat, windless water, but it captured my imagination. I got hold of a windsurfer and taught myself how to use it. That experience of seeing something new that you don't understand but you want to learn, and then having it become second nature and used by many, many people, is a model I have in my head that has been very helpful.

You were at the helm of VMware for about 10 years, and you led it to become one of the world's top software companies. What are some of the strategies for leading a software company that you developed over that period?

I think a lot of what made VMware so great was the very strong value-based culture that we had. It produced quality and innovation. We had a set of principles that we set down in our first month and followed all the way through. The culture was collaborative, respected people, and set very high standards. We also treated our partners and customers with equal respect, honesty, and straightforwardness. Because of that, people were very passionate about the company.

Really three things drove people internally. First was financial rewards. Second was that, from the engineering side, their work was having a big impact and, from the sales side, that this product they were selling was really going to help their customers. So people felt very good about what they were doing. They knew the company had very high integrity, and they were proud to be part of a high-integrity operation. Third, we had built together such an outstanding group of people and created a merit-based environment—no politics, but collaboration, and everything out in the open as much as possible. We all enjoyed coming to work. People liked the environment, and they liked the people they worked with and felt passionate about our products. When you put those three things together, people will maintain very high standards in their work and will innovate. Their hearts were in it; they were engaged.

In terms of scaling the culture, it was always about finding new mechanisms to have that collaboration and communication—and getting more sophisticated about communication and infrastructure because you have to start adding infrastructure and processes as you go. Also, you need to get everybody to keep reinventing their job. As we scaled, people needed to bring in new people to do the things they used to do. It really came down to some very simple first principles and making sure we were always consistent with them. I am proud of how seamlessly we scaled from 0 to 7,000 people plus well over a billion dollars. We were certainly working on adding more structure and processes, but it is a feat to grow a company 50%–100% year over year for 9 years straight and maintain high profitability throughout. We did that.

I think a value-based culture, opposed to a coin-operated culture, facilitates a group of people that care about what they are doing and are engaged by it. It then results in spectacular work from everybody.

What makes you feel successful about your work in software?

I'm goal-directed. I develop a vision, sometimes tactical and sometimes long-term—and am then relentless about getting to them because their achievement is my success. My goals are generally fairly big picture, but I have a sensitive antenna for issues. When things are not naturally tracking, I break them down into subgoals, to keep on track. I am compelled to see progress toward my goals. When I achieve a goal, I feel tremendous. People often asked me "How does it feel to have built VMware?" and it always jolted me because I was so involved in what was next for VMware that it didn't seem relevant.

I remember the day we launched our product. We received many incredible emails, like "not since man walked on the moon..." and "your brains must be bigger than Volkswagens...," numerous wonderful emails. It certainly felt great to be alive and part of VMware that day. We knew we had done something great that people loved, and that's just tangibly satisfying. When strong value is being delivered that I can actually see in either an objective or subjective way, and the people participating are happy, I feel successful. When something happens that sets you back, I sense it early and tend to get very agitated.

I like to have as much positive impact as possible in what I deliver and in how I work with and lead other people. That is what drives me.

"There are 24 hours in a day"

Technical leaders and executives are famous for being time-strapped. What strategies do you use to stay sane and use your time effectively?

I prepare for meetings ahead of time and then leave time after the meeting for follow-up via email. I regularly monitor my time, and when it is getting overly scheduled, I look for a way to offload certain categories of what I am doing, to either an existing person or a new hire. I set up certain rituals to keep myself and those I work with in sync and on track. At VMware, I reviewed my calendar daily with my assistant and met every Monday morning together with all my direct reports. That was valuable because everyone stayed aware of issues and knew we would work together to resolve them efficiently on a weekly basis. It also kept us in touch and collaborating with one another as a team. The required weekly meeting facilitated alignment and focus on execution as a given. I've also learned how to suggest other people for opportunities that come my way, and I regularly adapt my policy on what I'll do so that I can be consistent about how I focus my time.

How do you achieve a work-life balance? How do you keep your professional life from dominating everything?

I really did prioritize. On weekends and nights, I prioritized my family. Maybe I missed out on some dinner schmoozing I could have been doing, but I would always choose a lunch or breakfast meeting over a dinner meeting. I was fairly rigid about going home unless I was traveling or had a dinner that required my presence. That said, now that I've been away for a few months, I do see that even when at home, I was preoccupied with VMware and not entirely present for my family. I am enjoying bringing full focus to my family when I am with them and will focus on strategies to maintain that going forward.

There are 24 hours in a day; you make an arbitrary decision about how many of them you'll spend on what. If you don't make a thoughtful decision, it is unlikely that you will get to some things that you consider highly important. By consciously scheduling the life side of the equation, you find a way to work within that. I encourage people to have an outside life. I often attributed VMware's lack of politics to the fact that everyone was also engaged with their outside life. Creativity loves constraints. So you constrain yourself, and then you find a way to get everything done within that constraint. And it leaves no room for politics.

Even as a CEO, you weren't working more than 10 hours a day?

I was there from about 8 to 6:30, and then I often got up early before work, and before my family was up, to do email. I went through email when there was downtime and we weren't doing anything as a family. But I learned that if I refrained from sending emails or asking people to do things on the weekend, they would have a better weekend. So even on the weekends, I tried to do email in an offline mode so that it wouldn't go out until Monday morning.

What do you see as the coming changes in the software field over the next 10–15 years that will impact career opportunities or the way we develop software?

Software is getting a lot easier to build and use, which means it is being integrated into all aspects of how we live and work, and also integrated into all kinds of devices. Obviously, more and more software is a service, so the advantages of not having to run, maintain, and upgrade your own software are enormous—and for the software developer, not having to package the software for any installation and end-user maintenance and upgrade is huge. The way we use the software, the user interfaces are going through major advancements. Rich 3D visual and audio many-to-many immersive social experiences will be facilitated that allow for complete collaboration when people are not physically together. Software-based virtual worlds can take advantage of not being constrained by the laws of physics. The integration of social networking into how we do things is very powerful, being able to understand and benefit from how millions of others think. The information and tools at our disposal to process and extract meaningful new information will continue to make software front and center in our evolving world. We saw how software and the Internet transformed the 2008 U.S. election, we see how it continues to be used to facilitate an open and transparent administration, we see the explosion of phenomenally useful iPhone applications...it is an exciting time. I find it hard to keep up with all the change but am optimistic about it all being put to constructive use. Personally, I am excited about the potential for software and other technologies to transform education so that high-quality collaborative education is available to anyone who wants it.

"Be adventurous while also being disciplined"

What suggestions do you have for others on being successful in software (either R&D or business)?

Software is a wonderful medium because of the experimentation you can do with no dire consequences. To really be adventurous while also being disciplined is my advice. At VMware, we focused on quality, and everyone was very proud of it. We were able to do very innovative new things that nobody had ever done before, and do them with quality. The software industry is so interesting right now. The wonderful thing about software is that you can do pretty much any discipline because software is needed for almost everything. I would encourage people to think about what is deeply interesting to them and find a way to work in that area, so that they can be in a role where they feel productive and creative in what they are building. I think software is such an excellent base for whatever you're going to do, from research to management, because it provides a useful way to model and monitor and even re-create the world.

One piece of advice I would give people is to always make sure you're in an environment that leaves you feeling empowered to fully use your talents, and that you feel appreciated for the work you do. If you are not, work constructively to change your current environment so that it does meet these criteria; if you can't, make a change.

You have two graduate degrees. Do you feel that graduate degrees in computer science (or an MBA, for that matter) are beneficial to career success in software? Do you see it as a benefit when recruiting someone?

Certainly, a graduate degree never hurts anybody, but in software, I would never assume that someone wasn't immensely talented just because they don't have a graduate degree. In software, it's easier to excel based on merit. I think a graduate degree can be great training, but it tends to be more something you would do because you have a deeper interest rather than something to move your career forward. Of course, some positions, such as professor, clearly require it.

What final words of wisdom or caution do you have for people entering the field?

When working in software, be meticulous and think long-term about the consequences of what you are doing; don't sacrifice that ever. In terms of working in software, it is one of the best ways to be in a position to keep learning and creating, due to the flexibility and the increasing pace of new developments and discoveries.

Diane Greene

CHAPTER 21

Compensation: Kuh-ching!

"All I ask is the chance to prove that money can't make me happy."
—Spike Milligan (1918-2002)

Money makes the world go 'round, and most people who take the time to read a book called *Making It Big in Software* will be wondering about the bottom line at some point. Compensation is important, and it's good to know what's fair and what's possible wherever you are in your career.

In this chapter, I explore the following topics:

▶ How compensation varies between large and small companies

▶ The common forms of financial compensation (there's lots more than just salary and annual bonuses)

▶ The technical mechanics of stock options and grants

▶ The financial considerations that accrue through indirect compensation

▶ Typical salary ranges for the next few years for professionals with different levels of experience and expertise

After all that, you might be more confused than informed, so I wrap up the chapter with a planning tool that I've found helpful for thinking through the real pros and cons of different positions.

Compensation Differences Between Company Types

Compensation in any job is much more than the base salary, although the base salary is a major component (at least, in the short term). Aside from salary, employees are compensated with a wide range of other financial incentives, including bonuses, stock grants, stock options, retirement investments, and many direct and indirect benefits. Startup companies will generally offer higher base salaries and/or stock options for junior and intermediate programmers to attract top talent to their unproven company. However, in the mid-to-high-level positions, startups are unable to offer more than the larger firms for senior staff. As a result, the spread across base salaries is typically narrower in startups with a 2.3x difference between base salaries from the lowest- to highest-paid employees. The big differentiator is in the allocation of stock options, preferred stock, profit sharing or part ownership in the company that are given out more generously to the senior staff. If the company takes off, everybody wins. If not, aside from looking for a new job in a few years, the junior staff won't have lost much financially, but the senior staff might have earned substantially more had they worked at a larger firm. These are the cost benefits of working at a startup. Larger, more established companies tend not to pay salaries much beyond market rates, and opportunities for stock options and preferred stock are more rare, although they do exist. In large companies, you'll see about a 5.5x spread between the base salaries of the lowest- and highest-paid employees. Larger companies do distinguish themselves around significant bonus plans for a broad swath of employees (with bonuses in the range of 5%–25%) and lucrative bonuses, stock grants, or options for senior and executive staff that can aggregate to several times the value of the employee base salary in a good year.

Impact of Graduate Degrees on Compensation and Career Potential

New graduates always wonder how much they're losing out financially by getting a Master's degree or Ph.D. After all, instead of going to school they could use those years to build up both their professional experience and their salary. In my experience, employers generally offer new graduates with a Master's degree about 4%–8% more than new employees with a Bachelor's degree. Ph.D. recipients get anywhere from 5% to 15% higher. What the market is really saying is that the skill you've developed is about as valuable as the skill you would have developed in the workforce had you joined after your Bachelor's degree. Ultimately, the real reason to go to graduate school should be for your interest in learning and the advanced skills you'll develop there. Most people agree that getting a graduate degree is a great learning experience, but it's not for everyone. Whether it directly helps your career in software is a matter of debate.

My own feeling is that a Master's degree is particularly valuable, especially when the program involves a research thesis. The experience of doing independent research and learning to write a scientific thesis is hugely valuable. Ph.D.s offer the same value but take a lot more time and go into much greater depth. If you plan to build a career around the specialty of your Ph.D., using your deep domain expertise to found a company, or become an academic then a Ph.D. can be very valuable. If not, a Master's degree with a research thesis is the way to go.

Finally, some important corner cases are worth mentioning. Some positions require a Ph.D. For example, if you want to be a researcher at IBM Research, Microsoft Research, or HP Labs, you most likely need a Ph.D. Some companies also prefer a Ph.D., at least to do some of the more exciting work. Google and Sun are great examples of this. And of course, you almost certainly need a Ph.D. to teach at the college or graduate level.

It's certainly the case that in the software profession you can reach the highest professional levels, and develop some of the greatest breakthrough technologies, without a graduate degree. Don't take my word for it; review what the gurus had to proffer about graduate degrees. I asked many of the people I interviewed for their thoughts on the value of graduate degrees, and there's a pretty interesting mix of opinions.

Stock Options

Stock options give the bearer the right to buy a limited number of stocks at a specific price, regardless of the price at which the stock may be trading on the free market. Stock options were made popular by the growth of Silicon Valley startups who couldn't afford to pay large salaries to attract top talent. Instead, they began offering stock options during the company's pre-IPO and penny stock stages. The strategy works well for all parties. If the company does well and the stock value increases significantly, the options can become extremely valuable. On the flip side, during the company's growth years, while the stock is still low cost, the cost to the company is fairly limited. The philosophy is simple: Help the company become a success, and you can get rich.

Here's how stock options generally work. Stock options have three factors: a strike price, a vesting period, and an expiration period. The strike price is the price you can buy the stock shares for, and this is related to the value of the stock at the time the options are issued. For example, if the company stock price is $1.50, then the strike price of stock options issued might be the same. The vesting period is the time until you can actually exercise the options. Many companies have a 2-, 4-, or 10-year vesting period, with a percentage of the options vesting each year. Finally, there is an expiration period, usually 10–20 years, after which the options become useless. Here's how you can make a lot of money: Let's say your company gives you 5,000 options of stock at $1.50. Five years later, the stock price has grown to $87, but your options give you the right to buy 5,000 units of the stock at $1.50. If you buy 5,000 units for $1.50 and sell them the same day for $87, you'll earn $85.50 on each unit, or $427,500. Sweet.

What's the downside? There are three: First, you never know exactly when to sell—that's the nature of the stock market. The amount you earn is directly related to the difference between the strike price and the current stock price, so timing is everything. Second, if you fail to sell because you're waiting for the share price to climb a little higher, the stock might begin to drop for any number of reasons, and your options will expire. You have no guarantees you'll make a dime with stock options, but the potential is great, especially for new companies that have a low stock price. For more established companies with stock prices over $50, the odds of your stock value increasing by 50 times over the course of a few years are pretty slim, so stock options clearly favor high growth companies. Third, you can get into serious trouble by buying your vested options at the strike price and then deciding to hold them. The excess of stock price over strike price is ordinary income. But suppose you don't sell enough shares to cover your tax liability, your company doesn't do an automatic withholding, and the stock price drops—you can now owe more in taxes than the value of your stock. Even if this scenario doesn't occur, you should think seriously about the risk of exercising your stock options but not selling the stock. Your goal should be to minimize your risk exposure to your company's potential failure. You already have salary risk. Having a lot of your financial assets tied to the company's success as well is poor financial planning.

Stock Grants

Another option companies have to motivate employees is offering preferred stock, sometimes called preferred shares or preference shares. Unlike stock options, which have value only based on the difference between the strike price and the current price, preferred stock is actual stock and, therefore, always has value as long as the stock is being traded.

Dividends on preferred stock are generally paid out before dividends to common stockholders, which is why they are called "preferred." The shares do not usually provide voting rights. Much like stock options, these are usually offered in conjunction with a vesting period, so an employee can't make use of all the units for several years. Because they are guaranteed to have value, but can't be exercised until they vest, stock grants are a powerful incentive for top employees to stay with the company.

Bonus Plans

Most companies offer some form of bonus plan, usually tied to corporate results as well as individual performance. For regular employees, these are typically in the range of 5%–25%. For executives, the range is more dramatic, which is reasonable. The performance of the business does depend more on the decision making, leadership, and execution prowess of its executives. As a result, their compensation is more tightly coupled with business performance. The range for executives is usually 20%–200%, although it can be up to 1,000% for C-level executives (CEO, CTO, CFO, CIO, and so on). Because business performance tends to be cyclical. If an executive can last long enough to get just a few good years under the belt, the economic rewards can be dramatic. For example, consider being an executive for 10 years, 2 of which are during good economic times, when the company soars largely on the strength of the economy. As a result you might receive 500% bonuses for each of the two good years. If your base salary was $230,000, you'd be $2.3 million better off—not too shabby.

Retirement Plans

One of the least interesting topics for professionals in their 20s and 30s is retirement. It seems so vague and distant. Yet the difference in retirement plans varies hugely across companies. Retirement plans have generally fallen off in value over the past 15 years. A weak retirement package might accrue to only 1.5 times base salary by the time you retire, while a lucrative one could offer as much as 20 times base salary. The difference could be literally millions of dollars. It's understandable why young professionals pay this little mind, but it could be the single biggest long-term financial differentiator between jobs. Make sure you understand the pension plan your company offers and factor that into your job planning, even if you're under 40.

Typical Salary Ranges (2010–2013)

Salaries vary widely across geographies and companies. In general, though, some trends emerge. As a general rule, salaries are higher in the California, New York, and Boston areas, sometimes by as much as 40%. Salaries are higher in the United States than in Canada and the European Union, often by as much as 20%. However, the increased salaries available in some locations are usually concomitant with a higher cost of living. Carefully weigh tax rates, housing costs, and health benefits before making a fair assessment.

Table 21.1 shows some typical North American ranges in U.S. dollars for 2010–2013.[1]

TABLE 21.1   Salary Ranges 2010–2013

POSITION AND EXPERIENCE	COMPENSATION
New employees (Bachelor's degrees)	$45,000–$65,000
Seasoned pros, 5–10 years	$60,000–$120,000 (possible stock options)
Career professionals	$85,000–$130,000 (possible stock options)
Hotshots, 10–25 years	$90,000–$175,000, (and stock options)
Executives	$130,000–$1,000,000 (stock options or grants of preferred stock, with bonuses tied to profit and/or stock value)
CEO/CTO	$150,000–$4,000,000 ($230,000 is the current average in the USA. Stock options or grants of preferred stock, with bonuses tied to profit and/or stock value. Bonus plans up to ten times base salary.)

Indirect Compensation

Money is important—it puts food on the table, pays the bills, and reduces some of life's stresses. But other ways in which companies compensate

---

[1] Table 2.1 covers the typical ranges of salary in North America. It excludes outliers at both extreme of the scale. Examples can be found below and above these ranges.

employees are also worth considering. Some of these save you money by offering you benefits you would otherwise pay for out of pocket (such as health coverage, dental insurance, and fitness facilities); others give you opportunities that you would never pay for yourself but will enjoy at your employer's expense (such as business travel to exotic locations).

These indirect benefits vary by geography. In some countries, the following perks have become ubiquitous for software professionals:

▶ Company car (including gas and insurance coverage)

▶ Medical insurance

▶ Company-funded vacations

▶ Home office expenses, such as high-speed Internet connectivity, workstation equipment, and ergonomic furniture

Those perks tend to be geographic, based on the norms of the country. Some other perks vary by company more than geography:

▶ Fitness center facilities on-site or membership to nearby clubs

▶ Gaming facilities on-site (video games, pool, foosball, Ping Pong)

▶ Travel to technical conferences

▶ Travel to academic conferences

▶ Travel for public speaking engagements

▶ Customer travel

▶ Opportunities to publish

▶ Opportunities to patent

These might sound like minor issues, but take a look at the math. Let's say you're married and would like to take two traveling vacations a year and have a gym membership. Many people bring their spouse with them on company business trips. It's not the same as being on a real vacation because you're working hard during the day, but nighttimes are available for exploring and enjoying a new place, and you can extend the stay a day or two after the business work is over to get some real vacation time. Table 21.2 illustrates a scenario in which you had two distinct three-day business trips and for each you tacked on an extra day of personal vacation. Your employer also covers your costs for a top-notch fitness membership.

TABLE 21.2   Side Benefits

ITEM	YOUR COST	BUSINESS-RELATED COST COVERED BY YOUR EMPLOYER
Trip 1, hotel fees for 4 days	$600	$450
Trip 1, flight	$1,200	$1,200
Trip 2, hotel fees for 4 days	$600	$450
Trip 2, flight	$1,200	$1,200
Gym fees	$3,500	$3,500
Total	$7,100	$6,800

You were able to get two semi-vacations and a fitness club membership and were only out of pocket $300. If your spouse joins you on the business trips you get a mini vacation for essentially the price of his or her ticket. Add to that the professional benefits of expanding your personal network internationally, seeing the world, and being able to meet some interesting and influential people, and it starts to add up to real value.

Fatherly Thinking

Deciding where to work is a personal choice. Some companies definitely pay more than others. It's all about supply and demand. Call me nuts, but I still believe the best choice is to take the position that offers the opportunities to work with the most talented people, provided that the pay is fair and the company doesn't look like it will be having a going-out-of-business sale in a few months. I also think everyone should experience having a job with a first-class firm, if they can. The long-term benefits of having worked for a top-tier firm are excellent; you'll be able to leverage those credentials for years (possibly decades) to come. Another consideration for professionals just starting out is that big firms usually operate with more revenue and resources than smaller ones, so they're more likely to "do things right" by following a comprehensive software engineering cycle. Additionally, the revenue base of larger firms allows them greater depth to attract and pay the best and brightest. The exposure to the best software engineering practices and the opportunity to work with a broader spectrum of top talent offers a superior staging ground for learning software tradecraft.

Table 21.3 can help you chart your way through the decision making.

TABLE 21.3   Considerations for Job Seekers

FINANCIAL BENEFIT	BENEFIT PER YEAR ($)
Salary	
Bonus plan (average expected amount)	
Stock options	(Estimate value over 10 years then divide by 10.)
Stock grants	(Estimate value over 10 years then divide by 10.)
Life insurance Health insurance Dental insurance Eye care insurance Company car benefits (car, gas, insurance) Fitness club Business trips to fun locations Home Internet coverage Cell phone, Blackberry expenses	(What would it cost you to get the same benefit if you paid for it privately?)
Pension and other savings plans (such as 401(k) plans)	(Evaluate this as the amount of money you would need to invest each year to achieve the post-retirement annual benefit this company purports to offer.)
Group insurance rates for home and auto	(How much will this save you, compared to the best you can arrange as an individual?)

NONFINANCIAL CONSIDERATIONS	YOUR RATING FROM 1 TO 10 (10 IS BEST)
Enjoyable/exciting work	
Long-term stability of the company	
Company track record	
Company reputation (and infrastructure) for innovation and research	
Opportunities for professional growth	
Opportunities for advancement	
Quality of the leadership team	
Work environment (offices/cubicles, informal/formal, intense/laid back)	
Work flexibility (hours and location)	
Talented coworkers	
Location (travel time, city)	

CHAPTER 22

Making It Big?

"Men who never get carried away should be."
—Malcolm Forbes (1919–1990)

Only a small percentage of people make it to the career heights they would really like to. I believe firmly that far more people could realize their dreams with just a touch more effort and a wee dose of tactical thinking. It's worth giving some thought to why some people seem to get there more naturally than others.

Who Makes It Big?

The people who make it big in software have some very clear qualities in common. They typically all are

- Goal-oriented
- Highly emotionally intelligent
- Darned smart
- Experts in their domains
- Sensationally tenacious, usually without being impolite

Another factor separates the world-famous gurus from the rest of the pack: luck. In my interview with James Gosling, I asked him what he attributed his own career success to. He answered with this:

I've been pretty lucky at building systems that people found interesting kinda at the right time. Certainly, the whole success of Java was 10% technology and 90% just dumb-assed lucky timing.

Luck—and, in particular, luck with timing—is a huge factor for most successful revolutionaries; it takes luck to be in the right place at the right time. But as the saying goes, "Fortune favors the prepared mind." It might have seemed like luck and circumstance even to them, but the combination of talent, hard work, analytic and emotional intelligence, innovativeness, and fierce goal-oriented determination would have made most of these people huge successes in any time or place.

Another trend you'll see clearly is that the fastest way to the top is to get in at the beginning. Many of the biggest names in software are innovators who founded their own products, organizations, or companies or at least got in very close to the start of these. In this book, you've seen examples such as Bjarne Stroustrup, James Gosling, Grady Booch, Diane Greene, Linus Torvalds, Marissa Mayer, Mark Russinovich, Richard Stallman, Marc Benioff, Robert Kahn, and Steve Wozniak, who all fall into that category. The correlation is high.

Finally, consider this sobering thought: Many of those who have helped to change the world the most, with world-spanning innovations, have at times received comparatively the smallest financial reward. That's a side effect of innovating within an established organization that owned the rights to what these great thinkers helped produce. That being said, financial rewards are more important to some people than others, and for some folks, the freedom to come to work and play, innovate, and dream is greater reward than money could ever buy.

What Does Making It Big Look Like?

I can tell you what it *might* look like. For John Schwarz, success is tightly correlated to leading people to action. For Robert Kahn, Steve Wozniak, Mark Russinovich, and Ray Tomlinson it's about the mental challenges they conquer. For James Gosling, Marissa Mayer, Peter Norvig, and Bjarne Stroustrup, success is more tightly coupled with the impact of their work on people and things. For others, it might be the opportunity to work with nice people and have a positive social experience. What's the point? What looks rather unsuccessful to you may be a rip-roaring success for someone else. Everyone is different.

I started this book by commenting in Chapter 1, "Making It Big," that success is different for everyone. It's important to have your own idea of success and make sure you know what you're going after. Sure, you can chart your road to success using someone else's model, but if you get there and are unhappy with where you are or who you are, what's it worth? A number of forces in society drive us to believe that success is directly connected to financial wealth. Some of the people I interviewed are certainly very wealthy, but none of them define their feeling of success by wealth. I don't think that was simply political correctness during the interviews, either. Most of us appreciate having a bit more money, or even a lot more, but it's not fundamentally what satisfies us. Getting to the top, regardless of what our personal top is, requires tenacity, smarts, and planning, which much of this book has been dedicated to. Even more so, it requires you to understand yourself and what will really satisfy you professionally. The ancient Greeks understood it. Inscribed in the courtyard of the Temple of Apollo at Delphi was the simple aphorism, "Know thyself."

Why Some People Don't or Can't

Career success isn't a high priority for many people. That's an admirable outlook—there's much more to life than work. However, there are those who *do* aspire but fail to achieve greatness in their careers. Their failure to accomplish high professional goals often stems from a few simple causes in some combination:

▶ They were unwilling to put in the effort to contribute at a high level. They dreamed of professional advancement, but never really made it a priority. Other aspects of their life dominated their passions and interest. Like an aspiring Olympian who refuses to train, or a doctoral candidate who indefinitely protracts his thesis, without the application of effort the dream remains a fantasy.

▶ Over their careers, they failed to continuously invest in their professional growth. Neither their technical skills nor their soft skills ever reached a level of competency that allowed them to progress to senior positions.

▶ They failed to be sufficiently proactive and tenacious in their approaches to starting and advancing technology projects.

▶ Poor communication skills impeded their ability to work the org, push through roadblocks, demonstrate leadership and communicate their accomplishments.

▶ They lacked the organizational savvy to navigate organizational and business situations with acumen.

▶ Their social interactions were negative or confrontational. They burned too many bridges and made too many foes.

▶ They operated as an army of one, never leveraging the multiplicative power of the team.

▶ They lacked the ability to lead and inspire others.

Some of these inhibitors are pretty mechanical, and any intelligent and motivated person could develop the skills and behaviors needed. Sadly, many ambitious and talented people fail to develop these skills simply because they are unaware of them or are unwilling to accept that they need to build them. In most cases, all they needed was a little awareness and a small but consistent effort to keep them on a path of personal growth.

Final Thoughts

From everything that we know, we can predict two things for the next decade: First, software innovation is thriving and huge opportunities await for further grow. Second, software development remains a lucrative and successful profession to be a part of. According to recent International Data Corporation (IDC) studies, there are 2.6 million software developers in the United States, with one of the fastest-growing professional growth rates. According to the United States Bureau of Labor Statistics (BLS), the number of software engineering jobs in the United States is expected to grow by 38% over the next ten years.

Software development is also popular throughout the European Union and the Middle East and has seen massive growth rates over the past five years in India and China due to increasing off-shoring of IT projects. IDC estimates the worldwide number of software developers at an astounding 14.9 million. Luckily, software developers are not only plentiful, but also well paid. As of May 2006, the average salary for software engineers was $85,370, and senior software architects earn in excess of $200,000.

Software is a lucrative profession and an exciting one. People often wonder if we have reached a plateau in software design and engineering innovation, but I think it's clear from everything we've seen over the past decade that great innovations and strong market demand lay ahead. As this book is heading off to print, massive R&D efforts are underway surrounding software as a service, and expanding the use of 3D gaming technology into communication and messaging infrastructure. Social networking software has exploded, and wireless mobile devices, GPS and Radio Frequency Identification (RFID) technologies have become mainstream. There will be 30 billion RFID tags deployed in 2010[1] alone. Computing has become sensationally portable, interconnected, and geographically locatable. The powerful growth of multicore CPU technology, along with emerging storage technologies such as solid state drives (SSDs), will soon take us to unheralded levels of computational resource, storage capacity, and access efficiency certain to enable a range of real-time software systems that were unimaginable four or five years ago. Current estimates project there will be nearly two billion people on the Web by 2011[2] and a trillion connected objects. The world is creating 15 petabytes[3] of new information daily, driving unprecedented demand for scalable information management. Our world is becoming increasingly instrumented and interconnected, and our technology has become more intelligent. The combined improvements to software and processing power may even allow automated cars to drive city streets more safely and reliably than humans within the next 25 years.[4] The more software develops as an industry, the more we realize that what we've seen so far is only the beginning. What a cool business to be in, indeed.

---

[1] Steve Mills, Senior Vice President, IBM Software Group, keynote address, IBM Analyst Connect Symposium (November 2009), Stamford, CT.

[2] *Ibid.*

[3] *Ibid.*

[4] Several companies and research groups are already working on prototypes for automated urban driving. You can see existing prototypes in action on YouTube, including Perrone Robotics' "Tommy Jr.," a robotic car programmed in Java. (Watch CEO Paul Perrone demo it with Java creator James Gosling here: http://www.youtube.com/watch?v=RYWMKwhZh8s.) Tommy Jr. was created for the 2007 DARPA Urban Challenge, where robotic vehicles compete for best time through the course as well as best adherence to California driving rules. (Watch the finals of the 2007 DARPA Urban Challenge here: http://www.youtube.com/watch?v=SQFEmR50HAk.)

Index

Symbols

@ symbol, 100, 105-106
"2008 Compensation and Entrepreneurship
  Report in IT," 379

A

accomplishments
  Bentley, Jon, 38
  Booch, Grady, 238
  communicating, 179-180
  Greene, Diane, 397
  Kahn, Dr. Robert, 325
  Malloy, Tom, 251-252, 257
  Mayer, Marissa, 26
  Norvig, Peter, 123
  Russinovich, Mark, 195
  Schwarz, John, 156
  Stallman, Richard, 81
  Stroustrup, Bjarne, 63
  Tomlinson, Ray, 102
  Torvalds, Linus, 171
  Wozniak, Steve, 355
achieving work-life balance, 249
  assessing, 249
  Benioff, Marc, 377
  Bentley, Jon, 40
  Booch, Grady, 241
  defining yourself, 245
  Gosling, James, 285
  Greene, Diane, 401
  Kahn, Dr. Robert, 330

life impacts work, 247-248
  Malloy, Tom, 256
  Mayer, Marissa, 29
  Norvig, Peter, 125
  organizational culture, 246-247
  repartitioning time, 245
  Russinovich, Mark, 197
  Schwarz, John, 159
  Stallman, Richard, 83
  stressors, 248
  Stroustrup, Bjarne, 65
  tips, 246
  Tomlinson, Ray, 108
  Torvalds, Linus, 174
  Vaskevitch, David, 217
  work environment, 247
  working backward, 249
acquisition of startups
  benefits, 392
  categories, 392-393
  getting the word out to potential
    buyers, 394
  growth comparison, 390-392
  problems, 394-395
adaptability (startups), 389-390
Advanced Logistics Project (ALP), 101
advancement
  accomplishments, communicating,
    179-180
  credibility, 178
  evaluations, 177
  goal-oriented careers, 181-184
  management peer impact, 187-188

manager influence, 185
  career discussions, 186-187
  helping managers look good, 185
  technical/organizational assistance, 185
promotibility inversion, 189-191
promoting others, 189
advice
  executives
    Benioff, Marc, 372-373
    Greene, Diane, 399
  field opportunities, 30
  startups, 372
  success
    Benioff, Marc, 371, 375, 378
    Bentley, Jon, 41-42
    Booch, Grady, 242-243
    Gosling, James, 286-287
    Greene, Diane, 403
    Kahn, Dr. Robert, 328, 331
    Malloy, Tom, 257-259
    Mayer, Marissa, 27
    Norvig, Peter, 126
    Russinovich, Mark, 198-200
    Schwarz, John, 159-160
    Stallman, Richard, 83
    Stroustrup, Bjarne, 66
    Tomlinson, Ray, 106, 109
    Torvalds, Linus, 175
    Vaskevitch, David, 216-218
    Wozniak, Steve, 358-359
affiliative leadership, 292
affinitizing, 319
aggressive estimates, 228
agile development process methodology, 272
agreements, 151-153
All the President's Men, 300
ALP (Advanced Logistics Project), 101
angel funding, 384
Apple
  computer development, 336
  iPhone, 310
  Jobs, Steve
    academics, 53
    business fluency, 337
  stock growth, 337
  Wozniak, Steve
    accomplishments, 355
    advice, 358-359
    biography, 352-353
    debugging, 354
    future of software, 357
    inspirations, 356

    personal future, 357
    personal success, 356
    pet peeves, 355
    Tetris, playing, 357
    time management, 357
    trends/innovations, 358
    viewing self as hardware person,
      353-354
architects, 112
The Art of Japanese Management
  (Pascale), 302
assertions, 89
assessing, work-life balance, 249
attracting new customers, 15
audiences. *See* customers
authority
  leadership, 291-294
  visionaries, 333-334
  world-class status, 334
awards (resumés), 47

B

bad projects, 11-12
balancing work-life, 244
  achieving by working backward, 249
  assessing, 249
  Benioff, Marc, 377
  Bentley, Jon, 40
  Booch, Grady, 241
  defining yourself, 245
  Gosling, James, 285
  Greene, Diane, 401
  Kahn, Dr. Robert, 330
  life impacts work, 247-248
  Malloy, Tom, 256
  Mayer, Marissa, 29
  Norvig, Peter, 125
  organizational culture, 246-247
  repartitioning time, 245
  Russinovich, Mark, 197
  Schwarz, John, 159
  Stallman, Richard, 83
  stressors, 248
  Stroustrup, Bjarne, 65
  tips, 246
  Tomlinson, Ray, 108
  Torvalds, Linus, 174
  Vaskevitch, David, 217
  work environment, 247
BARC (Microsoft Bay Area Research Center), 7
believing in yourself, 336-337

benefits
  big shots, 7-9
  CEOs, 379
  publishing, 342
  startup acquisitions, 392
Benioff, Marc
  advice for success, 371, 375, 378
  attraction to software as a service, 371
  biography, 369-370
  future of software, 377
  getting started, 370
  graduate degrees, 376
  listening to customers, 21
  philanthropy, 373-374
  platform independence, 375
  SaaS, 374
  software executives, 372-373
  startups, 372
  time management, 377
  trends/innovations, 376
  work-life balance, 377
Bentley, Jon
  accomplishments, 38
  advice for success, 41-42
  biography, 37-38
  future of software, 41
  getting started, 38
  personal success, 39
  pet peeves, 39
  time management, 40
  trends/innovations, 40
  work-life balance, 40, 249
  writing code, 39
best and worst programmers differences, 295
betterment of society, 4
big shots, 7-9
biographies
  Benioff, Marc, 369-370
  Bentley, Jon, 37-38
  Booch, Grady, 236-237
  Gosling, James, 281
  Greene, Diane, 396
  Kahn, Dr. Robert, 323-325
  Malloy, Tom, 252
  Mayer, Marissa, 23-24
  Norvig, Peter, 122-123
  Russinovich, Mark, 192-193
  Schwarz, John, 154-155
  Stallman, Richard, 79-80
  Stroustrup, Bjarne, 62-63
  Tomlinson, Ray, 100-101
  Torvalds, Linus, 170
  Vaskevitch, David, 214-216
  Wozniak, Steve, 352-353

bloggers, 342
bonus plans, 408
Booch, Grady
  accomplishments, 238
  advice for success, 242-243
  biography, 236-237
  future of software, 241-242
  getting started, 237
  knowledge, 239
  personal success, 239
  pet peeves, 240
  Rational Software beginnings, 238
  time management, 240
  trends/innovations, 239
  work-life balance, 241
book publishing, 342
brainstorming, 312-313
Brin, Sergey, 380
Brooks, Frederick, 225, 349
browser engines, rendering, 25
buggy code, writing, 133
building
  emotional caches, 189
  teams, candidates, 295
    attracting, 295
    filtering, 296
    interviewing successfully, 296-298
    keeping best people happy, 298-299
    mix, 299
    prima donnas/superstars, 300
  trust, 140
burning bridges, 128
business of software, learning, 70
business plans, 381-382
business skills, 337-338

C

C/C++, 63, 87
The C++ Programming Language
  (Stroustrup), 64
candidates
  attracting, 295
  filtering, 296
  interviewing successfully, 296-298
careers
  advancement
    accomplishments, communicating,
      179-180
    credibility, 178
    evaluations, 177
    goal-oriented careers, 181-184
    management peer impact, 187-188
    manager influence, 185-187

promotibility inversion, 189-191
promoting others, 189
early years
business of software knowledge, 70
career paths, choosing, 74
expertise, 70
job satisfaction, 76-78
low-level programming skills, 71
mentors, 74-75
networking, 72-73
tradecraft skills, 69-70
watching leaders, 72
paths, choosing, 74
planning/placement, 49
roles
architects, 112
CEOs, 111
channel salespeople, 114
chief architects, 112
CTOs, 111
department managers, 113
direct salespeople, 114
directors of engineering, 111
directors of marketing, 111
fellows, 111
function verification testers, 114
product managers, 113
program managers, 113
programmers, 113
release managers, 112
research staff members, 113
second-line managers, 112
system verification testers, 114
technical evangelists, 115
technical managers, 112
technical salespeople, 114
usability engineers, 113
Vice Presidents, 111
visibility, 116
satisfaction, 8, 76-78
statistics, 416
success. *See* success
CDAs (confidential disclosure agreements), 381
CEOs, 111
benefits, 379
salary ranges, 409
changing career goals, 183
channel salespeople, 114
chief architects, 112
choosing
career paths, 74
companies, 43-46, 411-412
Circles of Concern/Influence, 205-206

climbing the corporate ladder, 45
cloud computing services, 383
co-opetition, 115
coaching
interviews, 60
leadership, 291-292
code
debugging, 88-90
reuse
innovation, 320
schools versus industry, 34
writing, 39
coercive leadership, 291-292
cold calling, 50
collaboration
agreements, 151-153
communication, 149
development environment, 238
innovation, 317
columnists, 342
commercially available components (COTS), 320
communication
effective, 117-118
email, 117
four modes of in-person, 118-120
importance, 116
interviews, 57
managers, 121
near-real-time, 179
personal accomplishments, 179-180
personal requests, 118
post-factum, 180
working the org, 149
companies. *See also* industry
choosing, 43-46, 411-412
communication
effective, 117-118
email, 117
four modes of in-person, 118-120
importance, 116
managers, 121
personal requests, 118
core competencies, 162-163
culture
core competencies, 163
work-life balance, 246-247
high/low performer differences, 115
impressions, 121
roles, 110
architects, 112
CEOs, 111
channel salesperson, 114

chief architects, 112
CTOs, 111
department managers, 113
direct salespeople, 114
directors of engineering, 111
directors of marketing, 111
fellows, 111
function verification testers, 114
product managers, 113
program managers, 113
programmers, 113
release managers, 112
research staff members, 113
second-line managers, 112
system verification testers, 114
technical evangelists, 115
technical managers, 112
technical salespeople, 114
usability engineers, 113
Vice Presidents, 111
visibility, 116
visiting, 51
working the org
agreements, 151-153
communication, 149
dressing for success, 150-151
emotional motivators, 140-143
getting people on-side, 140
negotiations, 144-149
problems, 130
social networking, 143
compensation
bonus plans, 408
companies
choosing, 411-412
differences, 405
financial
industrial, 33
rewards, 3-4
salary ranges 2010–2013, 409
schools versus industry, 35
graduate degrees, 405-406
indirect, 409-411
larger companies, 405
preferred stock, 407
retirement plans, 408
startups, 405
stock options, 406-407
competitive offerings, 18
complainers, 129
confidence in interviews, 57
confidential disclosure agreements (CDAs), 381
constraints (time and resource), 319

contacts
building, 72-73
finding jobs, 49
Convolution Principle, 227
coop students, 266
core competencies, 162-163
corporate influence, 4
costs
patents, 338
software defects, 276, 279
startups, financing, 383-385
COTS (commercially available components), 320
creating opportunities, 366-367
credibility, 121
career advancement, 178
project proposal success, 164
critical success factors (CSFs), 203
cross-disciplinary studying, 334-336
crossing the chasm, 386-389
customer focus, 387
demos, 388
Internet, leveraging, 388
looking big, 389
Crossing the Chasm (Moore), 17, 368
CSFs (critical success factors), 203
CTOs, 111, 409
culture (companies)
core competencies, 163
work-life balance, 246-247
curriculum, 32
customers
attracting new, 15
criteria, 18
existing, 15
feedback, 21-22
focus, 16
listening, 21
product development influence, 16
startup focus, 387
types, 16

D

databases, 10
debugging, 88-89
assertions, 89
code inspections, 90
Design by Contract, 89
Wozniak, Steve, 354
decision making, market-driven, 14
defects, 276, 279
delegation, 303

democratic leadership, 291-292
demos, 388
department managers, 113
dependency management, 227
Design by Contract, 89
developing
    emotional intelligence, 98-99
    goals, 183
    growth skills, 92-94
    hard skills, 84
    soft skills, 84, 95, 99
    technical skills, 85
        debugging, 88-90
        programming languages, 86-88
        reviews, 91-92
    time-management skills, 93-94
development
    based on existing customers, 15
    customer criteria, 18
    customer focus, 16
    defects, 276, 279
    maturity, testing, 275-276
    methodologies, 270-274
    popularity, 416
    quality, 18, 279-280
    SaaS example, 19-21
    technical skills, 85
    technologies, 17-18
    user feedback, 21-22
    value, 16
direct salespeople, 114
directed career path example, 181
directing others, 304
directors of engineering, 111
directors of marketing, 111
disruptive technology, 18
domain expertise skills, 86
dressing for success, 150-151
drivers, schools versus industry, 35

E

early adopters, 17
early career years
    business of software knowledge, 70
    career paths, choosing, 74
    expertise, 70
    job satisfaction, 76-78
    low-level programming skills, 71
    mentors, 74-75
    networking, 72-73
    tradecraft skills, 69-70
    watching leaders, 72

early majority adopters, 17
education. *See* school
EI (emotional intelligence), 95, 99
    developing, 98-99
    maturity and common sense, 96
    personalities, 98
    self-assessment, 98
    side-by-side comparison example, 96-97
Eisner, Michael, 319
elevator pitches, 164, 381
Ellison, Larry, 53
email
    @ symbol, 100, 105-106
    discussions, 117
    evolution, 102
    future, 104
    invention of networked, 103-104
    length, 117
    managing, 210-213
emotional caches, building, 189
emotional intelligence. *See* EI
emotional motivators, 140-143
    face time, 142
    giving something for nothing, 141
    inspiring self-worth in others, 141
    sharing glory, 142
employment agencies, 49
engines, rendering in browsers, 25
enjoying work, 5-6
enthusiasm, 8, 58
estimates, 227-228
evaluations (employee), 177
executives
    advice
        Benioff, Marc, 372-373
        Greene, Diane, 399
    salary ranges, 409
    schedule overruns, 221
existing customers, 15
expertise
    defined, 190
    early career, 70
external business plans, 382
extracurricular activities
    resumés, 48
    value, 54-55

F

face-saving exits, 265
face-to-face private meetings, 118
Fagan, Michael, 90

failures
  rates, 12
  startups, 380
  success, 416
  visionaries, 348
fame, 8
feedback, 21-22
fellows, 111
financing startups, 383
  angel funding, 384
  fourth-stage, 385
  investment capital, 385
  second-stage, 384
  third-stage, 385
finding
  innovation opportunities, 311-312
  jobs. See job searches
  mentors, 74-75
first few months at work, learning curve,
  361-362
  colleagues, 364
  good mentors, 362
  managers, 362-363
  managing your boss, 366
  opportunities, creating, 366-367
  pushing yourself, 368
following the money, 301
formal code reviews, 90
FORTRAN, 86
four modes of in-person communication,
  118-120
  face-to-face private meetings, 118
  large group presentations, 119-120
  small group discussions, 118
  small group presentations, 118
fourth-stage funding, 385
free software, 82
freedom of motion, 35
fun work environments, 76-78
function verification testers, 114
fundamental technical skills, 85
future
  email, 104
  software, 416
    Benioff, Marc, 377
    Bentley, Jon, 41
    Booch, Grady, 241-242
    Gosling, James, 285-286
    Greene, Diane, 402
    Kahn, Dr. Robert, 330
    Malloy, Tom, 258
    Mayer, Marissa, 29
    Norvig, Peter, 125

    Russinovich, Mark, 199
    Schwarz, John, 158
    Stallman, Richard, 83
    Stroustrup, Bjarne, 66-67
    Tomlinson, Ray, 108
    Torvalds, Linus, 174
    Vaskevitch, David, 217
    Wozniak, Steve, 357

G

Gates, Bill
  academic grades, 53
  business fluency, 337
Gerstner, Lou, 13, 208
getting people on-side, 140
getting started
  Benioff, Marc, 370
  Bentley, Jon, 38
  Booch, Grady, 237
  Gosling, James, 282-283
  Greene, Diane, 397
  Kahn, Dr. Robert, 325
  Malloy, Tom, 252
  Mayer, Marissa, 24
  Norvig, Peter, 123
  Russinovich, Mark, 193
  Schwarz, John, 155
  Stallman, Richard, 80
  Stroustrup, Bjarne, 63
  Tomlinson, Ray, 101
  Torvalds, Linus, 171
  Vaskevitch, David, 216
getting to revenue, 385-386
Gladwell, Malcolm, 73, 334
goal-centric time management, 202-203
goal-oriented careers, 181-184
  changing with time, 183
  developing, 183
  directed career path example, 181
  trying different jobs, 183
  undirected career path example, 181
  working backward, 184
goal-oriented project management, 261-264
goals, 226-227
good ideas versus good business, 380-381
good software
  market embracing, 12
  market-driven, 14-15
Google
  founders, 380
  successful innovation, 315
  work environment, 247

Gosling, James
    advice, 286-287
    biography, 281
    future of software, 285-286
    getting started, 282-283
    graduate degrees, 287
    Java inspirations, 283
    personal success, 284
    pet peeves, 284
    time management, 285
    trends/innovations, 284
    work-life balance, 285
gossiping, 128
government agencies, 50
GPS, value perception cycle, 314
graduate degrees
    Benioff, Marc, 376
    compensation, 405-406
    Gosling, James, 287
    Greene, Diane, 403
    Malloy, Tom, 255
    Mayer, Marissa, 28
    Russinovich, Mark, 199
    Schwarz, John, 160
    Stroustrup, Bjarne, 65
    Tomlinson, Ray, 106
    Vaskevitch, David, 216
graphical user interface, 340
Gray, Jim, 7
Greene, Diane
    accomplishments, 397
    advice for success, 403
    architecture degree, 397
    biography, 396
    future of software, 402
    getting started, 397
    graduate degrees, 403
    influences/inspirations, 399
    leading software companies, 399
    personal success, 400
    pet peeves, 397
    starting VMware, 398-399
    time management, 401
    work-life balance, 401
growth
    problems, 135-137
    skills, 92-94
    startup acquisition comparison, 390-392
    statistics, 416
gurus. *See* visionaries

H

halo-effect, 121
Hamilton, James, 12, 211-212
hard skills, 84
high performers, 115
higher-level programming languages, 87
human nature, managing, 264-266
    face-saving exits, 265
    making people feel loved, 264
    status reports, 265
humility in interviews, 57

I

IBM
    Gerstner, Lou's guiding principles, 13
    IMS, 10
    patents, 341
    successful innovation, 315
identifying successful innovations, 309
images, revitalizing, 121
impressions, 121
IMS, 10
In Search of Excellence, 303
incremental improvements, 18
indecision (time management), 207
indirect compensation, 409-411
individual work (schools), 32
industry. *See also* companies
    compared to schools, 34-36
        code reuse, 34
        drivers and shapers, 35
        financial compensation, 35
        freedom of motion, 35
        innovation, 35
        interpersonal networking, 35
        leadership, 35
        learning/doing, 35
        personal portfolios, 36
        productivity, 36
        recognition, 36
        risks, 36
        teamwork, 34
    compensation. *See* compensation
    culture
        core competencies, 163
        work-life balance, 246-247
    early careers
        business of software knowledge, 70
        career paths, choosing, 74
        expertise, 70

job satisfaction, 76-78
low-level programming skills, 71
mentors, 74-75
networking, 72-73
tradecraft skills, 69-70
watching leaders, 72
four modes of in-person communication,
118-120
influence, measure of success, 4
leaders, watching, 72
limited field of vision, 33-34
publications, 341
influences
Greene, Diane, 399
managers on employee success, 185-187
Mayer, Marissa, 24
Vaskevitch, David, 216
informal code walkthroughs, 90
innovation, 17
2005 McKinsey report on corporate
success concerns, 307
benefits, 306
brainstorming, 312-313
business advantage, 308
fostering successful
affinitizing, 319
avoiding dictating solutions, 318
best people, 316
carrying through, 322
collaboration, 317
current state of the art, 321
data, 319
Google, 315
IBM, 315
iteration, 318
market as source, 321
Microsoft, 315
reusing existing components, 320
rewards, 316
studying other fields, 321
time and resource constraints, 319
keeping up
Benioff, Marc, 376
Bentley, Jon, 40
Booch, Grady, 239
Gosling, James, 284
Malloy, Tom, 255
Mayer, Marissa, 28
Norvig, Peter, 125
Russinovich, Mark, 197
Schwarz, John, 157-158
Stallman, Richard, 82
Stroustrup, Bjarne, 65

Tomlinson, Ray, 107
Torvalds, Linus, 173
Vaskevitch, David, 217
Wozniak, Steve, 358
opportunities, 311-312
resumés, 48
schools versus industry, 35
self-made innovators, 336-337
successful, 309-311
identifying, 309
iPhone example, 310
marketing, 309
OS/2 flop example, 310
value perception cycle, 313-315
inspections (code), 90
inspirations
Greene, Diane, 399
Wozniak, Steve, 356
interface designs (Mayer, Marissa), 26
internal business plans, 382
Internet
finding jobs, 50
frequency of top 24 programming
languages and platforms, 87
leveraging for startups, 388
release cycles, 29
server warehouses, 30
internship students, 266
interpersonal networking, 35
interviews, 56-61
candidates, 296-298
coaching, 60
communication, 57
company negativity, 59
confidence/humility, 57
enthusiasm, 58
falsifying information, 60
follow-up etiquette, 60
interest in software, 57
knowing the competition, 58
Norvig, Peter, 124
personal/medical information, 59
positive, 58
research, 56
selling yourself, 59
skill-testing questions/brainteasers, 56
investment capital, 385
iPhone, 310
IQ, 96
iteration
development methodology, 271
innovation, 318

J

Java, 87. *See also* Gosling, James
Jericho, 101
job roles, 110
    architects, 112
    CEOs, 111
    channel salespeople, 114
    chief architects, 112
    CTOs, 111
    department managers, 113
    direct salespeople, 114
    directors of engineering, 111
    directors of marketing, 111
    fellows, 111
    function verification testers, 114
    product managers, 113
    program managers, 113
    programmers, 113
    release managers, 112
    research staff members, 113
    second-line managers, 112
    system verification testers, 114
    technical evangelists, 115
    technical managers, 112
    technical salespeople, 114
    usability engineers, 113
    Vice Presidents, 111
    visibility, 116
job satisfaction, 8, 76-78
job searches
    career planning/placement offices, 49
    choosing companies, 43-46
    cold calls, 50
    employment agencies, 49
    extracurricular activities, 54-55
    friends/contacts, 49
    government agencies, 50
    importance of grades, 52-54
    Internet searches, 50
    interviewing, 56-61
        coaching, 60
        communication, 57
        company negativity, 59
        confidence/humility, 57
        enthusiasm, 58
        falsifying information, 60
        follow-up etiquette, 60
        interest in software, 57
        knowing the competition, 58
        personal/medical information, 59
        positive, 58
        research, 56
        selling yourself, 59
        skill-testing questions/brainteasers, 56
    newspaper postings, 51
    professors, 50
    resource effectiveness, 51-52
    resumés, 46-48
        mailing, 51
    school performance, 46
    student positions, 55
    visiting companies, 51
Jobs, Steve
    academics, 53
    business fluency, 337

K

Kahn, Dr. Robert
    accomplishments, 325
    advice for success, 328, 331
    biography, 323-325
    future of software, 330
    getting started, 325
    networking contributions, 326
    personal success, 327
    pet peeves, 326
    pivotal career point, 326
    software scale, 327
    technology/trends, 329
    time management, 329
    work-life balance, 330
Kay, Alan, 350
Kennedy, John F., 261

L

laggards, 17
large group presentations, 119-120
late majority adopters, 17
lateness. *See* overruns
Law of the Few, 143
leadership. *See also* visionaries
    authority, 293-294
    delegation, 303
    directing others, 304
    following the money, 301
    innovation
        2005 McKinsey report on corporate
            success concerns, 307
        affinitizing, 319
        avoiding dictating solutions, 318
        benefits, 306
        best people, 316
        brainstorming, 312-313

business advantage, 308
carrying through, 322
collaboration, 317
current state of the art, 321
data, 319
Google, 315
IBM, 315
identifying valuable, 309
iPhone example, 310
iteration, 318
market as source, 321
marketing, 309
Microsoft, 315
opportunities, 311-312
OS/2 flop example, 310
reusing existing components, 320
rewards, 316
studying other fields, 321
successful, 309-311
time and resource constraints, 319
value perception cycle, 313-315
managing, compared, 288-290
proceeding without formal support, 294
resumés, 47
rewards, 301-302
schedule overruns, 235
average example, 223
avoiding, 235
causes, 224-231
effects, 223
executive perception, 221
handling, 232-233
leadership, 235
right people, 235
statistics, 222
schools versus industry, 35
shared values, 303
styles, 290-292
teams, building, 295-300
lean development methodology, 273
learning
business of software, 70
expertise, 70
low-level programming skills, 71
programming languages, 86-88
schools versus industry, 35
tradecraft skills, 69-70
learning curve (first few months at work),
361-362
colleagues, 364
good mentors, 362
managers, 362-363
managing your boss, 366

opportunities, creating, 366-367
pushing yourself, 368
length
emails, 117
resumés, 48
life impacts work, 247-248
Lightstone's Convolution Principle, 227
limited field of vision, 32
industry, 33-34
school, 33
school as, 32
Linux, 173. See also Torvalds, Linus
LogAD (Logistics Anchor Desk), 101
low performers, 115
low-level programming skills, learning, 71

M

mailing resumés, 51
Malloy, Tom
accomplishments, 251-252
advice for success, 257-259
biography, 252
chief software architect role, 254
future of software, 258
getting started, 252
graduate degrees, 255
personal success, 254, 257
pet peeves, 259
risk-taking decisions, 253
technical accomplishments, 257
time management, 256
trends/innovations, 255
work-life balance, 256
The Management of Innovation, 303
managers
communication, 121
employee's first few months, 362-363
influences on employee success, 185-187
managing, 366
peer impact, 187-188
managing
dependency, 227
leadership, compared, 288-290
managers, 366
projects
defects, 276, 279
development methodologies, 270-274
goal-oriented, 261-264
human nature, 264-266
maturity, testing, 275-276
plans, changing, 269-270
quality, 279-280

SMART, 262
   students, 266
   value, measuring, 267-269
schedule overruns, 232-233
marketing, 309
marketplace
   driving software, 14-15
   embracing good software, 12
   influence on schools, 33
Master's degrees, 406
maturity, testing, 275-276
Mayer, Marissa
   accomplishments, 26
   advice for success, 27
   biography, 23-24
   choosing Google, 43
   field opportunities, 30
   future of software, 29
   getting started, 24
   graduate degrees, 28
   influences, 24
   listening to customers, 22
   personal success, 27
   pet peeves, 25
   time management, 29
   trends/innovation, 28
   women in computing, 26
   work-life balance, 29
measuring
   success, 3-6
   value, 267-269
mentors, 74-75, 362
methodologies (development), 270
   agile development process, 272
   iterative development, 271
   lean development, 273
   rapid prototyping, 274
   scrum, 271
   waterfall development process, 274
   XP, 273
Meyer, Bertrand, 89
mezzanine funding, 385
Microsoft
   Bay Area Research Center (BARC), 7
   stock growth, 337
   successful innovation, 315
   work environment, 247
mistakes
   fundamentals versus incidentals, 137
   growth
      excessive self-promotion, 136
      self-marketing wrong messages, 136

   technical skills, 135
   unimportant roles, 137
people, 127
   burning bridges, 128
   complainers, 129
   gossiping, 128
   inappropriate decision making, 131
   snitching on coworkers, 129
   too many suggestions, 130
   working the org, 130
productivity, 133
   buggy code, 133
   lack of productivity, 134
   missing dates consistently, 134
   skunkworks focus, 135
   time management, 135
team, 131-132
Moore, Geoffrey, 17, 386
motivation, emotional, 140-143
   face time, 142
   giving something for nothing, 141
   inspiring self-worth in others, 141
   sharing glory, 142
The Mythical Man Month, 225

N

NDAs (nondisclosure agreements), 381
near-real-time communication, 179
negotiating, 144
   meeting in the middle, 145-147
   mutual gain options, 147-148
   outcomes, estimating, 145
   quitting while ahead, 149
   seeking first to understand, 144
networked email, 103-104
networking
   early career, 72-73
   Kahn, Dr. Robert's contributions, 326
   wasting time, 209
   working the org, 143
new customers, attracting, 15
new graduates
   career paths, choosing, 74
   finding jobs, 52-54
   industry leaders, watching, 72
   job satisfaction, 76-78
   learning
      business of software, 70
      expertise, 70
      low-level programming skills, 71
      tradecraft skills, 69-70

mentors, 74-75
networking, 72-73
resumés, 46
school performance, 46
new writer advice, 344-345
newspaper job postings, 51
nondisclosure agreements (NDAs), 381
North American salary ranges 2010-2013, 409
Norvig, Peter
accomplishments, 123
advice for success, 126
biography, 122-123
future of software, 125
getting started, 123
job interview example, 124
personal success, 124
pet peeves, 124
time management, 125
trends/innovations, 125
work-life balance, 125

O

OOP (object-oriented programming), 63
languages, 88
Stroustrup, Bjarne, 63
open source, 383
opportunities
creating, 366-367
innovations, 311-312
Mayer, Marissa, 30
OS/2 flop, 310
Outliers, 334
overruns
average example, 223
avoiding, 235
causes, 224
adding manpower, 225
aggressive estimates, 228
bad estimates, 227-228
dependency management, 227
fundamentals, bypassing, 230
human performance, 224
scope creep, 224
social dynamics, 229-230
strategic changes, 231
time away from deliverables,
forgetting, 231
unclear goals, 226-227
effects, 223
executive perception, 221
handling, 232-233

leadership, 235
right people, 235
statistics, 222

P

pacesetting leadership, 291-292
Page, Larry, 380
paralysis by analysis, 207
Parkinson's Law, 230
passion, 350-351
patents, 338
career success, 341
costs, 338
criteria, 338
graphical user interface example, 340
names, 341
style-mixing pants example, 339
worthy ideas, 340
Patton, General George, 207
people problems, 127
burning bridges, 128
complainers, 129
gossiping, 128
inappropriate decision making, 131
snitching on coworkers, 129
too many suggestions, 130
working the org, 130
performance (schedule overruns), 224
Perlis, Alan, 86
personal portfolios, 36
personal success, defining, 415
personal tenacity (proposals), 168
personal walkthroughs, 90
pet peeves
Bentley, Jon, 39
Booch, Grady, 240
Gosling, James, 284
Greene, Diane, 397
Kahn, Dr. Robert, 326
Malloy, Tom, 259
Mayer, Marissa, 25
Norvig, Peter, 124
Russinovich, Mark, 199
Schwarz, John, 160
Stallman, Richard, 81
Stroustrup, Bjarne, 65
Tomlinson, Ray, 109
Torvalds, Linus, 172
Vaskevitch, David, 217
Wozniak, Steve, 355
Peters, Tom, 303

Ph.Ds, 406
philanthropy (Benioff, Marc), 373-374
pitching proposals, 166-168
plans (project), changing, 269-270
platforms
    independence, 375
    Internet frequency of top 24 programming
        and platforms, 87
popularity of software development, 416
post-factum communication, 180
preferred stock, 407
presentations
    large group, 119-120
    small group, 118
    summary, 381
proactiveness (urgency), 208
problems
    acquisitions, 394-395
    fundamentals versus incidentals, 137
    growth
        excessive self-promotion, 136
        self-marketing wrong messages, 136
        technical skills, 135
        unimportant roles, 137
    people, 127
        burning bridges, 128
        complainers, 129
        gossiping, 128
        inappropriate decision making, 131
        snitching on coworkers, 129
        too many suggestions, 130
        working the org, 130
    productivity, 133
        buggy code, 133
        lack of productivity, 134
        missing dates consistently, 134
        skunkworks focus, 135
        time management, 135
    team, 131-132
product development
    based on existing customers, 15
    customer criteria, 18
    customer focus, 16
    quality characteristics, 18
    SaaS example, 19-21
    technologies, 17-18
    user feedback, 21-22
    value, 16
product managers, 113
productivity
    problems, 133-135
    schools versus industry, 36
professional activities, 48

professors, 50
program managers, 113
programmers
    9-to-5 job, 108
    high/low performers, 115
    role, 113
programming languages
    Internet frequency of top 24 programming
        languages and platforms, 87
    learning, 86-88
Programming Pearls, 38
project management
    defects, 276, 279
    development methodologies, 270
        agile development process, 272
        iterative development, 271
        lean development, 273
        rapid prototyping, 274
        scrum, 271
        waterfall development process, 274
        XP, 273
    goal-oriented, 261-264
    human nature, 264-266
    maturity, testing, 275-276
    plans, changing, 269-270
    quality, 279-280
    SMART, 262
    students, 266
    value, measuring, 267-269
projects
    failures, 11-12
    good
        market embracing, 12
        market-driven, 14-15
        managing. See project management
    overruns
        average example, 223
        avoiding, 235
        causes, 224-231
        effects, 223
        executive perception, 221
        handling, 232-233
        leadership, 235
        right people, 235
        statistics, 222
    proposals
        connecting privately with decision
            makers, 164
        converting naysayers to believers, 163
        core competencies, 162-163
        credibility, 164
        elevator pitch, 164
        example, 165

executive commitment, 169
others' ideas, including, 164
personal tenacity, 168
pitching, 166-168
skunkworks, 135
promotibility inversion, 189-191
promoting others, 189
promotions. *See* advancement
proprietary software, 194
proposals
connecting privately with decision
makers, 164
converting naysayers to believers, 163
core competencies, 162-163
credibility, 164
elevator pitch, 164
example, 165
executive commitment, 169
others' ideas, including, 164
personal tenacity, 168
pitching, 166-168
public speaking, 345-348
adapting to audiences, 346
antagonists, 348
clarity and pace, 346
engaging audience, 346
first person, 347
hand motions, 347
purpose, 348
smiling, 347
speaking the charts, 347
understanding audience, 346
publishing, 343
benefits, 342
books, 342
columns/blogs, 342
impact, 341
industrial/trade publications, 341
new writer advice, 344-345
research papers, 341
value, 343
whitepapers, 342
pushing yourself, 368

Q-R

quadrants of time, 93-94
quality
products, 18
testing, 279-280

R&D, bootstrapping, 382-383
rapid prototyping development
methodology, 274

Rational Software beginnings, 238
recognition, 36
recruiting candidates
attracting, 295
filtering, 296
interviewing successfully, 296-298
relational databases, 156
release cycles, 29
release managers, 112
remote workers, 383
rendering browser engines, 25
research papers, 341
research staff members, 113
resources
constraints, 319
finding jobs
career planning/placement offices, 49
cold calls, 50
effectiveness, 51-52
employment agencies, 49
friends/contacts, 49
government agencies, 50
Internet searches, 50
mailing resumés, 51
newspaper postings, 51
professors, 50
visiting companies, 51
responsiveness (startups), 389-390
resumés
awards, 47
details, 47-48
extracurricular activities, 48
grades, 52-54
innovations, 48
leadership roles, 47
length, 48
mailing, 51
new graduates, 46
professional activities, 48
technical domain skills, 47
retirement plans, 408
revenue (startups), 385-386
reviews (technical), 91-92
revitalizing images, 121
rewards, 301-302, 316
risks
schools versus industry, 36
toleration, 17
roles (companies), 110
architects, 112
CEOs, 111
channel salesperson, 114
chief architects, 112

CTOs, 111
department managers, 113
direct salespeople, 114
directors of engineering, 111
directors of marketing, 111
fellows, 111
function verification testers, 114
product managers, 113
program managers, 113
programmers, 113
release managers, 112
research staff members, 113
second-line managers, 112
system verification testers, 114
technical evangelists, 115
technical managers, 112
technical salespeople, 114
usability engineers, 113
Vice Presidents, 111
visibility, 116
Russinovich, Mark
  accomplishments, 195
  advice for success, 198-200
  biography, 192-193
  future of software, 199
  getting started, 193
  graduate degrees, 199
  Microsoft recruitment, 195
  personal success, 196
  pet peeves, 199
  proprietary software, 194
  time management, 196
  trends/innovations, 197
  Windows incorporation of tools, 195
  Winternals development, 193-194
  work-life balance, 197

S

SaaS (software as a service), 19, 374
  Benioff, Marc, 374
  technology adoption example, 19-21
salary ranges 2010-2013, 409
Salesforce.com, 369
satisfaction, 76-78
schedule overruns
  average example, 223
  avoiding, 235
  causes, 224
    adding manpower, 225
    aggressive estimates, 228
    bad estimates, 227-228
    dependency management, 227

fundamentals, bypassing, 230
human performance, 224
scope creep, 224
social dynamics, 229-230
strategic changes, 231
time away from deliverables,
  forgetting, 231
unclear goals, 226-227
effects, 223
executive perception, 221
handling, 232-233
leadership, 235
right people, 235
statistics, 222
Schmidt, Eric, 380
school
  career planning/placement offices, 49
  compared to industry, 34-36
  curriculum, 32
  importance of grades, 52-54
  individual work, 32
  limited field of vision, 32-33
  market influences, 33
  performance, 46
  student positions, 55
Schwarz, John
  accomplishments, 156
  advice for success, 159-160
  biography, 154-155
  career goals, 184
  future of software, 158
  getting started, 155
  graduate degrees, 160
  path to CEO position, 156
  personal success, 160
  pet peeves, 160
  time management, 158
  trends/innovations, 157-158
  work-life balance, 159
scope creep, 224
scrum development methodology, 271
second-line managers, 112
second-stage funding, 384
self-made innovators, 336-337
server warehouses, 30
shapers, 35
shared values, 303
sharing glory, 142
Sharpen the Saw story, 92-94
skills
  business, 337-338
  communication
    effective, 117-118

email, 117
four modes of in-person
  communication, 118-120
importance, 116
managers, 121
personal requests, 118
growth, 92-94
hard, 84
leadership
  authority, 293-294
  delegation, 303
  directing others, 304
  following the money, 301
  innovation. *See* leadership, innovation
  managing, compared, 288-290
  proceeding without formal support, 294
  rewards, 301-302
  schedule overruns, 235
  shared values, 303
  styles, 290-292
  teams, building, 295-300
low-level programming, 71
soft
  defined, 84
  developing, 84, 95
  emotional intelligence, 95-99
technical
  debugging, 88-90
  development, 85
  domain expertise, 86
  fundamental, 85
  growth required, 85
  problems, 135
  programming languages, 86-88
  reviews, 91-92
  tradecraft, 86
time-management, 93-94
tradecraft, 69-70
skunkworks projects, 135
small group discussions/presentations, 118
SMART (specific, measurable, attainable,
  realistic, timely), 262
SMPs (symmetric multiprocessors), 267
socializing
  dynamics, 229-230
  networking, 143, 349-350
  wasting time, 209
soft skills
  defined, 84
  developing, 84, 95
  emotional intelligence, 95-99
    developing, 98-99
    maturity and common sense, 96
    personalities, 98

self-assessment, 98
side-by-side comparison example,
  96-97
software
  as a service. *See* SaaS
  scale, 327
space program project management example,
  261-264
specific, measurable, attainable, realistic,
  timely (SMART), 262
Stallman, Richard
  accomplishments, 81
  advice for success, 83
  biography, 79-80
  free software champion, 82
  future of software, 83
  getting started, 80
  personal success, 81
  pet peeves, 81
  time management, 83
  trends/innovations, 82
  work-life balance, 83
startups
  acquisition
    benefits, 392
    categories, 392-393
    getting the word out to potential
      buyers, 394
    problems, 394-395
  adaptability, 389-390
  Benioff, Marc advice, 372
  business plans, 381
  compensation, 405
  crossing the chasm, 386-389
  elevator pitches, 381
  external business plans, 382
  failures, 380
  financing, 383
    angel funding, 384
    fourth-stage, 385
    investment capital, 385
    second-stage, 384
    third-stage, 385
  getting to revenue, 385-386
  good ideas versus good business, 380-381
  growth versus acquisition, 390-392
  internal business plans, 382
  R&D, bootstrapping, 382-383
  responsiveness, 389-390
  summary presentations, 381
statistics
  job growth, 416
  overruns, 222
status reports, 265

stock options, 406-407
stressors, 248
Stroustrup, Bjarne
    accomplishments, 63
    advice for success, 66
    biography, 62-63
    The C++ Programming Language, 64
    future of software, 66-67
    getting started, 63
    graduate degrees, 65
    personal success, 64
    pet peeves, 65
    time management, 65
    trends/innovations, 65
    work-life balance, 65
students
    limited field of vision, 32
    managing, 266
    positions, 55
styles, leadership, 290-292
success. *See also* advancement
    advice
        Benioff, Marc, 371, 375, 378
        Bentley, Jon, 41-42
        Booch, Grady, 242-243
        Gosling, James, 286
        Greene, Diane, 403
        Kahn, Dr. Robert, 328, 331
        Malloy, Tom, 257-259
        Mayer, Marissa, 27
        Norvig, Peter, 126
        Russinovich, Mark, 198-200
        Schwarz, John, 159
        Stallman, Richard, 83
        Stroustrup, Bjarne, 66
        Tomlinson, Ray, 106
        Torvalds, Linus, 175
        Vaskevitch, David, 216
        Wozniak, Steve, 358-359
    characteristics, 8
    credibility, 121
    defining, 415
    dressing for success, 150-151
    enthusiasm, 8
    failures, 416
    fame, 8
    freedom, 7
    fun work environment, 76-78
    innovation, 309-311
        affinitizing, 319
        avoiding dictating solutions, 318
        best people, 316
        carrying through, 322
        collaboration, 317

        current state of the art, 321
        data, 319
        Google, 315
        IBM, 315
        identifying, 309
        iPhone example, 310
        iteration, 318
        market as source, 321
        marketing, 309
        Microsoft, 315
        OS/2 flop example, 310
        reusing existing components, 320
        rewards, 316
        studying other fields, 321
        time and resource constraints, 319
    IQ, 96
    job satisfaction, 8
    luck, 414
    management peers impact, 187-188
    manager influence, 185-187
    measures
        betterment of society, 4
        corporate/industrial influence, 4
        enjoyment, 5-6
        financial compensation, 3-4
    patents, 341
    personal
        Bentley, Jon, 39
        Booch, Grady, 239
        Gosling, James, 284
        Greene, Diane, 400
        Kahn, Dr. Robert, 327
        Malloy, Tom, 254, 257
        Mayer, Marissa, 27
        Norvig, Peter, 124
        Russinovich, Mark, 196
        Schwarz, John, 160
        Stallman, Richard, 81
        Stroustrup, Bjarne, 64
        Tomlinson, Ray, 103
        Torvalds, Linus, 172
        Vaskevitch, David, 218
        Wozniak, Steve, 356
    positive impressions, 121
    project proposals
        connecting privately with decision
            makers, 164
        converting naysayers to believers, 163
        core competencies, 162-163
        credibility, 164
        elevator pitch, 164
        example, 165
        executive commitment, 169
        others ideas, including, 164

personal tenacity, 168
pitching, 166-168
qualities, 413-414
rates, 12
summary presentations, 381
symmetric multiprocessors (SMPs), 267
Sysinternals, 195
System 360 project, 349
system verification testers, 114

T

task-centric time management, 203-205
teams
building, 295
attracting, 295
filtering, 296
interviewing successfully, 296-298
keeping best people happy, 298-299
mix, 299
prima donnas/superstars, 300
co-opetition, 115
problems, 131-132
schools versus industry, 34
technical domain skills, 47
technical evangelists, 115
technical managers, 112
technical salespeople, 114
technical skills
debugging, 88-89
assertions, 89
code inspections, 90
Design by Contract, 89
development, 85
domain expertise, 86
fundamental, 85
growth requirements, 85
problems, 135
programming languages, 86-88
reviews, 91-92
tradecraft, 86
technology. See also innovation
adoption lifecycle, 17
customer criteria, 18
quality characteristics, 18
SaaS example, 19-21
technologies, 18
disruptive, 18
tenacity (urgency), 208
TENEX, 102
testing
maturity, 275-276
quality, 279-280

thinking inside the box, 319
third-stage funding, 385
time
constraints (innovation), 319
management
1950s-1980s, 201
1990s, 201
Benioff, Marc, 377
Bentley, Jon, 40
Booch, Grady, 240
Circles of Concern/Influence, 205-206
email, 210-213
goal-centric, 202-203
Gosling, James, 285
Greene, Diane, 401
indecisions, 207
Kahn, Dr. Robert, 329
Malloy, Tom, 256
Mayer, Marissa, 29
Norvig, Peter, 125
problems, 135
Russinovich, Mark, 196
Schwarz, John, 158
skills, developing, 93-94
Stallman, Richard, 83
Stroustrup, Bjarne, 65
task-centric, 203, 205
time wasting, 209-210
Tomlinson, Ray, 107
Torvalds, Linus, 173
urgency, 208-209
Vaskevitch, David, 217
Wozniak, Steve, 357
wasting, 209-210
time-shared computing, 100
The Tipping Point: How Little Things Can
Make a Big Difference (Gladwell), 73, 143
Tomlinson, Ray
@ sign, 103-106
accomplishments, 102
advice for success, 106, 109
biography, 100-101
evolution of email, 102
future of email, 104
future of software, 108
getting started, 101
graduate degrees, 106
invention of networked email, 103-104
personal feelings toward email, 104
personal success, 103
pet peeves, 109
programming as a 9-to-5 job, 108
time management, 107

trends/innovations, 107
    work-life balance, 108
Torvalds, Linus
    accomplishments, 171
    advice for success, 175
    biography, 170
    future of software, 174
    getting started, 171
    personal success, 172
    pet peeves, 172
    time management, 173
    trends/innovations, 173
    work-life balance, 174
trade publications, 341
tradecraft skills, 69-70, 86
trends, keeping up. *See also* innovation
    Benioff, Marc, 376
    Bentley, Jon, 40
    Booch, Grady, 239
    Gosling, James, 284
    Kahn, Dr. Robert, 329
    Malloy, Tom, 255
    Mayer, Marissa, 28
    Norvig, Peter, 125
    Russinovich, Mark, 197
    Schwarz, John, 157-158
    Stallman, Richard, 82
    Stroustrup, Bjarne, 65
    Tomlinson, Ray, 107
    Torvalds, Linus, 173
    Vaskevitch, David, 217
    Wozniak, Steve, 358
trust, 140
types
    audiences, 16
    leadership, 291-292

U–V

unclear goals, 226-227
undirected career path example, 181
urgency (time management), 208-209
usability engineers, 113

value
    extracurricular activities, 54-55
    perception cycle, 313-315
    products, 16
    publishing, 343
    shared, 303
    software, measuring, 267-269
Vaskevitch, David
    advice for success, 216-218
    biography, 214-216

future of software, 217
    getting started, 216
    graduate degrees, 216
    influences, 216
    personal success, 218
    pet peeves, 217
    time management, 217
    trends/innovations, 217
    work-life balance, 217, 249
vice presidents, 111
visibility, 116
visionaries. *See also* leadership
    authority, 333-334
    believing in yourself, 336-337
    business skills, 337-338
    cross-disciplinary studying, 334-336
    defined, 333
    failures, 348
    passion, 350-351
    patents, 338
        career success, 341
        costs, 338
        criteria, 338
        graphical user interface example, 340
        names, 341
        style-mixing pants example, 339
        worthy ideas, 340
    public speaking, 345-348
        adapting to audience, 346
        antagonists, 348
        clarity and pace, 346
        engaging audience, 346
        first person, 347
        hand motions, 347
        purpose, 348
        smiling, 347
        social networking, 350
        speaking the charts, 347
        understanding audience, 346
    publishing, 343
        benefits, 342
        books, 342
        columns/blogs, 342
        impact, 341
        industrial/trade publications, 341
        new writer advice, 344-345
        research papers, 341
        value, 343
        whitepapers, 342
    self-made innovators, 337
visiting companies, 51
VMware foundation, 398-399

W–Z

wasting time, 209-210
watching industry leaders, 72
waterfall development process, 274
Welch, Jack, 186
whitepapers, 342
Winternals, 193-194
women in computing, 26
work environment, 247
work-life balance, 244
    achieving by working backward, 249
    assessing, 249
    Benioff, Marc, 377
    Bentley, Jon, 40
    Booch, Grady, 241
    defining yourself, 245
    Gosling, James, 285
    Greene, Diane, 401
    Kahn, Dr. Robert, 330
    life impacts work, 247-248
    Malloy, Tom, 256
    Mayer, Marissa, 29
    Norvig, Peter, 125
    organizational culture, 246-247
    repartitioning time, 245
    Russinovich, Mark, 197
    Schwarz, John, 159
    Stallman, Richard, 83
    stressors, 248
    Stroustrup, Bjarne, 65
    tips, 246
    Tomlinson, Ray, 108
    Torvalds, Linus, 174
    Vaskevitch, David, 217
    work environment, 247

working the org
    agreements, 151-153
    communication, 149
    dressing for success, 150-151
    emotional motivators, 140-143
    getting people on-side, 140
    negotiations, 144
        meeting in the middle, 145-147
        mutual gain options, 147-148
        outcomes, estimating, 145
        quitting while ahead, 149
        seeking first to understand, 144
    problems, 130
    social networking, 143
world-class authority status, 334
worst and best programmers differences, 295
Wozniak, Steve, 336
    accomplishments, 355
    advice, 358-359
    biography, 352-353
    debugging, 354
    future of software, 357
    inspirations, 356
    personal future, 357
    personal success, 356
    pet peeves, 355
    Tetris, playing, 357
    time management, 357
    trends/innovations, 358
    viewing self as hardware person, 353-354
writing code, 39

XP development methodology, 273

FREE Online Edition

Your purchase of *Making it Big in Software* includes access to a free online edition for 45 days through the Safari Books Online subscription service. Nearly every Prentice Hall book is available online through Safari Books Online, along with more than 5,000 other technical books and videos from publishers such as Addison-Wesley Professional, Cisco Press, Exam Cram, IBM Press, O'Reilly, Que, and Sams.

SAFARI BOOKS ONLINE allows you to search for a specific answer, cut and paste code, download chapters, and stay current with emerging technologies.

Activate your FREE Online Edition at
www.informit.com/safarifree

> **STEP 1:** Enter the coupon code: QBBJPXA.

> **STEP 2:** New Safari users, complete the brief registration form.
> Safari subscribers, just log in.

If you have difficulty registering on Safari or accessing the online edition, please e-mail customer-service@safaribooksonline.com